JOURNAL FOR THE STUDY OF THE OLD TESTAMENT
SUPPLEMENT SERIES
253

Sheffield Academic Press

1 and 2 Chronicles

Volume 1
1 Chronicles 1–2 Chronicles 9
Israel's Place among the Nations

William Johnstone

Journal for the Study of the Old Testament
Supplement Series 253

לבני אדם שׂר צבא
ולבתי חנה רופאה

כפי שׂהם מבינים מי שׂהם
כן הם מבינים מה שׂבספר הזה

Published by
Sheffield Academic Press Ltd
Mansion House
19 Kingfield Road
Sheffield S11 9AS
England

Typeset by Sheffield Academic Press
and
Printed on acid-free paper in Great Britain
by Bookcraft Ltd
Midsomer Norton, Bath

British Library Cataloguing in Publication Data

A catalogue record for this book is available
from the British Library

ISBN 1-85075-693-7

CONTENTS

ABBREVIATIONS

ANET	J.B. Pritchard (ed.), *Ancient Near Eastern Texts*
AV	Authorized Version
BBB	Bonner biblische Beiträge
BDB	F. Brown, S.R. Driver and C.A. Briggs, *Hebrew and English Lexicon of the Old Testament*
BHK	R. Kittel (ed.), *Biblia Hebraica*
BHS	*Biblia hebraica stuttgartensia*
BKAT	Biblischer Kommentar: Altes Testament
BZAW	Beihefte zur *ZAW*
C	Chronicles (1 and 2); 'The Chronicler', the assumed final editor/author of 1 and 2 Chronicles
CAH	*Cambridge Ancient History*
ExpTim	*Expository Times*
FOTL	The Forms of the Old Testament Literature
GKC	*Gesenius' Hebrew Grammar*, ed. E. Kautzsch, trans. A.E. Cowley
JPSV	Jewish Publication Society Version
JSOT	*Journal for the Study of the Old Testament*
JSOTSup	*Journal for the Study of the Old Testament*, Supplement Series
KBS	L. Koehler, W. Baumgartner, *Hebräisches und aramäisches Lexikon* (ed. J.J. Stamm *et al.*; Leiden: Brill, 3rd edn, 1967–90)
LBA	Late Bronze Age
NEB	New English Bible
NIV	New International Version
NRSV	New Revised Standard Version
OTG	Old Testament Guide
SJLA	Studies in Judaism in Late Antiquity
ST	*Studia theologica*
ZAW	*Zeitschrift für die alttestamentliche Wissenschaft*

INTRODUCTION

The Challenge of Chronicles

Chronicles (C) is a challenging work, not just in its format but in the way in which it throws widely held views into question.

On the forgiveness of sins, for instance, C insists that, while God in grace preserves the sinful people of Israel—and humanity as a whole—alive, there is no easy blotting out of the guilty past. Rather, he focuses realistically on the lasting effects of sin, the cost of reparation and the long process of rehabilitation.

Then again, C rejects the order of the books in the standard English Versions of the Bible. In the standard English Versions of the Old Testament it is associated with the 'historical books', with Samuel–Kings coming before it and Ezra–Nehemiah following it. But in the conventional order of the Hebrew Bible it stands at the end of the canon as the last word of the Hebrew Scriptures. It thus comes *after* Ezra–Nehemiah, despite, ostensibly, dealing with the period *before* them.

In the Hebrew Bible it is not, thus, part of a series of history books merely giving a connected account of the past. Rather, it is a theological work. As the final work of the canon, it looks forward to a future yet to be realized. It offers a theology of hope in the dawning age that only God can bring about through the transformation of the present conditions of human life. And it endorses a pattern of life to be followed meantime as Israel awaits the fulfilment of these hopes.

C in its Hebrew Bible form rejects, too, many of the chapter and paragraph divisions of the standard English translations, and even the division of the work into two books after 1 Chronicles 29. Such divisions often run counter to the structure of the traditional Hebrew text (the 'Masoretic Text' [MT]): this leaves one free to find, for example, that the more natural break in the work is after 2 Chronicles 9, not at the end of '1 Chronicles'. This commentary will, on the whole, adopt the paragraphing of MT.

1 and 2 Chronicles is treated as one work in MT. This is shown by the fact that it notes the total number of verses in the work (1765) only at the end of 2 Chronicles, a number which obviously includes 1 Chronicles, and identifies the mid-point of the work as 1.27.25a.

The Chronicler's Theology

Though C is working on a very broad canvas with a host of details, he nonetheless presents, I believe, a highly integrated theological statement, a single dominant complex of ideas, which binds the whole work together. There are many sides to that statement and these are worked out in a variety of ways in different parts of the book; but all the elements cohere as parts of the one system.

1. *The Overall Argument of the Work*

C is a theological work: it is concerned with the universal relationship between God and humanity, and the vocation of Israel within that relationship. It begins with Adam, the father of humankind (1 Chron. 1.1), and ends with an edict by the gentile world emperor of the day in the name of the LORD as cosmic deity, who has given him 'all the kingdoms of the earth' (2 Chron. 36.23). In between it sketches the ideal form of the life of Israel, but also Israel's failure to attain that ideal, and the relations of Israel with the nations of the world.

Although the elements of the argument are closely interwoven, it will be convenient to divide the presentation into two volumes: 1, *Israel's Place among the Nations* (1 Chron. 1–2 Chron. 9); and 2, *Guilt and Atonement* (2 Chron. 10–36). The first, in broad terms, deals with Israel's attempt to realize the ideal; the second with Israel's failure to attain that ideal and the hope that lies beyond that failure.

This theme is appropriate for the times and conditions under which C is writing. The indications are that C is writing in the fourth century BCE, that is, 200 or so years after the edict of the Persian emperor, Cyrus, in 538 BCE (2 Chron. 36.22-23) allowing the return of the Jewish exiles from their deportation to Babylon. Large numbers of émigré Jews still live abroad and the hopes of the 'return from the exile' have been realized only to a limited degree. Though a 'return from exile' has occurred under figures like Sheshbazzar, Zerubbabel, Ezra, and Nehemiah (see the book of Ezra–Nehemiah), the definitive 'Return' is still awaited. Historically speaking, C is a post-exilic work; but theologically speaking it is 'exilic', written when

Israel is still 'in exile', whether among the nations of the world or even in its own land, and it ends with the hope of the Return, which is about to dawn.

For the date of the writing of C, see the genealogy of the line of David in 1 Chronicles 3. The reuse of Neh. 11.1-17 in 1 Chron. 9.2-16 makes it clear that C is written after the account of the governorships of Nehemiah in Ezra–Nehemiah had been completed (Nehemiah's second governorship some time after 432 BCE, Neh. 13.6).

The relationship between C and Ezra–Nehemiah (Ezra–Nehemiah is also treated by MT as a single work; for example, it notes at the end of Neh. that 'the book' contains 685 verses) has been the subject of intense scholarly discussion. The fact that C ends at the point at which Ezra–Nehemiah begins (the edict of Cyrus; cf. Ezra 1.1-4 and 2 Chron. 36.22-23) has led to the seemingly obvious conclusion that Ezra–Nehemiah is the continuation of C (cf. the sequence of the English versions). But here is already an indication of the importance of adhering to the guidance of the traditional MT for the understanding of the work: for MT the books are separate and come in the sequence C—Ezra–Nehemiah. This is not a historical sequence but a theological one. The attempt at the realization of a return to the land in practical political terms has been tried under Ezra and Nehemiah and the other leaders. But that 'return' has been only a limited success: Ezra–Nehemiah deals with an aspect of the central problem, *ma'al*, 'unfaithfulness', that C is seeking to solve (1 Chron. 2.7; cf. Ezra 9.2, 4 ['the *ma'al*', of those still referred to as 'the exiles']; 10.2, 6, 10; Neh. 1.8; 13.27; the rearrangement of historical sequence also in Ezra–Nehemiah, which this topic illustrates, shows that it, too, is fundamentally a theological work). C is now reinterpreting the edict of Cyrus in eschatological terms. The edict of Cyrus is, thus, not an 'overlap' that links C, and Ezra–Nehemiah together in that historical sequence, but a framework (an *inclusio*) in which the realized Zionism of Ezra–Nehemiah is contrasted with the eschatological Zionism of C (two poles of Jewish life that continue to this day).

The genealogical section with which the work opens in 1 Chronicles 1–9 sketches in the factors of the situation. It acts as a preface to the whole in which the major themes of the work are announced: it presents an ideal, exposes a problem and proposes a solution.

As can be seen from the reuse of much of the genealogical data from Genesis to Kings in 1 Chronicles 1–9, these apparently arid chapters presuppose the content of these earlier works and are referring to them here in a kind of shorthand: the allusion to a name is enough to conjure up incidents in the earlier works in which that named individual was involved. C is the last word in the Hebrew Bible also in this sense, that it presupposes the content of the earlier canon.

Thus, C presupposes much if not all of the present Pentateuch and the 'Deuteronomistic History' of Joshua–Kings, including primeval and patriarchal stories, Moses and the Law-giving at Sinai, the worship of the Tabernacle and the conquest of Joshua. Passages like Exod. 30.11-16; Lev. 5.14-6.7; 25; 26; Numbers 4, and Josh. 5.13-15 and 7 will figure significantly in the discussion below; Samuel–Kings provides the basis for C's account of the monarchy. The Book of Psalms, as an expression of the Jerusalem tradition of messianic and Zionist theology, is also of fundamental importance (cf. the composite Psalm at 1 Chron. 16.8-36).

The human race was created in Adam for fellowship with God but the history of that relationship has, from the beginning, been marked by false starts and unsuccessful restarts. Already in 1 Chron. 1.1, Adam is succeeded by Seth, 'the substitute son'. 1 Chronicles 1.1-3 records the names of the ten generations which mark the progressive degeneration of humanity from Adam to the destruction of the universal flood. Noah, the second father of humanity, makes a new beginning. 1 Chronicles 1.4-27 records the further ten generations from Noah's son Shem to Abram, that is, Abraham, 'the father of many nations'. There are narrative asides included already within these verses (vv. 10-12, 19) which show that the ordered life of the world is always under threat: especially from the international powers in Assyria and Babylon (Nimrod) and Egypt (Cush), at the practical limits of the known world; and from the Philistines (and Edomites, 1 Chron. 1.43) at Israel's local level at the centre of the world. This sets the pattern which is to recur repeatedly throughout the work. Within this vast triple 'coaxial pyramid' of all the nations of the world—formed by the descendants of Noah, the descendants of Shem and the descendants of Abraham—Israel takes its place with its vocation to become what all else had hitherto failed to become, a people dedicated to God and the agent of the restoration of the relationship between God and humanity. Israel's destiny is to be vicarious not in its suffering but in its holiness.

For Israel, too, the genealogies lay out the fundamental factors in the situation (1 Chron. 2–9). An ideal is presented. In a unique arrangement of the tribes of Israel, C places Levi, the sacral tribe, in the centre of the tribal system (1 Chron. 6; the climactic role is also assigned to them also in 1 Chron. 9.10-33). It is through the presence of the Levites in the midst of the people that Israel is to be enabled to live the life of holiness that expresses the ideal harmony in the relationship between God and humanity.

But within Israel also the pattern of repeated false starts and unsuccessful restarts recurs. Once again, within the shorthand of the genealogies, the fundamental problem of Israel's life is exposed and the solution to that problem presented. A thematic term, which is to dominate the whole work, is introduced already at 1 Chron. 2.7: *ma'al*, 'unfaithfulness'. Judah has taken over the leadership of the tribes from Reuben, the first-born. But immediately, in the first incident in the process of the conquest of the Promised Land, Judah is plunged into *ma'al* by the action of one of its own tribesmen.

That term, *ma'al*, recurs twice more in the genealogies. It provides the explanation for the loss of the East Bank in the Assyrian exile in the eighth century BCE in 1 Chron. 5.25 and for the deportation of Judah in the Babylonian exile in the sixth in 1 Chron. 9.1. The genealogies of the tribes of Israel thus begin and end in *ma'al*; from first to last, on West Bank and on East, Israel has been guilty of *ma'al* and it is that *ma'al* that accounts for her forfeiture of her land.

Is there any solution to the problem of *ma'al*? *Ma'al*, and the means of coping with it, are defined in a section of the laws on sacrifice in Lev. 5.14–6.7. It is failure to give to God what is rightfully due to him. But there are differences of scale and quality between the defrauding of God envisaged in that legislation on *ma'al* in Leviticus and that of which Israel is accused in C. In Lev. 5.14–6.7, *ma'al* is defined as the accidental defrauding of God by the individual Israelite of what is due to him from offerings in kind (defined in Num. 18), broadened in Lev. 5.17 to include unwitting breach of any of the commandments. Lev. 5.14–6.7 also specifies the means of rectifying the *ma'al*: the sacrifice of the guilt-offering (a yearling ram), plus the payment of the equivalent of the amount by which God has been defrauded, plus the addition of 20 per cent. Here already is a reminder by C of a fundamental element in sin and forgiveness: repair of the damage inflicted and compensation to the wronged person are duties laid on the wrong-doer and are essential ingredients in reconciliation.

But Israel as a whole is in a far worse predicament than that envisaged in the legislation of Leviticus 5–6 which relates to individual, accidental defrauding of God in offerings in kind: Israel is guilty of national, premeditated defrauding of God, not in the mere symbols of the dedication of life, but in the substance of life itself, compounded over the generations. The extension of the application of *ma'al* from the careless individual to the premeditated acts of the guilty nation has already been undertaken also in Leviticus, in the curses at the end of the Holiness Code (Lev. 26.40-45). If the whole land has been polluted generation after generation, there is no possibility of rendering what is due in 'holy things', let alone of paying compensation. The only consequence of such compounded premeditated national failure to accord God his due can be forfeiture of the land, 'so that the land can enjoy its sabbaths' (Lev. 26.43; cf. 2 Chron. 36.21). The land as gift is withheld by the Giver. But hope resides precisely in that application of *ma'al* in Leviticus 26: for there it is related by context immediately to the legislation on the hope of Return in the Jubilee in Leviticus 25 and to the gracious response by God to the repentance of Israel.

The pattern of Israel's life for good and evil, which has been laid out in the genealogical preface, is repeated in the rest of work. The narrative section, 1 Chronicles 10–2 Chronicles 36, is dominated by the Davidic monarchy: once again the tribe of Judah, from which the house of David springs, takes the role of leadership. It is under David and Solomon (1 Chron. 10–2 Chron. 9), that Israel attains its destiny, or its nearest approximation to its destiny, among the nations of the world. The restoration of harmony between God and humanity in and through Israel is expressed through 'sacramental' theology: the Davidic king sits on no mere human throne but on the throne of the LORD himself (e.g. 1 Chron. 28.5); he is the representative on earth of the LORD himself, as his 'son' (e.g. 1 Chron. 17.13); under his leadership, the host of Israel becomes the LORD's host (cf. 1 Chron. 5.18); Jerusalem itself, at the centre of the earth, becomes the focal point for all nations (cf. the climactic verses on both David and Solomon, 1 Chron. 29.30; 2 Chron. 9.23).

Once again the Levites are at the centre of life, supremely now in the institution of the Temple in Jerusalem, the building of which dominates the account from 1 Chronicles 17–2 Chronicles 7. As already indicated in the genealogies, the balance—and equilibrium—between Judah and Levi is critical. But also, once again, *ma'al* dominates the presentation: it occurs another fourteen times (see on 1 Chron. 2.7 for references) to account for the disaster of the reign of Saul and the failure of the rule of the house of David from Solomon's successor, Rehoboam, down to the last individual to bear the title 'king', Zedekiah. Even David is not exempt from guilt (1 Chron. 21.3):

three times (1 Chron. 13; 17; 21), culminating in the presumptuousness of the census, he violates—or threatens to violate—the holy.

The Temple is built as the place where the triumphs of the LORD through his representative David are celebrated, focused on the liturgy surrounding the ark. But, because of his guilt, David is debarred from practising the cult of the altar. David has the authority to organize the Levites, including the priests, in their rotas of service; but the sphere of holiness is theirs alone to promote. The Levites thus provide the officiants at the altar, where whole burnt offerings, sin and guilt offerings are presented, and the Temple musicians for the liturgy celebrating and anticipating the LORD's triumphs; more fundamentally, they are the teachers who remind Israel of its duties regarding what it owes to God (2 Chron. 35.3), and the monitors of Israel's practice in according God these rights (1 Chron. 9.26).

In his study of the fifteen subsequent reigns from Rehoboam to Josiah and the sequel (2 Chron. 10–36), C undertakes an exhaustive exploration of the potentiality of the sacramental theology of the royal house of David, with its messianism and related Zion theology (for example, in 2 Chron. 13.12, cf. Isa. 7.14; 2 Chron. 20.20, cf. Isa. 7.9), to express and to realize Israel's destiny among the nations of the world. The critical point in the appraisal of these fifteen reigns is the priority given to the maintenance of the Temple and the loyalty of the respective kings of the house of David to the tradition of Jerusalemite theology implied by the Temple (cf. the disastrous departures from Jerusalem by Rehoboam, which inaugurates the period [2 Chron. 10], through Jehoshaphat [2 Chron. 18] and Ahaziah [2 Chron. 22.5], down to Josiah [2 Chron. 35.22]). Even the greatest of the reforming kings, Hezekiah and Josiah, are fallible, the latter catastrophically so (2 Chron. 32.24-31; 35.20-24). The whole edifice of royal theology lies in ruins: Zion is sacked; the Temple is destroyed along with its twin foci, the ark and the altar; the Davidic line is cut.

But out of the failure of the Davidic house, C again produces a message of hope. The chronology with which he works[1] is related to the jubilee (Lev. 25.8-55): in the fiftieth year 'you shall return, every one of you, to your property and every one of you to your family' (Lev. 25.10). For C, the exilic generation is the fiftieth generation

1. Cf. S. Japhet, *The Ideology of the Book of Chronicles and its Place in Biblical Thought* (Frankfurt: Peter Lang, 1989), pp. 74-75 n. 203, although this chronology is not applied by her.

since Adam (10 generations from Adam to Noah; 10 from Shem to Abraham; 30 from Abraham to Josiah, makes, by the deduction of one for the repetition of Abraham, the generation after Josiah—the exilic generation—the fiftieth generation).

> For C, the exile begins already with the death of Josiah (see on 2 Chron. 35.24-25). The 70 years of the exile, as foretold in Jer. 25.11-12, is calculated by C as the period from the death of Josiah in 609 to the edict of Cyrus in 538.

The exilic generation—to which he himself and all his readers after him belong—is, thus, the one to whom the proclamation of eschatological jubilee is made (cf. the parallels between Cyrus's edict in 2 Chron. 36.22 and the proclamation of the jubilee in Lev. 25.9). The last word of C is, 'Let him go up', from the root of *'aliyyâ*, 'return, immigration into the land of Israel'. But, in the interim of waiting for that consummation, that is an ascent to the land which any can begin now through the pursuit of the life of holiness as defined in the Law. It is life under the Levites that provides Israel with the realized eschatology under which it can live a life of the practice of holiness now, while it awaits the definitive 'Return' in God's future.

2. *The Chronicler's Key Terms*

A feature of the highly integrated and tightly conceived character of C's work is his use of an extensive network of key terms in cross-reference and allusion ('semantic fields'). These terms may be arranged as follows to reflect the outline of C's theology given above:

- (a) the nature of the relationship designed by God with his world through his people, Israel;
- (b) the blessings that flow from that relationship realized;
- (c) the actions that constitute breaches of that relationship;
- (d) the consequences that follow from the breakdown of the relationship, culminating in the forfeiture of those blessings;
- (e) the programme of reconstruction.

> Only a selection of the key terms is given. The references below are far from exhaustive but cross-refer to discussions in the body of the commentary, which, in turn, provide further cross-references.

(a) The nature of the relationship of God to his world through his people is defined primarily in terms of the Jerusalem tradition of theology:

- Israel affirms a duality in the one Deity: 'God' who is the cosmic power; 'the LORD' who relates himself to Israel (2 Chron. 26.5);
- God's sovereignty is universal (1 Chron. 29.11-12; 2 Chron. 36.23);
- Israel's life is sacramental: God's cosmic reign is discharged on earth by his representative and agent, the Davidic king, who sits on the LORD's own throne in Jerusalem (1 Chron. 28.5; 29.23; 2 Chron. 9.8; 13.8);
- the land is God's land (2 Chron. 7.20), the LORD's 'inheritance' (2 Chron. 20.11); it is the physical theatre for working out the concept of holiness and degrees of holiness by the metaphor of space (1 Chron. 6.49);
- Israel is the visible, physical expression of the universal dominion of God: it is a *qāhāl*, a sacral assembly (1 Chron. 13.2), 'gathered' for concerted action (1 Chron. 11.1); God's 'host' on earth (1 Chron. 12.22; 2 Chron. 14.11-13), his 'camp' (1 Chron. 9.18-19), mustered for action (root *pqd*, 1 Chron. 21.5), which 'sallies forth' to war (2 Chron. 26.11; also in peace 2 Chron. 1.10); the opposite is the *hāmôn*, the rabble, the horde of the nations (2 Chron. 20.2);
- as such, nothing must interpose between the immediacy of the interchange between Israel and God, the privileged sphere of the fusion of the divine and human on earth; hence the need for 'enrolment' (*hityaḥēś*), the definition of the membership and limits of the people of Israel (1 Chron. 9.1);
- this relationship requires exclusive reliance upon God (for the model, cf. 1 Chron. 5.20), consultation of him in all things (*drš*, *š'l*, *bqš*, *niš'an* (1 Chron. 10.13-14 [28.9 for a 'sacramental' application]; 2 Chron. 7.14; 13.18; 14.11; 15.4). The evidence of this reliance is in symbol (the store-houses for the dedication of the 'holy things', 1 Chron. 9.26) and thus in reality. The criteria are the traditional Law of Moses (1 Chron. 22.11-13; 2 Chron. 6.16; 23.18). God provides unbroken sourcesof guidance in the prophetic word in warning (2 Chron. 18) and in Scripture (Introduction to 2 Chron. 10–36).

(b) The blessings which flow from the immediacy of the relationship are also stated in terms of the Jerusalem tradition of theology.

For Israel itself:

- God is 'with' his people (1 Chron. 11.9);
- God 'establishes' (*kûn*) his king; the verb *kûn* also expresses sacramental correspondence: the establishment of the dynasty is the establishment of the people that enables the establishment of the Temple (1 Chron. 14.2);
- his king is 'helped' (*'zr*, 1 Chron. 5.20), becomes 'strong' (*ḥzq*, both in himself and in the support from his people, 1 Chron. 11.10; *'mṣ*, 1 Chron. 22.13), 'succeeds' (*hiṣlîaḥ*, 1 Chron. 22.11), enjoys 'victory' (1 Chron. 11.14), 'health' (*rp'*, 2 Chron. 7.14; 30.20), 'capability' (*'āṣar kōaḥ*, 1 Chron. 29.14; cf. 2 Chron. 13.20), 'riches and honour' (1 Chron. 29.12);
- Israel enjoys possession of the land (*'ḥz*, 1 Chron. 9.2; the use of the principle of correspondence 'inherit'–'disinherit', *yrš*, 2 Chron. 20.7; *nḥl*, 1 Chron. 28.8; cf. 'people of the land' of the indigenous population which Israel then becomes, 1 Chron. 11.4, cf. 2 Chron. 23.13);
- as God is good (2 Chron. 30.18), so 'good things' happen in the land (2 Chron. 10.7); in security (2 Chron. 26.8), the arts of agriculture flourish (2 Chron. 26.9-10); peaceful commerce (2 Chron. 15.5);
- the land is held in uninterrupted succession by succeeding generations (1 Chron. 28.8);
- security from threats from without and within (garrisons sacramentally represent the pacification of the land by God, 2 Chron. 8.5): use of Exodus vocabulary as archetype of the LORD's victory over the nations—security from the 'destroyer' (*mašḥît* 2 Chron. 24.23), experience of 'judgments' (*šᵉpāṭîm*, 2 Chron. 24.24), the king as the recipient of 'signs' (*môpᵉtîm*, 2 Chron. 32.24);
- the hall-mark is 'joy' (1 Chron. 12.40).

For Israel's relations with the other nations of the world:

- pacification and peace: the ark is laid up in the Temple of Jerusalem as its 'place of rest' by Solomon, 'the man of peace' and 'quietness' (1 Chron. 22.9); cessation of the tumults of the nations (2 Chron. 15.5, the destiny of Israel and the destiny of the nations are inseparably bound up with one another);

- the love of God for Israel is recognized to be of benefit for the world (2 Chron. 2.11; 9.8);
- acknowledgment from all the nations of the world (1 Chron. 22.5): the trophies of victory laid up in the Temple (the shields of the earth, 2 Chron. 12.9); tribute from the nations (1 Chron. 16.29) and consultation by the kings of the nations (2 Chron. 9.23-24);
- 'fear of the LORD' is the inevitable regard in which the loyal Davidic king is held (1 Chron. 14.17);
- the motif of the 'righteous gentile', Tou (1 Chron. 18.9), Ornan (1 Chron. 21.23), Huram (1 Chron. 14.1), Cyrus (2 Chron. 36.22), even Neco (2 Chron. 35.21); the inclusion of the innocent non-Israelite in Solomon's prayer (2 Chron. 6.32-33);
- confirmation of the status and possessions of the nations (2 Chron. 20.10).

(c) The actions which constitute breaches of that relationship:

- resorting to other gods (*ma'al*, 1 Chron. 2.7; *'zb*, 1 Chron. 28.9); wickedness/non-righteousness (*rš'*) is exemplified by Ahab and his family (2 Chron. 18–24), by contrast to David's righteousness (*ṣdq*, 1 Chron. 18.14);
- consulting the physicians (2 Chron. 16.12);
- parleying with other nations (1 Chron. 1.10).

(d) The consequences that follow from the breakdown of the relationship:

- the anger of the LORD (1 Chron. 27.24);
- forfeiture of possessions and land: sacramental correspondence is again the key concept—failure in the symbol (the 'holy things') means, by that act inevitably, simultaneous forfeiture of the substance (2 Chron. 15.2);

The commonly applied term, 'retribution', the punishment that *follows* a crime, is too narrow a concept. It is instinctive to look at cases where 'retribution' does not follow, in particular the end of the reign of Ahaz (2 Chron. 28.22-27). Forfeiture of status has already taken place. The

Augustinian 'from whom to be turned *is* to fall; to whom to be turned *is* to rise', expresses well the indivisible nature of the two sides of the one reality. Cf. *šûb*, 2 Chron. 30.9: to turn in repentance *is* to be granted a restoration; or 2 Chron. 34.15: to render *is* to receive.

- cumulative rejection across the generations (1 Chron. 28.9b; 2 Chron. 36.15);
- sickness and premature death (1 Chron. 10.3);
- the invasion of the chaotic horde of the world of the nations (Nimrod and Cush are the emblematic international enemies, the Philistines and Edomites the local, 1 Chron. 1.10-12; 2 Chron. 20.2);
- defeat and even death at the hands of the nations (1 Chron. 10);
- negative Passover–inverted exodus: the 'destroyer' is aimed at Israel herself (1 Chron. 21.12); what the foreign invaders do not succeed in doing, Judah's own kings do (2 Chron. 21.14, Jehoram as new Pharaoh);
- invasion from the world of the nations, for punishment and correction (2 Chron. 12; 24.23-24);
- death penalty mitigated in the forfeiture of those blessings and submersion in the world of the nations (1 Chron. 5.26).

(e) The programme of reconstruction:

- much of the Law of the Pentateuch is expounded in narrative form in C in terms of Israel's past history, especially the legislation and the blessing and curse of the 'Holiness Code' in Leviticus 17–26. C is the story of an ideal (holiness) and of a succession of superseded models for the attainment of that ideal. For C's understanding of reconstruction, see Lev. 26.40-45: even without king, Temple and land, restoration can be anticipated; the symbols may not endure, but the reality remains; sacramental theology has to be transposed from the monarchical system into that of Torah; it is by obedience that Israel becomes what it is destined to be;
- acknowledgment of sin (*kn'*, cf. Lev. 26.41; 2 Chron. 7.14; the opposite of arrogant refusal to confess, 2 Chron. 16.10; or of presumptuousness, 2 Chron. 32.26);
- the sovereignty of God as the universal God who, when his own people let him down, can use the empires of the world as the instruments of his sovereignty (2 Chron. 36.23);

- the pursuit of the life of holiness; the patient waiting of the people poised for the Return (2 Chron. 30.9).

What Kind of Literature is C and with what Expectations Should it be Read?

Unlike most of the rest of the Hebrew Bible, the process by which C has come into being lies close to the surface: the balance between C's own contribution and its reuse of earlier sources, especially Samuel–Kings, is clear from the comparison of texts.

This is not to say that C's relation to these underlying texts is not extremely complex. Since the use he makes of them—how far he adopts, adapts, adds to or suppresses—is an important indicator of his purpose, much space will have to be given to the purposes that can be inferred to lie behind that selection and adaptation. But in order not to impede the flow of the presentation of C's own thought too badly, the details of the comparison between the two versions will usually be placed in smaller print.

I have tried to maximize the significance of details in the text as it stands in MT; for example, minute differences in the parallels between C and Samuel–Kings. It is sometimes said that it is a mistake to regard all such changes as significant. One of the issues in modern study is how far the variations in Samuel–Kings have arisen in the course of the history of the transmission of the text of Samuel–Kings after the time of C: it is argued that Hebrew MSS of Samuel among the Dead Sea Scrolls support the reading of C rather than the MT of Samuel. That is not the only deduction from the evidence that might be made: it could be that in certain circles an attempt was made to harmonize the text of earlier Samuel with the later C. But, while the debate about the original character and content of the Samuel–Kings and C texts is wholly valid, in terms of this commentary it is irrelevant. The reader is presented with two given texts—Samuel–Kings and C—and these two texts will endure as the received texts for interpretation. It is thus wholly appropriate that every last variation between these two texts be taken with seriousness as evidence for the differing purposes for which both texts have been received as holy Scripture.

This is not to say that on—rare—occasions one is not driven to suspect that the received text has become corrupted (such as in 1 Chron. 6.57-60). One must be constantly aware that there may be entirely accidental reasons for the variation between texts. But the onus of proof lies with the interpreters—among whom, on occasion, I must be counted—who propose to change the received text in either version.

The question of the unity of C is also not a question on which time will be spent. It is the function of C as it now stands in MT that will be the focus of attention. This is a congenial position, for on grounds of content, as outlined above, there seem in any case to be strong indications of coherence in the work. No space will, then, be given to the defence of unity of C—it is a given—nor to arguments about any editorial history through which the work might have passed.

Critical questions of history and geography also need not be opened in this context. C is not a manual of either (for C's use of geography, cf. e.g. 1 Chron. 5.1-2). To attempt to use C as a historical source, or even to defend the historicity of his work, is at best a distraction and, with no doubt the best of intentions, to run counter to the purpose of the work (e.g. taking the genealogies as actual statements of lineage rather than metaphors for historic, geographical and social conditions—for instance, Samuel as the grandfather of Heman, 1 Chron. 6.33; Obed-edom as the son of Jeduthun, 1 Chron. 16.38; cf. the impossibly large figures in the Tables at 1 Chron. 29.4, 21 or C's invention of a repentance of Manasseh, 2 Chron. 33.12-17, or of an exile for Jehoiakim, 2 Chron. 36.6-7; the data here are moveable counters). C smoothes and streamlines the profile of historical events; to force the material back into its historical mould—for example, to speculate about the social policies of the historical Solomon, or even to allow the more historical account in Samuel–Kings to print through—is to deprive it of the configuration through which C is expressing his theology. One must refuse to adjust the received text of either version in the light of the other, even when there is external evidence that supports one reading over the other. It might be held that, where there are two texts that diverge (e.g. Samuel–Kings has Josiah die at Megiddo, C in Jerusalem), both cannot be 'right' and one must be amended in the light of the other (or both, in the light of outside evidence). I have little sympathy with that view: the worst thing that one can do to a biblical text is—understandable though it may be and motivated with the highest of purposes—to propose a harmonizing reading. For, in so doing, one may be destroying the very point that the respective writer is trying to make. Only by the willing suspension of historical considerations can one do justice to his intention. On the above example, all historical probability supports the likelihood that Josiah was killed at Megiddo, as Samuel–Kings says he was. But to adjust the text of C in the light of Samuel–Kings would be, as I shall argue below, to negate the theological (not historical) argument that C is presenting, namely, that the death of Josiah marks the death of the Davidic dynasty in Jerusalem.

Given the nature of C, space will be given to the elucidation of historical, geographical and other data only in so far as that seems to contribute to the understanding of the theological statement intended. As for kind of writing, C's must be termed a work of theology. That is probably as far as one need go, but the point can be reinforced by the suggestion that the work bears some relationship to the type of Jewish literature known as midrash. Midrash is the reinterpretation of a given biblical text, that is, a text which has received some kind of status as canonical Scripture. The task of the midrash is not to incorporate new historical data; it is to reinterpret the given data in such a way that new insights for the edification of the community are achieved. J. Neusner's definition of midrash is, it seems to me, highly illuminating:[2]

> *Midrash*... represents... creative philology and creative historiography. As creative philology, the *Midrash* discovers meaning in apparently meaningless detail. It... uses the elements of language not as fixed, unchanging categories, but as relative, living, tentative nuances of thought. As creative historiography, the *Midrash* rewrites the past to make manifest the eternal rightness of Scriptural paradigms. What would it be like if all people lived at one moment?... *Midrash* thus exchanges the stability of language and the continuity of history for the stability of values and the eternity of truth.

There will be repeated points of contact with this definition in the commentary. It may be noted that the word midrash occurs in the Hebrew Bible only in C and there it is used, in all probability, in connection with the authoritative written work penned by the prophets as the running commentary on the reigns of the kings of Judah until the death of Josiah (see Introduction to 2 Chron. 10–36). The likelihood is that this work also belongs to C's idealistic and ideological presentation. No such work is extant; probably no such work ever existed; but that in no way invalidates the point that C wishes to make: throughout the course of Israel's history, God interposed his word through his prophets at every critical juncture.

2. J. Neusner, *Between Time and Eternity* (Encino: Dickenson, 1975), p. 52.

1 CHRONICLES 1: ISRAEL'S PLACE WITHIN THE HUMAN FAMILY

1 Chronicles 1 is C's preface to his work. Despite its discouraging appearance as a catalogue of unfamiliar names, it deserves careful attention. In the selection and arrangement of these names, it will be argued, C presents the framework and some of the central ideas of his work as a whole.

The chapter is carefully constructed to show by means of genealogies the descent and interrelationship of the one family of the human race. But there is a gradual focusing of interest: side branches are mentioned, but many are then left undeveloped; only very selective lines of descent are traced. Twice under the wider umbrella of the whole human race (first Adam, then Noah), then once again under the umbrella of the population of the immediate geographical area (Abraham), the chapter narrows down attention to the one family, Israel, mentioned for the first time in v. 34b. It is Israel, both in itself and in its relations with the rest of humanity as sketched through the genealogies, that is to be the subject of the whole work.

One vital clue to the understanding of how the names in 1 Chronicles 1 have been selected and arranged must be the fact that they are all derived from the book of Genesis.

Sometimes this information is drawn from the narratives, sometimes from the genealogies of Genesis:

vv. 1-4 Adam to Noah and his sons, Shem, Ham and Japhet; see the narratives and genealogies of Genesis 2–9;
vv. 5-23 the descendants of Japhet, Ham and Shem; see the genealogies of Gen. 10.2-29;
vv. 24-27 Arpachshad to Abram; see the genealogies in Gen. 11.10-26;
vv. 27-28 Abraham, Isaac and Ishmael; see the narratives in Genesis 16–17;
vv. 29-34 the descendants of Ishmael and Keturah; see the narratives and genealogies in Gen. 25.13-16;
vv. 35-54 the descendants of Esau; see the genealogies and other data of Genesis 36.

Wherever possible C has compressed this parent Genesis text (some cases will be noted below). Frequently, it is the selection of texts and the differences between the parent text and the use to which C puts that text that highlight his intention.

In this context, and in many contexts later in C's work where there are parallels with other passages in the Hebrew Bible, the significance of these differences will be maximized in the effort to understand the distinctive message of C. It may be argued that many of these differences are trivial, even accidents of the transmission of the text (such as in this chapter the odd collocation 'Esau and Israel' in v. 34, where for consistency one would have expected either two personal names 'Esau and Jacob'—as in the LXX tradition—or two national names, 'Edom and Israel', but not the mixture of the two as in the present text), and cannot, therefore, be confidently used as evidence of C's intention. The assumption made here, however, is that, unless other considerations compel one to consider that unlikely, any changes that exist are deliberate, no matter how small, and do reflect the mind and purpose of the author.

It is an important observation for the understanding of 1 Chronicles 1 that C knows both the names embedded in the Genesis narratives and those in the genealogies that provide the chronological framework for these narratives. It may thus be assumed that he is familiar with the narratives themselves and is presupposing their content.

C's audience must also have been well-versed in the traditions of Genesis: his use of its genealogical framework must have functioned for his readers (and for such a highly sophisticated work of learning with its detailed modification of a written text one must assume an audience primarily of readers) as a kind of cryptic code, allusively bringing to mind in the most condensed form possible the stories of the primeval and of the patriarchal periods.

The structure of the chapter is made clear by the unusually large number of paragraph markers in the MT; these help the reader to break up the sheer volume of the material into its constituent elements (NRSV gives only a modified form).

Vv. 1-4 The ten generations from Adam to Noah; the sons of Noah: Shem, Ham and Japhet.

V. 5 Japhet's seven sons.

Vv. 6-7 Three sons of Japhet's oldest son, Gomer, and four sons of his fourth son, Javan.

Vv. 8-9 Ham's four sons; five sons of Ham's oldest son, Cush; two sons of Cush's fourth son.

V. 10 Note on Nimrod, another son of Cush.

Vv. 11-12 Seven sons of Egypt, Ham's second son, including a note on the origin of the Philistines.

Vv. 13-16 Eleven sons of Canaan, fourth son of Ham.

V. 17 Shem's nine sons.

Vv. 18-23 The lineal descent of Shem's third son, Arpachshad, is traced through four generations to the brothers Peleg and Joktan, 'in whose days the earth was divided'; thirteen sons of Joktan are then listed.

Vv. 24-27 The ten generations from Shem to Abraham (through Arpachshad and Peleg).

V. 28 Two sons of Abraham: Isaac and Ishmael.

Vv. 29-31 Twelve sons of Ishmael.

V. 32 Abraham's six sons by his concubine; the two sons of the second of these, Jokshan.

Vv. 33 The five sons of the fourth of these, Midian.

V. 34a 'Then Abraham begat Isaac'.

V. 34b Isaac's two sons: Esau and Israel.

V. 35 Five sons of Esau.

V. 36 Seven sons of Eliphaz, oldest son of Esau.

V. 37 Four sons of Reuel, second son of Esau.

Vv. 38-39 Seven sons of Seir; two sons and a daughter of Lotan, oldest son Seir.

V. 40a Five sons of Shobal, second son of Seir.

V. 40b Two sons of Zibeon, third son of Seir.

V. 41a One son [MT 'sons'] of Ana, fourth son of Seir.

Vv. 41b Three sons of Dishon, son of Ana.

V. 42 Three sons of Ezer, sixth son of Seir; two sons of Dishon, fifth son of Seir.

The change in paragraph marker at the end of v. 42 coincides with the introduction of quite different material: there is no genealogical element in the list which follows of the successive monarchs in Edom nor of the regions where chieftains ruled after the monarchy.

Vv. 43-51a The succession of eight kings who ruled in Edom before a king ruled in Israel. These are presented within a stereotyped framework: 'X died and Y reigned in his place', with a note on his place of origin and/or his father's name. Only once is an incident recorded: the fourth king's massacre of the Midianites. Only in the case of the last king is the name of his wife mentioned.

Vv. 51b-54 The list of the eleven regional chieftains of Edom, who then followed the kings.

V. 34a gives a very good example (among others) of the importance of noting how the MT uses paragraph markers to throw material into sharp relief.

The significance of the names in vv. 1-54 is both chronological and geographical. The lineal descent marking the succession of generations provides C with the beginnings of his overall chronological framework: the twenty generations of the general history of the human race from Adam to Abraham; the twenty-second generation, Isaac's sons, Esau and Israel, sharpen the focus on the central line of Israel. The lateral lines show the geographical diffusion of the human race and the central location of Israel within it. What, then, is the statement which C is thus indirectly making through the shorthand of this genealogical framework?

The story of the human race begins with an ideal stated (1 Chron. 1): Adam, the human creation of God, who is destined for a life of perfect harmony with God, as expressed, for example, in the figure of God walking in the Garden of Eden in the cool of the day and seeking the company of his human creatures (Gen. 2; for Adam again as the focus of C, cf. 2 Chron. 6.18; 32.19).

But the following name, Seth, is unexpected: instead of the first sons of Adam, Cain and Abel, it is Seth, the 'replacement'—as his name implies—for Abel murdered by Cain (Gen. 4), who is then listed. Here already a theme that is to recur again and again in C's work is sounded: the purpose of God for good is continually frustrated by the perversity of the human race. God constantly attempts to restore, repair or contain the damage by means of some alternative provision; secondary figures, like Seth, through no intrinsic merit of their own are repeatedly called upon to fill the role originally intended for favoured primary figures, like Cain.

The story of God's dealing with the human race continues to be one of false starts and repeated restarts: the line of succession is traced through the ten generations of wickedness rampant from Adam, the first father of humanity, to Noah, the second father of humanity. After another ten generations, Abraham, the 'father of many nations', is reached. Out of his descendants only one line is chosen, that of his grandson, Israel. It is intended that at last in that people the ideal will be realized on behalf of the other nations of the world, to whom it is related by the genealogies and amid whom it is set. The remainder of C's work is to explore how far Israel is successful in realizing this double destiny both in itself and on behalf of others. 1 Chronicles 1 thus states Israel's place amid the whole family of humanity, its election by God's free choice for God's special blessing and for special responsibility. What should have been first achieved under Adam and what might then have been attained under Noah, only begins its possible realization in the third beginning under Abraham, with his grandson, Israel.

C, thus, wastes no time reporting the descendants of Cain from Genesis 4. Instead, he proceeds directly through a period of ten generations from Adam to Noah (v. 4), who, as the survivor of the Flood with his sons, is the second father of humanity. At the sons of Noah, C pauses: they provide the three great divisions into which the population of the earth now falls. They are further subdivided into seventy-one ethnic or geographical groups and sub-groups (vv. 5-23). Noah's sons are listed in reverse order to v. 4, so that Shem, the ancestor of Israel, now comes in climactic position at the end. These lands and nations are listed from the perspective of the land of Israel: Israel stands at the centre of the world of the nations and their territories.

Japhet (vv. 5-7) is listed for three generations, with seven sons and seven grandsons. The lands represented by Japhet lie to the north and west along the northern side of the Mediterranean, as the most familiar of these names, the Medes (so closely linked with the Persians elsewhere in the Hebrew Bible, e.g. Dan. 5.28) and Javan (= Greece; see, for example, Dan. 8.21), make clear.

> Other standard identifications of names in the list confirm the general geographical region (cf. KBS). For example, Gomer (the Cimmerians of Cappadocia and Armenia), Magog, Tubal, Meshech and Togarmah are all mentioned in Ezekiel 38–39, as terrifying invaders from the North who will fall with great slaughter in the land of Israel. Tiras may be the same as the Tursha, among the 'Sea Peoples' fought by Ramesses III at the beginning of the twelfth century BCE. Ashkenaz, the Scythians from the Caucasus, has since the Middle Ages supplied the name for the Jews of northern and eastern Europe. Elishah and Kittim echo the towns of Alashiya and Kition known from the Late Bronze Age in Cyprus, just as Rodanim echoes Rhodes. Tarshish, wherever it was located in the Mediterranean, is constantly related to ocean-going vessels (2 Chron. 9.21; 20.36-37).

Ham (vv. 8-16), listed with four sons, twenty-three grandsons and four great-grandsons, is located on the southern side of the Mediterranean, in north Africa and across the land bridge into the Arabian peninsula, Palestine and Syria, as, again, the most familiar names, Egypt and Canaan (v. 8), make clear. Ham thus represents also the pre- and non-Israelite population of the Land of Israel.

Only some of the names mentioned can be identified: Cush with Nubia, Put with Libya. The association of Canaan with Egypt and these surrounding areas in v. 8 is scarcely surprising in view of the imperial claims of Egypt in the New Kingdom and later to Canaan. Verse 9 leads into the area of S Arabia (for Sheba cf. 2 Chron. 9.1, also Ezek. 27.22). The Egyptian sphere is elaborated in vv. 11-12: Patros, v. 12, is Upper Egypt, Caphtor perhaps Crete, Lydia in western Asia Minor. Places and peoples in Canaan follow in vv. 13-16: for example, Sidon; the succession of Hittites (cf. the Assyrian reference to Syria-Palestine as 'Hatti-land'), Jebusites and Amorites, all associated with Jerusalem (cf. Ezek. 16.45), is notable; places on the north Lebanon coast are listed—Arqa, Sin and Zemar with the offshore island of Arvad, and Hamath inland on the Orontes.[1] Hamath is to feature in 1 Chron. 13.5 and 2 Chron. 7.8 as marking the northern frontier of the Davidic kingdom.

Shem (vv. 17-23) is listed with nine sons (or five sons and four grandsons through Aram, if the parallel in Gen. 10.23 is followed). Out of these nine only one line is then traced—that of Arpachshad, whose lineal descendants for four generations are then given. Shem's great-grandson through the line of Arpahshad is Eber, the father of the Hebrews. From Eber there 'split off' two branches: the branch of Peleg ('splitting'), from which Israel is eventually to spring, which is resumed in vv. 24-27; and the branch of Joktan, whose thirteen sons are now listed in this context. Shem spreads west from Mesopotamia, as the most familiar names in v. 17 make clear: Elam, east of the lower Tigris; Asshur, on the upper Tigris; the Aramaeans, on the upper Euphrates; Uz (if it is the same name), the homeland of Job (Job 1.1), in the steppes east of the Jordan

Shem in part overlaps with Ham: Havilah, now associated with Ophir, the source of legendary wealth in the Arabian Sea (cf. 1 Chron. 29.4; 2 Chron. 8.18; 9.10), and Sheba occur in both lists, vv. 9 and 22-23; so Lud in vv. 11 and 17 (cf. Sheba and Dedan, v. 9, as sons of Ham yet also grandsons of Abraham by his concubine, v. 32). Meshech, v. 17, has already been given under Japhet in v. 5. Most of the remaining names are of uncertain location.

The most important issue is C's viewpoint. Many of these names, so unfamiliar and obscure to the modern reader, were presumably commonplace to C and to his audience and merely part of their awareness of the world in which they lived. Others may have been traditional and even in C's day long since defunct, so that this world is partly also

1. L.H. Grollenberg, *Atlas of the Bible* (London: Nelson, 1956), map 4.

a world of the mind, of the memory and imagination. No matter what the actual conditions of outward life may be (one may think of C writing in the very circumscribed circumstances of the Persian Empire of the fourth century BCE), here is a landscape of rich association from which replenishment can constantly be drawn. From a 'scientific', ethnographic, point of view nations are associated which can have very little to do with one another: a clear example is the listing of Canaan among the descendants of Ham when knowledge now available shows that the Canaanites in language, religion and culture belonged firmly within the Semitic tradition, that is, to the Semites, the descendants of Shem.

C's ideological statement is clear. With its central role, symbolized by its location at the very centre of the earth, Israel has the task of realizing in its life the ideal once intended by God for all. But that restart is under constant threat from the menacing world of the nations, among whom Israel is to be born. The fearsome reputation of the warring nations of the north as in Ezekiel 38–39 has already been noted. The Canaanites and the other indigenous populations of what is to become the land of Israel will pose the closest, insidious, threat of dragging Israel back down to their own level, of preventing Israel from attaining its true identity as part of, yet separate from, the world of the nations.

C's purpose is also clear from the occasional snatches of narrative interspersed among the genealogies. The first of these is the statement in 1 Chron. 1.10 about Cush and his son Nimrod, who 'began to be a tyrant upon earth' (the meaning 'tyrant' is recognized for the term in Isa. 49.25 [KBS], significantly a text of the Babylonian exilic). Cush, as has been noted, represents the Nile valley south of the first cataract. Later in his work C is to refer to Egyptian armies invading Israel as 'Cush' (2 Chron. 12.3; 14.9-13; 16.8; 21.16; it is another Egyptian, Neco, who is to bring about the death of Josiah and so inaugurate the exile [see on 2 Chron. 35.20-24]). Nimrod is identified with Babylon and the valleys of the Tigris and Euphrates in general (Gen. 10.10), and thus with the power that is ultimately to be responsible for the downfall of Israel (1 Chron. 9.1; 2 Chron. 32.31; 33.11; 36; for Assyria see 1 Chron. 5.6, 26; 2 Chron. 28.16-21; 30.6; 32; 33.11). Nimrod and Nebuchadnezzar, the first and the last Babylonian tyrants to be mentioned in C (1 Chron. 1.10; 2 Chron. 36.6-13; cf. 1 Chron. 6.15), thus form, with Cush, an *inclusio*—a matching beginning and end—of the destructive foreign forces threatening the very existence of Israel, which dominate the entire work.

It is to be noted that C omits Nimrod's more innocuous pursuit—that he was 'a mighty hunter' (Gen. 10.9). The word 'tyrant' (*gibbôr*) may also be translated 'mighty man, hero, warrior': it will be C's purpose to record the 'warriors' of Israel (from the same word, e.g., 1 Chron. 11.10–12.40), that is, the forces God has at his disposal to counter the threat to his purposes posed by the nations of the world.

Another discursive item retained from Genesis concerns the origin of the Philistines (1 Chron. 1.12). If the Canaanites are the indwelling pre-Israelite population ever ready to subvert from within, and the Egyptians and Babylonians are the first and the last of the international enemies threatening Israel with annihilation from without, the Philistines on the western coastal fringe are the nearest alien neighbour constantly probing and seeking to detach territory. Their interventions in the fortunes of Israel are to be repeatedly noted from the reign of the first king, Saul, to that of Ahaz, the last king under whom they appear (1 Chron. 10.1 to 2 Chron. 28.18).

Verse 12 introduces another thematic term—the verb *yāṣā'*, in its military sense of 'to sally forth': the Philistines invade from across the sea and are in a state of constant readiness to attack. The verb is also to be used of Israel doing battle in the name of the LORD: Israel are to be the LORD's agents in the pacification of the earth; when they fail to realize that purpose, they themselves fall victim to invasion by the very forces which it is their task to subdue.

yṣ': 1 Chron. 5.18; 7.11; 11.2; 12.36; 14.8, 15; 19.9, 16; 20.1; 2 Chron. 1.10; 6.34; 14.9-10; 19.4; 20.20-21; 23.14; 25.5; 26.6, 11; 28.9; 35.20.

In this extended account of the sons of Noah, C sticks very closely to his terse source in Gen. 10.2-29, but with some abbreviation. After v. 7 he omits the material from Gen. 10.5, which stresses the natural division of humanity by language and geography; after v. 10, Gen. 10.9-12, which tells of the positive achievements of Nimrod as huntsman and city-builder; and, after v. 16, Gen. 10.18b-21, the note on the boundaries of the Canaanites which spread down the coast from Sidon to Gaza and east to the Dead Sea, the diffusion of the families of Ham, and the heading to the section on Shem emphasizing the fact that he is the ancestor of Eber. After v. 23 Gen. 10.30–11.9 is omitted—resumptive material and the Tower of Babel narrative. C is about the possibility of harmony within humanity, not what divides.

Already, from his handling of his sources, one begins to form an impression of C as a writer driven by a powerful purpose to select ruthlessly from his sources the materials that are relevant to his theme, yet whose vigour at times outruns his consistency: the last phrase of v. 23, resuming the foregoing, is unnecessary and is similar to material that he has earlier omitted from his Genesis source (e.g. Gen. 10.20 after v. 16).

C, having thus indicated the geographical disposition of the human race, returns in vv. 24-27 to trace out of this mass of humanity a second period of ten generations, which brings the narrow line of Israel's direct descent from Shem, son of Noah, down to Abram. Verse 24 thus resumes the lineal descent broken off at v. 4.

This double resumption of Shem in vv. 17 and 24, in the first case to complete the genealogy of the sons of Noah, in the second to lead the narrative off in the direction of the decisive events under Israel, is reminiscent of the double resumption of Benjamin at the end of the genealogies in 1 Chronicles 8 and 9.35-44, the first of which rounds off the genealogy of the Israelites and the second of which prepares for the history of the monarchy.

The source behind vv. 24-27 is Gen. 11.10-26; its ceremonious recital of the ages of the successive fathers at the birth of their sons and of the years of their survival thereafter has been suppressed by C: it is with the succession of the generations not their lengths that he is concerned. Out of his voluminous source C reproduces a bare list of names.

At Abram (v. 27), the tenth generation from Noah and twentieth from Adam, C must again broaden out his genealogical presentation to include collateral branches. By means of the merest mention of the change of Abram's name to Abraham, he is making allusion to the covenant of promise which God made with Abraham in Gen. 17.4-5 by which he is to become the father of many nations:

'Your name will no longer be called Abram;
Your name shall be Abraham,
because I make you the father of a host of nations.'

The phrase, 'Abram, that is, Abraham' (v. 27), is actually, for all its modest character, the first for whose very verbal formulation C is himself responsible and which is not dependent *verbatim* on the Genesis source.

Having prepared the way for the location of Israel within the three broad divisions of humanity as a whole, as represented by the sons of Noah, C now turns to locate Israel within the 'many nations' represented by Abraham's descendants.

The wording of the introductory phrases to the genealogies of Abram's descendants in vv. 28 and 32a is again C's own: Israel's line of descent is only one of three stemming from Abraham, and even that is shared with Edom. Abraham's two sons, Isaac and Ishmael, are mentioned first (v. 28); the third line from Abraham's concubine follows in v. 32. As under Noah, Shem, the first of the three lines to be named, is then treated last in order to throw it into greater prominence, so here Isaac, though named first (v. 28), has his descendants listed only from v. 34.

Ishmael with his twelve sons (vv. 29-31; the list is derived from Gen. 25.13b-16aα) is to be Israel's neighbour in the desert and desert fringes of Syria and Arabia to the east and south.

The most familiar of the names mentioned are: Nebaioth and Kedar, see Isa. 60.7 for the association with sheep-raising; perhaps Massa is to be related to Prov. 30.1; 31.1, in which case there is here another association with the wisdom tradition (cf. Uz in v. 17) for which the 'people of the East' are proverbial (1 Kgs 4.30); Tema is the important oasis in N Arabia (Job 6.19), perhaps the home of Eliphaz (Job 2.11), see v. 32 for Shuah, the origin of Bildad (Job 2.11).

By his concubine Keturah, Abraham has a third line of descent: six more sons and seven more grandsons (vv. 32-33 = Gen. 25.2aβ-4 with the omission of Gen. 25.3b, perhaps by textual error) in the remoter desert area (Midian, for example, is located on both sides of the Gulf of Aqaba [Grollenberg, map 9]; Sheba and Dedan overlap with the descendants of Ham in v. 9).

The isolated paragraph of v. 34a, noted above, throws the birth of Isaac, and the two branches which stem from him, into greater prominence.

C's formulation of v. 34a, '*Then* Abraham became the father of Isaac' marks a phase in developments more strongly than the mere listing in the Genesis text, 'Abraham became'. By contrast, in C there is an abbreviation of this formulation at the beginning of vv. 36 and 39: the Edomites are simply listed (cf. the omission of 'These are' at the beginning of vv. 37, 38, 40a,b, 41a,b, 42a,b).

Even in the line through Abraham's son Isaac there is yet another choice to be made: this time the preference of one twin, Israel, over his older brother, Esau.

C continues (v. 34) his use of the genealogical framework of Genesis by adapting Gen. 25.19b for the birth of Isaac; the names of Isaac's twin sons, Esau and Israel, assumes the narrative in Gen. 25.20-26 with the substitution, not in fact made in Genesis until 32.28/35.10, of the name 'Israel' for 'Jacob'.

But the list of Israel's descendants cannot yet be given: it must be delayed by an extensive account of the rival family of Esau with its prior claim by right of birth to status and preference.

The list of Esau's five sons (v. 35) C constructs from Gen. 36.4, 5a, 10; he provides him with eleven grandsons (vv. 36-37) to Genesis's ten by including, seemingly through another lapse in attention to detail, among the list of Eliphaz's sons one Timna, whom Genesis 36.11-12 states to be Eliphaz's concubine. The relationship to Esau of Seir, whose descendants are now listed in vv. 38-42, is not made clear: although C follows Gen. 36.20-28 for the twenty-eight names themselves, he omits the notes in Gen. 36.9, 'Esau the father of Edom in the hill-country of Seir' (so Gen. 36.43b for the first part) and 36.21, 'the sons of Seir in the land of Edom', which go some way in explaining it. For a further discussion of the relations between Israel, Seir and Edom, see on 2 Chron. 25.11-12.

Several of the places listed in vv. 43-50 can be identified with Arab place-names in the area to the south of the Dead Sea, e.g., Bozrah (v. 44) with Buseirah.

The list of the eight kings of the Edomites, which follows in vv. 43-51a, is prefaced by the phrase, included in the parent text in Genesis 36.31-43, 'before any king ruled the Israelites'. This comment, noting the advanced state of Edom's political development compared to Israel's, may be intended to heighten the marvel of the fact that it was to this long-settled and socially mature people that, nonetheless, Israel, in all its rawness and the restlessness of its nomadic life, was preferred.

But the point is more far-reaching. C faithfully reproduces material in the full form that it has in Genesis, including a seven-times recurring phrase, 'then king so-and-so died and there reigned in his place…', which seems redundant to his purpose, given his striving for economy of expression that is so evident earlier in the chapter. Thereby the stress on monarchy is all the greater. The reason for its inclusion may be found in the subtle addition to his Genesis source of an echoing phrase after the eighth and last king: 'Then Hadad died'. This is followed by a paragraph marker. The new paragraph then begins: 'Then there were tribal chieftains in Edom…'

The text in Genesis merely gives the list of names of the chieftains of Esau at this point, 'by clan, locality and name' (the phrase is omitted by C in v. 51b, as he omits 'according to their settlements in their land-holdings' along with a final reminder that Esau is the ancestor of Edom at the end of v. 54). C may be wishing to convey the impression that as there had been a succession of kings, so now there is a succession of national chiefs—as opposed to the contemporary regional chiefs of Genesis.

By the eighth and last king of Edom C has reached the thirteenth generation from Abraham (Abraham + Isaac + Esau +s ons + grandsons + eight generations of kings), at precisely the moment in Israel of the emergence of David as king in the fourteenth generation from Abraham (cf. 1 Chron. 2.1, 4-5, 9-15). At that moment, as C makes explicit beyond Genesis, the rule of the Edomites passes from kings to tribal chieftains and monarchy itself passes from Edom to Israel.[2] The specific way in which Israel is preferred to Esau is in kingship. The contrast is also in legitimacy: Edom's kings are all from different families and places; Israel's are to be from the one stock of the house of David.

The point is confirmed by the fact that at the end of v. 37 C omits material on tribal chieftains that Gen. 36.13b-19 inserts at this point; so also at the end of vv. 38, 42, where Gen. 36.21b; 29-30 are omitted. C abbreviates his source by also omitting Gen. 36.24b, 25b at the end of v. 40b, 41a.

It is through the Davidic monarchy that God's dominion is to be exercised on earth. That at least is to be the theory of the reign of the Davidic House—but it is eventually to be forfeited because of the faithlessness of the kings: thus under Jehoram, the Edomite monarchy is re-established (2 Chron. 21.8).

Thus it may be that C is making a still more subtle point in anticipation of the conclusion of his work. It is striking that the writer of Zechariah 12, surely a near-contemporary of C, twice (v. 5) uses the term for 'tribal chief' employed here (*'allûp*) of the future ruler of Judah. Just as Edom forfeited kingship, so, too, Israel is destined to forfeit the same institution.

Whether this connection with Zechariah is correct or not, the point undoubtedly stands. The mode by which the LORD's dominion is to be exercised on earth will, when Israel returns definitively to the land, no longer be monarchy, glorious experiment in its finest hours under David and Solomon though it has been. It can only come through the holiness of God's people. Thus, allusively and indirectly, the theme of the whole work has been sounded.

2. S. Japhet, *I & II Chronicles* (London: SCM Press, 1993), pp. 63-64.

The Narrowing Line of Choice: The Pattern of the Generations

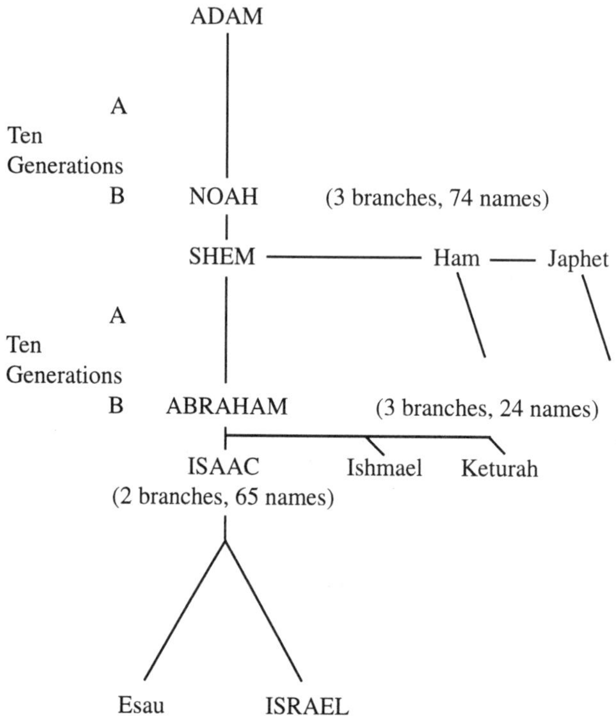

The pattern of use of the parent source in Genesis is ABAB: A, severe reduction to a mere list of names; B, close reproduction.

1 CHRONICLES 2.1-2: PREVIEW OF 1 CHRONICLES 2–8

In 1 Chron. 2.1, C resumes from where he has left off in 1 Chron. 1.34b: he has given 'the offspring of Esau' (1 Chron. 1.35-54). Now, having sketched the whole family of humanity, Israel's more distant relatives as well as her nearest kin, he is in a position to turn to the centre, to Israel herself, the focal point of his entire work (1 Chron. 2–8).

The list of the descendants of Israel in the opening paragraph, 1 Chron. 2.1-2, is given virtually in the standard order of the Hebrew Bible, as in Gen. 35.23-25 and Exod. 1.2-4, as the table below makes clear: the sons of Leah are followed by the sons of Rachel; then the 'concubine tribes' follow—the sons of Rachel's maid, Bilhah, and of Leah's maid, Zilpah. The only exception is Bilhah's son, Dan, who is here placed between the sons Leah and Rachel. It is a curious fact that, for Dan, C gives no list of descendants in the following chapters. Perhaps the location here, between the sons of the main wives, is in some kind of compensation for that omission.

Genesis 35.23-25/Exodus 1.2-4

LEAH	RACHEL	BILHAH	ZILPAH
Reuben|Simeon|Levi|Judah| Issachar|Zebulun	Joseph|Benjamin	Dan|Naphtali	Gad|Asher

1 Chronicles 2.1-2

LEAH	BILHAH	RACHEL	BILHAH	ZILPAH
	(Dan)		(Naphtali)	

But, if C thus lists the twelve sons of Israel more or less in conventional order in 1 Chron. 2.1-2, when he turns thereafter to deal with the tribes individually in 1 Chron. 2.3–8.40, he follows his own scheme, which begins with Judah, ends with Benjamin, and places Levi in the centre:

Judah Simeon Reuben	Gad [Reuben] Half-Manasseh	Levi	Issachar Benjamin Naphtali Half- Manasseh Ephraim Asher	Benjamin
(1 Chron. 2.3–5.10)	(1 Chron. 5.11-26)	(1 Chron. 6.1-81)	(1 Chron. 7.1-40)	(1 Chron. 8.1-40)

What is C communicating by means of this unique arrangement of the tribes of Israel? C is presenting a problem and proposing a solution.

As 1 Chronicles 1 has already indicated, the question with which C's whole work is concerned is the relation between God and his human creation, the recognition of God's dominion on earth. The ideal lost under Adam is to be recovered, after several false starts, through Israel.

Judah is the first tribe to be handled, because through it the model of monarchy for the realization of divine dominion on earth is to be presented. Just as Judah, the tribe from which the royal house of David springs, heads the first list of tribes, so Benjamin, from which the unsuccessful first attempt at monarchy—that of Saul—emerged, heads the last list of tribes, and also concludes that last list in order to form the link into the story of the unsuccessful monarchy which begins in 1 Chronicles 10 with the reign of Saul, the Benjaminite. Another factor in this arrangement is that Judah and Benjamin conjointly constitute the southern kingdom, the part of Israel to survive longest in the land. They encompass the more vulnerable tribes round Levi, the true centre of the nation.

But the problem, which C now poses, is that the tale of human failure evidenced in the broad mass of humanity in 1 Chronicles 1 continues even in the chosen people. Reuben has already been demoted from the dignity of the first-born because of moral outrage (1 Chron. 5.1; cf. Gen. 35.22; 49.3-4). But in Judah, too, elevated to first position thus secondarily, there is a recurrence of the tribulations of humankind: there is again false start, restart, and supplanting in morally dubious circumstances, as will be seen below. The problem is starkly stated in terms of the fate of Judah under the Davidic monarchy—exile. Judah thus forms a dark *inclusio* round the entire tribal system (1 Chron. 2.3; 1 Chron. 9.1).

But C's purpose is not simply to expose a problem; it is also to propose a solution. He is not concerned simply to set a censorious tone for the account of Israel's long slide to ultimate disaster that follows. The enormous scale of the detailed record of family descent and settlement, which he now gives, is evidence not of an arid antiquarianism but of an ardent zeal to preserve in the fullest possible detail an account of Israel as it once was and ideally is—its wide territories and flourishing people, which are in sharpest contrast to the pitiful remnant that survives in his own day. The downfall of Israel is made the more poignant by being placed against a background of the full potentiality that she has failed to realize. But this record is also the basis for hope: for it is also the register of those entitled to belong to Israel in the Return, the definitive resettlement of the land (cf. 1 Chron. 9.1).

C indicates as the only true basis for hope the tribe whom he places at the centre of his genealogical presentation of Israel—Levi. Impressive an agency though it is for Israel to realize its destiny, the monarchy is ultimately, and even intrinsically, flawed. It is only through the status and role of Levi that, in the end, Israel is to achieve its status and role amid the nations of the world.

In order to make that clear a new, pyramidal, arrangement of the tribes has to be worked out. Levi is supported on either side by the tribes adopted by Israel as his first-born after the failure of Reuben and the inadequacy of Judah—the sons of Joseph, Ephraim and Manasseh (Gen. 48). The tribes in ch. 5 thus climax appropriately in the half-tribe of Manasseh: they are involved in exemplary incidents of how the sovereignty of God may be expressed and recognized on earth, but also in cautionary incidents of defrauding God, which require precisely the agency of the Levites to restore, as is indicated in ch. 6.

The matching flank of the pyramid in chs. 7–8 does not seem to be so well worked out. One would have expected Ephraim and Half-Manasseh on the West Bank to be similarly immediately associated with Levi as Half-Manasseh is on the East Bank. But, if the MT paragraphing is carefully followed, the disorder is less than at first appears and principally concerns the position of Benjamin. The major paragraph marker after Levi is not, in fact, reached until the end of Issachar, with the result that Issachar is bound up closely with Levi (in the standard genealogy Issachar is the brother next to Levi once Judah has been removed to first position, 1 Chron. 2.1). The first 'free-standing' tribe to follow is Benjamin, who, in the standard biblical presentation, is the younger brother of Joseph, with whom he shares Rachel as mother. Again, in the MT paragraphing, Naphtali is included in Benjamin. It is only then that Half-Manasseh and Ephraim are reached. Asher, as the other son of Zilpah, appropriately enough matches his full brother, Gad, with whom the inner group of the pyramid had started (Benjamin in ch. 8 is tied up closely with Asher). There is a not dissimilar aggregation of tribes on the 'left side' of the pyramid: Simeon and Reuben are grouped with Caleb, son of Jephunneh (1 Chron. 4.15–5.10).

The agenda for the whole of C's work is now to be set by the genealogies: the exposition of the ultimate failure of the model of monarchy for the realization of the dominion of God upon earth; the primary model of Israel's life turns out to be the life of holiness under the teaching of the Levites, their officiating at the altar and their monitoring of Israel's observance of that holiness. The holiness expected of God's people, but violated by them, is defined as in the 'Holiness Code' of Leviticus 17–26, which ends in Leviticus 26 with the same eschatological expectation of restoration as in C's work.

1 CHRONICLES 2.3–4.23: JUDAH AND THE HOUSE OF DAVID

Since monarchy is to be the interim model of the means whereby God's dominion on earth is to be exercized, C first turns to consider the tribe from which the monarchy in its most ideal form is to spring—Judah.

But in Judah, from its very origin, from the very first generation born in the promised land, there is corruption. For the sons of Judah C has at his disposal a bald, morally neutral list in Gen. 46.12, which he cites in 1 Chron. 2.5. But once again he makes clear the drift of the argument by including snatches of narrative (as in 1 Chron. 1). He has chosen to excerpt his material on the birth of Judah's sons (vv. 3-4) from the sordid tales in Genesis 38 (3a is freely composed from Gen. 38.1-5: 3b is virtually identical with Gen. 38.7). Judah's first act of disloyalty is to marry a Canaanite wife, that is, on C's reckoning, a non-Semite descended from Ham (1 Chron. 1.8). By her he has three sons. The first is cut off in his prime by the LORD for unspecified wickedness; so too is the second, for his refusal to fulfil the duty of brother-in-law to his deceased brother's wife. Judah himself, having compromised himself by resorting to one whom he takes to be a common prostitute, is by that act seduced by his daughter-in-law because of his earlier failure to provide her with his third son as husband. It is from this irregular levirate union, consummated because of failure in different ways by the original husband, his brother and his father, that there are born twin sons. Like Israel and Esau, they are contentious even from the womb: Perez ousts Zerah from his position as first-born (Gen. 38.29). It is from Perez that the main lines of Judah's descendants are traced, including not least the royal house of David. The fact that this line, so dubious in its origins, at length culminates in David already hints at C's central statement about the foundation of the monarchy: the long-suffering of God; his merciful provision in response to human depravity; the instability of the institution.

The details of the account of Judah's descendants and their settlements (1 Chron. 2.3–4.23) thus inauspiciously inaugurated are complex and, in part, obscure and inconsequential because of textual corruptions and, perhaps, the imperfections of the traditions available to C. But the overall pattern is clear. Concerns similar to those that govern the general layout of the entire section on Israel's genealogies in 1 Chron. 2.3–8.40 are reflected in the detail of this section. There C, having first set out the sons of Israel in a conventional order, rearranges them in such a way as to place Levi in the centre with Judah and Benjamin, with the tribes of the southern kingdom, who also provided the monarchy, forming the outer framework and the tribes of the northern kingdom the inner. So here in the presentation of Judah, there is a combination of straightforward listing of names according to strict genealogical sequence and of patterning of these names in order to show their significance in relation to one another. As Levi stands at the centre of the twelve tribes, so David stands at the centre of Judah.

1 Chronicles 2.3-4 gives the five sons of Judah in conventional order (see, for example, Gen. 46.12):

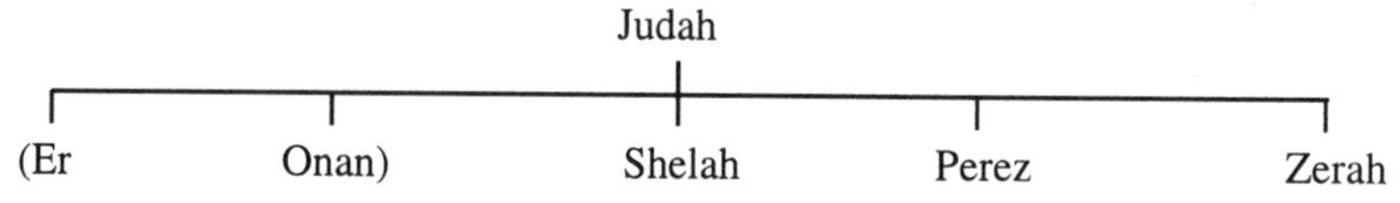

But in the presentation of the following generations patterning immediately takes place: the descendants of Shelah, the oldest surviving son, are relegated to the end of the entire list of Judah's descendants (1 Chron. 4.21-23). It is Tamar's twin sons, Perez and Zerah, who gain prominence. Again, their descendants are first listed in conventional order (vv. 5-6):

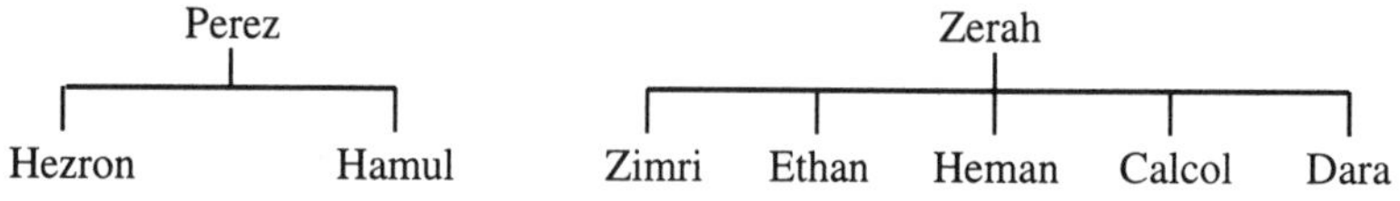

But the discussion that follows does not trace their descendants even according to this sequence. The sons of Perez have been announced first and of them Hezron has been given the first position: this prominence is about to be explored in 1 Chron. 2.9–4.20. Perez's other son, Hamul, plays no further part in C. But the subsidiary branch of Zerah is to be disposed of first (cf. the order of treatment of Noah's sons in 1 Chron. 1.4-17 and of Abraham's in 1 Chron. 1.28-34). The effect of this arrangement is to bring into prominence once more the failings of Israel from the start; the tone of the whole subsequent history is once again set. The line stemming from Zerah leads through Zimri and Carmi to Achar, 'the troubler of Israel, who transgressed in the matter of the devoted thing'.

As in vv. 2-3 C has presupposed the disgraceful tale recounted in Genesis 38, so now in v. 7 he alludes in the tersest possible way to the deplorable events recorded in Joshua 7.

Only the genealogical data in Josh. 7.1 make clear that Carmi is the grandson of Zerah (Zimri occurs in the form Zabdi; see LXXa, Zabri).

The battle at Jericho is the very first campaign of the military conquest of the Promised Land, at the very outset of the settlement of the West Bank under the leadership of the commander of the LORD's cosmic army (Josh. 5.13-15). The spoils of victory ought, accordingly, to be devoted in their entirety to God, the Giver of Victory and the Bestower of the Land. Achar, this wretched descendant of Judah, by taking some of the spoils for himself is guilty of *ma'al*, that failure to accord God his rights, which is to run its destructive course through the entire subsequent history of Israel down to the exile (1 Chron. 5.25; 9.1; 10.13 [2×]; 2 Chron. 12.2; 26.16, 18; 28.19 [2×], 22; 29.6, 19; 30.7; 33.19; 36.14 [2×]).

The theme is not simply confined to the word *ma'al*. The sacramental idea, that the leader of the armies of Israel, in this case Joshua, is but the human counterpart of the cosmic power of God and the agent of his dominion on earth, is to dominate the ideology of monarchy in C (e.g., 1 Chron. 28.5; cf. 1 Chron. 21.16).

The Achar incident thus already marks the beginning of the end. To make the point even more emphatic, C uses the name in the form 'Achar', rather than the 'Achan' of Joshua 7; 22.20. This form of the name picks up the name of the Valley of Achor (Josh. 7.24, 26), where the culprit was stoned to death with all his family and burned with all his possessions, and also the play on words in Josh. 7.25, 'Why did you bring trouble on us (*'ᵃkartānû*)? The LORD brings trouble on you (*ya'korᵉkâ*) today.' Achar is the troubler (*'ôkēr*) of Israel.

Yet, once again, the failure of Israel is brought into conjunction with the gracious provision of God, for the remaining sons of Zerah have entirely wholesome and constructive associations with wisdom and the Temple musicians in Hebrew Bible traditions (the non-chronological relation of these names is striking and is to be a recurrent feature of the genealogies).

> The four names occur in identical form (except that Darda appears for Dara) and sequence in 1 Kgs 4.31 of men renowned for their folk wisdom (appropriately to the sequence of C's genealogical arrangement by importance rather than by chronology, Solomon, son of David, surpasses them in wisdom). There they are said to be 'the sons of Mahol', a name that does not recur as a personal name and which should be perhaps taken in its meaning as a common noun 'dance', that is, 'liturgical dance', as in Ps. 149.3; 150.4: in this case, 'sons' will mean 'members of a guild'. This association with the music and dance of the cult seems to be confirmed by the attribution of Psalm 89 to Ethan and Psalm 88 to Heman where the form of their patronymics 'the Ezrahites', which is presumably an adjectival form of their father's name, Zerah, could also be a common noun meaning 'native', alluding to their part-Canaanite descent. The recurrence of the names Ethan and Heman (apart from 1 Kgs 4.31 Calcol and Dar[d]a do not reappear in the Hebrew Bible) in lists of levitical musicians (e.g. 1 Chron. 15.19) in the Temple may be further confirmation of their association with the liturgy of the cult (and, indeed, further suggestive that 'Levite' is, in part at least, also a guild term).

These associations thus bring the failure of Achar to accord God his rights into conjunction with the Temple service, specifically the atoning rites of the altar (cf. David's arrangement of the musicians in 1 Chron. 16: Heman and Jeduthun [= Ethan] at the altar; Asaph with the ark).

> Ethan's son bears the impeccably orthodox name, Azariah ('the LORD has helped', v. 8; cf. 1 Chron. 5.20). It is tempting to suggest that Zerah's descendants are to be seen as beginning with a Zimri, the regicide and usurper (1 Kgs 16.9-20), who became proverbial in Israel by his act of sacrilegious disloyalty (2 Kgs 9.31).

The major line of descent from Judah has now been reached (v. 9)—that of David through Hezron. C again first sets out the three sons of Hezron, presumably in order of birth (cf. v. 25)—though the source of the information is unknown:

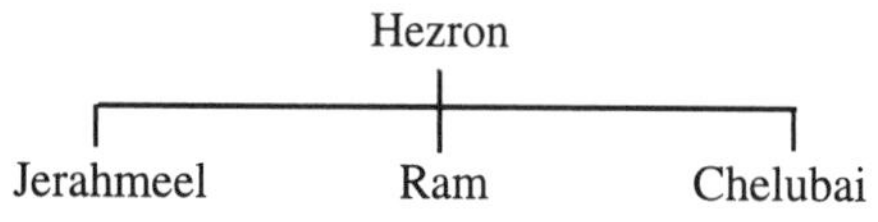

Thereafter C imposes a pattern on the genealogical data to give Ram, from whom the Davidic house is descended, both pre-eminence and centrality. The unique form, 'Chelubai', is perhaps meant as a signal of the complexity and non-coherence of the 'Caleb group' that becomes clear especially in ch. 4.

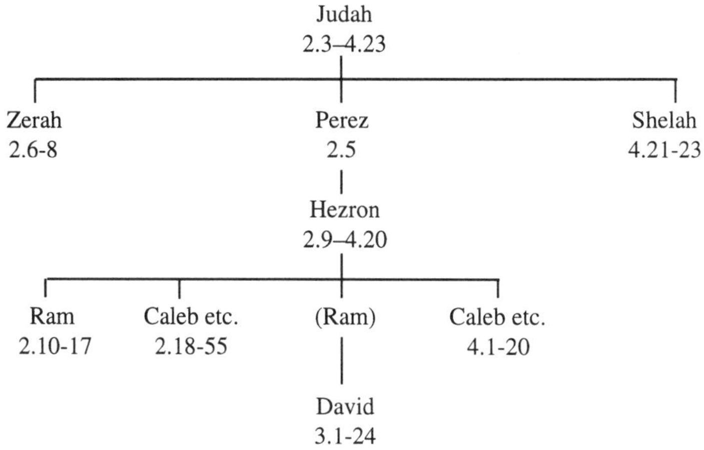

David and his house are placed in the centre of C's presentation of Judah, with the peripheral sons of Judah forming the outer framework, and the remainder of the descendants of Hezron the inner.

But David is not only given centrality, as in 1 Chron. 3.1-24. He is also accorded pre-eminence: already in 1 Chron. 2.10-17, pride of place is given to the direct descent of David through eight generations from Ram (cf. the eight generations of kings of Edom—but none from the same stock, 1 Chron. 1.43-51). The stark directness of this lineage is in contrast to the elaborate complexity of the many lines descending from Caleb and in itself expresses the significance of the chosen line (cf. the directness Adam–Noah–Abraham in 1 Chron. 1).

For his information for this line of descent from Ram to David in 1 Chron. 2.10-17, C is dependent upon the genealogy in Ruth 4.19b-22. He makes two additions to it, however. At the end of v. 10 he alludes to Num. 2.3 where Nahshon is identified as 'prince of the sons of Judah'. The rule of the house of David is, thus, a resumption of the pre-eminent role of David's ancestor, Nahshon, in Judah, and, indeed, in the nation as a whole, at the time of the Exodus and the wilderness wandering. Nahshon's sister, Elizabeth, was Aaron's wife (Exod. 6.23); in the camp of the Israelites Nahshon had the most honorific place of all at the east of the Tent of Meeting (Num. 2.3); he was the leader of his tribe (Num. 1.7) and his tribe took the leading place among the twelve in bringing offerings at the dedication of the altar (Num. 7.12) and in setting out on the stages through the desert (Num. 10.14). If—as is likely—the form in which this Numbers material is cast derives from the post-exilic period, the eventual subordination of the civil leader (Nahshon the prince) to the levitical line (Aaron the priest) that it reflects is striking and in complete harmony with C's thinking.

To the bare list of Ruth 4, C also adds the names of David's brothers and sisters (1 Chron. 2.13-17). He alludes to the romantic tale of the choice of David in preference to his older brothers, which is told in 1 Samuel 16. But, besides the names of the first three recorded there, he now supplies from some otherwise unknown source the names of the rest of David's brothers.

> The difference between 1 Samuel—David is the eighth son—and 1 Chronicles—David is the seventh—is resolved by the Syriac version, which supplies here a seventh brother, Elihu (cf. 1 Chron. 27.18).

Some of the doughtiest warriors of the early monarchical period are also ascribed by this list to this dominant household as sons of David's sisters: Ab(i)shai, Joab and Asael, as sons Zeruiah, and Amasa, as son of Abiga(i)l. This is the first time in the Hebrew Bible that these mothers are identified as sisters of David.

In 2 Sam 17.25 the sisters, Zeruiah and Abigail, are daughters of one Nahash. Commentators (e.g. Mandelkern) have tried to harmonize that passage with 1 Chron. 2.16-17 by assuming that Nahash was the name, otherwise borne by men, of David's father Jesse's wife. In Samuel–Kings Zeruiah is so redoubtable a mother that the first three are routinely referred to as 'sons of Zeruiah' (e.g. 1 Sam. 26.6).

Having thus ascribed pre-eminence to David by tracing his genealogical descent from his forebear, Ram, before the descendants of Ram's older brother, Jerahmeel, C now turns to expressing the centrality of the Davidic house by placing David and his descendants centrally in ch. 3 in the context of the other Judaeans, Caleb and Jerahmeel (the latter are incorporated into the former to indicate relative significance). This framework of Caleb–Jerahmeel runs from 2.18-55 and 4.1-20.

The broad pattern within which the descendants of Caleb and Jerahmeel are presented is relatively clear, though there is considerable complexity of detail. The entire material 2.18–4.20 falls into sixteen sections which show a degree of symmetry in their arrangement around the pivotal section on David in ch. 3:

Caleb I		2.18	1
Caleb II		2.19-20	2
Hezron's late marriage		2.21-23	3
Caleb III		2.24	4
Jerahmeel		2.25-41	5
Caleb IV		2.42-45	6
Caleb V		2.46-47	7
Caleb VI		2.48-49	8
= Caleb II (a) and (b)	(a) 2.50-53	(b) 2.54-55	9
DAVIDIC HOUSE		3.1-24	10
= Caleb II (a) and (b)	(a) 4.1-2	(b) 4.3-4	11
= Caleb III		4.5-8	12
= Caleb II (b)		4.9-10	13
Chelub		4.11-12	14
Kenaz		4.13-14	15
Caleb son of Jephunneh		4.15-20	16

It is apparent that, though it is not slavishly adhered to or mechanically contrived, there is a clearly conceived structure in these chapters. As in the case of descendants of Ram, where both pre-eminence and centrality are assigned to the Davidic house, so here in the presentation of the remaining descendants of Hezron, pre-eminence and centrality are assigned to Caleb II and III, the inhabitants of the region of Ephrath–Ephrathah, especially Kiriath-jearim, Bethlehem, and Tekoa. Caleb not only heads the list in rows 2 and 4 but is also in rows 9 and 11-13 brought into closest proximity to the central figure, David, whose native town was Bethlehem. There is also an indication, that, as in the case of humanity in general in 1 Chronicles 1 and of Judah as a whole in 1 Chron. 2.3, there was a false start (row 1 and especially row 3), which, however, provided the context for the new creative beginning of rows 2 and 4.

Once rows 1-4 have been removed, the purpose of which is to give Caleb II and III pre-eminence, a clear pyramidal structure, grouped around the central figure, is left (the Arabic numerals refer to the rows in the above diagram):

10
DAVID

9
Caleb II — 11-13
Caleb II/III

6-8
Caleb IV-VI — 14
Chelub–Kenaz

5
Jerahmeel — 15-16
Caleb b. Jephunneh

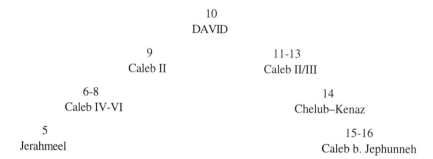

It is notable that the two names at the foot of the pyramid mean, respectively, 'May God be merciful' (Jerahmeel) and 'May he be turned [in compassion]' (Jephunneh).

But, while the overall structure is relatively clear, the passage contains many complex and obscure details. Of the two hundred or so persons, peoples and places named in 2.18-55 and 4.1-20 less than one quarter (some 45) occur again in the Hebrew Bible: the exact number of proper names intended, indeed, must remain uncertain since the text in some verses can hardly be intact and probably needs to be emended, especially in the light of the ancient versions (so already 2.18 and many other places, e.g. 2.24, 52b; 4.3, 7, 12-13). Such geographical names as are paralleled elsewhere bear out C's pyramidal design: the population of David's city of Bethlehem is considered within the further flung populations of Judah in the Negev and in the Shephelah.

The first branch, Caleb I (1 Chron. 2.18), is very shadowy. As it stands, the text is inconsequential: 'Caleb…begat Azubah a woman and Jerioth. These were her [whose?] sons: Jesher, Shobab, and Ardon. Then Azubah died'—but no mention is made of the fate of Jerioth. The Vulgate and the Syriac suggest that the name of only one wife, Azubah, is mentioned, Jerioth being her child. None of the other five names recurs as belonging to a Calebite and this very lack of knowledge, coupled with the (early?) death of Azubah ('desolate one'; cf. Isa. 6.12), suggests a peripheral and, perhaps even, fleeting element.

The second branch, however, Caleb II (1 Chron. 2.19-20), belongs to the core of the Calebites. Despite unpromising beginnings—its mother, Ephrath, is a substitute wife for the dead Azubah—it is destined to attain central significance in both geographical and historical terms. Its mother's name, Ephrath, in that form, or in the longer form, Ephrathah, may be presumed to be the same as the geographical region in which not only Bethlehem, home of David (cf. Gen. 35.19; 48.7), lay, but also Kiriath-jearim (1 Chron. 2.50), sometime location of the ark of the covenant (1 Sam. 7.1; Ps. 132.6). The historical significance of Caleb II lies through the line of descent through Hur. This Hur may be the same figure, who, at the time of the wilderness wandering and the covenant-making at Sinai, stood in closest proximity to Moses and Aaron, assisting at the battle against Amalek and acting as stand-in for Moses as magistrate (Exod. 17.10, 12; 24.14). His grandson, Bezalel (Uri of the intervening generation is only known in this genealogical connection), occupied a key position later in the same period as chief craftsman in metal, stone, wood and cloth, in charge of the design and construction of Israel's first sanctuary, the tabernacle in the wilderness, and of supplying its furnishings, including the ark, table of shewbread, lampstand, incense altar, and altar for burnt offerings, the vestments of the priests, and preparing the anointing oil and incense (Exod. 31.1-11). It was to Bezalel's tabernacle that Solomon went on his coronation (2 Chron. 1.3-5). The preeminence of Caleb II thus lies not simply in the fact that it comes from the same region as the Davidic dynasty, but also in the fact that there springs from it the man who was chief craftsman of the first sanctuary, the tabernacle, which remained in being until the time of the building of the second sanctuary, the Temple in Jerusalem. Caleb II thus links Moses and David, the two phases of Israel's religious history in the pre-exilic period.

The following verses on Hezron's late marriage (1 Chron. 2.21-23) recount the abortive attempt to settle the furthest north-east of the country, the region of Argob in northern Bashan on the East Bank (for the locality cf. Deut. 3.4, 14; 1 Kgs 4.13). The weak hold by these Judaeans on this area is indicated by a number of factors. Jair, the principal figure involved (Segub does not figure elsewhere), originates from a marriage contracted by his progenitor Hezron in his declining years. He is of mixed tribal stock, stemming from the female side of the descendants of Machir, the first-born of Manasseh, conqueror and possessor of the whole of Bashan and Gilead (Josh. 17.1). This mixed origin results in Jair being called on occasion, 'son of Manasseh' (e.g. Num. 32.41). His possession is twenty-three (thirty, Judg. 10.4; sixty, Josh. 13.30), *ḥawwôt*, a word that occurs in the Hebrew Bible only in connection with Jair and probably implies temporary settlements (the still more obscure Kenath and its satellites recur in Num. 32.42). These were located in the part of the country most vulnerable of all to invasions from the neighbouring states of the Aramaeans (Geshur lay immediately to the north of Bashan in the Golan Heights).

The general outcome of the sequel in 1 Chron. 2.24 is clear though the text is, unfortunately, obscure. The text apparently runs: 'After the death of Hezron with Caleb in (?) Ephrathah—now Hezron's wife was Abijah—she bore him Ashhur, father of Tekoa'. The verse could possibly be interpreted to mean that 'the daughter of Machir', now named Abijah, bore a son posthumously to Hezron. However, 'him' may refer to Caleb. Either way, out of the debacle of the unsuccessful attempt to settle the East Bank, Caleb produced descendants for Hezron on the West Bank around Tekoa.

> NRSV makes Ephrathah the wife of Hezron; but such a name for a wife of Hezron is not otherwise known, and is indeed, borne by Caleb's wife in 1 Chron. 2.19, 50. NRSV further emends Abijah, the name of Hezron's wife actually given here, to *aābîhû* 'of his father' and follows the reading suggested by the Vulgate and LXX, 'Caleb went in to Ephrathah'.

1 Chronicles 2.24 thus recounts the origins of Caleb III and continues the themes of false starts made good and of the pre-eminence of Caleb. The phrase of the type 'X the father of Y', which recurs frequently in this chapter (here, 'Ashhur the father of Tekoa'), doubtless means that the population of town Y regard themselves as descended from or belonging to the clan of X (so now repeatedly, e.g. 1 Chron. 2.42-45 for the towns of Ziph, Mareshah, Hebron, Jorkeam and Beth-zur).

C having thus given Caleb II and III a position of pre-eminence among the non-royal lines of Judah now turns to his pyramidal presentation of the families of Judah: at the apex stands David flanked immediately on each side by the same Caleb II and III.

The genealogy of Jerahmeel (1 Chron. 2.25-41) is a striking example of C's careful preservation of the identity of even the obscurest parts of Israel by recording the names of at least some of the founding ancestors. Of the thirty-seven male descendants recorded by name, not to mention the three wives, not one recurs elsewhere in the Hebrew Bible. Jerahmeel itself, as the name of a tribal group, only occurs again in 1 Sam. 27.10 and 30.29, in the context of David's forays in the Negeb, when he was in the service of Achish of Gath. These passages at least serve to locate the Jerahmeelites in the southern extremities of the country. The genealogy itself is divided into two sections (marked also by MT): vv. 25-32 indicate the lateral spread of the clan, though by no means completely, since out of the six immediate sons only one is traced, and that only in part, to the seventh generation, and another to the second (the 'dead ends' are noted, vv. 30, 32); vv. 33-41 continue the lineal descent of one son from the seventh to the twentieth generation.

A notable feature of these last thirteen generations is that they are not only ultimately derived from Jerahmeel's second wife, but they are also descended from an Egyptian slave (v. 34): here, in this outer fringe of the people, Israel merges with the world of the nations. This Egyptian slave, matching symmetrically the daughter of the Egyptian Pharaoh in 1 Chron. 4.17, married to a descendant of Caleb's son Jephunneh, serves to mark the base of C's pyramid, at whose apex stands David. That the Jerahmeelites belonged to the more nomadic element within Israel is indicated by the fact that none of them, in contrast to many of the sons of Caleb (e.g. 1 Chron. 2.24, 42, etc.), is called 'father of such-and-such a location', that is, of the settled population there.

There now follows in 1 Chron. 2.42-55 the presentation of a number of branches of the Calebites. The overall use of the term 'Caleb' no doubt expresses a sense of community between the various branches; nonetheless, variations in the title may indicate a sense of distinctions. Thus, 'Caleb' on its own is confined to the centrally placed Caleb II and III (1 Chron. 2.50-55; 4.1-10), while Caleb IV, V and VI (1 Chron. 2.42-49) is referred to under 'brother of Jerahmeel', indicating a sense of community also with the Jerahmeelites (cf. the other term, 'Chelub', and 'Caleb son of Jephunneh' in 1 Chron. 4.11, 15, which also express community yet distinctiveness).

The text of the material on Caleb IV (1 Chron. 2.42-45) begins in some disorder. By analogy with v. 43, v. 42 might have been expected to read: 'And the sons of Caleb the brother of Jerahmeel were Mesha his first-born (he was the father of Ziph; and the sons of Ziph were A,

B, C...), and X (he was the father of Maresha; and the sons of Maresha were D, E, F...), and Y (he was the father of Hebron; and the sons of Hebron were G, H, I...)'. Nonetheless, the overall meaning is clear. Caleb IV represents the population in some half-dozen localities that constitute the outer ring of settlements in southern and south-western Judah.

It is not possible to determine exactly which elements represent personal names and which place names: Tappuah may be the name of a clan within Hebron, cf. the locality of that name in the Shephelah in Josh. 15.34; but in that case the names alongside Tappuah should also be regarded as place names.

The location of these settlements is for the most part clear from the other contexts in the Hebrew Bible in which they occur: Hebron itself in south Judah, with Beth-zur to its north (Josh. 15.58), Ziph and Maon to its south (Josh. 15.55; 1 Sam. 23.14-24, etc.; Jorkeam, otherwise unknown, is perhaps to be equated with Jokdeam in the light of Josh. 15.56, which associates it with Ziph and Maon), and Maresha in the Shephelah (Josh. 15.44; Mic. 1.15). The strategic significance of Beth-zur, Hebron, Ziph and Maresha as the outer ring of the fortresses round the heartland of Judah is underlined by the fact that they all appear in the list of the fortresses constructed by king Rehoboam at the end of the tenth century BCE (2 Chron. 11.7-10).

1 Chronicles 2.46 gives the list of Caleb V, that is, the sons of Caleb, 'brother of Jerahmeel' by his first concubine. It is not stated what the relationship of the 'sons of Jahdai' in v. 47 is to Caleb V, whether they are a group loosely attached (in which case Caleb V should be subdivided into Va and Vb), or genuine descendants whose precise genealogical connection has been lost in the tradition or through textual corruption. At all events, it is striking that none of the ten names in vv. 46-47 recurs in the Hebrew Bible either as a personal or as a place name; like Jerahmeel's descendants, Caleb V must, therefore, represent a nomadic element in the population of the south and south-west of the country.

1 Chronicles 2.48-49 records the names of Caleb VI, a further branch of the descendants of Caleb, 'brother of Jerahmeel', this time by his concubine Maacah, whose name has strong Aramean associations (cf., e.g. 1 Chron. 3.2: 19.7; Gen. 22.24; Josh. 13.13). The relationship of the individuals of Caleb VI is not clear: are Sheber, Tirhanah, Shaaph and Sheva four sons of Caleb, or is Tirhanah, as befits the feminine form of the name, a daughter who in turn was

mother of Shaaph and Sheva? In addition, the text of v. 49 may be defective: the proper name of the father of Gibea, corresponding to Shaaph and Sheva, may have fallen out. At all events, the formula, 'father of…', suggests that the names thus prefaced are place-names: Madmannah figures in a list of twenty-nine cities 'in the extreme south, toward the boundary of Edom' in Josh. 15.21-32; Machbenah is otherwise unparalleled, but has been associated with Cabbon in the Shephelah in Josh. 15.40 (Mandelkern); while Gibea does not recur elsewhere in the Hebrew Bible in this precise form, it is related to the common noun for 'hill' and to a number of place names from the same root, Geba, Gibeon, and, in particular, Gibeah (cf. Josh. 15.57 for a locality of that name again associated with Ziph and Maon).

Caleb's daughter Achsah fits perfectly into C's pyramidal presentation, since she was given in marriage to Othniel, son of Kenaz, the conqueror of Kiriath-sepher/Debir, who is recorded in matching position in 1 Chron. 4.13 by C. The location of her territory in the deep, waterless South is graphically indicated by her request to her father for springs of water (Josh. 15.16-19; Judg. 1.12-15).

With 1 Chron. 2.50 C reaches the uppermost tier of the pyramid next to David himself. The Calebites of Caleb II and III have already been presented in the position of pre-eminence in vv. 19-24; they are now placed in honorific centrality flanking the royal house in 1 Chron. 2.50-54 and 4.1-10.

> The NRSV relates the first phrase of v. 50 to what goes before. But this not only violates the paragraphing of the MT but obscures C's structuring of the material.

The pre-eminence and centrality of this uppermost tier are expressed geographically in terms of their settlements in the heartland of Judah: Caleb II in the central hill country in the main townships of the area, Kiriath-jearim, Bethlehem and Beth-gader, and Caleb III in Tekoa on the eastern fringe of the wilderness of Judah.

Caleb II, as descended from Hur the grandfather of Bezalel, the craftsman of the first sanctuary of Israel in the Wilderness, is disposed in 1 Chron. 2.50-55; 4.1-4, 9-10, symmetrically on either side of the royal house in 1 Chronicles 3, in closest proximity to David, the founder of the later, supreme sanctuary of Israel, the Temple in Jerusalem.

Even within Caleb II there is a hierarchy. The Calebites of Beth-gader are dismissed with a mere mention. Not only does their ancestor not figure again in the Hebrew Bible (neither do the ancestors of Kiriath-jearim or Bethlehem), the very locality does not recur, at least, in this form, though there are a number of similar place names derived from the same common noun, *gādēr*, 'stone wall'.

Kiriath-jearim is treated in some detail: the four primary population sub-divisions, about which little or nothing is otherwise known, are noted and the secondary sub-divisions of Zorah and Eshtaol.

> Eshtaol recurs in the Hebrew Bible only in conjunction with Zorah. They were the original settlement area of the Danites (Josh. 19.41), where Samson was born and brought up (Judg. 13–16). Zorah was the site of another of king Rehoboam's fortresses (2 Chron. 11.10).

C is interested in Kiriath-jearim for its associations with the ark of the covenant. This interest is subtly indicated in v. 52b by the puns on the names of Shobal's first-born, Reaiah (1 Chron. 4.2), and of an element of the population, 'half of the Manahathites' (*ḥ*^{a}*ṣî hammānaḥtî*, the proper form of the name given in v. 54; cf. 1 Chron. 8.6 and Samson's father Manoah). For these C reads here *hārō'eh ḥ*^{a}*ṣî hamm*^{e}*nūḥôt*: '(Shobal)...who sees half of the resting places'. This is a clear reference to the fact that Kiriath-jearim was a temporary 'resting place' for the ark of the covenant immediately before David brought it to Jerusalem, where it was thereafter given its final 'resting place' in the Temple (for C's use of *m*^{e}*nûḥâ* for the resting place of the ark in the Temple, cf. 1 Chron. 6.31 [16, MT]). Here a fundamental aspect of the significance of the Jerusalem Temple as planned by David is anticipated: the 'resting' of the ark symbolizes the pacification of the earth in the name of the LORD.

From Kiriath-jearim, the township fleetingly dignified by the presence of the ark, C passes to Bethlehem, birth-place of David himself. Verse 54 may allude to the military support afforded David by the Bethlehemites: his nephew Joab (if this is the same individual) was his army commander; the place-name Ataroth, the plural of the common noun meaning 'crown' and applied to settlements as crowning the hills on which they stood (so of Samaria in Isa. 28.1, 3, and Jerusalem in Isa. 62.3), may refer to his family's hilltop strongholds (cf. 1 Chron. 4.3-4); Netophah was the home of two of David's mighty men (1 Chron. 11.30), who were also superintendents of the royal service (1 Chron. 27.13, 15), besides being the residence of a Levitical musician (1 Chron. 9.16; Neh. 12.28). This last association prepares the way for the climax in v. 54.

The text of v. 54 seems to have lost at least one phrase: 'the sons of Salma, *the father of* Bethlehem, were... *and*...' Cf. the structure of v. 52 and the resumption in 1 Chron. 4.3, below.

Those brought most nearly into association with David are scribes of Kenite origin and affiliated to the Rechabites. In a manner similar to that envisaged in Deut. 17.18, David, as model king, has at his side the scribes (cf. 1 Chron. 18.16), the authoritative teachers of the Law, who belong by their Kenite origin to the most original form of Yahwism and by their Rechabite association to its purest version.

C shares here the strong association of the origins Israel's faith in the LORD, Yahweh, with the Kenites: Moses received the revelation of the divine name Yahweh while tending the flocks of his Kenite father-in-law Jethro (Exod. 3), priest of Midian, who officiated at the altar at the 'Mountain of God' and gave advice on legal matters in Exodus 18. Genesis 4.26 associates the invocation of Yahweh with the generation of Cain, the father of the Kenites. For the zealous and conservative Yahwism of the Rechabites, cf. Jeremiah 35; that zeal was directed specifically against the royal house of the north which broke away from the house of David, 2 Kgs 10.15-17.

The basis of David's rule lies in a Yahwism that remains conscious of its desert origins and does not compromise with the debilitating influences of Canaan.

At the apex of C's pyramid in historic, institutional and theological significance, and occupying the position of centrality in Judah, stands the house of David (1 Chron. 3). David in his descent has already been given the position of pre-eminence under his ancestor Ram in 1 Chron. 2.10-17; now his own descendants in the house of David are listed. The chapter falls into three sections marked by the way in which the names of the various descendants are listed:

(1) The names of twenty children of David himself are given in vv. 1-9.

(2) The direct line of descent of sixteen generations of the House of David from Solomon to Josiah is given in vv. 10-14. This is marked from Rehoboam in the tersest possible way: 'A, his son, B, his son...'

(3) Verses 15-24 then continue in a looser structure which includes both lateral and lineal elements, perhaps to the thirtieth generation after David.

The handling of the first generation (vv. 1-9) is striking. C again uses the device of centrality to underline significance: whereas in the parallels in 2 Samuel David has but seventeen sons (six born at Hebron, eleven at Jerusalem), C provides him with nineteen (Eliphelet and Nogah, vv. 6-7 being the extra ones): the six born at Hebron, the four sons of Bathshua daughter of Ammiel (= Bathsheba daughter of Eliam, 2 Sam. 11.3), plus nine others born in Jerusalem. Solomon, as the last son of Bathshua and designated crown prince, stands in the centre of the pattern 9 + 1 + 9. That these additional sons belong deliberately to C's pattern is indicated by his insertion of the sub-totals six, four and nine (vv. 4, 5, 8). C retains these additional sons in his reuse of the material in 1 Chron. 14.4-7.

The material in 1 Chron. 3.1-9 is paralleled in 2 Sam. 3.2-5; 5.5,14-15. C makes a number of more minor adjustments, of which only the most significant can be noted. In v. 1a the informal narrative style of 2 Sam. 3.2, 'There were sons born to David in Hebron', is replaced by a formal definitive record, 'These were the sons of David who were born to him at Hebron'. Minor detractions in character or incident are omitted. In 2 Samuel Abigail is identified as 'the wife of Nabal of Carmel'; here the discredited Nabal disappears. The phrases in 2 Sam. 5.5 that in Hebron David reigned 'over Judah', while in Jerusalem he reigned 'over all Israel and Judah', are also suppressed: for C David is simply king of Israel; initial difficulties do not signify. C retains the fact that David's six sons at Hebron were born of as many wives, a tribute at once to the king's virility and to his diplomatic contacts. The differentiation between those born in Jerusalem and those in Hebron suits his purpose of stressing the centrality of Solomon and is also retained. In v. 5b he identifies the first four sons born at Jerusalem as offspring of David's union with Bathshua, which in 2 Samuel 11, but not Chronicles, begins in the dubious circumstances of adultery and contrived death (hence even the change of name in C?). To the list of names of David's sons, C appends in v. 9 a note that all nineteen were of high and comparable status, being born of David's wives, not his concubines, a point not made clear in 2 Sam. 5.13, which could imply that some at least were by his concubines. Tamar, who figures only in 2 Samuel 13, as Absalom's sister, is added to the list without specification of who her mother is to complete a total of twenty offspring.

The significance of the direct sequence in vv. 10-14 is clear from earlier lists of a similarly economical kind that C has given: the ten generations from Adam to Noah (1 Chron. 1.1-4); the ten generations from Shem to Abraham (1 Chron. 1.24-27). By such lists C traces the direct line of those through whom God's purpose is being worked out, in this case the royal house of David. The six generations Isaac–Israel–Judah–Perez–Hezron–Ram have necessarily included many lateral elements to include the full picture of Israel's nearest kin (1 Chron. 1.34–2.9), but thereafter the six generations from Amminadab to Jesse have been listed in direct succession (1 Chron. 2.10-12). Again, lateral spread is required to locate David within the family of Jesse, and Solomon as his successor within the family of David (1 Chron. 2.13-17; 3.1-9). The sixteen names in succession from Solomon to Josiah in 1 Chron. 3.10-14 bring C, as will be argued in connection with 2 Chron. 35.25–36.23, to the exile, forty-nine generations after Adam. The goal of C's entire work is the fiftieth generation in which eschatological release is proclaimed to the exiles, as in the Jubilee of Leviticus 25.

In the account of the succession of the kings of the House of David down to the exile C adheres to the order as recounted in the books of Kings. The Abijam of 1 Kgs 14.31 appears here as Abijah (v. 10; so 2 Chron. 12.16–14.1).

Verses 15-24 list exilic and post-exilic descendants of the House of David. The text is not without its difficulties: it is not altogether clear how many generations of David's line are being listed. Perhaps this lack of clarity is not surprising given C's purpose. In his ideological chronology, just noted, these figures all belong to the 'exilic generation'. It is thus not of first importance to C to clarify the actual chronology, the historical inner succession within this genealogy. Here, then, is another example of that 'timeless contemporaneity', most evident in 1 Chronicles 9 (but see already Solomon's contemporaries listed in 1 Chron. 2.6), the ideal population of Jerusalem, where individuals of widely separated historical epochs rub shoulders with one another (the wilderness period, David and Nehemiah).

Josiah has an additional son Johanan attributed to him. The form and sequence of his other sons Jehoiakim, Jehoahaz and Zedekiah (2 Kgs 23.30–24.18) is altered to Jehoiakim, Zedekiah and Shallum (= Jehoahaz, cf. Jer. 22.11) (v. 15). Jehoiachin (2 Kgs 24.6), the form used in 2 Chron. 36.8, appears here as Jeconiah (= Jer. 28.4; 29.2), and a second son, Zedekiah, otherwise unknown, is attributed to Jehoiakim (v. 16; the reason for the addition of this Zedekiah is discussed under 2 Chron. 36.1, 10). A further divergence from data given elsewhere in the Hebrew Bible is that here the father of Zerubbabel is identified as Pedaiah, the third of the seven sons of Jehoiachin, whereas in Hag. 1.1 it is the eldest, Shealtiel (v. 19).

Apart from Zerubbabel, Shecaniah, and Hattush, probably none of those listed in vv. 18-24 is mentioned elsewhere in the Hebrew Bible. In v. 21 the links at the twenty-second to the twenty-fourth generations after David are problematic. A minimal adjustment of the text, supported by some ancient textual and versional evidence (*BHK*), and followed by RSV, still does not make clear whether Rephaiah, Arnan, and so on, are successive generations, as 'his son' would imply as in vv. 10-14 above (though whose son then is Rephaiah?), or are further sons of Hananiah. On the first assumption there are indeed thirty generations after David recorded in this chapter; on the second, there are only twenty-six. Adjustments of a similar kind have to be made in v. 19b, where MT reads 'son of Zerubbabel', though two sons actually follow; so in v. 23, where three names follow. Contrariwise, in v. 22a 'sons' is followed by one name! Further obscurities are in v. 20, where the five named, through whom the direct line of descent is not in fact traced, seem to have been added as an afterthought to Zerubbabel (*BHS* suggests they were born in Judah; *BHK* that the phrase 'and sons of Meshullam' has dropped out before them), and in v. 22b where, though a total of six is given at the end of the verse, only five names in fact appear. *BHK* suggests that, if a sixth name has not fallen out, the phrase 'and the sons of Shemaiah' be omitted as a gloss derived from Ezra 8.2, the six named then being sons of Shecaniah. This would involve the loss of a still further generation of the descendants of David, bringing the number down to twenty-five.

This material on the descendants of David might be expected to provide some indication of the date of C's work: it cannot have reached its present form until after the last-named in the list. This expectation is heightened by the cross-reference to Hattush, who belongs to the third last recorded generation (v. 22). In Ezra 8.3 he is listed as the head of a household accompanying Ezra back to Judah. Unfortunately neither the date of Ezra's coming to Jerusalem (458 or 398 BCE are the dates most usually given) nor the age of Hattush at the time is known. A fixed point is provided by the notice that Jeconiah (v. 16) was eighteen years of age in 597 (2 Kgs 24.8; 2 Chron. 36.9 gives eight years). Assuming approximately twenty years between father and son, the last-named generation in v. 24 would be born about 375, 455 or 475 BCE, depending on whether 30, 26 or, even, 25 generations are meant by v. 21. That is to say, C is not likely to have been written earlier than the mid-fifth century and may be as late as the mid-fourth. As Hattush was already a head of household at the time of Ezra's arrival, his sons, and even his grandsons, may have been already born. C's work can then at least be associated quite closely with Ezra's mission, even if a more absolute date is unobtainable. It is not certain that the Anani mentioned in 1 Chron. 3.24 is the same person referred to in the Elephantine papyrus dated 408 BCE.

The question must arise at this point as to why C retains so many of the descendants of the house of David after the demise of the last effective Davidic monarch, Josiah, and the last to bear the title, 'king', Zedekiah. Does this retention indicate that C held some hope of the restoration of the Davidic dynasty, some messianic expectation? The view taken in this commentary is that it does not. The layout of the genealogies already makes the point that is about to be expounded in detail in the narrative section of the work as a whole. The primary model of Israel's life whereby the sovereignty of God is to be recognized is the Law of Moses; the Levites are the instructors of Israel and monitors of its giving to God of all that is due to him. It is that system which, in the manner of Lev. 26.40-45, carries Israel beyond *ma'al*, of which most kings of the Royal House are to be guilty, into the future, towards the fulfilment of the hope of Return. In the genealogies, the Levites are located centrally among the tribes of Israel (1 Chron. 6). Monarchy, with all the far-reaching affirmations and expectations attaching to it of sovereignty in God's name, represents the most intensive attempt to express the ideal that Israel is called to attain, but it remains a subordinate, and in practice defective, instrument, perhaps even intrinsically so. Thus, the two attempts at kingship, that stemming from Judah, associated with David, and that stemming from Benjamin, associated with Saul, remain on the outer limits of the definition of those who belong to Israel (1 Chron. 2–4; 8). But just as the descent of the failed dynasty of Saul is traced for many generations after his death (fifteen? see discussion on 1 Chron. 8.29-40), so too is that of David. Even the families of discredited royal houses retain their right to be counted as members of the people of God.

Having thus placed the house of David in pre-eminence and centrality within its own tribe of Judah, which is itself pre-eminent in Israel, and having brought David's descendants down to perhaps the thirtieth generation, near to his own time in the wake of Ezra's mission, C now returns in 1 Chron. 4.1-23 to document, in descending order of geographical proximity to the royal house, the other members of the tribe of Judah in the mirror image of the sequence employed in ch. 2.

After the complexities of the royal house in ch. 3, C begins 4.1 with a résumé of his argument in ch. 2, using the chief personages of that presentation, Judah (2.3), Perez (2.4), Hezron (2.5), Carmi (2.7) and Hur (2.19), the father of the craftsman of the tabernacle.

Carmi is a surprising choice given that he is not on the direct, narrowing line of the other names in v. 1. Caleb of 2.18, to whom the bulk of the Judah material of chs. 2 and 4 is assigned, would have been expected. But perhaps C deliberately chooses Carmi to remind his audience of the fateful note of doom arising from the deed of *ma'al* perpetrated by Carmi's son, Achar.

Shobal, the father of Kiriath-jearim (cf. 1 Chron. 2.50), picks up the record of Caleb IIa precisely at the point where it has been interrupted in order to bring Bethlehem into closest proximity to David. 1 Chronicles 4.2 thus resumes 1 Chron. 2.52-53 (Reaiah's name was used for a pun in the earlier passage): there it had not been made completely clear from which elements of these clans of Kiriath-jearim the Zorathites (as a sub-clan) were in fact sprung. These are now identified (though none of them occurs elsewhere in the Hebrew Bible): the 'these' of 4.2 is thus the specification, at least in part, of the 'from these' of 2.53.

If 1 Chron. 4.2 functions as the specification for 2.53, then 4.3-4, the beginning of which, 'these are the father of Etam', seems to be textually corrupt, may be expected to provide further definition of 2.54 (Caleb IIb). Both certainly concern the population of Bethlehem. Whereas 1 Chron. 2.54 expresses the population in collective terms, whether by clan names ('Netophathites..., half of the Manahathites, the Zorites') or by settlements ('the crowns of the house of Joab'), 4.3-4 provides the names of individual persons and locations, the latter perhaps the very strongholds which were the power base of the house of Joab. Etam was the crag to which Samson retired (Judg. 15.8, 11) and which king Rehoboam fortified as another of his fortresses (2 Chron. 11.6); Jezreel and Gedor both figure among the settlements of Judah (Josh. 15.56, 58), the first as the home of David's first wife (1 Chron. 3.1), the second as the home of one of those joining David at Ziklag (1 Chron. 12.7); while Hushah is the place of origin of one of David's warriors (1 Chron. 11.29; 20.4), who was also a superintendent of the royal service (1 Chron. 27.11; cf. above 1 Chron. 2.54 under Netophah). The other names in 1 Chron. 4.3-4 do not recur of these individuals in the Hebrew Bible.

The restoration of the text at the beginning of v. 3 remains uncertain. On the above discussion it might have run somewhat as follows: 'These are the sons of Salma, father of Bethlehem...? father of Etam...' *BHK* notes that the Syriac Version begins the verse with, 'These are the sons of

Abinadab', which may refer to the custodians of the ark of the covenant at Kiriath-jearim (1 Sam. 7.1; 2 Sam. 6.3-4).

1 Chronicles 4.5-8 incorporates Caleb III, previously announced in 1 Chron. 2.24 in a position of pre-eminence, that is, occupying part of the heartland of Judah, as its major settlement, Tekoa, situated between Bethlehem and Hebron, makes clear. None of the following dozen names of offspring of Ashhur recurs in the Hebrew Bible. Since they are all proper names or gentilics, they suggest a mostly nomadic population on the eastern edge of the territory of Judah.

1 Chronicles 4.9-10 resumes 2.55 (Caleb IIb) and, as there, completes the account of Caleb II–III with a statement, now in the form of an anecdote, justifying the supreme significance of the office of scribe, versed, like Ezra, in the Law, to study and perform it and to teach statute and ordinance in Israel (Ezra 7.10). By means of a play on the name Jabez (from a root *'bṣ*, which does not occur in Hebrew), the pain and hardship (*'ṣb*) of the birth and early experience of the guild of professional scribes is referred to (the position of the Levites in Israelite society lies to hand for illustration). Verse 10a is a model of what makes for acceptable prayer: it is a cry to God (1 Chron. 5.20; 16.8; 21.26; 2 Chron. 6.33; 14.11), an expression of fundamental trust and outright dependence on the part of the petitioner. In form it is a conditional clause, 'If...your hand is with me', which amounts to a wish, 'If only you would...' The perfect submission is made clear by the fact that the sentence has no principal clause stating human action or response. This is the first time the term 'God' occurs in C's work ('the LORD' has already appeared in 1 Chron. 2.3). 'God' is used by C when the cosmic and international significance of the Deity is affirmed, often in competition with rival claims, a sense appropriate here in a context of expansion of territory (even the preposition 'with' is important in such a context; cf. 1 Chron. 11.9).

1 Chronicles 4.11-12 begins C's account of the next tier down the pyramid, matching Caleb IV–VI in 1 Chron. 2.42-49. The sense of loose affiliation, yet distinctiveness, is indicated by the form of the name Chelub, which recurs only in 1 Chron. 27.26.

None of the other eight names of persons or places in this section recurs in the Hebrew Bible; presumably they belong to the outer ring of settlements in Judah.

More information is available concerning Kenaz (1 Chron. 4.13-14). It is information, however, which well illustrates the complexity of the interrelationship of the various branches and suggests that they may be associated by the similarity of catchwords rather than by actual blood-tie. Kenaz's first born, Othniel, features in the conquest narratives (Josh. 15.17; Judg. 1.13), where, in recognition of his exploit in reducing Kiriath-sepher, he is given in marriage Caleb's daughter, who also appears in the matching position in 1 Chron. 2.49. He is also one of the first judges of Israel (Judg. 3.9-11). In the latter reference, Othniel is identified as 'son of Kenaz, Caleb's youngest brother', a reference that leaves ambiguous whether Othniel or Kenaz is the brother of Caleb. The matter is still further complicated by the fact that Caleb, son of Jephunneh (1 Chron. 4.15), is called a Kenizzite (Num. 32.12; Josh. 14.6,14): is this gentilic to be associated with Othniel's father or with that other (related or unrelated?) Kenaz, the grandson of Esau (1 Chron. 1.36) (cf. yet another Kenaz in 1 Chron. 4.15)? Of the other descendants of the present Kenaz, none recur in the Hebrew Bible, though Ge-harashim, 'a valley of craftsmen', reappears as a locality in Benjamin in Neh. 11.35, presumably on the frontier of Judah. No indication is given of the special skill of the craftsmen who lived in this region. The name is, however, suggestive of the development of the distinct trade guilds, perhaps under royal patronage (cf. under 1 Chron. 4.21-23).

The final group of Calebites (1 Chron. 4.15-20) begins with Caleb son of Jephunneh, again linked, presumably merely by means of his name, with Caleb son of Hezron = Caleb II–III, and with Caleb brother of Jerahmeel = Caleb IV–VI. It was this Caleb, son of Jephunneh, who was the hero of the wilderness and conquest periods (Num. 13.6; 14.6, 30, 38; 26.65; 32.12; 34.19; Deut. 1.36; Jos. 14.6, 13-14; 15.13; 21.12). Because of his exemplary trust in the LORD and obedience to him, and his consequent optimism, energy and success, he was the only survivor of the wilderness generation, along with Joshua son of Nun, to set foot in the promised land. Under Caleb son of Jephunneh there appear to be no fewer than six groups, listed under different ancestors, whose relationship to one another is not explained: Caleb himself (v. 15) with three sons and a grandson; Jehallelel (v. 16) with four sons; Ezra (vv. 17-18) with some ten (?) offspring, and four associated place names; Hodiah (v. 19) with two associated place names; Shimon (v. 20a) with four sons and Ishi (v. 20b) with two. Apart from Caleb, none of the other personal names recurs, at least of these individuals, elsewhere in the Hebrew Bible.

The difficulty of the passage is compounded by the fact that the text is poorly preserved in a number of places, for example, in v. 15b, where the MT reads, 'and the sons of Elah and Kenaz', at least one name has fallen out; v. 17 should begin 'the *sons* of Ezrah' (MT has only the singular); v. 17b runs in the MT 'she conceived Miriam and Shammai', but who is 'she'? [unless Ezrah is a woman; cf. Mandelkern]; v. 18 begins 'And his Jewish wife...', but whose? It is tempting to restore the text in such a way as to produce coherence in the genealogical material, somewhat as follows: in v. 15b read, 'and the sons of Elah were Jehallelel, Ezra and Kenaz', which would provide the necessary link with vv. 16 and 17; the note in v. 18b, 'these are the sons of Bithiah, daughter of Pharaoh, whom Mered married' cannot go with the immediately preceding in v. 18a, since these are identified as the offspring of a Jewish wife; by transposing v. 18b before v. 17b a subject is provided for the verb 'and she conceived' (so NRSV); in v. 19 the phrase 'the sons of the wife of [the otherwise unknown] Hodiah' should perhaps be read as 'the sons of the Jewish wife' (so *BHK*), which the verse goes on to identify by the fact that she is sister of 'Noham the father of Keilah... and Eshtemoa...'; the two missing sons are supplied from v. 20a and b, Shimon and Ishi.

As noted above, the half-Egyptian parentage of some of these Calebites (v. 17) corresponds to that of some of the Jerhameelites (1 Chron. 2.34). Of the place-names mentioned, Eshtemoa occurs twice (vv. 17 and 19), cf. the place in the south of Judah mentioned as one of the recipients of David's spoils in 1 Sam. 30.28 and the Aaronic city of refuge in 1 Chron. 6.57 (cf Josh. 21.14; is this place to be identified also with the Eshtemoh of Josh. 15.50?); a Gedor has already occurred in v. 4; the Soco is presumably the place of that name in the southern hill-country (Josh. 15.48) rather than the one in the Shephelah (Josh. 15.35); Zanoah, the place mentioned in Josh. 15.56 rather than the one in Josh. 15.34; Keilah recurs in Josh. 15.44, 1 Sam. 23.1-13, Neh. 3.17-18.

C ends his account of Judah in 1 Chron. 4.21-23 by returning to Shelah, Judah's oldest surviving son, but not belonging to the dominant line of Perez–Hezron–Caleb. 1 Chronicles 4.21-23 thus forms with 1 Chron. 2.3 the immediate outer bracket within which the material on Judah is handled.

1 Chronicles 4.21-23 provides within brief compass a good example of the problems of interpretation posed by much of C's genealogical material, those of source, text and reference.

The difficulty of retaining the thread of the presentation amid the elaboration of the genealogies is illustrated by a rare misprint in the Collins edition of RSV in 1 Chron. 4.21, where 'the' is without a capital letter, thus making the verse look like the continuation of the immediately preceding section.

There is no parallel passage to these verses in the Hebrew Bible; C must be basing his work on now no longer extant sources, which may be being referred to in v. 22b, 'the records are ancient'. The antiquity of these traditions and the way in which they were handed down (unlike the parallels in Genesis, Kings, etc., they were not enshrined in 'Scriptures') may account for at least some of the difficulties in the text and the obscurity of the references. The content is a tantalizing jumble of geographical, ethnic, military and social information, stemming from a variety of periods.

The interconnection of the phrases is quite unclear. Is v. 21b an explanation of v. 21a, or independent of it? Does 'and Jokim...' (v. 22) continue the immediate sons of Shelah? Is Jashubi-lahem in v. 22 a proper name or a bowdlerised form of 'they returned to Bethlehem' (*BHK* and *BHS*)? Does 'these were the potters...' (v. 23) refer to all the people in v. 22? Does the phrase, 'and the inhabitants of Netaim...' (v. 23) refer to the preceding or the succeeding?

The geographical area is located by the references to Mareshah, Cozeba (presumably = Chezib, probably to be identified as the birthplace of Shelah himself in Gen. 38.5 = Achzib) and Gederah, as in the western fringes of the lowlands of Judah (cf. the gazetteer Josh. 15.36, 44; the other place-names are not mentioned again in the Hebrew Bible).

The population is described as being descended from Shelah through Er (he bears the same name as his uncle, the oldest brother of Shelah, who was 'wicked in the sight of the LORD') and Laadah (otherwise unknown). But the ethnic connection of the other elements is not clear: it is not explicitly stated whether Jokim, Joash and Saraph (also otherwise unknown), 'the men of Cozeba' and 'the inhabitants of Netaim and Gederah' are later descendants or merely other loosely affiliated groups.

The historical reference to Joash and Saraph's rule over Moab seems to imply a brief colonial expansion on the East Bank (compare the peaceful migration of Ruth's father- and mother-in-law, Ruth 1.1-3, or David's parents, 1 Sam. 22.3-4; the Targum takes the verb, 'were lords of...', v. 22, to mean 'married'). See also the fact that the paragraphing of MT in 1 Chron. 5.1-2 associates the East Bank tribe of Reuben with these West Bank tribes.

An interesting insight is given into the economy of the region during the time of the monarchy: the local craft guilds in the linen workshops and the potteries enjoyed royal patronage. If Netaim and Gederah are taken to be common nouns, 'plantations' and 'pens' (so the Vulgate), then the nurserymen and stockbreeders, it would seem, also depended upon crown concessions. Specific mention of Mareshah as a royal fortress is made in 2 Chron. 11.8 in connection with Rehoboam, so that this royal patronage could extend back at least to the late tenth century. With this reference to the potentiality of Judah to fulfil its role in Israel as the tribe of origin of the royal house the account is appropriately rounded off.

1 CHRONICLES 4.24–5.2: SIMEON

In accordance with C's overall plan of the tribes of Israel (1 Chron. 2.3), the account of Simeon now follows (1 Chron. 4.24–5.2). It is striking, however, that in this section Judah still remains a major focus of attention.

This focus on Judah is made even sharper by the paragraphing of MT. It divides the material into two sections: 1 Chron. 4.24-27, the list of Simeon's descendants; 1 Chron. 4.27–5.2, the impact of Judah's leadership. Notably, against the chapter division, that second section includes the first two verses of material on Reuben. The reason for this paragraphing is clear: the two paragraphs of the MT thus climax in the statements concerning, on the one hand, the size of Judah (that Simeon's 'whole clan never attained the size of the descendants of Judah', v. 27); and on the other, its significance—though it took over the position of power and leadership among its brothers, yet it was never accorded Reuben's status of the first-born (5.2). Judah thus remains essentially the centre of interest from 1 Chron. 2.3–5.2, just as it dominates the genealogies as a whole by the *inclusio* 1 Chron. 2.3; 1 Chron. 9.1; see also 1 Chron. 6.15.

Given C's attitude to the monarchy, there is a certain negativity in the presentation of Judah. Being weaker, Simeon has to submit to Judah's political leadership and suffer from its territorial growth. Yet the weak shepherds of Simeon are to outlast the royal power of Judah.

The exposition begins with the names of Simeon's five chief ancestors (v. 24).

This list is closest to that of Num. 26.12-13, where, however, Jachin appears for Jarib. It varies more markedly from the lists in Gen. 46.10 and Exod. 6.15, where a sixth ancestor, Ohad, is added after Jamin, and Zerah appears as Zohar. C also omits the fact that the last named, Shaul, was 'the son of the Canaanite woman' (Gen. 46.10), which, given that Judah's son Shelah, with whom he has just dealt, was also the son of a Canaanite woman (Gen. 38.2, 5) might have been thought to suit his purpose. It may be part of his favourable treatment of Simeon as opposed to Judah that leads C to omit this point.

The lineal descent of only one branch (Shaul) through six succeeding generations is then detailed (the names of none of these individuals recur in the Hebrew Bible, but it is striking that the succession Mibsam–Mishma occurs among the Ishmaelites, 1 Chron. 1.29-30). By the seventh generation, C contents himself with recording, unnamed, that Shimei had 'sixteen sons and six daughters'. The relative weakness of Simeon is the point: 'his brothers did not have many offspring' (v. 27a). In terms of numbers Simeon can stand no comparison with Judah (v. 27b).

The second section deals with Simeon's territories (1 Chron. 4.28–5.2). Elsewhere in the Hebrew Bible the picture is one of the gradual assimilation of Simeon by Judah. In the gazetteer of Josh. 15.26-63, all of the localities mentioned, or some variation of their names, with the exception of Bethuel, Beth-marcabot, Hazar-susim and Etam, occur among the possessions of Judah. Beer-sheba to Rimmon (Josh.15.26-32) are located on the frontier with Edom and the Negeb (the territory of Caleb VI and Caleb son of Jephunneh, cf. 1 Chron. 2.49; 4.18), while Tochen/Ether and Ashan (Josh. 15.42) are placed in the Shephelah (the territory of Caleb IV, Caleb son of Jephunneh and Shelah, cf. 1 Chron. 2.42; 4.19, 21), that is, on the outer fringe of the settlements of Judah.

> The situation at Ziklag (v. 30) may be taken as a signal example: before the rise of David, the Simeonites were unable to hold this territory because of Philistine pressure, and, possibly, Amalekite incursion (1 Sam. 30.1). Ziklag passed into the hands of the Philistine ruler of Gath, who was thus able to grant it as a feudal territory to David, to whose house it thereafter belonged in perpetuity (1 Sam. 27.6).

In C it is more a matter of Simeon's being forced by Judah's dominance and by pressure of their own growing numbers to seek for new pasture-grounds and settlements at the expense of their non-Israelite neighbours to the south.

For the list of Simeon's territories (vv. 28-33), C refers to Josh. 19.2-8. But he uses this source in a highly significant way. First, he cuts off its outer framework (Josh. 19.1, 9), which places Simeon's inheritance within the larger inheritance of Judah (cf. Judg. 1.3, 17). Then, in place of two static lists of towns in Joshua, each accompanied by its villages, C introduces a sequence of events. By a simple change in the gender of the suffix, C makes the first list refer to towns and the second to towns with lands (the pronominal adjective '*their* villages',

v. 32, no longer refers to the cities but to Simeon). C thus relates these lists to two different periods: the period of settled life before David; and the period of pastoral life thereafter.

The first list of thirteen towns represents the period up to the reign of David (vv. 28-31; v. 31b, 'these were their cities until the reign of David', is C's own, replacing the simple enumeration of 'thirteen' in Joshua; elsewhere in the genealogies the reign of David marks the beginning of the definitive realization of the pattern of Israel's life, 1 Chron. 6.31; 7.2). After the list of further five cities (Joshua has only four; C adds Etam at the head of the list), C adds a long independent section on the significance of these places (vv. 33b-43).

It is in relation to these places that the heads of households are recorded in the register. Thirteen names are given in vv. 34-37 (three of them with pedigrees, extending to one, three and five generations; none of those named recurs in the Hebrew Bible). The coincidence of the number thirteen suggests that these heads of households are meant to be related to the thirteen original towns of the period before David. If so, the force of the information is again that Simeon, originally a settled tribe in the pre-Davidic era, has become a shepherd tribe in the post-Davidic period. But this does not mean a diminution in their numbers. On the contrary, so greatly have their numbers increased (v. 38b) that they have been forced to expand into two new areas, where they have displaced the original population: in the region of Gedor they displace Hamites in the time of Hezekiah (vv. 39-41; Mandelkern distinguishes this Gedor from that in 1 Chron. 4.4, 18 and, following LXX, equates it with Gerar, cf. 2 Chron. 14.13-14; for the Meunim as traditional enemies beside the Philistines and the Arabs, cf. 2 Chron. 26.7); subsequently, in Mount Seir they displace Amalekites (vv. 42-43). The leaders of their successful colonization in this far south are otherwise unknown.

The names of localities occupied by Simeon are virtually identical with those listed in Josh. 19.2b-8a, with one or two variations: for example, the Sheba repeated in Josh. 19.2, probably in error (cf. the total of thirteen given in v. 6 despite fourteen names being listed), is omitted; Bilhah now appears for Balah, Tolad for Eltolad, Bethuel for Bethul, Beth-biri for Beth-lebaoth and Shaaraim for Sharuhen. The five 'villages' show the addition of Etam at the head of the list as contrasted with Josh. 19.7, and the substition of Tochen for Ether.

Of particular interest are the names Bethmarcaboth ('chariot depot': in Josh. 19.5 the form of the name is still with the definite article, suggesting a common noun in process of development into a place name) and Hazar-susim ('horse depot'), which suggests a significant role for the region in the deployment of the cavalry forces (of the Israelite crown or the Egyptian imperial army?). Baal (v. 33) may be identified with Baalath-beer (Josh. 19.8). It is striking that place names compounded with Baal mark the territories of Reuben and Half-Manasseh on the East Bank in 1 Chron. 5.8, 23: it may not be fanciful to see in this an expression of the idea that the alien force of Canaanite religion lurks at the gate.

The last comment in v. 43, that the Simeonites 'are there till this day' (cf. v. 41 where they laid the people East of the Arabah under ban 'to this day') may be intended to mean that small and mobile though the population of Simeon may be, it actually outlasts its more illustrious neighbour, Judah. Ousted by the Davidic monarchy to the lands of Ham and Edom, they actually outlive it. Here is a paradigm of the ambiguousness of monarchy for Israel: the two greatest monarchs of the Davidic House, David himself and Hezekiah, as C himself will later acknowledge, have merely brought dispossession to Simeon; yet, despite their dispossession, this element of Israel survives, long after the monarchy itself has disappeared.

Verse 33b introduces one of C's key terms, *hityaḥēś*, 'to be registered' (1 Chron. 5.1, 7, 17; 7.5, 7, 9, 10; 9.1, 22; 2 Chron. 12.15; 31.16-19), which is immediately tied up with the significance of the whole genealogical section in 1 Chronicles 2–8 (cf. 1 Chron. 9.1). It is essential for the role of Israel, as the people of God and as his agents in the world, that those who may claim to belong to that people can be identified and that claims of belonging can be validated. Further, because holiness is expressed through the metaphor of space in the Hebrew Bible (see, for example, Solomon's prayer in 2 Chron. 6.22-39 for the degrees of holiness), it is equally essential that claims to territory are confirmed and that the relation of people to territory is established. By possession of land identity is established. This registering of the people is thus a sacral undertaking: see the legislation for the muster of the people in Exod. 30.11-16, which is later to play a significant part in the fit organization of the life of the people (e.g. 2 Chron. 31.4-6, 19, for Hezekiah himself). It is precisely an infringement of the character of the people as sacral that lies at the heart of David's guilt in the census in 1 Chronicles 21, the hinge chapter on the presentation of the whole of the monarchy.

> By means of this material, C gains a striking parallel to the experience of the Danites, who were equally forced out of what was subsequently to become Judaean territory, and who acquired a homeland for themselves in a peaceful region by force of arms in the far north (Judg. 18; there are some verbal correspondences, 'land broad on either hand', v. 40/Judg. 18.10; 'quiet', v. 40/Judg. 18.7, 27; 'they smote', v. 41/Judg. 18.27; 'they dwelt', v. 41/Judg. 18.28; statistics of forces, v. 41/Judg. 18.2, 11). Dan and Beer-sheba thus mark not simply the geographical limits of the land in the far north and south but reflect similar processes for Israel's possession of that land.

The final verses of the section (1 Chron. 5.1-2), have nothing directly to do with Simeon, but return to the problem of the status of Judah. Reuben, the first-born of Israel, has been deprived of his birthright because of an act of gross indecency (intercourse with his father's concubine Bilhah, Gen 35.22; 49.4; the vocabulary of the latter passage is reflected here). Judah takes over the position of political leadership within the community, but is not granted the status of first-born. The birthright is no mere intangible right to precedence; it is expressed physically by a double portion (Deut. 21.16-17), in this case possession of central lands on the West and East Banks. But this right to the most favoured territory is taken over, not by Judah, even though the royal house is descended from it, but by Joseph's sons, Ephraim and Manasseh.

It is unlikely that the fundamental point for C is geographical. Rather, as his arrangement of the tribes indicates, the transfer of the birthright implies the right of closer association with Levi at the centre of the tribal system. The most notable descendant of the House of Joseph is the Ephraimite Joshua (cf. 1 Chron. 7.27), who, as servant and successor to Moses, does indeed stand, in the role that he played in the early history of Israel, in closest association with the Levites. It is to be Joshua who not only leads the successful invasion of the land (Josh. 1–12; cf. 1 Chron. 2.7), and apportions the land to the people of Israel (Josh. 13–22), but also mediates a covenant to all Israel (Josh. 24) at Shechem in the territory of Ephraim (1 Chron. 7.28). In Deuteronomy the custodians of that covenant at Shechem are precisely the Levites (Deut. 27.14).

Joshua the Ephraimite thus fulfils the acquired birthright of the house of Joseph by settling Israel in its land and mediating to that newly created Israel the Mosaic covenant whose officers are none other than the Levites. Despite the failure of Reuben and the flawed pretensions of Judah, the means have been provided, through the passing of the birthright to Joseph, for Israel yet to fulfil the purpose of God—settlement to the limits of the land with the Levites at the centre.

1 Chronicles 5.3-26: The East Bank Tribes: Reuben, Gad and Half-Manasseh

In terms of content, 1 Chronicles 5 as a whole deals with 'the East Bank tribes' of Reuben, Gad and Half-Manasseh. But C's interest is not merely in a systematic geographical description of the tribes; it is primarily in questions of hierarchy. Thus, as already announced by the paragraphing of MT, the opening verses (1 Chron. 5.1-2) inextricably bind Reuben up with Judah over the question of the right of precedence by birth. That right should have gone to Reuben as the first-born, but it was forfeited by an act of gross immorality (v. 1). Judah then becomes the dominant tribe by virtue of the fact that the monarchy springs from it. But that historical fact does not weigh with ultimate importance: the monarchy as the agency through which Israel can realize its destiny is flawed. The true means by which Israel will find its identity and role is the Levites.

In order to make that clear, a new pyramidal arrangement has to be worked out. As David stands at the apex of the pyramid of monarchy, flanked on both sides by Caleb (1 Chron. 2.25–4.20), so Levi has now to be supported in the inner tier of the pyramid of the tribes of Israel as a whole by Israel's adopted first-born, Manasseh and Ephraim. This, then, is the main task of 1 Chron. 5.3-26: to show how the East Bank tribes appropriately flank the Levites, who will be dealt with in 1 Chronicles 6, at the apex of the pyramid of the tribal system. This they do by being involved in incidents that are both exemplary, in showing how God's sovereignty is to be expressed and recognized on earth, and cautionary, in that they too, like Judah, defraud God and suffer exile (the thematic term *ma'al* occurs at the beginning of v. 25). Thus, they also share in the general predicament of Israel which it is the function of the Levites to handle, as is indicated in preliminary fashion in 1 Chronicles 6.

MT divides the material in 1 Chron. 5.3-26 into four major sections:

A. vv. 3-10: Reuben;
B. vv. 11-17: Gad;
C. vv. 18-22: war on the Hagrites: the exemplary incident;
D. vv. 23-26: Half-Manasseh: the cautionary experience.

A. *Verses 3-10: Reuben*

The record of Reuben's descendants begins with a phrase resuming v. 1, which still retains the honorific title, 'first-born', for Reuben despite the intervening verses. These verses recounting Reuben's loss of status explain his position on the vulnerable East Bank and his need to expand his territories eastward into the Syrian desert (vv. 9-10).

The spread of Reuben's sons (v. 3) is almost exactly reproduced from Exod. 6.14b (cf. Gen. 46.9; Num. 26.5), but the descent for eight generations through one line only (vv. 4-6) is peculiar to C.

At the beginning of v. 4 'Joel his son' must be read with LXX^L (*BHK* and *BHS*), otherwise the relationship of Joel is unknown.

This relatively short genealogy leads directly to the disastrous invasion of the northern and eastern tribal territories by the Assyrian king, Tiglath-pilneser III, during the course of the Syro-Ephraimite War about 732 BCE (cf. v. 26; 2 Kgs 15.29), when their chief was deported (v. 6). The narrative contrasts this loss of territory with earlier prosperous days at the end of the eleventh century BCE, when opposition was easily overcome and grazing-grounds for the numerous flocks were secured along the desert fringes as far as the Euphrates. This war on the Hagrites, the descendants of Sarah's Egyptian maid-servant, Hagar (Gen. 16.1, etc.) is used in vv. 18-22 as the model of the successful campaign (for the activities of the Hagrites as one of Israel's traditional eastern nomadic adversaries, cf. Ps. 83.6). It is striking that this expansion is associated with Saul, otherwise used by C as a foil for David.

The remaining prominent Reubenites mentioned in vv. 7-8 are otherwise unknown. It may be by deliberate design that C lists climactically in v. 8 a place name associated with Baal (cf. Num. 32.38; Josh. 13.17) as a reminder of the temptations to worship other gods that constantly assailed the Israelites on settlement and to which they finally succumbed (cf. vv. 25-26).

The geographical region and the territories assigned to the East Bank tribes as a whole are described in Josh. 13.8-31 (cf. 2 Kgs 10.33): the land from Aroer on the Arnon, the traditional northern boundary of Moab, north through Gilead and Bashan, with Reuben in the south, Gad in the centre and Half-Manasseh in the north. C's much shorter list at v. 8 is indicative only.

B. *Verses 11-17: Gad*

The second of the East Bank settlers is the 'concubine tribe' of Gad.

In vv. 11 and 16 C defines Gad's territories. Other sources (Deut. 3.12ff.; Josh. 12.5) place Gad for the most part to the south of the Jabbok, the valley running down from the hills of Gilead to the Jordan between the Dead Sea and the Sea of Galilee. C alone in the Hebrew Bible locates him in Bashan, the old kingdom of Og, stretching north from the Jabbok, across the valley of the Yarmuk to the Golan Heights and the foothills of Mount Hermon.

These foothills are the 'outlets' of v. 16, where perhaps Sirion (= Hermon; Deut. 3.9; Ps. 29.6) is to be read for 'Sharon' (*BHK*).

Salecah, the limit of Gad's expansion, is the traditional eastern frontier of Og's kingdom.[1] C thus heightens the insecurity of Gad: for Bashan, highly desirable for its proverbial oak forests (Isa. 2.13, Zech. 11.2) and fatstock (Ezek. 39.18, Amos 4.1), was the area on that far-flung north-eastern frontier most bitterly fought over by Israel and her near neighbours, the Aramaeans of Damascus. Gad, on C's view, stands in the forefront of the battle. The experience of the historical Gad is here being extended to become typical of the East Bank tribes.

Between his definitions of geographical area in vv. 11 and 16, C records numerous names of individuals and clans, none of whom is otherwise known in the Hebrew Bible; the relation between the two lateral and the two lineal groups is not fully clear (vv. 12-15).

C imparts the information (v. 17) that it was not until towards the middle of the eighth century BCE, in the reigns of Jotham of Judah and Jeroboam II of Israel, that Gad was enrolled by its genealogies (cf. Hezekiah's similar undertakings two generations later in 1 Chron. 4.41). There is no mention of this in the account of Jotham in 2 Chron. 27.1-9, where, however, the enrolment might be brought

1. Deut. 3.10 and Josh. 12.5; cf. L.H. Grollenberg, *Atlas of the Bible* (London: Nelson, 1956), map 12.

into relation with the muster of the army for his campaigns against Gad's neighbours, the Ammonites.

It is hardly surprising that it was at this time and from this insecure area, that no fewer than three of the usurpers of the throne of the Northern Kingdom emerged in the mid-eighth century, Shallum, Menahem, and Pekah (2 Kgs 15.10, 14, 25).

C. *Verses 18-22: War on the Hagrites. The Exemplary Incident*

While in v. 10 it was Reuben alone who made war on the Hagrites, here it is a joint expedition by all three Israelite tribes on the East Bank: Reuben, Gad and Half-Manasseh. This concerted action gives C the opportunity to illustrate in brief compass central themes of his theology on the role of Israel in the world. The section is thus particularly rich in association with other parts of C's work, as will be indicated below.

Israel is the agent of the LORD's rule on earth. It is the 'outward and visible sign', the earthly counterpart, of the hidden cosmic reality and power of the LORD of hosts. In a word, C's theology of Israel is sacramental. Since the seen and the unseen are but the two sides of the one indivisible reality, in order to be the fitting agent of this cosmic power, Israel must be totally prepared and equipped with the best of all the temporal forces available. But, at the same time, Israel must be wholly reliant upon God, not upon her own strength. This paradox can only be resolved in sacramental terms: it is because Israel is totally in tune with the cosmic direction of the universe that she is unconquerable on the field of battle.

It is these ideas that are expressed in this section. The forces of Israel on the East Bank are portrayed in terms of total battle readiness: the very first phrase to describe them, *b*^{e}*nē ḥayil* ('valiant warriors' [NRSV], v. 18), already has a sacramental significance expressing both the innate calibre of the troops and the outward status and armaments that perfectly express that inner quality.

That outward equipment is specified in terms of the most up-to-date defensive and offensive arms available: shields, swords and bows.

The descriptions of the standard military equipment of the infantryman vary slightly in other contexts: for *māgēn* ('shield') and *ḥereb* ('sword') used here, a larger shield (*ṣinnâ*, 1 Chron. 12.24 [25, MT]) and spear (*rōmaḥ*, 1 Chron. 12.24 [25, MT]; *ḥ*^{a}*nît*, 1 Chron. 12.34 [35, MT]; cf.

2 Chron. 11.12; 14.8; 25.5). Instead of 'treading the bow', that is, stringing it by bracing it with the foot, as here, there is also the expression 'kissing the bow', namely, drawing the already strung bow, in 1 Chron. 12.2; 2 Chron. 17.17 (where 'kissing' is also incongruously associated with shield).

Not only are they equipped; they are battle-hardened, skilled in the use of their armaments (v. 19a).

The number of troops mentioned, 44,760, presumably indicates the total mobilization of the males of arms-bearing age (though see the figures in the table below for 1 Chron. 12.38, the early period of David).

As so often throughout C, the statistics for armies can only be appreciated in comparative terms. The following are the main sets of figures for Israel given by C:

1 Chron. 5.18	Reuben, Gad and Half-Manasseh	44,760
1 Chron. 7.1-5	Issachar	145,000
1 Chron. 7.6-11	Benjamin	59,434
1 Chron. 7.40	Asher	26,000
1 Chron. 12.24-36	West Bank	219,600
1 Chron. 12.37	Reuben, Gad and Half-Manasseh	120,000
1 Chron. 21.5	David's census: Israel	1,100,000
	Judah	470,000
2 Chron. 11.1	Rehoboam's army: Judah and Benjamin	180,000
2 Chron. 13.3	Abijah's army (S)	400,000
	Jeroboam I's army (N)	800,000
2 Chron. 14.8	Asa's army: Judah	300,000
	Benjamin	280,000
2 Chron. 17.14-18	Jehoshaphat's army: Judah	780,000
	Benjamin	380,000
2 Chron. 25.5	Amaziah's army (S)	300,000
2 Chron. 26.13	Uzziah's army (S)	307,500

The last phrase in v. 18, 'ready for service' (NRSV), may be translated literally, 'the advancers of the host'. Two key terms are involved. The verb 'to advance' (*yṣ'*) has already been met in 1 Chron. 1.12. The term 'host', introduced for the first time, perfectly expresses sacramental theology: the plural 'hosts' (*ṣ^{e}bā'ôt*) is part of the divine title, 'LORD of hosts', which occurs in 1 Chron. 11.9 and elsewhere, where the reference is to the cosmic powers that God has at his disposal. Israel's army on earth is thus—ideally, at any rate—the local expression of those powers, embodying God's will and discharging his purpose. It is no wonder that those who are called to this service must have the Levites in their midst.

'Host' (*ṣābā'*) is again used of Israel, or a part of it, in 1 Chron. 7.4, 11, 40; 12.8, 14, 21, 23-25, 33, 35-36; 18.15; 19.8; 20.1; 25.1; 26.26; 27.3, 5, 34; 2 Chron. 17.18; 25.5, 7; 26.11, 13-14; 28.9, 12. It is also used of hosts rivalling Israel, and, by implication, Israel's God: Aram, in 1 Chron. 19.16, 18; Assyria, in 2 Chron. 33.11.

The opponents are the Hagrites, already introduced in v. 10, and associated Ishmaelites (v. 19; Jetur and Naphish have already occurred in 1 Chron. 1.31; Nodab does not recur in the Hebrew Bible).

But how can success in battle be secured? Verse 20 provides the pattern. These East Bank tribes are, in this campaign, a model of co-operative submission. The fundamental attitude is indicated in the last phrase, 'because they trusted in [God]' (cf. 2 Chron. 32.10): they acknowledge that the outcome of a battle is a matter of God's decision, regardless of the relative strength of the forces involved (the point is repeated in a similar 'because' clause at the end of v. 22a: 'because the battle is from God': it is fought at his instigation, in his name, in his power, and the successful result is the inevitable consequence of his decision). Thus, with a sense of total dependence, in the heat of battle they 'cry' to God, that is, they invoke his help (*z'q*, 2 Chron. 18.31; 20.9; 32.20; compare the similar use of the verb *qr'* in 1 Chron. 4.10); God allows himself 'to be entreated' (cf. the repentant Manasseh in 2 Chron. 33.13,19) and 'sends help'.

The verb 'to help' (*'zr*) is common in C, not least in connection with the support given to David: 1 Chron. 12.1, 18-19, 20, 21-22; 15.26; 22.17; also 2 Chron. 14.11 (the model case of Asa); 18.31; 19.2; 26.7, 13, 15; 32.8 (the model case of Hezekiah); contrast Ahaz in 2 Chron. 28.16, 21, 23 and elsewhere.

The passive verbs with which the verse opens are significant: it is only because Reuben, Gad and Half-Manasseh 'were helped' by God, and the enemy 'were delivered' by him, that the victory is secured.

It is significant that in this international incident it is 'God' who is invoked—the Deity in his international title. In this light even the apparently vague phrase for the opposition, 'and all who were with them', is significant. The preposition 'with' (*'im*, included in the messianic title, 'Immanuel', 'God is *with* us' [Isa. 7.14]) possesses an important range of affirmations about the presence and power of God in support of the Davidic king against any who would oppose him (1 Chron. 11.9; cf. already 1 Chron. 4.10, and 2 Chron. 36.23).

The consequences of the victory thus granted by divine approval are spoils in vast abundance (v. 21).

Again, only comparative statistics enable the scale of the triumph to be appreciated; the huge quantities show the ideological nature of the writing.

	Recipient	*Spoils/Tribute*	*Source*
1 Chron. 5.21	Reuben, Gad, Half-Manasseh	50,000 camels, 250,000 sheep, 2,000 donkeys, 100,000 prisoners	Hagrites
1 Chron. 18.2	David	unspecified tribute	Moab
1 Chron. 18.4, 7-8	David	1,000 chariots, 7,000 horsemen, 20,000 infantry; gold shields, bronze	Zobah
1 Chron. 18.6	David	unspecified tribute	Damascus
1 Chron. 20.2	David	unspecified	Ammon
2 Chron. 9.24	Solomon	unquantified silver, gold, silver, garments, equipment, spices, horses, mules (tribute)	'all the kings of the earth'
2 Chron. 14.15, 15.11	Asa	700 (?) cattle, 7,000 (?) sheep, camels (unspecified)	Gerar
2 Chron. 17.11	Jehoshaphat	silver (tribute)	Philistines
2 Chron. 17.11	Jehoshaphat	7,700 rams, 7,700 he-goats (tribute)	Arabs
2 Chron. 20.25	Jehoshaphat	unspecified property	Moab, Ammon, Meunites (?)
2 Chron. 25.11	Amaziah	10,000 prisoners	Seir
2 Chron. 26.8	Uzziah	unspecified tribute	Ammon
2 Chron. 32.23	Hezekiah	unspecified tribute	'all the nations'

The concluding statement of the section restates the reality: 'the outcome of war depends on God' (v. 22a). But as soon as apostasy creeps in, forfeiture of territory is, according to sacramental theology, inevitable (v. 22b). It is such apostasy that the following section is about to expound.

For the modern reader the war language is offensive; the vocabulary of 'defence' and 'pacification' by military means arouses unease and cynicism. It is hard to see how the purposes of God for peace and justice can be achieved by such means. The offence may be partly blunted by the character of the writing, suggested by the fact that the incident is neither dated nor located and by the huge quantities of the spoils claimed: this is ideology, not history. But, however objectionable the language, the sacramental force of the war metaphor must be allowed to stand. It is not quietism or passivity that is being commended: only those who are in that state of receptivity which comes from total commitment and preparedness, yet who are convinced that the outcome depends entirely upon the being and nature of God, can expect to prevail over adversity and circumstance.

It should also be noted that C too regards bloodshed in war as a regrettable necessity, permissible only within the context of the sacral muster (cf. 1 Chron. 21)—and as excluding David from building the Temple (1 Chron. 28.3). It is only Solomon, the 'man of peace' (1 Chron. 22.9), who will have that honour. The fragility of conquests by war is suggested also by the last phrase of 1 Chron. 5.22. The ideal is that peace is a given (even at the hands of the world emperor, 2 Chron. 36.23) and that God's sovereignty expressed through the wisdom of his vicegerent on earth is acknowledged by the rulers of the earth, not imposed on them (2 Chron. 9; see the table above, showing tribute received in recognition as well as spoils gained by force).

D. *Verses 23-26: Half-Manasseh. The Cautionary Experience*

C completes his exposition of Israel's settlement on the East Bank with his account of the half tribe of Manasseh (vv. 23-26). Those who had been chosen as substitute for the renegade first-born, Reuben (v. 1), turn out to be no better themselves.

The ambiguousness of Manasseh's record in this part of the land is skilfully indicated. On the one hand, they prospered and became numerous (v. 23); their seven heads of households (otherwise unknown) are meticulously recorded and generously appreciated as renowned for their valour and substance (v. 24; cf. v. 18; the vocabulary is to be frequently used of effective warriors in 1 Chron. 7–8). But on the other, they became conformed to the tradition of the indigenous population who had been destroyed that they might settle in the land and they themselves forfeit that land (vv. 25-26).

The temptations of the land where they settle is suggested by the unique way in which its frontiers are defined (v. 23b). Just as Gad is quite exceptionally allotted the area of Bashan north of the Jabbok in v. 11 (otherwise in the Hebrew Bible assigned to Half-Manasseh, Num. 32.39-40, Deut. 3.13-15, Josh. 13.29-31), so now here Half-Manasseh is crowded around Hermon, a famous seat of Baal: C is using geography ideologically.

The association of Hermon with Baal is indicated by Pss. 42.6; 89.12 and 133.3, and especially here in the place name Baal-hermon ('Baal of Hermon'), located in Judg. 3.3 at the southern end of 'Mt Lebanon'.

Senir is a synonym for Hermon (Deut. 3.9; cf. Song 4.8 and the parallelism in Ezek. 27.5).

In this area contaminated with the worship of Baal, Manasseh succumbs. They commit the archetypal sin of *ma'al* (1 Chron. 2.7), the depriving of God of his rights. The title used here for God, 'the God of the fathers', indicates the specific rights violated: his rights of sole worship claimed by his victory on behalf of his people in giving them their land in the teeth of opposition from the indigenous population. The incomprehensible element is how Manasseh could abandon its own strong tradition and surrender to the allures of a system thus discredited. C uses the standard vivid biblical metaphor of 'fornication' for this religious pluralism (Exod. 34.15-16; Hos. 2.7, etc.; used again in 2 Chron. 21.11, 13).

C is to make much use of the title, 'the God of the fathers', with reference both to the founding ancestors of the people of Israel and also to David and Solomon as the prime agents of God in Israel's victories in war and the pacification of the earth and as the founders of Temple worship in Jerusalem, through which God's sovereignty thus established on the field of battle is thereafter expressed: 1 Chron. 12.17; 29.20; 2 Chron. 7.22; 11.16; 13.12, 18; 14.3; 15.12; 19.4; 20.6, 33; 21.10; 24.18, 24; 28.6, 9, 25; 29.5; 30.7, 19, 22; 33.12; 34.32-33; 36.15.

In v. 26, the condemnation is broadened to include Reuben and Gad, as well as Half-Manasseh. They succumbed to the same temptations of the worship of Baal as had the indigenous population whom God had driven out before them. Thus they neglected not simply God, but what he had done for them and the injunctions he had given them. Their penalty too should be the destruction once meted out on the earlier population (the technical term for the destruction of the pre-Israelite population recurs in 2 Chron. 20.10 [cf. 2 Chron. 20.23]; 33.9). The fact that Israel 'merely' forfeits the land they have so unworthily occupied by being taken into exile, rather than suffering death, is in itself an expression of the grace of God. The action of Tiglath-pilneser as agent of God (contrast 2 Kgs 16.7 where he comes at Ahaz's request) in ejecting his people from his land picks up v. 6 and rounds off the whole account in vv. 3-26 of Israel's catastrophic attempt to settle the East Bank. It is notable that the expression 'to arouse the spirit' is always used in C of the initiative of God in inspiring the action of foreigners against (here and 2 Chron. 21.16) or for (2 Chron. 36.22) Israel.

'Spirit' belongs to the standard vocabulary of 'inspiration'. As God breathed into clay to create a living being (Gen. 2.7), so he can animate the action of these beings by his spirit (thus prophetic inspiration is accounted for, 2 Chron. 15.1; 20.14; also the 'possession' of the warrior, 1 Chron. 12.18).

In v. 26, Pul is not necessarily to be regarded as a separate king of Assyria: the verbs 'took captive' and 'brought' are singular in Hebrew; the conjunction between the phrase, 'The God of Israel aroused the spirit of Pul *and* the spirit of Tiglath-pilneser...' is to be taken in the sense of 'namely' as elsewhere in the Hebrew Bible (e.g. Deut. 9.8, 22 as the specification of Deut. 9.7). Pul is Tiglath-pilneser's Babylonian throne name.[2]

For the places of exile (except Hara, which does not recur in the Hebrew Bible), see 2 Kgs 17.6//Isa. 37.12.

Verse 26 ends on the grim note of the unatoned guilt and the perpetuation of the loss, 'to this day'. In the light of C's whole work, 'this day' is the exilic generation, which is for him the time of the dawning of the eschatological Return (2 Chron. 36.23).

2. J. Bright, *A History of Israel* (London: SCM Press, 3rd edn, 1981), p. 270.

1 CHRONICLES 6: LEVI

This tale of the frustration of the providence of God by the unfaithfulness (*ma'al*) of his people is brought into immediate association with the genealogy of the Levites. As has been already noted, the central role of the Levites in providing the priesthood at the altar, the religious teachers throughout the community at large and the monitors of Israel's practice of holiness is recognized by the central position of Levi among the genealogies of Israel.

However, not only the position, but also the structure of the chapter is designed to make these key levitical functions clear. Once again the overwhelming list of names and the complexity of its detail must not be allowed to obscure the clear arrangement of the data.

The chapter falls into three main sections:

A. vv. 1-30: the genealogy of the Levites;
B. vv. 31-49: the chief duties of the Levites;
C. vv. 50-81: the settlements assigned to the Levites throughout the other tribes.

MT provides subdivisions of this material, most of which will be noted below.

A. *Verses 1-30: The Genealogy of the Levites*

Within the first section C again uses devices now familiar from the earlier chapters of the genealogies: centrality, pre-eminence and false start (see, for example, David in 1 Chron. 2–4). In the centre stands the family of Kohath from whom the priests of the Temple descend. Within that central family there is pre-eminence, the line of descent of the high priests from Aaron. But even within Aaron's family there is a false start: the first two sons are eliminated and it is only from the third and fourth sons who survive that the priesthood descends. The remaining Levites are grouped around this central family of Aaron.

The MT paragraphing makes this focusing of interest clear:

vv. 1-2:	out of Levi it is Kohath that is central;
v. 3a:	pre-eminence in this line moves through the first-born of two generations from Amram to Aaron;
v. 3b:	the four sons of Aaron;
vv. 4-15:	after a false start, the line of descent of the high priests from Eleazar, the oldest that survives;
vv. 16-28:	the Levites of Gershom and Kohath; the descent of Samuel;
vv. 29-30:	the Levites of Merari.

The material can be conveniently divided into two parts:
(1) the descent of the high priests (vv. 1-15);
(2) the descent of the non-priestly Levites (vv. 16-30).

(It is notable that no account is given of the ordinary priests descended from Aaron, through his surviving sons Eleazar and Ithamar, to complement the line of high priests. Only a brief note is later given in 1 Chron. 24.1-6.)

(1) *Verses 1-15: The Descent of the High Priests*
The three sons of Levi are first given (v. 1) in their usual Hebrew Bible order (cf. Gen. 46.11, Exod. 6.16, Num. 3.17; 26.57):

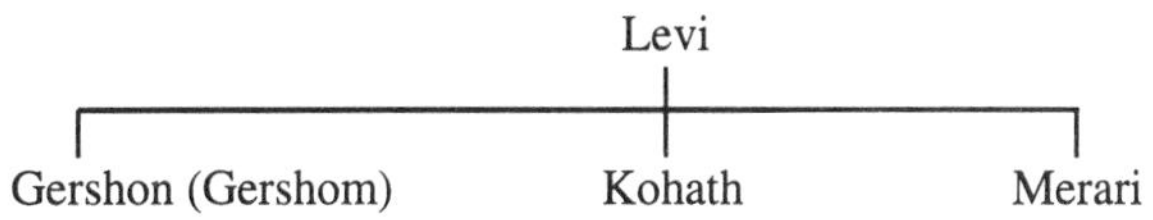

Kohath's central role, as ancestor of the line of Aaron, is then immediately indicated by the fact that it is his descendants who are traced first (vv. 2-15). But even within his descendants there is an order of precedence: only some are destined for the supreme role of officiating at the altar. Of the sons of Kohath the priesthood is traced only through the family of Amram and of the children of Amram only through Aaron.

Even Moses takes second place, as does Miriam (Moses' older sister, Exod. 2.4, if the unnamed sister there is Miriam).

Of the four sons of Aaron (v. 3), only Eleazar and Ithamar are to survive and of these Eleazar is to be the dominant partner. It is this line that is now traced in direct descent through the succession of high priests, to the twenty-sixth generation from Levi.

As must be the case so often in such genealogies (cf. 1 Chron. 1), the original audience to whom Chronicles was addressed were so well-versed in the traditions of their people that the mere mention of a name was sufficient to conjure up an entire episode. So, in the case of the succession of the priesthood, associations must have been brought immediately to mind: Eleazar (v. 4), who with Joshua and the heads of the tribes apportioned out the Promised Land by lot to the people (e.g. Num. 34.17); Phinehas his son (v. 4), whose zeal for the exclusiveness of the worship of the LORD averted the LORD's anger (Num. 25.7-13) and who led the inquiry into the alleged *ma'al* of the East Bank tribes (Josh. 22.13, 30-34); Zadok (v. 8), who anointed Solomon as king (1 Kgs 1.45); Azariah (v. 10), who officiated in Solomon's brand new temple (1 Kgs 4.2) at the high point of the fortunes of God's people.

But there is also a darker side indicated: the history of the priesthood begins with the elimination of Nadab and Abihu (v. 3), the older pair of Aaron's own family, who, despite having been present on Mt Sinai itself at the very moment when the covenant between God and Israel was concluded (Exod. 24.1,9), failed in their service at the altar and were destroyed (e.g. Lev. 10.1). The history of the priesthood is then traced only as far as Jehozadak (v. 15), who was in office at the time of a disaster of still greater magnitude, the exile of 587 BCE (cf. Hag. 1.1, Zech. 6.11, Ezra 3.2). The priestly sacrifices had not sufficed to atone or to avert the crisis, not even for the officiants at the altar themselves. There is nothing mechanical about the cult in ancient Israel; the priests share in the captivity of their people. Yet the section ends (v. 15) with the seed of hope: the exile was caused not by the mere whim of a human world conqueror, Nebuchadnezzar—he was merely the instrument—but by the will of God himself as the punishment for his people's faithlessness. Correspondingly, any return must depend upon an act of restoration by God himself (2 Chron. 6.36-39). It is to be noted that the fate of Judah, which provides the framework for the entire genealogical section (1 Chron. 2.3; 9.1; cf. 5.25), is here brought directly into relationship with the function of the central line of the Levites.

The line of priests of Aaron can hardly be complete, at least in its second part: only nine names are recorded for the period of nearly four hundred years from the foundation of the Temple to the exile (from Azariah, v. 10, to Jehozadak, v. 15). The incompleteness of the information is made still more clear by the fact that the sixth named of these last nine (Hilkiah, v. 13) is in office at the time of Josiah's reformation in the 620s (2 Kgs 22; 2 Chron. 34), thus leaving the preceding five to span more than three hundred years back to Solomon's time (in the list of kings of the house of David in 1 Chron. 3 for the equivalent period there are sixteen names). The information may be even more defective in that three of the names (Amariah–Ahitub–Zadok, vv. 11-12) recur in the same sequence in the time before Solomon (vv. 7-8).

Other occurrences of the genealogy of the priests do not significantly help to clarify the matter: 1 Chron. 6.50-53 merely repeats the line for the first twelve generations from Aaron to Ahimaaz; 1 Chron. 9.10-11 provides only a selection of names with the added complication that Meraioth is inserted between Zadok and Ahitub (cf. also Ezra 7.1-5; Neh. 11.11).

The two Azariahs in vv. 9-10 are also puzzling: the Azariah who officiated in Solomon's Temple was the son of Zadok, according to 1 Kgs 4.2, not his great-great-grandson as here. Ahimaaz is known in the Samuel–Kings narrative only as a young son of Zadok who acted as courier (2 Sam. 15–18); nothing is said of his officiating in the Temple or of his son Azariah or grandson Johanan.

On the other hand, C's genealogy of the Aaronic high priests is notable for its omissions: one would have expected Jehoshaphat's high-priest, Amariah (2 Chron. 19.11), and, especially, Jehoiada (2 Chron. 22.11–24.25), the priest who was loyal to the LORD in the testing days of Athaliah, to deserve a mention; so, too, the martyred Azrikam (2 Chron. 28.7), if he was indeed high priest.

The leaving out of Uriah, the no doubt unwilling accessory to Ahaz's apostasy, is perhaps less surprising, given that C makes no mention of him at the appropriate point in 2 Chronicles 28. Abiathar also, who in Samuel is portrayed as the last survivor of the priesthood of the pre-monarchical period (1 Sam. 22), receives no mention: his place as descendant of Ahitub is taken by Zadok (cf. 2 Sam. 8.17).

(2) *Verses 16-30: The Descent of the Non-priestly Levites*

Verse 16 resumes v. 1: the Levites are now to be considered in their breadth through their three branches and not just in the main central line that produced the specialized office of priesthood, as in vv. 1-15.

There is the trifling variant of Gershom for Gershon: the latter is the commoner form and probably the more original; compare the clan name derived from it, 'Gershonite' (Num. 3.21, etc.); the former is perhaps introduced under the influence of Moses's son of the same name, see Exod. 2.22.

The first generation of the descendants of the three branches, Gershom, Kohath and Merari, are now listed in their usual Hebrew Bible sequence (vv. 16-19).

The material is a slightly abbreviated version of Num. 3.17-20, with some influence from Exod. 6.19 in v. 19.

Thereafter (vv. 20-30), only one line out of each of these branches is followed: Gershom's through Libni for eight generations (vv. 20-21); Kohath's now through a second son, Amminadab, for some twenty generations (vv. 22-28; because of textual difficulties the exact number of generations is uncertain); Merari's through Mahli for eight generations (vv. 29-30). The symmetry of the presentation, 8–20–8, is striking: as Kohath was the major branch in that it produced the priestly line of Aaron through Amram and was therefore given the position of pre-eminence (vv. 1-15), so now (vv. 16-30) it retains its position of centrality and prominence among the non-priestly Levites through Amram's younger brother, Amminadab.

The first line listed is that of Gershom (vv. 20-21). Apart from Libni, already mentioned in v. 17, the names given are unique to C. Clearly only a selection of names is given. Some of them recur (in reverse order) in vv. 39-43 of this chapter as forebears of the Gershonite musician, Asaph. The list surely coincides sufficiently to refer to the same genealogy (the four identical names in the lists are underlined):

vv. 20-21	vv. 43-39 (*sic*)
Gershom	Gershom
Libni	
Jahath	Jahath
	Shimei
Zimmah	Zimmah
Joah	
	Ethan
Iddo	
	Adaiah
Zerah	Zerah
Jeatherai	

There may be another coincidence between the two lists: Iddo and Adaiah resemble one another closely in Hebrew.

Joah son of Zimmah recurs in 2 Chron. 29.12 as a contemporary of Hezekiah in the last quarter of the eighth century BCE, a date which confirms that the list of names for the preceding centuries back to Gershom is incomplete (cf. 1 Chron. 15.5-7).

The next line listed is that of Kohath (vv. 21-28). As befits the dominant family, the list of names for the non-priestly Levites descended from Kohath is much fuller than for those descended from Gershom and Merari. It does, however, present a number of problems, as can be appreciated by comparing the list with vv. 33-38, where it recurs in reverse order as the genealogy of the Kohathite musician, Heman. In this second list the difficulties of the first are ironed out:

vv. 22-28	vv. 38-33 (*sic*)	
(Israel)	Israel	
(Levi)	Levi	
Kohath	Kohath	
*Amminadab	Izhar	
Korah	Korah	
Assir		
Elkanah		
Ebiasaph	Ebiasaph	
*Assir	Assir	
*Tahath	Tahath	
*Uriel	Zephaniah	
*Uzziah	Azariah	
*Shaul	Joel	
*Elkanah	Elkanah	
*Amasai, *Ahimoth	Amasai	
	Mahath	1 Sam 1.1
*Elkanah	Elkanah	
Zophai	Zuph	Zuph
Nahath	Toah	Tohu
Eliab	Eliel	Elihu
Jeroham	Jeroham	Jeroham
Elkanah	Elkanah	Elqanah
Samuel	Samuel	Samuel (8.2)
*Vashni, Abijah	Joel	Joel Abijah
	Heman	

Whereas in vv. 33-38 the descent passes uninterruptedly from father to son, there are some gaps in the information in vv. 22-28, especially concerning the three last Elkanahs. One is introduced in v. 25 without explicit mention of who his father was; he is credited with a second son whose name is reminiscent of the grandson of this Elkanah in the second list. The MT of v. 26 seems to preserve two readings concerning another Elkanah: 'As for Elkanah, the sons of Elkanah were Zophai his son and Nahath his son' and 'As for Elkanah, his son was Elkanah, Zophai his son, Nahath his son'. The genealogical link of Samuel is likewise missing.

Ten of the names (marked *) are peculiar to C. Of particular note is the name given here to Kohath's son: elsewhere it always appears as Izhar (v. 38; Exod. 6.18, 21; Num. 16.1); here, uniquely, it is Amminadab. Has this form been influenced by the name of Aaron's father-in-law (Exod. 6.23), or by that of one of the Levites commissioned by David to be one of the bearers of the Ark (1 Chron. 15.10-11), or, even, by that of Abinadab, in whose house the Ark rested while it was at Kiriath-jearim (1 Sam. 7.1)?

There is also a striking coincidence between the name Shaul and that of Saul, first king of Israel. The parallel Uzziah–Azariah between the two lists also reminds one of the Judaean king of the mid-eighth century who bore this double name. The remaining names fall into two groups:

(1) Korah to Ebiasaph, who are paralleled in Exod. 6.24, where, however, Assir, Elkanah and Ebiasaph appear as brothers, not, as here, father–son–grandson. The second list in vv. 33-38 follows the Exodus view in recognizing here only one generation. The Korah of v. 22 is none other than the opponent of Moses and Aaron in the narrative of Numbers 16 and with whose sons (guild?) are associated Psalms 42–49, 84, 85, 87 and 88.

(2) Zophai to Abijah, who correspond to data in 1 Sam. 1.1; 8.2. The text of v. 28 is probably to be emended in the light of 1 Sam. 8.2: the name Joel has fallen out; Vashni is a corruption of *w^eš ēmišnēhû* 'and his second'.

The introduction of Samuel here as a descendant of Kohath shows that C regarded him as a Levite, as befitted his function as a minister in the Temple in which Eli officiated as priest. The material in 1 Sam. 1.1, which suggests that he was an Ephrathite/Ephraimite, may simply refer to the locality in which he functioned, rather than the stock from which he was sprung (cf. the Levite from Bethlehem in Judg. 17.7). In v. 33 he is listed as the grandfather of the musician Heman.

The line of Merari (vv. 29-30 a separate paragraph in MT, as in vv. 44-47; 1 Chron. 9.14; 15.17b; 16.38; in the transportation of the Tabernacle, the one sanctuary until the construction of the Temple, Merari are responsible for the strutural elements of tent and court, Num. 4.29-33): apart from Mahli (Exod. 6.19; Num. 3.20, 33; 26.58), the names are peculiar to C. Unlike Gershom and Kohath there is no close parallel between the genealogy given here and that of the chief musician of the clan that follows in vv. 31-48 (Mahli is again the only point of contact). There is a coincidence at least in name with Libni and Shimei of the sons of Gershom (v. 17).

B. *Verses 31-49: The Chief Duties of the Levites in the Sanctuary*

This section deals with the two main duties of the Levites in leading worship—the liturgy and the sacrificial rites at the altar. The word *'ᵃbôdâ*, 'service', covers both of these activities (frequently in C: already in this passage, v. 32, for the liturgy; v. 48 for the rites of the altar):

(1) vv. 31-47: the institution by David of the chief musicians (who are divided by MT into two subsections: Heman of Kohath with Asaph of Gershom, vv. 31-43; Ethan of Merari, vv. 44-47; the separate subsection, vv. 44-47, thus matches the earlier subsection on Merari in vv. 29-30);

(2) vv. 48-49: the appointment by Moses of the priests and their assistants for service in the sanctuary.

(1) *The Institution of the Musicians (Verses 31-47)*

The duty of the non-priestly Levites is first and foremost to take charge of the music (*šîr*) of the sanctuary (v. 31; for examples of their leadership of the liturgy see 1 Chron. 15.16; 2 Chron. 5.12; 20.21; 35.15). *šîr* is used primarily of vocal music, the song of hymn and thanksgiving (for an example of their songs see 1 Chron. 16.8-36). The accompaniment with musical instruments (*kᵉlê šîr*, e.g. 1 Chron. 15.16) is implied.

The high authority of David, who was himself 'the sweet singer of Israel' *par excellence* (2 Sam. 23.1), as organizer, provides the basis for this service. Here (v. 31), C introduces one of his key terms: 'institute' (*he'ᵉmîd*).

It is used, for example, in 1 Chron. 15.16-17; 22.2; 2 Chron. 8.14; 11.22; 19.5,8; 20.21; 23.10,19; 24.13; 29.25; 30.5; 31.2; 34.32; 35.2; also of heterodox practice, 2 Chron. 11.15 (Jeroboam); 25.5, 14 (Amaziah); 33.19 (Manasseh). It is also used of God's appointment: his oath (1 Chron. 16.17); the king (1 Chron. 17.14; cf. 2 Chron. 9.8), the land (2 Chron. 33.8).

It is a term of royal authority which extends not simply to putting into effect what the LORD has ordained through Moses, but to carrying out innovations that transpose the Mosaic tradition appropriately into new circumstances.

It is notable that C brings the institution of music into connection with the ark of the covenant, here and throughout his work. The ark is, initially, the symbol of God's prevailing power on the field of battle (Num. 10.35-36). When the world has been pacified (the fundamental question with which C grapples is how the relationship of peace between God and humanity can be restored), the ark can be laid up in its place of 'rest' (here C introduces yet another key term). The Temple in Jerusalem is to be that place of rest (*m*[e]*nûḥâ*, e.g. 1 Chron. 22.9; 28.2): the building of the Temple will thus finally mark the pacification of the world thanks to the victories of God through his vicegerent on earth, the Davidic king. But, if the opening of the Temple marks the completion of this pacification, its rites are integral to its maintenance. The song of the levitical musicians is to proclaim and celebrate the LORD's victories. But the appointment of the singers does not have to wait until Solomon has built the Temple in Jerusalem; they are installed in office at the moment when David brings the ark into Jerusalem (see 1 Chron. 13; 15). The song of the Levites celebrates not just the end result, but the process; they anticipate the completion; they are ordained, indeed, even before David sets out on his wars of pacification (1 Chron. 18–20). It is for this reason that Levitical song is equated with prophecy in C (1 Chron. 25.1).

This passage concerns arrangements for the liturgy in the period between the moment when David pitches a tent for the ark in Jerusalem (1 Chron. 15.1) and the moment when Solomon opens the Temple in Jerusalem (2 Chron. 5). The place where the liturgy is to be celebrated meantime is defined here as the 'dwelling of the tent of meeting' (v. 32), the portable sanctuary which had its origins in the time of the wilderness wandering (Exod. 25–31). As the sequel will show (1 Chron. 16.37-42), David actually divides the musicians: one family (Asaph) is to conduct the liturgy in connection with the ark in Jerusalem, and two families (Heman and Ethan/Jeduthun) with the altar at Gibeon. In Solomon's Temple these two institutions will be recombined (2 Chron. 5.5).

Each of the three great levitical families has its leader in connection with this responsibility for the music of the liturgy: the families are now arranged in order of precedence, Kohath–Gershom–Merari. The Davidic authority for the organization is underlined by the way in which the genealogies of the three main figures, Heman, Asaph and Ethan, one for each of the three levitical families, are traced backwards from the time of David (vv. 33-47). The stress is on the fact that they belong to the generation of David (cf. 1 Chron. 15.16-17); only then are their pedigrees traced backwards to their origins.

The names largely reproduce those already given in vv. 22-30 except in the case of Merari, where a new list appears containing names mostly otherwise unknown. In other texts Mahli is a brother of Mushi, not a son, for example, in 1 Chron. 23.21.

The relative importance given here to the leaders of the three levitical families or guilds of musicians (the emphasis on 'these and their sons' in v. 33 is to be noted) is indicated by the fact that, while Heman's genealogy (Kohath) is traced through 23 generations back to Israel, Asaph's (Gershon) is traced through only 15 to Levi and Ethan's (Merari) through 14, again to Levi. This relative importance is not, in fact, matched by the Psalms with which they are explicitly associated in the Psalter: Heman is associated with only one Psalm (Ps. 88); so, too, Ethan (Ps. 89); but Asaph has twelve (Pss. 50, 73–83; possibly more are 'Asaphite', cf. 1 Chron. 16.7-36).

It is hard to distinguish this Heman and Ethan from the individuals mentioned in 1 Kgs 4.31-32 whom Solomon surpassed in wisdom, not least in the skill of composition of *šîr* (but cf. 1 Chron. 2.6). Ethan, son of Kushaiah = Kishi, recurs only in 1 Chron. 15.17, 19; he is replaced later in C by 'Jeduthun' (e.g. 1 Chron. 16.41). Jeduthun's genealogical descent is never given and his name may simply be a variant of Ethan. Even in C Asaph tends to appear more frequently than Heman and he, alone of the three, recurs in Ezra (2.41, 3.10) and Nehemiah (7.44; 11.17, 22; 12.46).

(2) *The Appointment of the Priests and their Assistants (Verses 48-49).*

The supreme task is that of the priestly Levites at the altar. Their work belongs, beyond any Davidic institution, to the fundamental model of how Israel's life is to be maintained, that is associated with the revelation of Moses himself (v. 49; cf. v. 31). Moses is here introduced functionally for the first time (cf. v. 3) and is given the title of a prophet, 'the servant of God' (cf. Amos 3.7); Moses is indeed *the* prophet *par excellence*, '*the* servant of God'. To impart full sanction, Aaron himself, the chief priest and founding father of the priesthood, is also mentioned as though he were still present.

First, the work of the priests' Levitical assistants is noted (v. 48). Their duties are not specified here: door-keeping to guard rights of entry; supervising the treasuries to monitor Israel's practice of offering 'holy things' would be expected (cf. 1 Chron. 9.17-32); perhaps, even, assisting in sacrifices (2 Chron. 30.15; 35.11).

> The more menial status of these Levites is indicated by the participle 'appointed' (Hebrew, *n*[e]*tûnîm*, 'given'), with the overtone 'as assistants'. The term is probably not to be confused in this context with *n*[e]*tînîm*, the technical term for the menial Temple servants: 1 Chron. 9.2, and especially in Ezra and Nehemiah (e.g. Ezra 8.20).

The duties of the priests themselves are defined (v. 49): 'to make smoke upon the altar of burnt offerings and upon the altar of incense for all the service of the holy of holies, and in order to make atonement for Israel'.

C introduces here ideas that are central to his work. The ideal for Israel's existence is total harmony with God. This harmony is expressed through the primary model of the system of holiness.

The exposition of Israel's place in the world involves the metaphor of space. Israel uses space to express degrees of holiness: the 'nearer' one comes to God, the more awesome the experience, and the greater the sanctification of the person who so approaches. The most holy place of all is the 'holy of holies', the inner sanctuary, in the Temple. It is made holy because that is where the ark of the covenant, the symbol of God's all-prevailing power in his battle for righteousness in the world, is installed. And even it is but the 'footstool' of his cosmic throne (1 Chron. 28.2).

Next in holiness is the nave of the Temple, where the altar of incense is, then the inner court of the Temple where stands the altar of burnt offering. Beyond, lies the outer court where the laity may come; then the city of Jerusalem; then the land of Israel; then the great mass of the generality of humanity (cf. the degrees of holiness implied in the prayer of Solomon, 2 Chron. 6.22-39).

Matching this hierarchy of sacred space there are degrees of holiness required in those who are admitted to them. Thus, the high priest, 'Aaron', alone has access to the 'holy of holies', and that only once a year on the Day of Atonement. The other priests, 'the sons of Aaron', officiate at the altar of incense in the nave and at the altar of burnt offerings in the inner court. The Levites control entry from the outer to the inner court, and to the outer court itself, according to consecration and purity (impurity is caused by the facts of 'biological existence':[1] bodily emissions, illness, death, Lev. 11–15).

The holiness of objects corresponds to the holiness of the space where they are brought and to the consecration of the personnel who handle them. These objects include the furnishings of the sanctuary and, especially for C's purpose, the offerings in kind that are brought to it. The 'most holy offerings' are those brought into contact with the 'holy of holies'; the 'holy offerings' are those brought into contact with the inner court of the Temple and the nave (see Num. 18, especially, for the definition of these offerings).

These offerings dedicated at the Temple are the symbol of the practice of holiness by Israel as a whole throughout the length and breadth of the 'holy land' (Zech. 2.12).

It is the institution of this whole ideal Temple system, which expresses sacramentally through the rites of the priests at the altars Israel's total fulfilment of its duty, that is being referred to here. As the supreme expression of that system, C focuses above all on the rites on the Day of Atonement (Lev. 16): the stated annual rites at the altar of burnt offerings and the incense altar and on the 'mercy seat', the lid of the ark of the covenant in the holy of holies, for the purification of the Temple, the Temple personnel and the community from all the accumulated inadvertent impurity that is inseparable from human existence (the problems arising from biological existence are but the signal examples). There is here a distinction of fundamental importance for C's argument: the distinction between inadvertent and deliberate wrong-doing. For inadvertent impurity a mechanism lies to hand for restoration. For deliberate defiance, like the *ma'al* of which C has already accused Israel (1 Chron. 2.7), there can be no such recovery. In Leviticus 16, the rites are not specific measures for the atoning for particular sins, when Israel falls away deliberately from its primary ideal of existence; these are stated annual rites, designed not as response to specific offences but as regular acts of penitence with which to begin another year of commitment to the LORD and his Law. 'Atonement' in this sense is the reinstatement of the community which is conscious to the highest degree of the possibilities of infringing the standards of purity required.

It is with the breakdown and the possible re-establishment of this

1. The phrase is Mary Douglas's, e.g. 'Sacred Contagion', in J.F.A. Sawyer (ed.), *Reading Leviticus* (JSOTSup, 227; Sheffield: Sheffield Academic Press, 1996), p. 96.

primary model of Israel's existence that C is concerned throughout his work. Israel has not only failed to maintain the primary model, the faithful observance of the requirements of absolute purity, which may be inadvertently infringed; it has deliberately violated the Law not merely in the external expressions of religion, the laws of purity, but in the whole cast of its life. The only possible consequence of that scale of guilt is forfeiture of its own holy land (as the litany of curses at the end of the 'Holiness Code' in Lev. 26 makes plain).

C. *Verses 50-81: The Settlements Assigned to the Levites throughout the Other Tribes*

Yet another resumption (vv. 50-53 pick up vv. 3b-8) marks the beginning of a new section. Having given the identity and the function of the Levites, C now turns to record their settlements. The Levites are not simply the clergy who officiate in liturgy and cult in the Temple: in the lands of their dispersion and in their settlements throughout the land, they constitute an indwelling presence of local teaching and example. Thus, in this respect also, they contribute to the well-being of the community.

Verses 50-53 resume the genealogy of the chief priest only as far as Ahimaaz son of Zadok, that is, to the time of David. The settlement patterns of the Levites are thus appreciated in conjunction with their other roles.

C introduces his own title in v. 54a: 'The following are their settlements listed according to their dwellings throughout their territory'. By the rather rare word for 'dwellings' (*ṭîrôt*), used only seven times in the Hebrew Bible, typically in connection with nomadic populations (e.g. Gen. 25.16 of Ishmael, Num. 31.10 of Midian, Ezek. 25.4 of 'the sons of the east'), C underlines the fact that in their settlements the Levites do not have arable land, but only pasture grounds for the grazing of their livestock. This point is made very clear in connection with Hebron, the very first place mentioned (vv. 55-56): on the one hand 'the cultivable fields of the city and its villages were given to Caleb' (cf. 1 Chron. 2.42-50), while for the sons of Aaron, on other hand, a home in the city and the use of the grazing grounds must suffice. In the midst of the settled community the Levites retain the witness of the nomad: they do not share in the agriculture of the settled population, nor are they immersed in the attitudes and pursuits of a fully settled life. They remain as shepherds and are thus able to fulfil a duty in connection with fundamental institutions: they supply animals for the Levites for the Passover sacrifice, as 2 Chron. 35.8-9 points out.

The list of settlements in vv. 54-81 is adapted from Joshua 21. C feels free to rearrange and adapt his source to suit his purposes.

Joshua 21.4-42 is laid out in two sections within which the material is handled with great regularity:
(1) vv. 4-8: general statement of the number of cities which the several groups of Levites received from the different tribes of Israel:

v. 4	Aaron and his sons receive 13 from Judah, Simeon, Benjamin;
v. 5	the rest of Kohath 10 from Ephraim, Dan and Half-Manasseh;
v. 6	Gershon 13 from Issachar, Asher, Naphtali, Half-Manasseh;
v. 7	Merari 12 from Reuben, Gad, Zebulun;

(2) vv. 9-42: specification of the actual names of these 48 cities:

vv. 9-19	Aaron and his sons;
vv. 20-26	rest of Kohath;
vv. 27-33	Gershon;
vv. 34-40	Merari.

C borrows vv. 5-39 of this material, with some further omissions, and rearranges them in the order vv. 10-19, 5-9, 20-39. The result of this rearrangement is that the general statement of the number of the cities that Aaron and his sons receive from the southern tribes is suppressed in favour of the detailed list which is transferred to the beginning of the whole (vv. 54-60). By this means C lends greater emphasis to Aaron and his sons at the outset. The three families of Levi are then each given twice, each initially with a single verse: the rest of Kohath (vv. 61; 66-70); Gershom (vv. 62; 71-76); Merari (v. 63; vv. 77-81).

C has not, however, proceeded with great attention to detail. Verse 9 (= 1 Chron. 6.65), which should have gone with v. 10 as the preface to the specification of the names of the cities of the southern tribes allotted to Aaron and his sons, is now stranded between the summary verse of the general statement (v. 8) and the beginning of the list of specific cities given to the non-Aaronic families of Kohath.

There are other obvious signs of inattention, which may, however be due to copyists' errors rather than to carelessness by C himself. Thus in 1 Chron. 6.57-60 the sum total of cities allotted to Aaron and his sons is given as thirteen but only eleven are listed (Juttah is omitted in v. 59 from its parallel in Josh. 21 and Gibeon, presumably because of the similarity of its name to the following Geba, in v. 60). Similarly, a whole verse

(= Josh. 21.23) has been omitted between vv. 68 and 69 thus reducing the required number of cities for the rest of the Kohathites from ten to eight.

More seriously, this omission involves the entire disappearance of Dan from the tribes of Israel among whom the Levites settled. The omission of the verse may be due to the entirely mechanical reason (homoeoteleuton) that the end of vv. 22 and 24 in Joshua 21 are identical ('four cities'), so that the copyist's eye may have passed unconsciously from the first to the second. Yet it is striking that on two other occasions Dan is omitted: so in the immediate context in v. 61 where C reads the barely comprehensible, 'And to the remaining Kohathites ten cities by lot from the clan of the tribe, from the half of the tribe of the half of Manasseh', for Josh. 21.5, 'And to the remaining Kohathites ten cities by lot from the clans of the tribe of Ephraim and from the tribe of Dan and from the half of the tribe of Manasseh'. Dan is also omitted, as has been noted above, from C's entire tribal system in 1 Chron. 2–8. The Dan of Josh. 21.23 is still located in the lowlands west of Jerusalem and not at the headwaters of the Jordan, a geographical situation which had by C's time ceased for so long to correspond to reality that he may have omitted it for no more complicated reason than that.

A still further omission affecting the sum total of levitical cities occurs in v. 77 where the first two place names in Zebulun have been left out, leaving Merari with only ten named settlements in place of the requisite twelve.

On at least one occasion C preserves a better text than Joshua: in v. 65 the phrase 'and from the tribe of Benjamin' is accurately added to the statement of Josh. 21.9. C makes deliberate additions in v. 78 to the data of Josh. 21.36, to stress that the writ of the Levites also extended as far as the steppe-lands to the east of the Jordan opposite Jericho.

But for the rest, C is concerned to abbreviate his parent text. After 'cities of refuge' the expression 'for one guilty of manslaughter' is left out. Indeed, the plural 'cities of refuge' is read in vv. 57 and 67, perhaps with the deliberate intent of implying that the system had been extended. The whole phrase is omitted in vv. 71, 76, 80. The sub-totals of cities from the various tribes are also omitted (vv. 59, 68, 69, etc., and at the end of the chapter), except in the case of Aaron only (v. 60). The retention of the number here underlines C's purpose in enumerating Aaron's holdings at the head of the list for the sake of emphasis. Other omissions of carelessness (e.g. 'and their pasture-grounds', a phrase otherwise consistently retained because of its significance in underlining the pastoral associations of the Levites, in v. 57) or design (explanatory phrases, e.g. on the name Hebron/Kiriath Arba in v. 55) have the same effect of abbreviation.

There are variations in the names of about one third of the cities listed here from the parent text in Joshua 21. But these differences in no way impair the portrayal of a settled levitical presence and influence in forty-eight key centres throughout the length and breadth of the land. The system needful for the nurture of Israel in the ways of God has been fully provided. The last-named city, Jazer, recurs as the centre on the East Bank for the implementation of the system in 1 Chron. 26.31.

Of particular note is the presence of the cities of refuge for the unintentional homicide (cf. Num. 35.6-34) in vv. 57, 67, in both cases in the territory of Kohath: the protection of even the inadvertent killer, by the ultimate death of the high priest, is assured within the ideal people. Once again the distinction, of fundamental importance for C's argument, between inadvertent and deliberate wrong-doing is made. For inadvertent crimes, even manslaughter, a mechanism lies to hand for restoration. For deliberate defiance, like Israel's *ma'al* (1 Chron. 2.7), there can be no remedy but forfeiture. The Israelites could live, if they chose, by the instruction of the Levites not only centrally but also integrally located dispersed among them.

1 CHRONICLES 7–9: THE WEST BANK TRIBES AND JERUSALEM

With the central and northern West Bank tribes in 1 Chronicles 7–8, C reaches the second half of his presentation of Israel as grouped symmetrically about the Levites in the midst; with the population of Jerusalem in 1 Chronicles 9, he is poised to present the history of the monarchy—and beyond.

As in the layout of the tribes as a whole (cf. on 1 Chron. 2.1-2), so in this section C follows a sequence all of his own:

Issachar	Benjamin	Naphtali	Manasseh	Ephraim	Asher	Benjamin
(7.1-5)	(7.6-12)	(7.13)	(7.14-19)	(7.20-29)	(7.30-40)	(8.1–9.44)

But, once again, the paragraph arrangement of MT shows that, beneath this surface appearance, there are still further dimensions in C's layout.

It is obvious from the number of verses assigned that not all the tribes are being dealt with equally (Naphtali with only one verse is especially cursorily treated). MT actually links Issachar with Levi.

> One has to go by the paragraph markers: the opening conjunction of 1 Chron. 7.1, '*And* to the descendants of Issachar belonged...', does not by itself confirm the link (Gad, Half-Manasseh and Ephraim begin with a conjunction in 1 Chron. 5.11, 23; 7.20; but cf. a similar situation with paragraph markers in 1 Chron. 5.1). The anomalous feature is actually the preposition, 'to'.

With that link, the descendants of Rachel, Benjamin and the two sons of Joseph, Ephraim and Manasseh, form the inner tier of the pyramid around Levi (see introduction to 1 Chron. 5.3-26). In the MT paragraphing Benjamin subsumes Naphtali (and possibly Dan as well, see below on 1 Chron. 7.12). The limit of that inner tier is clearly marked by the words of 1 Chron. 7.29b, at the end of Ephraim, '...among these dwelt the sons of Joseph, son of Israel'. Asher is then linked with the second treatment of Benjamin in 1 Chronicles 8, before the reference to Judah in 1 Chron. 9.1, with its allusion to the

Babylonian captivity, rounds off the lower tier of the tribes begun with Judah in 1 Chron. 2.3.

There are a number of further interconnections that C has to make. The genealogical section of his work (1 Chron. 1–9), which propounds the problem of humanity as a whole and proposes a solution in which Israel has the key role, must now be linked to the narrative section of the work (1 Chron. 10–2 Chron. 36), in which the attempt of Israel to carry out that key role through monarchy is traced. Already in the genealogical section it has been announced that Israel as a whole has by its *ma'al* failed in its task. The narrative section seeks to portray how the ideal was attempted in monarchical terms but how the monarchy, too, failed in its purpose.

In this presentation, Benjamin plays a key role. It is not just the favoured son of the favourite wife, Rachel, with its time-honoured place among the tribes of Israel (hence its location in 1 Chron. 7.6-13). It also stands at the critical juncture of C's whole work. Benjamin constitutes the link between the genealogical section and the ensuing history in two additional vital respects: it is first, the tribe in whose territory Jerusalem, the site designated for the Temple and, therefore, for the capital of the Davidic kingdom and empire, is located; secondly, it is the tribe from whom the first king of all, Saul, whose story is about to be told in 1 Chronicles 10, was selected.

This multiple role of Benjamin is expressed by the complex arrangement of materials in 1 Chronicles 8–9. There is a resumption of the genealogy of Benjamin (1 Chron. 8.1-40 picks up, but in very different form, 1 Chron. 7.6-13); within Benjamin there is a resumption of the genealogy of Saul (1 Chron. 9.35-44 picks up, but in slightly briefer compass, 1 Chron. 8.29-40). There is also a resumption of the populations of Jerusalem (1 Chron. 9.2-34 resumes in very different terms 1 Chron. 8.14-28; 1 Chron. 8.29-32 overlaps the populations of Saul's Gibeon and Jerusalem). But the supratribal significance of Jerusalem, Benjaminite city though it is, is made clear by the description of its ideal, intertribal and levitical population (1 Chron. 9.2-34: the beginning of v. 3 and the end of v. 34 form a clear inclusio). This note on the population of Jerusalem, within the wider presentation of the interrelationship of Benjamin, ties in the note on the failure and fate of Judah, the tribe of David (1 Chron. 9.1).

The effect of C's inclusion of material on Benjamin in both 1 Chron. 7.6-13 and in 1 Chronicles 8 is that Benjamin becomes the dominant and integrating force among these northern tribes; compare the role of Caleb II and III first mentioned in 2.19-24 to be resumed in 2.50-55; 4.1-10, or that of the family of Ram recorded in 2.10-17 and resumed in the house of David in ch. 3. This corresponds to the facts of history, that Benjamin along with Judah alone survived the Assyrian captivity of 721 BCE and with Judah constituted the outer framework of the Israel that continued longest in the land.

1 CHRONICLES 7.1-5: ISSACHAR

Issachar, settled in the valley of Jezreel, is handled first of the tribes occupying the centre and north of the West Bank (1 Chron. 7.1-5). Names from only five generations are listed and only the family of the oldest in each generation is given.

The names of Issachar's immediate sons are paralleled in Gen. 46.13 and Num. 26.23-24. C agrees with Numbers against Genesis for the name of the third son.

There is a curious reminiscence between the names of the four sons of Issachar and the data on the judge from Issachar, listed in Judg. 10.1-2, Tola, son of Puah, who lived (*yōšēb*; cf. the name of the third son, Jashub, here) in Shamir (cf. the fourth son, Shimron). The names of the last three generations of Issachar's descendants are unique to C.

Not only is the list of Issachar's descendants clearly incomplete; there are also no details given of the tribal territories settled (contrast, for example, Judah in 1 Chron. 2–4). Instead, C picks up here the method of description of Israel as a war camp, organized, armed and ready for service, which he has used for the first time in connection with the exemplary campaign of the East Bank tribes in 1 Chron. 5.18-22.

Parts of this descriptive phraseology recur in different connections throughout 1 Chronicles 7 (especially vv. 2-5, 7, 9, 11, 40; also in 1 Chron. 8.6, 10, 13, 28, 40; the fullest form appears in 1 Chron. 7.40). A composite form of the presentation runs somewhat as follows: those specified by name are the leaders, variously termed, 'heads of households', 'the elite', 'men of substance/valour', 'princes', who exercise hereditary leadership by virtue of birth and status; then follow the statistics for their followers, their clansmen, 'those who were registered' (1 Chron. 4.33) by their 'lines of descent', 'to sally forth' (1 Chron. 1.12), as a 'host' (1 Chron. 5.18), 'in battle'. This is the mechanism in practical terms whereby the LORD's people become the LORD's host in the battles of defence and pacification. Here, for the only time in the enumeration of any of the tribes in 1 Chronicles

2–8, Issachar's armed forces are termed 'divisions' (v. 4), a word used elsewhere of small detachments of troops used as raiding parties (1 Chron. 12.21) or mercenaries (2 Chron. 25.9): Issachar (is there a play on the meaning of the name, 'man of hire', Gen. 30.18?) are ready to be of service at a moment's notice.

For Issachar, C supplies sum-totals for three groupings (vv. 2, 4-5; for comparative table see 1 Chron. 5.18). It is striking that the first two of these belong to quite different generations (Issachar's grandson and great-great-grandson, respectively). Because they both belong to the same line of descent, they should be regarded as recording growing relative strength, recorded in different periods (cf. the two sets of data on Simeon in 1 Chron. 4.24-43, one from David's time and the other from Hezekiah's). But that may be being over-logical. We have noted already how C is presenting Israel in ideal terms, of which 'timeless contemporaneity' (1 Chron. 9) is one aspect: for statistics the cross-section may be cut at any point on the time-line. It may be better, therefore, to take these numbers in aggregate as C's statement about the relative strength of the people in this part of the land. The totals here (145,600, or 123,000 if the statistics under David are not aggregated) may be contrasted with the total for Issachar of 64,300 in Num. 26.25. Issachar has played its full part in being fruitful and multiplying and filling the earth (v. 4b; cf. Gen. 1.28). C's use of statistics (cf. his cross-checking totals 'four' in v. 1, which is not in his parent text in Genesis or Numbers, and 'five' in v. 3, though only four names are mentioned) reflects his concern that not one of all the multitudinous families of Israel in its ideal extent should be lacking.

In relating the first group of statistics to the time of David (v. 3), C is defining Issachar in relation to the organization of the Levites by David in 1 Chron. 6.31 (a likely reason for the MT paragraphing that links Issachar with Levi). This is the period when the necessary forms of the people's life under monarchy are instituted, the hierarchy of the king and the heads of households. But under this leadership Israel are God's freemen, settled in God's land, eligible, responsible and equipped for the defence of their heritage and the furtherance of his work.

1 CHRONICLES 7.6-13: BENJAMIN (1) WITH NAPHTALI

The first section on Benjamin (1 Chron. 7.6-12) is markedly different from the second in ch. 8. In 7.6 there are three sons, whereas in 8.1-2 there are five, and only one name, Bela, is common to the two lists. The names of the sons of Bela are entirely different in 7.7 from those in 8.3-5.

Such divergencies in the names of Benjaminites are by no means peculiar to C: Gen. 46.21 and Num. 26.38-40 likewise show differences from one another.

Of the twenty-nine Benjaminites named in 1 Chron. 7.6-12, twenty-one do not recur elsewhere in the Hebrew Bible. No list of tribal territories is given; one at least of the personal names is identical with a place-name, Anathoth (v. 8); Alemeth has been identified with Almon (Josh. 21.18 [Mandelkern]).

Again, as in the case of Issachar, the strength of the Benjaminites is indicated by sum totals (59,434 in this context, as against 45,600 in Num. 26.41). Once again, the statistics are taken from different generations: Benjamin's grandsons in the first two cases, great-grandson in the third.

1 Chronicles 7.12, appearing after the sum totals, looks like an appendix.

The names Shuppim and Huppim, though reappearing in reverse order under Manasseh in v. 15, seem to recur, if in modified form, in Gen. 46.21 (Muppim, Huppim, of Benjamin) and Num. 26.39 (Shephupham, Hupham, again of Benjamin). Ir may be the same as Iri in v. 7.

Significantly, however, Hushim appears in Gen. 46.23 as a Danite: could v. 12, or at least v. 12b, therefore, be the sole vestige of Dan otherwise missing from the tribal system in 1 Chronicles 2–8? It is certainly geographically appropriate that Benjamin should occupy territory once belonging to Dan immediately to its west, after the Danite migration had taken place (cf. Judg. 18) and thus include material originally attributed to Dan within it (cf. Aijalon and the settlement of the eastern Philistine plain being attributed to Benjamin in 1 Chron. 8.13, though this area was originally allotted to Dan, Josh. 19.40-46). It is tempting also to take Aher not as a proper name but as the adjective, 'another', thus making the reference to Dan even more oblique.

The notice on Naphtali (v. 13) is of the utmost brevity and confines itself to the first generation only. The four sons are recorded as in the parent text of Gen. 46.24-25 (cf. Num. 26.48-50), with minor variations in the form of the names (Jahzeel for Jahziel, Shillem for Shallum). No territories are specified; no sum totals given. The implication is that this northerly tribe, located next to Dan itself in its new northern location, maintained only a precarious existence and a tenuous attachment to the Israelite tribal system.

One detail is preserved from the Genesis source: although none of the other matriarchs of Israel, Leah, Rachel and Zilpah, is mentioned by C, the name of Rachel's maid Bilhah is here retained. 'Sons of Bilhah' may be simply a mechanical transcription from Gen. 46.25; yet the analogous phrases, 'sons of Leah', and so on, are omitted in the Chronicler's transcription from Gen. 46.15, 18, 22. Here again, therefore, there may be a deliberate emphasis by C on the marginal status of Naphtali. The plural 'sons' is further evidence that not only Naphtali but Bilhah's other son, Dan, is included in this section.

1 CHRONICLES 7.14-19: MANASSEH

The section on Manasseh is very disjointed: no fewer than eight or nine different snippets of information are crammed into these six verses. Even with supplementary information available from other parts of the Hebrew Bible, especially Num. 26.28-34 and Josh. 17.1-13, some of these elements remain hardly comprehensible.

Verse 14a is abrupt: 'The sons of Manasseh: Asriel whom she bore' (the RSV ignores the punctuation of the MT). According to Num. 26.28-34, Asriel was the second son of Gilead, son of Machir, son of Manasseh (cf. Josh. 17.1-13). Nothing further is known of him or of his mother to whom C here obscurely refers. The proposal that the text is corrupt (*BHK* and *BHS*: Asriel has been inserted by dittography) is attractive.

Verse 14b is only slightly less abrupt than v. 14a: 'His (presumably Manasseh's) Aramaean concubine bore Machir father of Gilead'. Significant weight may be attached to this sentence: at this point in C's presentation of the tribes of Israel, it is a description of the position of the half tribe of Manasseh on the West Bank which is expected, not that of Gilead, part of the half tribe on the East Bank, whose position has already been dealt with in 1 Chron. 5.23-26. The emphasis here on Machir's mixed and menial racial origins (nothing further is known of Manasseh's Aramaean concubine) suggests the threat of military and racial assimilation of Israel by the Aramaeans, representing the ever-menacing world from which Israel took its origins (cf. 1 Chron. 1 and the pyramid of David with Egyptian influence at its extremities, 1 Chron. 2.34; 4.17). It would seem that C wants to suggest that Manasseh, half on the East Bank and half on the West Bank, can only be viewed as a whole: the fate of the nearer part is implicated in that of the farther.

Verse 15aα is very obscure. Does it mean, 'Machir took a wife for Huppim and for Shuppim' (NRSV)? But if Huppim and Shuppim were the sons of Benjamin referred to in 1 Chron. 7.12, what power did Manasseh have to provide them with wives? Does it refer to the infiltration of semi-

Aramaean influence even of Benjamin? Alternatively, if less likely, does it mean that Machir took for himself a wife from among Huppim and Shuppim? In this case the integrative role of Benjamin in that part of Israel may be the point.

The Aramaean associations of the name Maacah, borne by Machir's sister in v. 15aβ, again underlines the Aramaean connection (cf. 1 Chron. 2.48). In v. 16a Machir is also said to have had a wife of that name.

Before v. 15aγ, 'and the name of the second was Zelophehad', some phrases must have fallen out. According to Num. 26.33 and Josh. 17.3 Zelophehad was a grandson of Gilead. It may be that again by the use of a single name C is conjuring up a whole incident. Zelophehad is chiefly remembered for a question about land tenure. He had died in the Wilderness 'for his sin' (Num. 27.3) and had left no son to inherit his allotted portion of land. A ruling enabled his daughters to succeed to his inheritance, provided they married within their tribe, so that their portion could not pass with them on marriage outside the possession of their people (Num. 36). The bond between people and land must not be broken.

The names of Machir's (half-Aramaean?) descendants through Maacah (vv. 16-17a) are otherwise unknown. Likewise of Gilead's sister and her sons (v. 18) there is no further information in the Hebrew Bible: the Abiezer is presumably not the family of Gideon, who in Josh. 17.2 are simply called Manassites. Shemida, introduced without explanation in v. 19, is another son of Gilead, according to Num. 26.32. Again for Manasseh neither localities nor sum totals are given (contrast Num. 26.34).

A striking feature of this presentation on Manasseh is the prominent role played by women throughout. Given the patriarchal nature of the overall presentation of the tribes—the stress on the heroic heads of household and their leadership of their numerous clansmen in war, v. 2 and elsewhere, which is conspicuously lacking in this section (see the analysis of the descriptive phraseology under Issachar, above)—this emphasis can hardly be interpreted other than as further indication of weakness and vulnerability in this area.

1 CHRONICLES 7.20-29: EPHRAIM

The section on Ephraim provides a fairly complete example of the Chronicler's method in the genealogical section of his work. By genealogy he preserves material on obscure branches of his people, who otherwise would be lost. Thus of the twenty-one personal names given under Ephraim fully two-thirds do not occur elsewhere in the Hebrew Bible.

> Only Shuthelah, v. 20, and Tahan, v. 25, are known from Num. 26.35, Elishama son of Ammihud, v. 26, tribal leader of Ephraim in the time of the wilderness wandering, from Num. 1.10; 2.18, and elsewhere, and Joshua, son of Nun, v. 27, from the accounts of his appointment as servant and successor to Moses and leader of the conquests of the Land in Exodus 17–Judges 2.

The naming of these individuals and the listing of the settlements round the perimeter of their tribal territory suggest a keen interest in the full complement of all Israel as ideally constituted and inhabiting its land.

But these names also reveal how the destiny of this part of Israel reflects that of the nation in general. As in the case of Israel as a whole, and of Judah and Caleb in particular, there is a history of a substitution, a false start, and an ideally accomplished conclusion. Manasseh was, in fact, the first-born of Joseph but he was displaced in blessing by Ephraim (Gen. 48), who received the more favoured area for settlement on the West Bank (this background narrative is not explicitly referred to here but is implied in the climactic arrangement of the passage). The initial act of preference is followed by a false start: the first settlers (despite the formulation in vv. 20-21, which seems to indicate nine generations in lineal descent, 'their father' in v. 22 suggests that the names indicate a spread of contemporary brothers) were annihilated by the pre-Philistine indigenous Canaanite population of Gath (for whom cf. Josh. 11.22). Nothing is known otherwise of such an incident; it is particularly striking in that it suggests that, half a dozen generations before Joshua, Ephraim was present in some strength in the region at least in the form of Bedouin raiding parties, if not outright settlers. From this extremity of adversity (v. 23), reconstruction took place; new Ephraimites are born.

C in vv. 23-27 uses the same pattern as in vv. 20-21 but, at least at the end in the cases of Ammihud and Elishama, and Nun and Joshua (there is no corroboration from other Hebrew Bible passages that Nun was the son of Elishama), the list is clearly meant to give lineal descent. However, Tahan (v. 25), according to Num. 26.35, was a son of Ephraim. If so, there are no more than seven generations indicated by the list.

At all events, the second attempt by Ephraim is brought to a triumphant conclusion by Joshua (Josh. 8–12). The extent of the conquest is indicated by the enumeration of the towns on the southern and northern frontier (vv. 28-29).

On the southern frontier, Naaran, v. 28, is probably to be identified with Naarah of Josh. 16.7 and Ayyah, with Ai of Joshua 7–8. Bethel, Beth-horon and Gezer are frequently mentioned elsewhere in the Hebrew Bible. Uzzen-sheerah occurs only here and has not been identified (Grollenberg).

A peculiarity of the definition of the northern frontier is that the places mentioned in v. 29 are elsewhere assigned to Manasseh (e.g. Judg. 1.27). Does this represent a squeezing of Manasseh into the northernmost extremity of its territory on the West Bank, as in the presentation of Manasseh on the East Bank (see above on 1 Chron. 5.23)? The opening phrase of v. 29 implies that Ephraim settled alongside Manasseh in these towns situated in the sensitive area along the northern edge of the hill country of Samaria (see their presentation as brothers in Gen. 46.20 and Josh. 17.14-18 for their joint action). In the last analysis, it is Ephraim who is the dominant partner in the House of Joseph; they have 'a Shechem' (the place-name, v. 28, means, 'a shoulder'), above the rest of Israel (cf. Gen. 48.22). Thus, the section ends emphatically with an inclusio linking Ephraim and Manasseh together as the sons of Joseph, the favoured son of Israel himself.

The ideal has been attained under Joshua in the hill country of Ephraim: in v. 28 the technical term *'ᵃḥuzzâ*, 'holding', is used, which designates the territory to be held inalienably in perpetuity by a tribe as its share in God's land (again in 1 Chron. 9.2; 2 Chron. 11.14; 2 Chron. 31.1; it is return to the *'ᵃḥuzzâ* that is the hope of the jubilee,

Lev. 25.13). Once again all is prepared for the realization of God's purpose for his people.

A striking omission on the Chronicler's part in this section is any mention of Israel's *ma'al*, failure to give God his due, despite the fact that materials for such a point lay easily to hand, for example, in 2 Kings 17. The whole point of his presentation is to account for the fall of Judah and the house of David, that is more recent to his own time and is the pressing theological problem for him. The core of Israel remains and is the surviving growth point for the future.

1 CHRONICLES 7.30-40: ASHER

Asher, lying on the sea-coast in the far north-west, is the furthest flung of all the West Bank tribes. Once again, C has produced a little genealogical material that is familiar, much that is otherwise unknown.

The names of Asher, his four sons, his daughter, and his two grandsons by his youngest son, eight names in all (vv. 30-31a), are known from Gen. 46.17 (cf. Num. 26.44-46, which omits Ishvah). Possibly Japhlet is the progenitor of the Japhletites of Josh. 16.3, but they are on the wrong side of the Ephraimite boundary. The names of the remaining Asherites are not found anywhere else in the Hebrew Bible.

Once again this material, which is peculiar to C, has suffered damage in transmission: it is not certain that Shemer in v. 34 is the same as Shomer in v. 32, or that Helem in v. 35 is the same as Hotham in v. 32, or Jether in v. 38 as Ithran in v. 37, or Ulla in v. 39 as Ara in v. 38. It is not clear, therefore, just how many generations are represented here (a maximum of eight) or how many individuals are mentioned by name (forty, assuming the identity above, and provided that Birzaith in v. 31 is a place name—location unknown; for the formulation 'father of . . . ' before a place name cf. 1 Chron. 2.42-55. If these identifications do not hold, then the number of people mentioned rises to forty-five).

Of all the contexts in which the key term *hityaḥēś* 'be enrolled' (1 Chron. 4.33) is used, this is the fullest (v. 40). The names of ancient Israel are not recorded merely out of nostalgic interest. They express how all Israel was enrolled, each as belonging to his family, and each with his share in the LORD's land in the form of house and ground. The ideal Israel is a regulated patriarchal society, whose ordered descent ensures the orderly transmission of inherited property down the generations and its preservation inalienably within the family. Israel is organized as an effective fighting force with a suitably designated chain of command. Thus it was that Israel should have become, and should have remained, a free and responsible community, which, secure within its borders, and settled around the Levites, was fully equipped to be the LORD's agents on earth.

1 CHRONICLES 8: BENJAMIN (2)

1 Chronicles 8 is a complex chapter: first, a general presentation of its argument is in order, before some consideration of its detail.

1 Chronicles 8 belongs to the general pattern of resumptions visible in chs. 7–9 (see general introduction to 1 Chron. 7–9: The West Bank Tribes and Jerusalem, p. 98 above). It resumes the genealogy of Benjamin in 1 Chron. 7.6-12. Within the general context of C's work, in which he is presenting an ideal, the failure to attain that ideal, and yet the possibility of reaching it, C is showing how Benjamin too has a part to play in the whole process. As a 'favourite son' of a 'favourite wife' (the family terms are used as a metaphor for historical standing and geographical location), Benjamin, along with his full 'brother', Joseph, has a place in the upper tier of the pyramid that surrounds Levi (1 Chron. 7). Yet Benjamin's place within Israel also shows great ambiguity: while it participates in the expression of the ideal, it is also heavily implicated, as the homeland of Saul, in the failure to realize that ideal. Like Judah, it stands also in the lower tier of the failed mechanism of monarchy. Yet, still further, at the heart of Benjamin lies Jerusalem, which is itself part of the expression of the ideal, participant in failure, and key element in the ultimate realization of the ideal. This complex of ideas is expressed through the discussion of the population of Jerusalem and its relation to Benjamin.

In order to present these ideas, the chapter is divided into three main sections:

(1) verses 1-7: early phases in the life of Benjamin;
(2) verses 8-28: Benjaminite families in Jerusalem;
(3) verses 29-40: the family of Saul the Benjaminite and its relations with Gibeon and Jerusalem.

Sections (1) and (2) are both constructed in an inverted manner which makes their drift somewhat difficult to perceive: it is only from the conclusion of the section that the thread of the argument becomes clear. This is particularly the case with section (2): it is only in v. 28b that the 'punch-line' comes: 'these dwelt in Jerusalem'. It is only then that the reader realizes that five main families resident in Jerusalem are being itemized (vv. 14-16; 17-18; 19-21; 22-25; 26-27). These families are presented in an equally inverted way: unknown names are introduced first and only subsequently is it said, '...were the sons of X': for example, in vv. 14-16 there is a string of nine hitherto unknown names, and only at the end of v. 16 is it said that they are the sons of Beriah, who has already been introduced in v. 13, (probably) as a son of Elpaal (v. 12). Elpaal in turn is a son of one Shaharaim, introduced without explanation in v. 8.

The structure of section (2) thus only becomes relatively clear from its conclusion: from an ancestor Shaharaim, a Benjaminite resident in Moab, there descends through one son, Elpaal (but one of the ten sons by two of his three wives), five major households who are to become residents in Jerusalem. These five major families have themselves a complex inter-relationship: Beriah's own family has nine sons (vv. 14-16); among these is Shashak, who himself produces a family of eleven sons (vv. 22-25); it is possible (*BDB*) that Jeroham, the father of the fifth family in vv. 26-27, is to be identified with yet another son of Beriah, Jeremoth (v. 14); meantime Elpaal has another group of seven of his sons as an independent family (vv. 17-18) and yet another son of Elpaal, Shema, has a family of nine sons (vv. 19-21).

> This construction of these family relationships depends on the phrase, 'and Beriah and Shema', with which v. 13 begins, being the continuation of the list of Elpaal's sons begun in v. 12 but interrupted by the remark on Elpaal's second son, Shemer, that he was the one who 'had built Ono and Lod'.

The construction of section (1) is similarly best appreciated from its conclusion (v. 7). The point at issue is the expulsion of the inhabitants of Geba. Those responsible for that act include one Gera. Gera, as the earlier genealogy makes clear, is a son of Bela (v. 3), himself a son of Benjamin (v. 1). Others involved in the expulsion are related in the same way: Naaman (v. 7) is another son of Bela (v. 4); it is not so clear whether Ahijah in v. 7 is to be identified with yet another son of Bela, such as Ahoah, v. 4 (a connection made by one tradition of the LXX and the Syriac [*BHK* and *BHS*]).

It is probable that, though the present text is obscure on the point, there is meant to be a connection between sections (1) and (2). The family of Shaharaim, the ultimate progenitor of these five families in Jerusalem, is presumably one of these dispossessed from their homeland in Geba. Their subsequent dynamism in returning from Moab to Jerusalem is shown in a number of other accomplishments (the building of Ono and Lod on the Philistine Plain,[1] v. 12; the 'putting to flight', by another branch of the family settled in Aijalon, of the [Philistine?] population of Gath, v. 13).

The obscurity in the text particularly concerns v. 8a: 'And Shaharaim begot in the territory of Moab from his sending them away.' The interpretation above assumes that that last phrase means 'after he (Gera) had expelled [for the exceptional form of the verb, cf. GKC §52o] them (the population of Geba)'. It must be acknowledged that the continuation of the text is equally problematical.

The link proposed between sections (1) and (2) is supported by the paragraphing of the MT. It in fact separates off vv. 1-2: Benjamin and the list of his five sons. The remaining verses (vv. 3-28) are then all taken as one—presumably coherent—unit.

One may suggest reasons for C to include some of these further obscure details on the descent of five Benjaminite families in Jerusalem. First, a parallel is being drawn with the Moabite background of king David (cf. the book of Ruth); the Benjaminites also have similarly racially mixed origins; the world of the nations is ever present even in Jerusalem. Secondly, Geba is involved in a notorious atrocity that implicated the whole of Benjamin (Judg. 19–21; Geba figures in MT in Judg. 20.10, 33); again, one may assume knowledge by C and his readers of the earlier biblical traditions (cf. on 1 Chron. 1). Geba also figures in the narrative of Saul's kingship (1 Sam. 13.3, 16; 14.5; the point is unaffected by the complex question of the interrelationship of these similar sounding, and near located, places, Geba, Gibeah and Gibeon: if C is equating them, and there must be a case for so arguing—Saul's Gibeah of 1 Sam. 10.26, etc., is here equated with Gibeon—then the reason for the transition to the discussion of the population of Gibeon in vv. 29-40 is made even clearer).

The link to this complex of associations is through the resumption of Benjamin's son, Bela (vv. 1, 3), the only element in common between the genealogies of Benjamin in 1 Chronicles 7 and 1 Chronicles 8.

The motif of the Benjaminites resident in Jerusalem (v. 28) recurs

1. Grollenberg, *Atlas*, map 23.

in v. 32, in section (3) of the chapter (vv. 29-40). But this list is, in turn, only preliminary to ch. 9, where the complete list of the population of Jerusalem, which transcends affiliation to merely one tribe, is given. Properly speaking, Jerusalem stands within the southern edge of the Benjaminite territory (cf. the definition of tribal boundaries in Josh. 18.11-28), and therefore contains a substantial component of Benjaminites among its inhabitants. But, when its Temple becomes the integrating force of the total life of all Israel, it can no longer belong to one tribe alone; its population must number more than Benjaminites. Therefore, although ch. 8 brings the presentation of the tribal system to a conclusion, it is in turn merely anticipatory of a new regime.

That ch. 8 marks a transition to the following chapters as well as a conclusion to what precedes it is indicated by yet another resumption: vv. 29-40, the particular group of Benjaminites stemming from Gibeon, from whom C derives Saul, the first king of Israel, is repeated very closely in 1 Chron. 9.35-44. This section thus provides both the link back to the genealogies and the preface to the ensuing history of the Israelite monarchy beginning with Saul.

Some points of detail in 1 Chronicles 8 require further consideration.

The chapter begins clearly enough with the patriarch Benjamin himself, his five sons and nine grandsons by his first-born, Bela (vv. 1-5). Already of these names only some seven recur elsewhere in the Hebrew Bible (Benjamin, Bela [1 Chron. 7.6], Ashbel, Gera, Naaman [Gen. 46.21; Num. 26.38-40], Ahoah [cf. 1 Chron. 11.12, 29?], Shephuphan [cf. Num. 26.39?]). Down to v. 28 there are a further seventy or so individuals of whom nothing further is known in the Hebrew Bible.

The interrelationship and, indeed, exact number of these subsequent Benjaminites are not clear. 1 Chron. 8.6-8 is particularly obscure:

Verse 6a: 'These are the sons of Ehud': but who is Ehud? The *ḥ* in the name differentiates him from the Ehud of 1 Chron. 7.10 and the judge of Judg. 3.15-30; it is also different from the *h* in Abihud (v. 3), the name in the immediate context that is otherwise closest in form to it. The possibility that some material has fallen out before v. 6 is high.

Verse 6b is a parenthesis: it explains how this group who had once been settled in Geba (the Levitical city in the north-eastern group of Benjaminite towns, see Josh. 18.24, etc.) has been transported to Manahath (presumably related to the Manahathites of 1 Chron. 2.52, 54 on the north-western frontier of Judah with Dan).

Verse 7 begins, 'and Naaman...', suggesting that, once again, some material has fallen out—at least one other son must have preceded Naaman. Given that the context is thus uncertain, it is hardly surprising that the continuation is equally problematical: '... and Ahijah and Gera (he deported them)'. NRSV follows the unlikely view that 'deported them' should be read as the personal name Heglam (which is otherwise unknown as a personal name). Some kind of inner-Benjaminite tribal feud seems to be indicated.

The subject of the verb in v. 7b, 'and he begat', is uncertain—Ehud or Gera?

Verse 8 introduces another unknown figure, Shaharaim. By a mistake typical of this chapter (cf. v. 30 where Ner should be inserted and v. 31 where Mikloth should be added from 9.36 and 9:37, respectively), Shaharaim may have slipped out by haplography at the end of v. 7. Yet again the text of v. 8b must be incomplete as it stands in the MT: 'Hushim [without objective particle] and Baara [with objective particle] his wives'. (NRSV connects the pair by emendation of the text.)

Section (3), vv. 29-40, deals with the family of Saul, the Benjaminite and presumptuous first king of Israel, and its relations with Gibeon and Jerusalem.

MT subdivides the section into three paragraphs, vv. 29-32; 33-34; 35-40. In the first of these, the names of the wife and sons of Gibeon are given. The mixed racial origin of the Gibeonites is suggested here by the Aramaean-sounding name of Maacah, their matriarch (v. 29). The motif of the residence in Jerusalem of a section of these Gibeonites, which is otherwise unknown in the Hebrew Bible (but cf. the equation in 2 Chron. 1.13), binds this section in with 1 Chron. 8.1-28 and 9.2-44.

Six generations of the immediate family of Saul are then given in vv. 33-34 and the continuation of the line in vv. 35-40.

In vv. 29-40 forty-three of the family of Gibeon are named, including three (Jeiel, the father of Gibeon, and two of his sons Ner and Mikloth) supplied in their correct place in vv. 29-31 from the close parallel in 1 Chron. 9.35-44. Of these only nine recur elsewhere in the Hebrew Bible, Saul, his father Kish, his grandfather (or uncle?; cf. 1 Sam. 14.50) Ner, his sons Jonathan, Malchishua (1 Sam 14.49), Abinadab (1 Sam. 31.2) and Eshbaal (= Ishbosheth 2 Sam. 2.8, etc.), his grandson Merib-baal (= Mephibosheth, 2 Sam. 4.4, etc.), and great-grandson Micah (2 Sam. 9.12).

The striking feature of this material (unparalleled in the Hebrew Bible) is the statement that Saul's family originally belonged to Gibeon (contrast the quite different Benjaminite town Gibea of 1 Sam. 10.26, etc., noted above). The reason for this adaptation may be to stress Saul's lowliest status within the community and yet also to assign to him a role within it. The Gibeonites were in origin non-Israelite (cf. the narrative of the Conquest in Josh. 9). By a trick they made peace with the invading Israelites. In return, they were reduced to becoming the perpetual hewers of wood and drawers of water for the Israelite sanctuary (Josh. 9.23). They were, in other words, the founding fathers of the most menial class of Temple servants, the *n*ᵉ*tînîm*, subordinate to the priests and the Levites, whose task it was to prepare the wood for the altar of sacrifice and the water for the ablutions and the washing of the sacrificial victims. Significantly, C gives his only reference to these *n*ᵉ*tînîm* immediately after this section in 1 Chron. 9.2: the only other references to them in the Hebrew Bible are in Ezra and Nehemiah (e.g. Ezra 8.20). C here turns early political and social circumstances into explanations for the comparative status of the cultic personnel. Saul is by birth a member of the lowest class of ritual attendants; yet even they, humble as they are, have their essential part to play in the Temple's rites.

By the choice of the form of the names of Saul's family C stresses Saul's instrumentality in Israel's guilt. Whereas in 2 Sam. 2.8; 4.4 and elsewhere, Saul's son and grandson are given names compounded with the element *-bôšet*, 'shame' (Ish-bosheth and Mephi-bosheth), C indicates the full horror of the guilt of the house of Saul as implicated in the worship of Baal, by retaining the probably original forms of their names, Eshbaal, 'man of Baal', and Meribbaal, 'champion of Baal' (vv. 33-34; cf. the name of Saul's grand-uncle, Baal, v. 30). No wonder that Saul's son and heir, Jonathan, in calling his own son 'Meribbaal' could never succeed to the throne of Israel (called in 1 Chron. 29.23 'the throne of the LORD').

Yet once again genealogical data are uncertain. It is not completely clear how many generations of descendants of Saul's Gibeonite ancestor are intended.

> The material in 1 Sam. 9.1; 14.51 would suggest that Saul was son of Kish, son of Jeiel (=Abiel), that is, that there were only three generations between Saul and his Gibeonite ancestor, not four, as here. Again, in v. 37b it is not certain whether Raphah, Elasah and Ezel were son, grandson and great-grandson of Bina, or his brothers.

Assuming the longer genealogy, there are in this chapter some nineteen generations of Benjaminites indicated. It may seem strange that the line of the rejected king, Saul, should be thus carefully preserved in such detail. A further striking feature is that in the parallel version in 1 Chron. 9.35-44 the line is traced only to the sixteenth generation. One is tempted to suggest that the sixteenth generation (the thirteenth from Saul) is that contemporary with the exile of Judah in 587 (for a rough comparison it may be noted that the exile took place in the thirteenth generation from Zadok in the High Priestly line, 1 Chron. 6.8-15, and in the nineteenth generation after David, 1 Chron. 3). Even the ill-fated house of Saul continues into a future of promise with mighty warriors and numerous progeny (v. 40). Guilt can be expiated. They retain their status as sons of Benjamin.

1 CHRONICLES 9.1-34: THE POPULATION OF JERUSALEM

1 Chronicles 9.1: Summary and Preview

In MT 1 Chron. 9.1 stands in a paragraph by itself. It is a pivotal verse, facing both back to the genealogical section (1 Chron. 2–8) and forward to the narrative section (1 Chron. 10–2 Chron. 36). It thus encapsulates the range of theological issues with which C is dealing: ideal, actuality, and hope.

Verse 1aα picks up 'these are the descendants of Israel' in 1 Chron. 2.1 and acts as the concluding formula for all the intervening material: those with a claim to belong to Israel have now been duly registered (*hityaḥēś* 1 Chron. 4.33). A statement of the ideal Israel ideally prepared has been given. The preceding chapters have shown how all has been provided for Israel to realize her destiny among the nations of the world: all Israel have been registered in the land as the LORD's host in a patriarchal system of descent and inheritance, with the levitical system for the sanctification of the people, as founded by Moses and organized by David, in their midst.

But the statement in v. 1aβ that Israel thus registered 'are inscribed in the book of the kings of Israel' has some problematical implications. The organization under which the attempt is to be made to bring the ideal for Israel into reality is the monarchy and it is the fate of Israel under the monarchy that is about to be recounted. But it may be doubted whether the 'book of the kings of Israel' is merely a secular archive from the royal court. Later in C reference will be made to the running commentary penned by the prophets on the course of Israel during the monarchic period (see introduction to 2 Chron. 10–36; the formulation here is the same as the reference to that work in 2 Chron. 20.34): the word of counsel and judgment from the prophets as the messengers of the LORD has accompanied his people in this record throughout the monarchical period. The gap between ideal and actuality has been repeatedly exposed by them and the affirmation of ideal and hope constantly made.

Verse 1b therefore anticipates the disastrous course of the monarchy to come. Judah, from which the monarchy stems and the last part of the kingdom to remain politically independent (thus there is a resumption also of the first section of the genealogies, that on Judah, 1 Chron. 2.3–4.23), is eventually to forfeit its land because of its unfaithfulness (*ma'al*, 1 Chron. 2.7). The polarization of the reference to the people in the two half-verses, 'Israel' and 'Judah', implies hope, however: beyond the debacle of Judaean monarchy, the people of Israel remains.

1 Chronicles 9.2-34: The Population and Role of Jerusalem

Jerusalem is integral to C's statement of ideal, failure, and hope. Through its original Benjaminite associations Jerusalem is linked to the fate of the first king, Saul; thus this section picks up 1 Chron. 8.28, 31. But with David Jerusalem has a supratribal role to play; as the site of the resting place of the ark, the symbol of the pacification of the world, Jerusalem is the seat of the Davidic king, the representative of God on earth, and the location of the Temple. But it becomes the place where David himself incurs guilt through his census of the people (1 Chron. 21). Therefore the altar of sacrifice has now to be constructed in Jerusalem.

1 Chronicles 9.2-34, defines the population of Jerusalem in the ideal time of David (v. 22; cf. 1 Chron. 6.31; 7.2). MT divides the section into four paragraphs:

(1) vv. 2-9: the lay inhabitants;
(2) vv. 10-11: chief priests;
(3) vv. 12-32: other priests and Levites;
(4) vv. 33-34: summary on the Levites and other inhabitants.

(1) *Verses 2-9: The Lay Inhabitants of Jerusalem Come from Judah, Benjamin, Ephraim and Manasseh*

First (v. 2), the city of Jerusalem is firmly placed against the background of the ideal of Israel as a whole settled in its tribal territories throughout the length and breadth of the land with the Levites living dispersed among them. Israel as a whole is meant to enjoy its 'holding' (*'ᵃḥuzzâ*, 1 Chron. 7.28), its stake in the land, and thus its full participation and empowerment in the purpose of God for his people. This is made clear by a literal translation of 1 Chron. 9.2: 'The original inhabitants, who were in their holding in their cities, were Israel, the priests, the Levites and the *n*ᵉ*tînîm*' (for the last cf. 1 Chron. 8.29-40).

The force of this translation can be seen in contrasting the passage with its original in Neh. 11.3 (Neh. 11.3-19 is the source, considerably changed, for 1 Chron. 9.2-17): 'While in the cities of Judah there dwelt each in his holding throughout their cities, Israel, the priests and the Levites and the *n*ᵉ*tînîm*...in Jerusalem there dwelt some Judaeans and Benjaminites'. Whereas in the Nehemiah passage there is clearly an unfavourable comparison between the nine-tenths, who settled with lack of concern into their landed territories, and the pioneering one-tenth who gave up such delights in order to repopulate the capital, there is no such implication here. In C there is no hint of blame at enjoyment of the LORD's provision or of reluctance on the part of the appropriate Israelites to populate the capital.

The NRSV translation of 1 Chron. 9.2, 'Now the first to live again in their possessions...', would relate the passage exclusively to the resettlement period after the Exile in the sixth and fifth centuries BCE. This translation is no doubt conditioned by the assumption that, since the exile has been mentioned in 1 Chron. 9.1, the following verse must concern the post-exilic period, and, further, by the similarity of the passage to Neh. 11.3, which refers to the situation in Jerusalem under Nehemiah around 444 BCE. But NRSV's interpretation is unlikely. There is no word in the Hebrew of this verse corresponding to the 'again' in its translation: it has been inserted simply on the basis of the assumption about the date of the passage. The NRSV translation also ignores the fact that 1 Chron. 9.2 is in a different paragraph from 1 Chron. 9.1, that it picks up 1 Chron. 8.28, 32, and that the sequel to 1 Chronicles 9 is the early monarchy.

But, even more importantly, the NRSV translation misrepresents the Chronicler's intention in this chapter: 1 Chron. 9.2-34 portrays the population of Jerusalem in terms of the Davidic ideal; the similarity to Neh. 11.3-19 is not to be understood in a crass historicist way which assumes that the passage refers directly and exclusively to the situation in Nehemiah's time. In treating the population of Jerusalem in an ideal way, C freely makes use of names from a wide variety of periods from David to Nehemiah: the holders of the office of gatekeeper are appointed by David and Samuel the seer (v. 22), but some thirteen out of the twenty-five names mentioned in 1 Chron. 9.3-17 are paralleled in Neh. 11.4-19 as contemporaries of Nehemiah.

Many of the names are peculiar to C. Of the Judaeans only one, Uthai, is even reminiscent of the corresponding name, Athaiah, in Neh. 11.4, and of the Benjaminites only one, Sallu (but also two of his forebears, Meshullam and Hassenuah [Neh. 11.9]), is mentioned in Neh. 11.7. Five of the six priests recur in Neh. 11.10-14, though with some modification in family relationship and in forms of names. Of the seven Levites mentioned in 1 Chron. 9.14-16, three, Shemaiah, Nattanaiah and Obadiah/Abda, recur in Neh. 11.15-17 and there is a strong resemblance between the name of a fourth, Bakbakkar (v. 15), to the Bakbukiah of Neh. 11.17. Two of the five gatekeepers of 1 Chron. 9.17, Akkub and Talmon, appear in Neh. 11.19.

By relating these contemporaries of Nehemiah to the Davidic era, C is throwing a bridge across the generations. All are involved in the one perpetual cult of the Temple, whether in the age of David in the tenth century, or of Nehemiah in the fifth. In a global way, past and present are combined in timeless contemporaneity in order to express in the most adequate way possible—the solidarity that integrates the disparate generations across the ages—the enduring status and function of Jerusalem.

The lay element of the population is defined in vv. 3-9. It consists of elements that match the pyramid of the population as expressed in 1 Chronicles 2–8: Judah and Benjamin, of the outer framework; Ephraim and Manasseh among those immediately flanking Levi. The ideological character of C's writing is clear from that inclusion of Ephraim and Manasseh of whom there is no mention in the parallel passage in Neh. 11.4 (C in the sequel in fact lists no Ephraimite or Manassite). By Nehemiah's time, Ephraim and Manasseh, the house of Joseph which represented the central element in the old northern kingdom destroyed by the Assyrians in 721 BCE, had long ceased to exist in the land. Even before that, since the revolt of Jeroboam (2 Chron. 10) at the end of the tenth century, they had belonged to the schismatic state of the north. For C, however, beyond the accidents of history, the north remains inalienably part of God's people; one day it will be gathered in and thus it continues to make its contribution to the ideal population of the capital.

The three chief men of Judah (vv. 4-6) represent Judah's three main divisions: Perez, Shelah and Zerah (cf. 1 Chron. 2.3–4.24). The family of Perez, as the dominant line from which David also was descended, is here given priority. Only Uthai, of the family of Perez, is given a lineage: whereas David is in the eleventh generation from Judah, Uthai represents only the seventh mentioned (but the text at 'the sons of Perez' is problematical). It seems likely that, nonetheless, a contemporary of David is meant.

At the beginning of v. 4 the phrase 'of the Judaeans' should be supplied by Neh. 11.4 to bring the sub-section into line with the following subsections beginning with vv. 7, 10 and 14; cf. v. 17. At the beginning of v. 5, Shelahite is to be read for Shilonite [Mandelkern; *BHK* and *BHS*].

Benjamin is represented by a rather larger number than the Judaeans, with four major families (vv. 7-9a), as might be expected, given the original affiliation of the city. None of the names now listed repeats the earlier account of the Benjaminite population of the city in 1 Chron. 8.8-40. The totals of Judaean plus Benjaminite heads of households in Jerusalem, 690 + 956, are rather larger than in Neh. 11.6, 8 (468 + 928). The numbers, including not only hundreds and tens, but also units, are striking. Precise statistics reflect specific periods; do these very precise figures reflect the situation in C's own day in the fourth century BCE? At any rate, the numbers indicate realistically modest totals of the population of Jerusalem in comparison with the tribesmen enumerated in 1 Chronicles 7 (cf. Table at 1 Chron. 5.18).

(2) *Verses 10-11: Chief Priests*

The priests are divided between the four mentioned in this paragraph and the two in the next. One would assume that this reflects the relative proportion of the line of Eleazar as against that of Ithamar (for the proportion of 2:1, cf. 1 Chron. 24.1-19) and the predominance of the one line over the other. This is borne out by the fact that Azariah (v. 11) in the first group of four is presumably to be identified with the High Priest who officiated in the Temple at the time of Solomon. He is, thus, of the main Zadokite line descended from Eleazar from which the high priesthood was derived (1 Chron. 6.4, 10). He bears the title of the High Priest, 'leader of the House of God' (cf. the Azariah of 2 Chron. 31.10, 13).

Azariah is given as Seraiah in Neh. 11.11; the divergence is hardly great inasmuch as Azariah and Seraiah appear as father and son in 1 Chron. 6.14, again in the line of Zadok–Eleazar.

This association with the High Priestly line is confirmed for the first two of those mentioned in v. 10: Jedaiah is identified as belonging to the house of the high priest Joshua of the time of the return with Zerubbabel (Ezra 2.36). In the parallel in Neh. 11.10 the next mentioned, Jehoiarib, is also of the same line, being identified as the father of Jedaiah. The affiliation of Jachin is unknown.

These names give further confirmation that cross-generation integration is part of C's deliberate design (cf. already Azariah). Jedaiah and J(eh)oiarib are contemporaries of Nehemiah in Neh. 11.10 yet are also listed among the priests returning with Zerubbabel some eighty years earlier (Neh. 12.6), as well as among David's appointees in 1 Chron. 24.7. It is difficult to dismiss this as mere coincidence of names since Jachin, the third priest of 1 Chron. 9.10 and Neh. 11.10, also appears in 1 Chron. 24.17 (the same phenomenon is found in the next section with Immer, v. 12, 1 Chron. 24.14; Ezra 10.20; Neh. 7.40). Periods, distinct historically speaking, are overlapped in order to present a unified national institution in its ideal form.

(3) *Verses 12-32: Other Priests and Levites*

The family affiliation of the two remaining priests (v. 12) cannot be established from the names, despite the long pedigrees attached to them. On the hypothesis above they would belong to the line of Ithamar.

The likelihood of this hypothesis is increased by a number of considerations. The arrangements for the security and supervision of the sanctuary, which is the major preoccupation of this section, should be read in the light of the revision of these arrangements by David in anticipation of the building of the Temple in 1 Chronicles 26. There, after the discussion of the priesthood in their two major divisions of Eleazar and Ithamar (1 Chron. 24), the concern is with the musicians from the three families of Asaph, Jeduthun and Heman (1 Chron. 25) and with the gatekeepers and keepers of the treasuries from the families of Merari and Korah (1 Chron. 26).

A Table will serve as a reminder of the complex interrelationships of these descendants of Levi:

Levi

Gershom	Kohath		Merari
	Amram	Izhar	
	Aaron	Korah	
	Eleazar Ithamar		
Asaph		Heman	Jeduthun

In 1 Chronicles 9 there are parallel concerns: the musicians are listed in vv. 15b, 16; the gatekeepers and others, especially of the family of Korah, appear in vv. 17-32. It would not then be surprising if the family of Merari features here as well. Verse 14 makes it explicit that they do: the last of the three names in v. 15a, for whom no family affiliation is given and who are unknown in the rest of the Hebrew Bible, recurs as the name of one of the ancestors of the musicians of

Jeduthun, that is, of the family of Merari in v. 16. It is, therefore, probable that all of vv. 14-15a is dealing with the Merari group and their functions as caretakers of the sanctuary as defined in 1 Chronicles 26. If so, this would explain why two priests of Ithamar are included by MT at the beginning of this paragraph: for it was under the supervision of the priests of the family of Ithamar that the Levites of the family of Merari discharged their tasks (cf. Num. 4.33).

The capacity of these priests for undertaking their work in the cult is described (v. 13) in similar terms to those by which other tribesmen are described as fit for war in 1 Chronicles 7. The work of God in either cult or battlefield is analogous, the one a sacrament of the other (cf. 1 Chron. 26.6).

Seven Levites follow (vv. 14-16). On the above argument these represent four from Merari followed by three musicians (for which see 1 Chron. 6.29-47; cf. 1 Chron. 15.17-24): this is explicitly stated for Mattaniah (Asaph) and Obadiah (Jeduthun); Berechiah, by implication, is from the third guild of musicians, Heman (his place of residence, 'the villages of the Netophathites', is mentioned in Neh. 12.28 as the home of levitical musicians).

Mattaniah the Levite (v. 15) may be an even more spectacular example of the fusion of historically distinct periods. A Mattaniah son of Mica/h/iah is known from the fourth generation before Nehemiah (Neh. 11.22; 12.35, cf. Neh. 12.8), as well as contemporary with Nehemiah (Neh. 11.17). There is also a Mattaniah contemporary with David (1 Chron. 25.16) and with Hezekiah (2 Chron. 29.13; cf. BDB 682b, 'but much confusion and uncertainty').

Verses 17-32, the longest discourse in C so far, names the special group of four gatekeepers among the Levites. The gatekeepers are a specialized group of the family of Korah (v. 19), who also include a distinguished guild of musicians (cf. 1 Chron. 6.22). The narrative in Numbers 16 explains their subordinate role in the Tabernacle, which corresponds to their position here as directly under the supervision of the High Priest ('Phinehas, son of Eleazar the leader', v. 20).

The section contains a great variety of ways in which the sanctuary, or parts of it, is described, thus reflecting its long history and the long history of the institutions associated with it. The statement that 'formerly' the Korahites were in charge of the 'King's Gate' on the east side (v. 18; cf. 2 Chron. 23.4-15) implies C's own day in the post-monarchic period. But the vocabulary of the wilderness wandering period is much in evidence. The use of archaic language heightens the sense of institutional continuity back into remotest antiquity: the Levites dwell 'in camps' (v. 18; a thematic term, cf. 1 Chron. 12.22; 2 Chron. 31.2); the sanctuary is called 'the Tent' (v. 19), 'the Tent of Meeting' (v. 21); the forefathers of the present generation were in charge of 'the camp of the LORD' (v. 19); now David and Samuel have appointed them for service in the 'house of the LORD'/'the house of the tent' (v. 23, a term, unique in the Hebrew Bible [cf. 1 Chron. 23.32 and the *ketibh* of 1 Kgs 7.45], which comprehends in one phrase the entire history of the sanctuary both as tent and temple), 'the house of God' (vv. 26-27). This great variety of descriptive terms for the sanctuary shows that it is not being described at any one moment in its history, let alone clarifying the relationship between these moments, but in a 'panchronic' way, in its enduring significance as the mechanism for securing the holiness of the people.

This sense of continuity is heightened by the references in vv. 17-22 to the personnel appointed. The leader, Shallum, his son Zechariah (v. 21) and the whole group mentioned in v. 17, are associated with the immediately pre-Temple phase in the time of David. Yet other names, Phinehas, son of Eleazar (v. 20), David and Samuel (in that order, v. 22), and Akkub and Talmon, v. 17, who are contemporaries of Nehemiah (Neh. 11.19), are all brought into association with one another in timeless contemporaneity. Shallum and his 'brothers' constitute an enduring corporation within the Temple personnel that goes back to the founding fathers of the people, but which is ready to be reactivated under Nehemiah.

The phrase, 'and their brothers', stressing shared responsibility recurs more often in this chapter of C than any other (vv. 6, 9, 13, 17, 25, 32).

The equation of Meshelemiah and Shallum [so BDB] is probable, given that there were only four families of gatekeepers, as is indicated in v. 24, and that these four must be those specified in v. 17. Meshelemiah recurs in 1 Chron. 26.1, 2, 9 and appears in yet another variant as Shelemaiah in 1 Chron. 26.14.

The four groups of gatekeepers, one for each point of the compass, are mentioned only in Ezra, Nehemiah and Chronicles; the Tabernacle in the Pentateuch has only one gate (on the eastern side; Exod. 27.16, etc.). The specification here of one at each side of the sanctuary perhaps reflects an ideal symmetry of the holy place in the midst of the land, as in Ezekiel's vision of the future Temple (Ezek. 40–47; compare 2 Kgs 25.18, where there are only three keepers of the threshold). As the Levites of highest status (Moses and Aaron and his sons, Num. 3.38) were privileged to encamp on the eastern side of the tabernacle in the wilderness, so the gatekeepers of the highest rank (Shallum) are stationed at the eastern gate of the sanctuary (v. 21).

It is not clear—though perhaps it is likely—that the terminology reflects distinction in rank, which, in turn, may imply a specialization of office among the gatekeepers. Whereas all are called 'gatekeepers', only the Shallum group are called 'guardians of the thresholds', or alternatively 'guardians of the entrance' (v. 19). The plural 'thresholds' may imply the entrance to both outer and inner courts. It is they, too, who (again in the same verse) are described as 'having oversight over the work of the cult'. But this apparent distinction within the terminology seems to be ignored in v. 22, which speaks of all four groups being chosen as 'gatekeepers at the thresholds' (unless the Syriac version is followed, which reads 'in number' instead of 'at the thresholds' [*BHK* and *BHS*]).

The four leaders remain permanently in Jerusalem (v. 24); 'their brothers' live in their villages and come in relays on the sabbath to take up duties for seven day periods. Quite how the rosters were organized is not clear (cf. 2 Chron. 23.4-8). The number of the gatekeepers (212, v. 22) would allow for one for each group at each gate for each week in a 52 week year, plus four for the leaders permanently resident in Jerusalem (cf. v. 25).

As their professional title implies, the gatekeepers were primarily janitors and porters. First and foremost, they were security guards: the abstract term for guard duty (*mišmeret/-mārôt*) occurs in vv. 23, 27 (cf. 1 Chron. 23.32). They were in charge of the key and were responsible for locking up at night and opening first thing in the morning (v. 27). Their settlements surrounded the sacred precincts for security.

But the main threat was not usually from foes from without. Rather it came from those within the sacred community itself who were suffering from some ritual impurity that ought to have debarred them from entry. The safeguarding of the holiness of the Temple lay within the gatekeepers' responsibility: to restrict access to the different areas of the Temple to those with the requisite degree of sanctification and purity (cf. 2 Chron. 23.19b: to ensure 'that nothing impure as regards any matter should gain entry'). The impurity is defined not merely in external, physical terms (e.g. Lev. 15.31-33), but also in moral (e.g. Pss. 15; 24). But their task was not only to supervise the admission of the worshippers. They had also to ensure the correctness of their observance of the sacred rites once they had gained entry (cf. 2 Kgs 23.4, where the function of the 'keepers of the threshold' is to purge the cult of everything associated with false practice). For the gatekeepers were in charge of the *l*^e^*šākôt* (v. 26), the rooms opening onto the Temple courts where the laity ate their communion sacrifices (cf., e.g., 1 Sam. 9.22; Jer. 35.2,4). By the post-exilic period, these rooms are associated with officials of high rank in the cult and are mentioned (as here) in association with storerooms (Neh. 10.37-39; 13.4-9).

Verse 29, along with these passages from Nehemiah, gives a useful definition of the function of these storerooms and therefore of the further duties of the gatekeepers: they were responsible for the reception and storage of all the offerings in kind of the people, their first-fruits and tithes, the tokens of their sanctification.

Especially were these Levites responsible for the materials for the preparation of the cereal offering involving corn, wine and oil, the three staple products of the land, which accompanied a whole series of sacrifices, both national and individual, stated and *ad hoc* (Exod. 29.2; cf. Lev. 6.20-23, Exod. 29.40, Num. 28.5, 9; Lev. 2.1, 4, 5, 7; 5.11; 7.12; 14.10, 21; 23.13; 24.5-10; Num. 6.13-20; 7.13; 8.3; 15.4-10 etc.). The contents of the incense is given in Exod 30.34-38. Spices are an ingredient of the anointing oil (Exod. 25.6). The storing, issue and return of the vessels and utensils of the cult at the altar of burnt offering in the court of the Temple or the incense altar in the nave (for which see 2 Chron. 4) was regulated by them. A function of the gatekeepers not specified here (but cf., e.g., 2 Chron. 24.8-14; 34.9-14) is the gathering of funds from the laity for the maintenance of the fabric of the sanctuary. It is little wonder that stress should be laid on the honesty and reliability of these officials in charge of such large sums given as offerings: they perform their tasks 'in faithfulness' (vv. 22, 26, 31; cf. 2 Chron. 19.9; 31.12, 15, 18; 34.12). Their intrinsic qualities (v. 22) are, as before (v. 13), comparable to those of the warriors.

A hierarchy is here clearly in evidence: the gatekeepers have their tasks delegated to them (v. 29). Only the priests can prepare the anointing oil, since only priests, as themselves anointed, may touch it

(v. 30). Mattithiah (v. 31), as first-born of the chief gatekeeper, has the task of actually preparing the cereal offering on the griddle (cf. Lev. 2.5; 6.22; 7.9). The preparation of the twelve 'loaves of the arrangement ['showbread'] (v. 32; cf., e.g., Lev. 24.6-7) is equally vested in the hands of the central levitical family of the Kohathites.

It would appear that in this chapter the non-priestly Levites have received a promotion to the office of guardians of the thresholds. In the pre-exilic Temple, the guardians of the threshold are priests (2 Kgs 12.9, cf. Jer. 35.4: the Maaseiah, son of Shallum (!), there mentioned is a priest according to Jer. 21.1; 37.3, ranking immediately after the High Priest and his deputy, 2 Kgs 25.18). See also 2 Chron. 34.9, where the keepers of the threshold are now specified as Levites, in contrast to the parallel in 2 Kgs 22.4.

In this section, therefore, with its stress on the gatekeepers and the promotion of the non-priestly Levites to the office of guardians of the threshold, C places striking emphasis not so much on the sacrificial cult served by the priests or on the music of the liturgy rendered by other Levites (though both are given due place in vv. 10-16 but without discussion of their function), as on the personal holiness of the worshipper in physical and spiritual terms and on the punctilious honouring of his obligations in offering firstfruits and payment of tithes. As the perpetual guardians of the sanctuary, the Levites in their constant vigilance are, in the unchanging ideal expressed through the contemporaneity of all generations, in the forefront of the defence of the people against committing *ma'al* against their God.

(4) *Verses 33-34: Summary on the Levites and other Inhabitants of Jerusalem*

Verse 33 forms the concluding summary on the Levitical musicians, picking up vv. 15-16; v. 34a is the concluding summary on the Levites as a whole, picking up v. 14; v. 34b rounds off the whole account of the population of Jerusalem by matching the opening phrase in v. 3.

The whole genealogical section, 1 Chron. 1.1–9.34, thus brings Israel to the portals of the Temple, to the very point of access to the presence of God. The chapters culminate in the reverent weekly presentation to God of the 12 loaves of the shewbread, each loaf representing a tribe, by the Levites of the central family of Kohath (v. 32). All is prepared: the land is fully settled by God's people; the Levites dwell in the midst to guide and instruct and serve at the gates of the sanctuary to ensure the scrupulous fulfilment of every duty to God and so to protect the sanctity of Israel's relationship with God from any defilement because of carelessness, neglect or wilful error.

The ensuing history is to show the stubborn and intensifying refusal of Israel to accord God his rights. Yet beyond even the ultimate penalty of the forfeiture of the land itself, the institution of the Levites, as guardians and instructors of the Law, remains. In the end, it is the life of Torah, the study and practice of the Law, which is the context of life in the interim of waiting 'in exile' for 'the Return'.

1 CHRONICLES 9.35–10.14: THE REIGN OF SAUL

In the genealogical section, 1 Chron. 1.1–9.34, C has presented in a global, unitary way Israel's privileged place in the world of the nations, its territorial extent and its ideal tribal layout, with the Levites positioned in the centre. All has been given and prepared for Israel to realize its destiny as God's people in the world. But the premonitions, that Israel on the West Bank, on the East Bank and as a whole forfeited her land because of disloyalty (*ma'al*) to God the giver of all, have already been given (1 Chron. 2.7; 5.25; 9.1). The theme of Chronicles is the vocation of Israel to dedication to the LORD; its failure in this vocation; and the way towards the remedying of the situation. C has stated the theme in general terms in the genealogical section; he now expounds it in detail in terms of the history of the monarchy from the abortive first kingship of Saul down to the exile and the hope beyond exile. The themes of guilt and atonement, derived from Leviticus, provide C with the interpretative key by means of which the whole sweep of Israel's history within world history is to be understood.

The reign of Saul marks the first episode of Israel's past to be told in detail. It is provided with a framework of C's own material in 1 Chron. 9.35-44 and 10.13-14, by means of which he makes very clear his interpretation.

The first part, 1 Chron. 9.35-44, the family tree of Saul, seems, at first sight, merely to repeat 1 Chron. 8.29-40, apart from abbreviation and some insignificant variations in the list and spelling of names.

The MT paragraphing again separates the general Gibeonite background (vv. 35-38) from Saul's specific line of descent (vv. 39-44). The division between Saul's immediate family and his remoter descendants, marked in 1 Chron. 8.34, is no longer maintained. C is concerned here with the house as a whole.

The genealogy of Saul thus serves as a bridge passage linking the genealogical section, 1 Chron. 1.1–9.34, with the following narrative historical section in the rest of C's work (for C's method, cf. the double resumption of Shem in 1 Chron. 1.17, 24).

The genealogical data show that Saul belongs to a mainstream Benjaminite family, indeed to the middle of that family, his grandfather, Ner (omitted in the corresponding list in 1 Chron. 8.30), being fifth son out of ten. This placing may simply be a statement of the facts of the matter, with the implication that the best equipped, irrespective of his standing in his family, was chosen for the job. But it is possible that the central positioning indicates centrality of status, as in the case of David (1 Chron. 3), and thus the genealogy reflects the pyramidal structure of society.

There is, however, a significant difference between the genealogies of 1 Chron. 9.35-44 and 1 Chron. 8.29-40, and this difference signals C's deeper purpose. Whereas in 1 Chronicles 8 Saul's genealogy is traced for nineteen generations through the exile and beyond to show the continued existence of the family as full, if humble, participants in the restored and enduring community of Israel, here in 1 Chronicles 9 it stops short in the sixteenth generation in the catastrophe of the Exile itself (1 Chron. 8.39-40 is not reproduced after 1 Chron. 9.44). It is the house of Saul as disastrous that is recounted here: Saul is the chief link in a chain that leads from settled life and its support in hereditary possession of ancestral lands in Gibeon to death and dispossession.

The point is made explicitly in C's key terminology in the last part of his framework in 1 Chron. 10.13-14. Saul himself forfeited his life and was dispossessed of kingship because of his *ma'al* (1 Chron. 2.7), his failure to show God the exclusive service due to him. C specifies the two main areas of Saul's failure: he did not carry out the instruction of God; and he sought for guidance (*drš*, now to become one of C's key terms, indeed, distinctive terms—43 times in C out of 163 in the Hebrew Bible) from a source other than God himself. C does not trouble to recount the story of this double failure, but merely presupposes it from the existing account of Saul's reign in Samuel–Kings, already current as Scripture within the community.

> The major episodes are Saul's disobedience to the instruction of God through the prophet Samuel in the matter of sacrifice at Gilgal (1 Sam. 13; cf. Uzziah in 2 Chron. 26.16), and in the campaign against Agag, king of the Amalekites (1 Sam. 15, his massacre of the priests at Nob).

While C must certainly have these incidents in mind, he puts the condemnation in a more general and fundamental way: Saul 'did not consult the LORD'. By this he refers not simply to the consultation of the medium at Endor (1 Sam. 28; for the death penalty for such, see Lev. 20.6) but also to his neglect of the ark, the primary vehicle of God's presence among his people, not least in the context of his battles against the Philistines (cf. 1 Chron. 13.3).

> It is to be a curiosity of C's method of argument that he sometimes delays the full explanation for condemnation in an incident to a later chapter. Thus not only is the nature of Saul's failure not fully explained until 1 Chron. 13.3; David's own fault in the ark narrative in 1 Chronicles 13 is not explained until 1 Chron. 15-13-15; the reason why he cannot build the Temple in 1 Chronicles 17 is not fully clarified until 1 Chron. 22.7-10; and the nature of his guilt in conducting the census in 1 Chronicles 21 only becomes clear in the light of 1 Chronicles 27.

By such failure, Saul invalidates his rule on behalf of the LORD of hosts. The deeper significance of the outrage at Nob (1 Sam. 22.16-19) is that the priests there were the national custodians of the ark.

C passes over any detailed account of earlier episodes of Saul's denial of God and proceeds in his borrowed material in 1 Chron. 10.1-12 directly to the final episode of Saul's reign—his defeat and death at the hands of the Philistines at the battle of Mt Gilboa. For C, as already announced in 1 Chron. 1.12, 'Philistines' have an emblematic function: they are representative of the alien forces ready to break into the life of God's people and to reabsorb them into the generality of the world of nations from which they take their rise (so recurrently throughout C, e.g., 2 Chron. 21.16). But, as v. 14 makes plain, the Philistines are only the apparent agents: the untimely death of Saul arises from the breach in his relationship with God. It is God who is active throughout: the verb in the phrase, 'transferred the kingdom to David', recurs at crucial points in the ensuing story: 1 Chron. 12.23; 13.3; 2 Chron. 14.7; the related noun occurs in 2 Chron. 10.15. God himself, the wronged party, removes the disloyal king and entrusts his people to another.

The account here is based closely upon 1 Sam. 31.1-13, but with a few modifications, which, on the one hand, smoothe the profile of the historical record, yet, on the other, point up the significance of some of the detail. The destruction of the disobedient king is told with graphic and horrific realism. With a quick stroke of the brush the catastrophic slaughter of the whole host of Israel is indicated (v. 1): the Hebrew for 'men of Israel' is a collective singular implying 'all the men of Israel', as opposed to Samuel's plural, which merely implies 'some men of Israel'. Even so, the Philistines' chief quarry is the royal house: first, there are picked off three of Saul's sons, with their high-sounding names, 'The LORD gave', 'My father freely offered', 'My king is deliverance' (v. 2). Indeed, v. 6 suggests that the whole royal line was wiped out.

> 'And all his house died together' is C's substitution for the statement in Samuel–Kings that all his warriors in the field perished.

This was hardly literally the case, as the genealogy of Saul, twice repeated above, has made plain. Yet, so far as maintaining kingly power and a royal line was concerned, his house was hereafter in reality defunct. The fine detail that a fourth son of Saul, Eshbaal, actually succeeded his father, if only for a brief moment (2 Sam. 1–4), is irrelevant for C's purpose and is omitted by him.

But the ultimate target of the Philistines is King Saul himself (vv. 3-5). The narrative, however, now follows events from the point of view of the stricken king. His army has been routed, his sons slain, and he himself grievously wounded by the long-distance shots of the archers (this detail, again, showing the instrumentality of God; cf. Ahab, 2 Chron. 18.33). With the word 'wounded' C introduces another of his thematic terms. 'Health' is an expression of the quality of life of one in harmony with God's purpose: its opposite, disease, or, here, wounds suffered in battle by the one who is supposedly *ex officio* God's vicegerent on earth, is evidence of breakdown of the relationship (cf. Asa, 2 Chron. 16.12; for other occurrences of *ḥlh*, 'be sick, wounded', cf. Jehoram, 2 Chron. 21.15; Joash, 2 Chron. 24.25; and, especially, Josiah, 2 Chron. 35.23; for the contrast 'health...sickness', cf. 2 Chron. 21.18: NRSV 'incurable disease').

It is only a matter of time before the Philistines close in on Saul. Rather than face capture by the degenerate Philistines, who were by nature what he had reverted to by practice (cf. Lev. 26.41), and suffer a cruel death at their hands, he seeks a quick and humane dispatch from his own armour-bearer. But, as a subject, the armour-bearer cannot commit such a sacrilegious act and as a warrior it is his duty, not to kill his master, but to be killed, if necessary, for him and with him.

Saul can see no alternative to suicide (the decision by Saul himself is put into great prominence by the dramatic MT paragraph divider at the end of v. 4a): the doomed king is not merely destroyed; he is self-destroyed, self-betrayed into a final act of self-destruction. By his wilful acts, he has locked himself into a course that leads to an inescapable fate. C's spare narrative excludes any sympathy or regret for Saul's degrading death: his theme is the doom of the disobedient and apostate king, whose end is deserved and inevitable. The piety and loyalty of his armour-bearer provide a grim foil to the impiety and disloyalty of his master.

But no man dies to himself, least of all a misguided king (vv. 6-7). C is interested in preserving from his parent text in 1 Samuel the baneful effect of Saul's disloyalty to God. The chief of these consequences is loss of land. As the text now stands, the motives of the Philistines were clear: it was on their initiative that an attack had been launched at Mt Gilboa (v. 1), because of its strategic position at the northern end of the central hill country commanding the plains of Jezreel. He who controlled Gilboa controlled the settlements in the valley below. The loss of Mt Gilboa inevitably means that the Israelites settled in Jezreel (assigned to Issachar in Josh. 19.18) are dispossessed of their homes and territories by the victorious Philistines (v. 7; the parallel in 1 Sam. 31.7 reflects more realistically the settlement pattern that existed before the battle: the Israelites could not settle in the favoured valley floor because of the presence of the indigenous Canaanite, cf. Judg. 1.27, but were confined to the higher ground that ringed the valley). C gives no hint of the presence of the indigenous Canaanites in the land: when the Israelites are driven out the Philistines move in. The view of the land is that of the theologian not that of historical actuality. C finds here an explicit example of his principle: *ma'al* (in this case the king's own failure) unavoidably involves forfeiture (in this case not simply the king's life and crown but his subjects' heritage in the LORD's land; unclean aliens again possess and pollute their territory).

C preserves from 1 Samuel 31 yet one further consequence of Saul's unfaithfulness. His action brings dishonour and disrepute not only on himself, but also on the cause and on the name of the God, in whose service he was supposed to be engaged and whose representative he was supposed to be. In the gruesome aftermath of the battle (vv. 8-10), the stripping of the corpses of the slain foes by the victors takes place.

In pursuit of his purpose of portraying the total extirpation of the house of Saul, C omits the number 'three' before Saul's sons in v. 8 (contrast 1 Sam. 31.8).

The horror of the traditional tale at the barbarity of the Philistines is reflected in the Hebrew, where there is a play on the words 'the Philistines' (*pᵉlištîm*) and 'to strip' (*lᵉpaššēṭ*): the forces of the world live up to their name. But this act is not simply a dishonouring of the high-born dead and a plundering of their equipment and finery, it is also a dishonouring of the God of Israel. For behind the warring armies are competing gods. The defeat of the armies of Israel led by the LORD's anointed is a defeat for the LORD himself and a triumph for the gods of the Philistines. The spoils taken from the corpses of the royal house are no ordinary trinkets, but trophies marking the ascendancy of Dagon. C makes the point of the divine contest more directly than 1 Samuel by reading 'in the temple of Dagon' at the end of v. 10 for the 'to the wall of Beth-shan' of 1 Sam. 31.10. Saul's head and regalia are carried in triumph throughout the land to announce to gods and to humanity the supremacy of Dagon over the LORD (the severed head is displayed to prove beyond doubt the death of the troublemaker; cf. 1 Sam. 17.54; 2 Sam. 4.7-8). They are then deposited in Dagon's temple as his rightful due as giver of victory. The Philistines for their part scrupulously avoid committing *ma'al* against their god (contrast the reference to Achar in 1 Chron. 2.7)!

It is left to the men of Jabesh-gilead to salvage some honour out of the situation (vv. 11-12). There was a special reason why it should have been they who with great courage and skill came to retrieve the remains of the dead king and his sons and who with due observance gave them decent burial.

The controversial note in 1 Sam. 31.12 that they burned their bodies is omitted.

It was not simply that they were relatively near to hand, twenty or so kilometres away on the East Bank; that would have been more a reason to keep quiet lest the Philistines be attracted to turn their attention to them next and to their desirable settlements on the edge of the Jordan Valley (for the very real danger of those on the East Bank, cf. 1 Sam. 31.7). Rather, they had an old debt to Saul to pay off: it had been their plight when threatened by the Ammonites, which, according to 1 Samuel 11, had first stimulated Saul into a signal act of deliverance. C has not reproduced this incident in his work, but may be presupposing it, as he presupposes the unfortunate incidents at Gilgal, Endor and against the Amalekites in v. 13. As the text stands, the act of the men of Jabesh-gilead has become one merely of piety on their part and not of grateful acknowledgment of Saul's earlier effectiveness as the LORD's champion of his people. But the assumption that the earlier incident is presupposed adds point to the present: the demonstration of the ineffectiveness of Saul is now made complete by the role reversal. The very subjects who at the beginning of his reign had been so indebted to him for deliverance, for life, freedom and honour, now at the end deliver the lifeless, dishonoured body of the king and reverently lay it to rest with due ceremony. The celebrations at Gilgal (1 Sam. 11.14-15) have turned into lamentation and fasting.

The reign of Saul thus returns to the point whence it started. But with the loss of Jezreel Israel is in worse case than before. The deadly power of *ma'al*, which is to culminate almost a score of generations later in the total forfeiture of the land in the exile, has begun its work.

1 CHRONICLES 11.1–29.30: DAVID: ENABLER OF ISRAEL'S DESTINY AMONG THE NATIONS OF THE WORLD?

Preliminary Review

Chronicles is an essay in exploration of the potential of the monarchy to realize the purpose intended for Israel in the world.

> In 1 Samuel 8 the monarchy is presented as, at best, a concession by God to the weakness and faithlessness of Israel whose king God alone is, and, at worst, a tyrannical institution, whose interests as centralized government will inevitably lead to curtailment of the freeborn Israelites' liberty and to seizing of their property. C begins with no such negativity and reserve about the monarchy in principle. It is the practice of monarchy that will inevitably bring about the failure of the institution.

For C, the primary model of Israel's life is expressed in the Law of Moses; its exponents are the Levites (cf. the centrality of the Levites amid Israel in 1 Chron. 6). The monarchy, with the house of David as its exponents, is the secondary model (cf. the peripheral character of Judah as the tribe of origin of David and of Benjamin as the tribe of origin of Saul in 1 Chron. 2.3–4.23; 8).

Yet the monarchy bears within it all the power and validity of the tradition of theology focused on Jerusalem. That theology is fundamentally sacramental: king, Temple and people are all the physical expression of the cosmic theological truth that stands behind all appearances. The king sits on the LORD's throne; he is his manifestation on earth, his vicegerent among the nations of the world (1 Chron. 28.5); the Temple is the cosmos in miniature, the model on earth of the cosmic dwelling place of God (1 Chron. 28.11); the people are the LORD's host, the earthly counterpart of the cosmic hosts whom the LORD has at his disposal, whose symbol is the ark (1 Chron. 13.6).

This Davidic model of the dominion of God on earth is now brought to bear on the primary Mosaic model of Israel's life: the remainder of C's work is essentially a dialogue between the Levites and the Davidic kings, against the portrayal in 1 Chronicles 11–

2 Chronicles 9 of the highest and best that the monarchy is capable of in the reigns of David and Solomon. The vast scope and possibilities of the secondary model of monarchy are portrayed in all their fulness; but C, as a post-monarchic writer, shows how, inevitably in the end, monarchy failed to enable Israel to achieve its destiny.

In expressing these themes through his account of the reign of David, C deploys the greatest mass of materials in his whole work. To keep the thread of his argument clear, it is best first to preview the overall pattern of his presentation with a rough grouping of the materials (the MT paragraphing is considerably more complex and will be noted in the chapters concerned):

1 Chron. 11.1-9	All Israel gathers to David at Hebron; he is anointed king. Jerusalem becomes David's residence.
1 Chron. 11.10–12.40	Retrospect: David's chief warriors who joined him in four waves of accession.
1 Chron. 13.1-14	Summons to the remainder of the people to share in the culminating act of bringing the ark of God into Jerusalem. But the plan is mishandled, suspended and only to be resumed in ch. 15 after appropriate measures.
1 Chron. 14.1-16.43	The beginnings of international recognition (Tyre; Philistines and among 'all the nations', 1 Chron. 14.17); the installation of the ark and the appointment of the Levites as its custodians (the crucial link between international recognition and the ark is made by the MT paragraph 1 Chron. 14.13–15.15).
1 Chron. 17.1-27	Nathan's prophecy: David cannot build God a house; God has already built a house for David; Solomon shall build the Temple.
1 Chron. 18.1–20.8	Wars of subjugation and conquest: Philistines, Moabites, Aramaeans, Edomites, Ammonites, including the king of Hamath's grateful recognition that David has achieved peace on behalf of the nations (1 Chron. 18.9-10).
1 Chron. 21.1–22.4	David's presumptuous act of the census, leading to the designation of the site for the altar of sacrifice and the Temple in Jerusalem.
1 Chron. 22.5-19	The commissioning of Solomon to build the Temple.

1 Chron. 23.1–27.34	The organizing of the personnel for the Temple and the laity.
1 Chron. 28.1–29.25	David's farewell addresses.
1 Chron. 29.26-30	Concluding annalistic notes.

This outline of the content of C's account of the reign of David already suggests that the presentation is in two parts, hinged around the census in 1 Chronicles 21. In the first part, 1 Chronicles 11–20, David is viewed in the most favourable of lights: only hints of trouble ahead in his handling of the sphere of the holy (1 Chron. 13; 17), but still contained, lie across the portrayal of him. Through David, Israel's first king worthy of the name after the false start of Saul, Israel can realize its authentic existence as the people of God and can fulfil its role amid the world of the nations. He is the ideal king; he enjoys immediacy of access to God as priest (1 Chron. 15–16); he is the recipient of an everlasting covenant (1 Chron. 17.10-14); he is perfectly in tune with the purpose of God and, because in tune, invincible on the field of battle (1 Chron. 18–20). The dynamic focus of Israel's life is the ark, by which the power of God is symbolized. David perfectly exercises dominion among his own people and the nations of the world. The world is pacified and the nations of the world bring tribute, their tokens of recognition.

But then David plunges the monarchical regime into crisis. Through the presumptuous act of conducting the census in violation of the Law of atonement in Exod. 30.11-16, he incurs guilt (1 Chron. 21; *'ašmâ*, 'guilt', v. 3, is part of the material contributed by C himself to the presentation of David's reign; it belongs to the same circle of ideas as *ma'al*; cf., e.g., Lev. 5.14–6.7). Yet, at the very place where the guilt has been incurred, God provides the means of atonement, for David's sin leads directly to the building of the altar of sacrifice. Nonetheless, the fundamental flaw in the monarchy has been exposed.

The census in 1 Chronicles 21 thus marks the change in David's status: alongside the monarchy, the full system of holiness as practised by the Levites must be brought into operation. The balance of power between David and the Levites shifts: instead of merely acknowledging the action of God through his king on behalf of his people, the Levites move to centre stage as providers of the system through which Israel can realize its identity (note the change in the status of Zadok from royal official, dependent on the king's initiative, in 1 Chron.

15.11, to the one who now takes over the role of officiant at altar and blesser of the people [cf. 1 Chron. 23.13], to become joint-participant with David in 1 Chronicles 24 and anointed figure independent in the sphere of the Temple in 1 Chron. 29.22). The conditionality of the status of the monarchy now becomes apparent even to David (1 Chron. 22.7-13). In the end the levitical system will stand alone as that through which the affirmations and hopes once expressed through the monarchical model will be realized.

Some idea of the thoroughgoing way in which C has set about his theological purpose in this presentation of the reign of David can be gained from a tabulation of the parallels between 1 Chronicles 11–29 and 2 Samuel 5–24:

1 Chronicles 11.1-9	cf. 2 Samuel 5.1-3, 6-10
11.11-41	23.8-9, 11-39
13.6-14	6.2-11
14.1-16	5.11-25
15.25–16.3	6.12-19
16.43	6.19-20
17.1–18.17	7.1–8.18
19.1–20.1	10.1–11.1
20.2-3	12.30-31
20.4-8	21.18-22
21.1-26	24.1-4, 8-25

In addition, 1 Chron. 16.8-36 is parallel to Pss. 105.1-15; 96.1-13; 106.1, 47-48.

A mere tabulation of verses cannot do justice to the subtlety of C's exploitation of his sources, so that a bare count of verses cannot compute fully and accurately the proportion of the materials which are C's own and that which he owes to his sources. Nonetheless, in rough terms the proportions are as follows: total number of verses in 1 Chronicles 11–29 is 521 [English versions]; total of parallel verses is 202, or just under 40 percent; total number of independent verses is 319, or just over 60 percent.

C's independent sections are, in the main, 1 Chron. 11.10, 42–13.5; 14.17–15.24; 16.4-7, 37-42; 21.27–29.30. The largest and most sustained section is 1 Chron. 21.27–29.22, 24-26, 28-30 (232 verses), on the choice of the site of the Temple, the organization of its personnel, the designation of Solomon as David's successor. 1 Chronicles 15, also largely about the personnel responsible for the liturgy, and 1 Chronicles 12, part of the list of David's supporters, are the other main independent materials.

> Equally significant are the materials at C's disposal in Samuel–Kings, but not used by him. If the material on David in Samuel–Kings is delimited as 2 Sam. 5.1–1 Kgs 2.11, 649 verses in total, only some 170 of these (including the parallel in 1 Chron. 3.4-8 to 2 Sam. 5.5, 14-15), or just over 25 percent, are used by C. The materials omitted, in the main, concern some of David's dealings with the house of Saul (Michal, 2 Sam. 6.20-23; Mephibosheth, 2 Sam. 9) and the unruly behaviour of David's sons as rival claimants to the throne (2 Sam. 13–21.17; 1 Kgs 1–2.10). In C's account, which seeks to idealize the picture of David before the census, the story of his adultery with Bathsheba is omitted from 2 Sam. 11.2–12.29. C's own farewell addresses are substituted for the poetic compositions in 2 Sam. 22.1–23.7.

It is at once clear from this bird's-eye view how highly selective is the borrowing, how substantial the omission, how extensive the rearrangement and how significant a proportion of the whole material in C has no parallel in Samuel–Kings, but is C's own contribution.

1 Chronicles 11.1-9: David, King of 'All Israel'; Jerusalem, 'City of David'

In 1 Chron. 11.1-3, C stresses Israel's unanimity in recognizing David as king: '*all* Israel gathered...' The roll-call of those who so gather is about to be given in 1 Chron. 11.10–12.40.

C strengthens the unanimity by omitting any reference to the preliminary stages in which David's position was disputed by Saul's surviving son, Eshbaal, and in which, initially, he was recognized as king only by his fellow tribesmen in Judah (2 Sam. 1–4). C's interest in the final result rather than the process is also indicated by his shortening of the text in 2 Sam. 5.1, 'all *the tribes of* Israel': it is Israel as a concerted whole, not as the sum of its individual parts, who acts here.

Unanimity is to be a leading theme throughout the presentation of the rule of the house of David. It is sounded in the first word of the Hebrew of 1 Chron. 11.1: 'There gathered together...' (*qbṣ*) (cf. 1 Chron. 13.2; 16.35; contrast 2 Sam. 5.1, which has only 'came', and which C has retained at the beginning of v. 3, where it is the special representatives within the people who are now the agents).

The verb *qbṣ* is used also in connection with Asa's reformation, 2 Chron. 15.9-10; the crisis of foreign invasions under Jehoshaphat, 2 Chron. 20.4; Jehoiada's covenant with Joash, 2 Chron. 23.2; Joash's renovation of the altar 2 Chron. 24.5; Amaziah's muster of Judah, 2 Chron. 25.5; Hezekiah's resistance to Sennacherib, 2 Chron. 32.4, 6. The verb is also used negatively of the support for Jeroboam against the house of David in 2 Chron. 13.7.

Similar stress on gathering and acknowledgment, not only by Israel, but also by the world around Israel, is laid by means of similar words for gathering in 1 Chron. 13.2, 4-5; 15.3; 28.1, 8; 29.1, 10, 20 (*qhl*), 1 Chron. 11.13; 15.4; 19.17; 23.2 (*'sp*) and 1 Chron. 22.2 (*kns*). David's status was uncontested and uncontestable inside and outside Israel; all rally round to show their recognition.

The detail that this unanimous recognition of David by all Israel took place at Hebron is retained by the Chronicler. But the muster at

Hebron is only the necessary preliminary step before the immediately following concerted assault by 'all Israel' on Jerusalem (vv. 4-9). That the conquest of Jerusalem is the immediate goal is made clear by the paragraphing of MT: the whole of vv. 1-9 belongs to one major section, divided into two subsections, vv. 1-3 and 4-9.

David's people bring with them a statement of recognition of his status that operates at three levels (vv. 1b-2). First, there is the acknowledgment that he is their kinsman: 'we are your bone and flesh' (v. 1b). That vivid greeting can be taken even further: he is, in a sense, the embodiment of his people; in him, Israel finds its unity and the realization of its true being.

> Elsewhere, and possibly in the parallel in 2 Sam. 5.1, the expression is used in a context of reconciliation after estrangement (2 Sam. 19.12-13). But, in view of C's omissions, such cannot be the intention here.

The status of David is, secondly, recognized from his past record: from the very first he has been effectively the military commander (v. 2a). In the metaphor of Israel as the LORD's host, military command is the key role of the leader. The thematic term of Israel as the LORD's host on the march is used: David has been the one 'to lead out' (*yṣ'*, 1 Chron. 1.12) Israel in the LORD's battles (1 Sam. 18.17; 25.28). The antonym, 'to lead back', of the safe return of the victorious troops, is also used here (cf., e.g., Josh. 14.11; Ezek. 46.10; Ps. 121.8). David's right to leadership was thus proved in the field even under the reign of the so-called king, Saul.

> This is emphasized by C by a number of little touches in v. 2: he adds the 'even' in the phrase '*even* when Saul was king'; he omits the 'over us' of Samuel at the end of that phrase; he omits the verb in the past tense of Samuel, 'you *were* the one who led Israel out', turning the expression into the past continuous, '*you have been and still are*...'

Thirdly, the people cite (v. 2b) the prophetic oracle by which David has been designated leader by God himself; it is this divine designation that explains David's success. The formulation does not match precisely any of the recorded words of Samuel, whose authority C adds at the end of v. 3 (not in Samuel; cf. 1 Chron. 9.22). But in substance they convey the force of such incidents (not reproduced by C, but presupposed by him) as 1 Sam. 13.14; 16.11-13 and the terms of Nathan's oracle to David in 1 Chron. 17.7.

In the prophetic oracle cited by the people, traditional terms for the leadership of the people are used: 'shepherd', the time-honoured ancient Near Eastern royal title with associations in its pastoral imagery with Israel's own nomadic past, expressing guardianship of the people's welfare; 'leader', which expresses a directness of relationship with the people in their conflicts with the outside world (used of Saul, 1 Sam. 9.16). The people avoid the term 'king', lest it be misconstrued in terms of a remote absolute monarch.

C adds to this divine authority the phrase, 'The LORD, *your God*', in order to stress the immediacy of the bond between God and king: David is executive for God. He also changes the 'you shall become leader over Israel' of Samuel to the more pointed, 'you shall *be* leader over *my people* Israel': beyond even David himself lie the people of God themselves and their role in his purpose; the monarchy is but the instrument of the people's realization of their destiny (cf. 1 Chron. 14.2; 1 Chron. 17.7).

The ceremony of recognition is two-fold (v. 3). David 'makes a covenant' with the 'elders' (logistics now require the more limited number of the representatives of the people to be involved); they 'anoint David as king'.

> C preserves the reading, 'all the elders of Israel came *to the king* to Hebron', despite the fact that it is only in the Samuel account that David has already become king of Judah by this point in the narrative (see the material in 2 Sam. 2.4, which C omits). This may simply be oversight, or another indication of C's view that David has been in principle king from the beginning; he who has been and is king is now openly acknowledged as such. Perhaps as a concession to the logic of his presentation, C omits the title 'king' from the Samuel version in the following phrase, 'King David made a covenant with them'.

The covenant is the standard institution in the Hebrew Bible (and in the wider ancient Near East) whereby social and economic relations, which transcend the immediate tie of family, are formally concluded. An oath concerning the matter at issue is sworn between the parties concerned, Divine witness is invoked as the sanction of the agreement, and the whole is sealed in a sacrificial meal in which, in the presence of God and with the participation of God through the sacrifice, the bond between the contracting parties is confirmed through the shared hospitality of the table (a model of the practice can be found in, for example, Gen. 26.28-31).

On this pattern, many of the details of this particular pact which

David made '*for* them' are unclear. The precise terms of the manner in which David would exercize kingship and in which they would recognize him as king are not stated. One can only presume that C is assuming these terms in the most ideal manner possible: of Israel engaging themselves wholeheartedly to becoming the LORD's host under David's leadership.

> The force of the phrase '*for* them' does not necessarily imply that here David is the mediator of the covenant (the same expression occurs in 2 Chron. 21.7). Other covenants in C may be brought in for comparison: Asa's, 2 Chron. 15.12; Jehoiada's, 2 Chron. 23.1, 3, 16; Hezekiah's, 2 Chron. 29.10; Josiah's, 2 Chron. 34.31-32.

Also unclear is what is meant by the phrase 'before the LORD'. One would normally expect that phrase to imply that the action takes place in a sanctuary, including the ark, where the LORD's presence is surely to be found (cf. 1 Chron. 16.1 for the combination of 'before GOD' and the ark). C's view of the sanctuary in Israel's early period is highly ideological: there is no hint that there was any sanctuary other than the movable tabernacle constructed in the wilderness period. That sanctuary is later relocated by David to Gibeon (1 Chron. 16.39; cf. 1 Chron. 6.32; 9.18-23), when he installs the ark in a special tent in Jerusalem. In all probability, then, the tabernacle, including the ark, is envisaged by C as the sanctuary at Hebron where this covenant-making took place. (By 1 Chron. 13.5 the ark is located at Kiriath-jearim; how it got there, C again does not tell us.)

The presence of the ark here is suggested by two titles traditionally associated with it: 'the LORD of hosts', which C is to reproduce in v. 9 (see below) and 'the ark of the covenant' (1 Chron. 15.25-26, 28-29 ['covenant', not in the 2 Sam. 6.12-16 parallel]; 16.6, 37; 17.1 ['covenant', again not in the 2 Sam. 7.2 parallel]; 22.19; 28.2, 18; 2 Chron. 5.2, 7, cf. 6.11 ['covenant' only now in the 1 Sam. 8.21 parallel]). Since people and king are making a covenant here 'before the LORD', then the presence of the ark of the covenant would be appropriate.

The other element in the act of recognition of David's kingship is the rite of anointing. The significance of anointing is well expressed by the symbolism of the oil used in the ceremony. As olive oil was used in ordinary life for cleansing, healing, illumination and celebration, so all these elements are gathered together in the act of anointing. There is a divine and a human side. God imparts the cleansing and separation from the past, renewal for the future and the power and illumination necessary for the discharge of the office. The people, by the act of anointing, acknowledge the new status thus imparted by God to the king and transmit to the king all authority over them. Anointing is, thus, a good example of sacramental thinking: the outward human action only has validity because of the underlying divine sanction.

C's desire to emphasize what has been in principle the case—David's enduring status over the one people of Israel, which he has by right held from the beginning—is now reflected in his account of the next step: the immediate capture of Jerusalem and its establishment as David's capital (vv. 4-9).

> C therefore omits the intervening verses, 2 Sam. 5.4-5, which provide the chronological information that David's reign in Hebron lasted for seven and a half years.

Once again, C cuts through the materials inherited from 2 Samuel directly to the point. Whereas 2 Sam. 5.6 begins, '*The king and his men* went to Jerusalem', making it an act of military conquest in the first instance, C (v. 4) broadens out the significance of the act: '*David and all Israel* came…'

The addition after 'Jerusalem' of the phrase, 'that is, Jebus', is not just a note to explain the name of the pre-Israelite inhabitants of Jerusalem, 'the Jebusites', about to be mentioned. Rather, the point is to mark a sharp break between the past and the future, the radical discontinuity between Jebus which has been occupied up till now by one of the nations of the world (Hamites, according to 1 Chron. 1.14), and Jerusalem, which will be inhabited henceforth by Israel, the people of God (thus 'that is, Jebus' in v. 4 is counterbalanced by 'that is, the city of David' in v. 5). The last phrase of v. 4, 'the [original] inhabitants of the land', recurs in C to point up this contrast (1 Chron. 22.18; 2 Chron. 20.7; cf. already 1 Chron. 4.40); later, Israel will be called 'the people of the land' (2 Chron. 23.13).

> The point is reinforced by further tiny adjustments. C uses the plural, '*inhabitants* of the land', which is slightly at odds with the preceding collective singular, 'the Jebusite'; they thus become representative of the pre-Israelite population (so again at the beginning of v. 5). Samuel reads 'to Jerusalem, *to* the Jebusites', dignifying the Jebusites as the adversary; C notes in a colder, matter-of-fact way, 'to Jerusalem; *there* there were the Jebusites'—they happened to be the occupants.

David's capture of the citadel, on top of Mt Zion itself, is recorded as a single imperious act: 'they said', 'David took'.

In v. 5 the capacity of the Jebusites to resist David is again reduced. C omits their taunt, recorded in Samuel after 'You cannot come here': 'The blind and the lame could repulse you'.

At a stroke Jerusalem has achieved its destiny: it will now eternally be called 'the City of David' (cf. v. 7, where the act of naming by David himself in 2 Sam. 5.9 is replaced by the general, 'therefore they call it...'). It is called 'the City of David' not so much because David conquered it by force of arms (v. 5), but because from there David henceforth rules (v. 7).

Verses 6 and 8, deliberately disposed around v. 7 as locking piece, mark the transition to the next topic, the successive waves of warriors rallying to David's support. These warriors are about to be recorded in four sections in decreasing order of priority and rank (1 Chron. 11.11-47; 12.1-18; 12.19-22; 12.23-40). At their head, therefore, stands in chief importance, Joab, the leader of the free citizen army, introduced by C by means of a substantial adjustment of the text (he does not figure at all in the parallel text in 2 Sam. 5.8-9).

Joab, according to the genealogy in 1 Chron. 2.16, was David's nephew (the son of David's sister Zeruiah, and always called by his mother's name because of the early decease of his father, 2 Sam. 2.32). Apart from his appearance in lists of officials or of his family or in other incidental references, Joab appears functionally in C only in the present passage, in 1 Chronicles 19 in the account of David's campaign against Ammon, and in 1 Chronicles 21 in the incident of the census. On these occasions, Joab appears almost consistently in a good light, which contrasts strongly with the repeatedly negative judgments that David passes on him in Samuel–Kings (cf. 2 Sam. 3.29; 16.10; 19.22) and which culminate in 1 Kgs 2.5-6 in David's instruction to Solomon to have Joab put to death.

Joab's leadership is here explained by reference to his signal courage and military skill displayed at the capture of Jerusalem. By virtue of this act of leadership, he is appointed David's chief officer (*śar*, the term by which the leader of the LORD's cosmic forces is known, Josh. 5.14, and much to be used in the ensuing chapters, e.g. v. 21). David attends to the supreme tasks: here the construction of the city outwards from the *millô'*, 'the in-fill', the great platform on the summit on which the citadel stands (in Samuel the construction is described from the outside inwards). Joab is then left, in a note unique to C

(v. 8), to take charge of construction works in the remainder of the city (the verb, meaning suggestively, 'give life to, revive', is used again of rebuilding devastated cites only in Neh. 4.2). All Joab's activities, whether in war or in peace, are done in the name of David and in subordination to him.

Verse 9 sums up the essential element in David's accession to the throne and his ever increasingly realized dominion, by means of a traditional term taken over virtually unchanged from 2 Sam. 5.10: 'David grew ever greater, *because the* LORD *of hosts was with him*'. The title, 'the LORD of hosts' (*ṣ^e^ba'iot*), used here for the first time in C (it is, indeed, to be used again in C only in 1 Chron. 17.7, 24), provides one of the most important examples of sacramental thinking. The 'hosts' in the title are the cosmic powers available to God for the realization of his purposes (cf. 2 Chron. 18.18; Josh. 5.14; Ps. 103.21; 148.2); Israel's armies are the earthly counterpart to these cosmic forces (cf. 1 Chron. 27.3; Exod. 7.4; 12.17, 41; Deut. 20.9; 1 Sam. 17.45; 1 Kgs 2.5; Pss. 44.9; 60.10; 108.11). The earliest occurrence of the title in the Hebrew Bible is in 1 Samuel, in association with the sanctuary at Shiloh and the ark of God, where it is connected with the wars which God wages on behalf of his people against their enemies (1 Sam. 1.3; 4.4, etc.). Though C does not reproduce the narratives from Samuel, it had been in the name of the LORD of hosts that David had confronted Goliath (1 Sam. 17.45); from that day, David had indeed 'gone from strength to strength' to become Israel's leader in fighting the 'battles of the LORD' (1 Sam.18.17; 25.28). The title, therefore, expresses the effective zeal of the LORD on behalf of his people, the war he wages on their enemies, the control he exercises over the destinies of the nations and his upholding of justice even for the oppressed individual (e.g. Isa. 1.24; 3.15; 19.4; 1 Sam. 1.11). Within this context even the preposition 'with' (*'im*) in the affirmation that the LORD of hosts is 'with' David takes on significance; as noted in 1 Chron. 5.20, it cross-refers to the expectations associated with the messianic name, 'Immanuel'.

It is thus entirely understandable that in 1 Chronicles 13, after the retrospect in 1 Chron. 11.10–12.40, on the forces who, up to this point, have allied themselves to David, the next act that David plans is none other than bringing into Jerusalem, his new capital, the ark, with which this title 'LORD of hosts' is especially associated. The ark of the LORD of hosts expresses the theological framework within which

David's hosts are set. In Jerusalem, the ark will become the visible symbol that his reign is indeed founded upon the strength and support of the LORD and that this alone explains his irresistibly increasing power. This circle of ideas associated with the Jerusalem tradition of theology is now to be fundamental in C's exposition of the significance of the house of David.

1 CHRONICLES 11.10–12.40: THE ROLL OF WARRIORS WHO JOINED FORCES WITH KING DAVID

Before continuing, in 1 Chron. 13.1, his account of how David proceeded to put God's purpose into effect, C pauses to record the four main phases in which support grew for David among Israel's warriors until he has finally been recognized as king by all Israel. Those now to be listed are those 'who came to Hebron to make him king' (1 Chron. 12.38; cf. 1 Chron. 11.1, 3). Once again, by means of this 'flashback', there is a certain 'timeless contemporaneity' (cf. 1 Chron. 9.2-34): gradual growth in support is now presented as concerted action; statistics are used as unchanging counters.

C himself provides in v. 10 a title for the whole section, 1 Chron. 11.10–12.40: 'These are the leaders [possibly, "sum totals", as English versions at 1 Chron. 12.23] of David's warriors who joined forces (Hebrew root, *ḥzq*) with him'.

> The verb *ḥzq* is another of C's key expressions: of twenty-seven occurrences of this verbal form in the Hebrew Bible, fifteen are in C, all, except 1 Chron. 19.13, in material peculiar to C himself. It is once used of God (2 Chron. 16.9), as lending support to those who are steadfast towards himself. Typically, it occurs in contexts dealing with the establishment or confirmation of the Davidic king of the day in power, meaning, 'assume control, be confirmed, show resolve, grow in strength': thus, Solomon, 2 Chron. 1.1; Rehoboam, 12.13; cf. 2 Chron. 13.7; Abijah, 2 Chron. 13.21, cf. v. 8; Asa, 2 Chron. 15.8; Jehoshaphat, 2 Chron. 17.1; Jehoram, 2 Chron. 21.4; Amaziah, 2 Chron. 25.11; Jotham, 2 Chron. 27.6; Hezekiah, 2 Chron. 32.5 (the verbal root is present in the very name 'Hezekiah'); cf. Jehoiada, 2 Chron. 23.1. See the simple form of the root in the exhortation in, for example, 1 Chron. 22.13, of David to Solomon 'be strong'.

The word, 'warriors', is the same as that used for Nimrod as 'tyrant' in 1 Chron. 1.10: the emblematic force of the nations of the world is now to be met and countered by the Davidic monarchy and its supporters. It is only because it is the divine purpose that the coronation can proceed: as in the act of anointing there is the divine and human side (1 Chron. 11.3), so in making David king the human act derives its validity only from the divine authority. The sacramental principle is fundamental: David sits on the LORD's throne (1 Chron. 28.5).

Thus, the verb 'to make king' (*himlîk*) is used of the human act again in 1 Chron. 12.31, 38; 23.1; 29.22; 2 Chron. 10.1; 11.22; 22.1; 23.11; 26.1; 33.25; 36.1, 4, 10; but also of the divine act in 1 Chron. 28.4; 2 Chron. 1.8-9, 11.

All would be in vain, were it not that the goal of the whole process is 'as determined by the LORD concerning Israel'. Through David, God is providing the means by which, at last, Israel can achieve its destiny as God's people in the world.

MT divides the roll of supporters into four sections:

A. 1 Chron. 11.11-47 David's heroes;
B. 1 Chron. 12.1-18 David's supporters at Ziklag;
C. 1 Chron. 12.19-22 David's supporters from Manasseh;
D. 1 Chron. 12.23-40 David's supporters at Hebron.

The heading and sections A, B and D begin with the same phrase, 'Now these are…' (1 Chron. 11.10, 11; 12.1; 12.23). Section C is the odd one out in being emphasized by MT only by a separate paragraph. Cf. the recurrence of 'these' in 1 Chron. 11.19, 24; 12.14, 15 and the summary answering the title in 1 Chron. 12.38, 'All these…'

A. *1 Chronicles 11.11-47: David's Heroes*

Section A is divided into three main parts: vv. 11-21; 22-25; 26-47.

With many variations in detail, this passage, to the middle of v. 41, is parallel to 2 Sam. 23.8-39. Thereafter, it is independent.

Verse 11a, 'These are the number of David's warriors', provides the title for the whole of Section A. The list begins in the earliest period of the series of events that is to culminate in David's being anointed as king. At this stage David is a fugitive in the wilderness of Judah, supported by only a handful of followers, 'The Thirty' (vv. 11-21; the narratives of David's flight from Saul, 1 Sam. 19–30, not reproduced by C, are presupposed). These *gibbôrîm* (1 Chron. 1.10), individual warriors, are the first to recognize that the failing order of Saul is doomed and that only through David can the threat to Israel's existence from the Philistines be neutralized (cf. vv. 13-19; for the Philistines as emblematic foe, cf. 1 Chron. 1.12). Their perceptiveness about the trend of events energizes their natural gifts and enables them to triumph against seemingly impossible odds. Only in time will more concerted action be possible and call for more formal organization of fighting units (v. 26).

In the title in v. 11a C introduces a characteristic idea. The parallel in 2 Sam. 23.8 reads, 'These are the names', showing that the primary interest there is in the identity of the individuals. Here, by contrast, C prefers the word *mispār*, 'number'; the emphasis is on the scale of support—tiny to begin with, but gradually rising.

The NRSV rendering, 'account', matches the minority use of the word as in Judg. 7.15, and suits the present context only as far as v. 25. There are other passages in C where *mispār* is used, again to stress the size of groups: 1 Chron. 12.23 at the beginning of Section C; in 1 Chron. 23.3, 24, 27 of the Levites; in 1 Chron. 25.1, 7 of the musicians; in 1 Chron. 27.1, 23, 24 of Israel, with a note on the non-presumptuous way in which such a census is to be conducted; also in 2 Chron. 26.11-12 of the army of Uzziah, numbered by a *sôpēr*, 'scribe', basically, 'counter', a noun from the same root as *mispār*. Elsewhere in C it is used of the appropriate scale of offerings 1 Chron. 23.31; 2 Chron. 29.32; 35.7. The word has already occurred in 1 Chron. 7.2, 40; 9.28; and is to reappear in 1 Chron. 16.9; 21.2, 5; 22.4, 16; 2 Chron. 12.3. C's interest in numbers as indicative of scale of support is underlined by the fact that in Section A he gives 51 names as opposed to Samuel's 36 and adds a further 42 of his own in section B.

Other features of C's presentation emphasize this interest in the scale of support for David rather than in recounting feats of bravery of individual supporters. Verses 11b-14 should give the names and most famous actions of the greatest of David's mighty men (cf. the reference to the specific group of 'The Three' in v. 12b and the parallel in 2 Sam. 23.8-12). In the event, C omits the name of the third of the trio and conflates the actions of the second and the third (vv. 9bγ-11bδ of the Samuel parallel are missing in C).

It may be that the omission of the third warrior is due simply to the textual error (2 Sam. 23.9bβ and 11bα, emended, both end in the same word, *lammilḥāmâ*, and it may be assumed that a copyist's eye has slipped from the first to the second with the result that the intervening phrase has been left out by homoioteleuton). Yet it is striking that the first three verbs of v. 14 have been changed to the plural from the singular in Samuel. This means either that once the copyist's error had occurred further changes had to be made so that the text might yield fluent sense, or, more likely, that C has deliberately shortened the text, aided by the fact that the exploits of both heroes involved actions against the Philistines.

The effect of the change is that the heroic stand against the Philistines in the barley-field is no longer the signal feat of courage by one of David's heroes, but one in which David and the hero shared together (cf. the title in v. 10: they 'join forces'). Further, the mighty act of the first of 'The Three', 'he wielded his spear over three hundred slain at one time', is described in identical language to that of the leader of the next group of warriors in v. 20: actions are here being integrated and typified.

The first of David's mighty men is Jashobeam (v. 11b; suggestively, his name means, 'let the people return'). Ironically, little is known about him (because of the poor condition of the text, his very name has to be restored in the parallel in 2 Sam. 23.8). His father/place of origin ('son of Hachmoni') is also unknown (another Hachmonite is found in high position at David's court in 1 Chron. 27.32). Nor is any information given about the circumstances or the identity of the enemy, whether Israelite followers of Saul, or Philistine aggressors as in the case of the following mighty man; given the context, the latter is the more likely. Again C, perhaps through deliberate association with (or inadvertent contamination from?) the similar text of v. 20, greatly reduces the scale of the incident from the 800 of the Samuel–Kings parallel. Either way, the success of the warrior in the LORD's service against overwhelming odds is the point: that which is intrinsically right must prevail. The promise at the end of the Holiness Code, 'Five of you shall give chase to a hundred, and a hundred of you shall give chase to ten thousand' (Lev. 26.8; contrast Deut. 32.30) finds here its expression.

Some obscurity also surrounds Jashobeam's precise rank. It is not clear in what sense he is 'chief': the Hebrew might mean first in time or in prowess, as well as leader. The MT has a double reading: *kethib*, that he was 'chief of The Thirty'; *qere*, that he was 'chief of the chariot warriors' (cf. the footnote in NRSV). It would appear that David's élite fighting corps in this early phase was known as 'The Thirty' (cf. vv. 15, 25), seemingly a round figure, since 2 Sam. 23.39 notes that there were actually thirty-seven. The *qere* reading must be anachronistic for this period of raiding parties (cf., e.g., 1 Sam. 25), though it is perfectly conceivable that, subsequently, when David had opportunity to organize his army, he should have risen to high rank.

This is made the more likely by the fact that there is in eight cases an identity, and, in the remaining four, at least a strong similarity, between the names of David's heroes here and those of the high officials each in charge of 24,000 in the twelve month rota of royal service in 1 Chronicles 27. The list is Jashobeam (but there son of Zabdiel), Dodai (cf. v. 12), Benaiah son of Jehoiada (cf. v. 22), Asahel brother of Joab (v. 26), Shammoth (v. 27), Ira (v. 28), Helez (v. 27), Sibbecai (v. 29), Abiezer (v. 28), Maharai (v. 30), Benaiah (v. 31), Heled (v. 30). In 1 Chron. 27.6, Benaiah son of Jehoiada is expressly identified as commander of 'the thirty' and thus links 1 Chronicles 11 and 1 Chronicles 27 together.

The second in rank is Eleazar the son of Dodo, the Ahohite (vv. 12-14). Again, though he does figure in 2 Sam. 23.9-10, nothing is known of him beyond the present incident, which has, in any case, been fused with the notable event associated in 2 Sam. 23.11-12 with the third of these chief mighty men. His family name suggests that he was a Benjaminite (cf. 1 Chron. 8.4), that is, a deserter from Saul's own tribe.

Eleazar's prowess in battle is now commemorated: 'he was with David at Pas-dammim when the Philistines were gathered there for battle' (v. 13). Pas-dammim is probably the same as Ephes-dammim ('No blood-guilt'), the place in the Valley of Elah that runs up from one of the probable sites of Gath to the vicinity of Bethlehem, where, then, naturally enough, the youthful David of Bethlehem answered the challenge of the champion Goliath of Gath (1 Sam. 17). In C's account, the incident concerns a fierce infantry engagement over a barley field (2 Sam. 23.11 has 'lentils'; C's change may be meant to evoke associations with Passover/Unleavened Bread, the festival of the barley harvest commemorating the deliverance of Israel from Egypt at the exodus). The Israelites as a whole had fallen back before the Philistine advance: Eleazar and David together (so now in C's version as noted above; the RSV's rendering, now corrected in NRSV, destroys the point) 'took *their* stand in the midst of the plot, and defended it and slew the Philistines' (v. 14). Territory, even if it is only a barley-field, has been recovered from the representative power of the nations. The long slow process of the restoration of the land has begun.

The verb, *nṣl*, translated here by NRSV as 'defended', recurs a further eleven times in C: 1 Chron. 16.35; 2 Chron. 20.25; 25.15, plus eight times in 2 Chron. 32.11-17 (where it is used in the context of the LORD's contest with rival deities), all except 2 Chron. 32.11 and 14 in C's own material.

The account of the episode ends with a note on the basic factor in the situation: 'the LORD performed a mighty deliverance'. Once again, sacramental thinking is in play: the heroic prowess of David and his companion would count for nothing were it not that the underlying purpose of God is being furthered. Behind the physical force lies the metaphysical reality. In tune with this moral and spiritual power David and his companion triumph against the forces thus futilely ranged to challenge God's regime.

The root 'to deliver' (*yš'*) recurs in 1 Chron. 16.23, 35*; 18.6, 13; 19.12, 19; 2 Chron. 6.41*; 20.9*, 17*; 32.22* (* = C's own material).

C's narrative makes it clear that the next incident, vv. 15-19, the reckless bravery of the three heroes in drawing water from the cistern at Bethlehem despite the presence of the Philistine post there, is independent of the preceding passage. The fact that there were three involved in this incident is merely coincidental; they have nothing to do with 'The Three', to whom the two heroes previously mentioned belonged. The distinction between the two groups of three is important for the understanding of vv. 20-25, which provides the names of two of the three heroes involved in the Bethlehem incident, Abishai, the brother of Joab, who was the leader, and Benaiah, son of Jehoiada, but carefully distinguishes them from 'The Three'.

It is likely that the incident occurred in the earliest phase of David's rise to power (as its context in Section A would suggest). The cave of Adullam is where David found refuge from Saul for a time and was the first rallying point of his supporters (1 Sam. 22). Adullam is located in the Philistine lowlands outside the territory of Judah (1 Sam. 22.5). The stranglehold that the Philistines had upon the country is indicated (vv. 15-16) not only by their garrison at Bethlehem but by their army encampment in the Valley of Rephaim, which lies between Bethlehem and Jerusalem, and provided the Philistines with a favourite access route into the heart of the country (cf. 1 Chron. 14.9) even during David's reign in Jerusalem.

This is the moment of the nadir of David's fortunes: he is a fugitive on the run, with a body of desperadoes (cf. 1 Sam. 22.2) to provide for. His sense of deprivation of the basic necessities of life, as well as of home and of standing in the community, is symbolized for him by the water in the cistern of the gate, the hub of everyday social life, in his home town of Bethlehem. Three of his heroes, including Abishai his own nephew (1 Chron. 2.16), by an act of daring infiltrate the enemy lines at risk to their own lives to get the water to satisfy their leader's thirst. But David is sensitive to the wider and deeper factors. He will not satisfy physical need at the cost of underlying realities: to drink the water thus gained at risk of life would be equivalent to drinking the life-blood of the heroes who had brought it. The water has to be handled as if it were blood, and the proper handling of blood, the vehicle of life, is to pour it out on the ground in homage and acknowledgment to God, the giver of life (Deut. 12.16). By this act of submission (which is the very opposite of *ma'al*), David pours out before God the whole life and circumstances of himself and his followers.

The exploits of two more of David's early heroic followers are recorded in vv. 20-25. The more or less identical concluding comments on each in vv. 20b, 21 and 24b, 25 again interrelate the individuals (cf. the link between vv. 11 and 20). But these comments are undeniably puzzling in content: 'he had renown among the three (plus warriors, v. 24); he was more honoured than the three (thirty, v. 25)...though he did not belong to the three'. (Verse 21a is perhaps still more puzzling and may mean something like: 'he was preferred in honour by the other two heroes to the three, and became their leader'.) If it is assumed that two groups of 'three' are being spoken of here, then perhaps the difficulties can be ironed out (NRSV prefers textual emendation): vv. 20b and 24b refer to the three heroes who broke through the Philistine ranks to bring the water from the cistern of Bethlehem and give identity to two of them (Abishai and Benaiah); vv. 21 and 25 refer to 'The Three', that is, the three original supporters of David, two of whom are identified by name in vv. 11 and 12 (it is possible that one of 'The Three' was also one of the three heroes who brought the water from Bethlehem, thus accounting for the close association of these two groups). On this assumption, Ab(i)shai, the brother of Joab, becomes chief of the three, that is, the three Bethlehem heroes. Verse 21a may mean something like: 'he was preferred in honour by the other two heroes to The Three, and became their leader'.

Ab(i)shai (vv. 20-21), like his brother Joab (cf. 1 Chron. 11.6), is treated favourably in C (the passages in Samuel, which suggest that he was an uncontrolled firebrand, are omitted by C, for example, 1 Sam. 26.6-11, 2 Sam. 16.9; 19.21-22). In 1 Chron. 18.12 he is even promoted to the generalship in an important engagement with the Edomites (2 Sam. 8.13 is different at that point). His exploit is now referred to in stereotyped language, 'he wielded his spear against three hundred men and slew them' (cf. v. 11).

In 2 Sam. 23.18-19 the reference is presumably to the incident recorded in 2 Sam. 2.31, the slaying of 360 Benjaminites by Ab(i)shai and his brother Joab. Such an inner-Israelite feud is entirely alien to C's purpose.

Benaiah, the son of Jehoiada, rates a separate subsection (vv. 22-25). He is described as the son of a valiant man, or man of wealth, and a great entrepreneur (the phrase occurs only in this context and seems by the accents to refer to the father rather than the son [contra English versions]), from Kabzeel (in southern Judah, Josh. 15.21). Three notable deeds are recorded of him, each introduced in the Hebrew by the emphatic personal pronoun: 'It was *he* who…' The first exploit is uncertain: RSV, 'he smote two ariels of Moab', merely transliterates a Hebrew word understood by some (e.g. NRSV, 'two sons of Ariel') as a proper name (cf. Ezra 8.16 for this usage) and by others (e.g. NEB) as 'champion', literally 'lion (*'ᵃrî*) of God (*'ēl*)'. His next exploit was to fight a lion (again, *'ᵃrî*, which may suggest some connection with the first incident) in the close confines of a pit 'on a snowy day', in the adverse conditions of intense cold, poor visibility and treacherous footing, which must have tested his personal strength and courage to the limit (v. 22). The third exploit is described at greatest length: armed with only a stick, he disarmed a gigantic Egyptian, some 2.3 metres tall, took his spear and slew him with it (v. 23).

The description of the last exploit is reminiscent of David's own encounter with Goliath (not reproduced by C): the unequal single combat between an Israelite armed with a stick (1 Sam. 17.40, though a different word from here) and a gigantic enemy armed with a spear 'like a weaver's beam' (cf. 1 Sam. 17.7).

The crises that Benaiah had to face not only tested his personal courage but warded off two foreign invaders, Moab, and, still more significantly, Egypt. The land of Israel is now being defended not just from foes from within its borders, as in the case of the Philistine threat.

It is hardly surprising, then, that, given a man of such calibre, David is happy not only 'to set [him] over his bodyguard' (v. 25), the position which he himself had occupied in Saul's court (1 Sam. 22.14), but later to place him in command of the foreign mercenary troops (1 Chron. 18.17, these troops formed the power-base for Solomon's accession to the throne against his main rival, Adonijah, 1 Kgs 1–2, a point irrelevant to C). The strength of the nations once directed against Israel will be used in its defence and in the furtherance of its task. Later, Benaiah is also in charge of the service of the third month in 1 Chron. 27.5-6.

Verse 26 begins with the title, 'As for the warriors of the armies', for the subsection down to v. 47. Virtually without further anecdote, C lists a further forty-seven of these earliest warrior supporters of David.

MT divides the list into twenty-one sections, listing the names mostly in pairs. The sections coincide with the verse divisions, except v. 31a, vv. 31b-32a, vv. 32b-33, vv. 46-47. The effect of thus breaking up the apparently monolithic list is to emphasize the variety of locations from which support for David is now drawn.

Down to v. 41a the list adheres in the main to that given in 2 Samuel 23; the remaining 16 names come, presumably, from other sources (the formulation 'the Pelonite', probably literally, 'the so-and-so', in vv. 27, 36 adds a touch of authenticity: the individual is remembered but, unlike the others, not his background).

David is no longer the isolated guerilla leader of 'The Thirty': the scale of his support has increased to the extent that he is now at the head of substantial fighting forces (a similar expression occurs in 2 Chron. 16.4 of the divisions of the armies of Damascus). The note in v. 42, that one of these leaders had himself 30 troops with him, may give some idea of the scale of support these warriors bring with them—about 1500 men, if that figure is typical. As noted above, nine of the names in vv. 26-31 recur in more or less recognizable form in the list of supervisors of the new rota from the fourth to the twelfth month in 1 Chronicles 27. Occasionally something further is known of the individuals concerned from other sources: the untimely end of Asahel (v. 26) is recorded in 2 Samuel 2; Elhanan (v. 26) is credited with the slaying of the brother of Goliath in 1 Chron. 20.5, if not of Goliath himself (2 Sam. 21.19); Sibbecai (v. 29) slew another of the giants (1 Chron. 20.4); the presence of Uriah the Hittite, with whose name the list in 2 Samuel 23 ends, among these the earliest and most devoted of David's followers, adds still further piquancy to the narration of David's shameless adultery with his wife and the contrivance of his death (2 Sam. 11–12), incidents which, however, C passes over. A note is added about Joab's armour-bearer (v. 39), but nothing further is known of the individual concerned, still less of the remainder.

The list by including the far-flung places of origin of many of these heroes sheds, where these are identifiable, interesting light on the widespread influence David was now beginning to exert. They come not only from his home town of Bethlehem and its environs (vv. 20, 26, 30), but also wider Judah (vv. 22, 28, 32, 37, 40), Simeon (v. 43 cf. 1 Chron. 27.16 [Mandelkern]), Benjamin, Saul's own tribe! (vv. 12, 28, 29, 31, 33, 39), the original area of Dan (v. 33), Ephraim (vv. 31, 32), Reuben (v. 42), Half-Manasseh on the East Bank (v. 44), and even people of foreign extraction (besides Uriah the Hittite, Moab, v. 46, Ammon, v. 39, Ishmael, v. 38 and Aram (?) v. 47 are represented; see also the parallels in 2 Sam. 23.34, 36 to vv. 35 and 38). The presence of such foreigners recognizing David's role as leader of Israel among the world of the nations is integral to C's overall theme. Conspicuous by their absence meantime are Levi, Half-Manasseh on the West Bank, Issachar, Zebulun, Naphtali, Dan and Asher, in the main the tribes of the Jezreel Valley and Galilee. It is notable that they are those who figure later in the genealogical pattern (1 Chron. 6–7). They are threatened in the Philistine advance to Mt Gilboa and are represented below in Section C by Half-Manasseh.

B. *1 Chronicles 12.1-18: David's Support at Ziklag*

C now turns to record the second wave of the support that brings David to the throne. He provides the title for the section in v. 1a: 'Now these are the men who came to David at Ziklag, while he could not move about freely because of [JPSV: he was still in hiding from] Saul son of Kish'.

The section presupposes the narrative in 1 Sam. 27.1–2 Sam. 2.3, which tells how David sought refuge from the jealous Saul, now king in name only, as a feudal vassal of the Philistine king, Achish of Gath; how he was granted by him a fief at Ziklag, which he used as a base to send raiding parties against the Negev; and how, thanks to the suspicion of the Philistine chieftains, he was providentially prevented from taking part against his fellow Israelites in Saul's last battle at Mt Gilboa. Apart from the use already made of 1 Samuel 31 in 1 Chronicles 10, only v. 19

betrays the slightest verbal reminiscence of the Samuel passage (cf. 1 Sam. 29.4). None of the 42 persons named in the following lists is known from other sources in the Hebrew Bible.

The MT divides the section into five paragraphs:

vv. 1-8	the arrival of helpers at Ziklag: twenty-three named from Benjamin with a note on the quality of those Gad;
vv. 9-13a	the names of the first ten Gadites;
vv. 13b-15	the eleventh Gadite, with evaluation;
vv. 16-17	David's address to the arrivals from Benjamin and Judah;
v. 18	the reply on behalf of the arrivals.

The first three paragraphs of the MT at first sight cut somewhat across the logic of the material; one would have been inclined to divide the first three sections into two (one on Benjamin, vv. 1-7; one on Gad, vv. 8-15) and to combine the last two. The force of the MT division is to integrate the Gadites (and Judaeans) closely into the Benjaminites and to heighten the fact that the crucial question in the whole section is the loyalty of the tribesmen of Saul to David. The paragraphing of the MT suggests that the verse division at the beginning of the chapter is misleading: vv. 1-2a is a general introduction to the whole section; v. 2b is the subtitle on Benjamin, which matches v. 8, the subtitle on Gad.

The first three paragraphs are concerned with the organization of these new recruits (the key term, *'zr*, 'help' is used: vv. 1, 17, 18 [twice], not to mention the names of the leaders, Ahi-ezer, v. 3, and Ezer, v. 10, plus two further in v. 6; cf. 1 Chron. 5.20). The primal period of the heroic individual working on his own or in small groups is now past. An army with specialized functions has now to be created (cf. 1 Chron. 5.18), the archers and slingers in v. 2 (perhaps both right-handed and left-handed rather than NRSV's ambidextrous bowmen; for left-handed Benjaminites, cf. Judg. 20.16) and the foot-soldiers with spear and shield in v. 8. C thus interprets the 'six hundred' men, whom David took with him to Achish, according to 1 Sam. 27.2, in terms of an army, who freely came to commit themselves to him.

The source of these recruits is equally significant. The bowmen are Benjaminites! Not only Saul's fellow tribesmen, but even his kinsmen, are deserting to David (men from Gibeah, v. 3, or if C's view of Saul's homeland is followed, from Gibeon, v. 4; cf. 1 Chron. 9.35-39): the inexorable transfer of the monarchy from Saul to David is proceeding apace even within the family of the doomed king. Yet, despite v. 2, these bowmen are not exclusively from Benjamin: at least two of them are from cities located in Judah (for Gederah, v. 4, cf. 1 Chron. 4.23; for Gedor, v. 7, cf. 1 Chron. 4.4); the levitical Korahites, too, v. 6 (cf. 1 Chron. 6.22), are represented. This association of Judaeans with Benjaminites prepares for the fourth and fifth paragraphs in vv. 16-18.

The Gadites (vv. 8-15) are of interest to C from a number of points of view. The matter under consideration is David's formal organization of his forces, especially as raiding parties (v. 18; NRSV, 'troops'): the old pun on Gad and *g^e^dûd*, 'raiding party', may be lurking in the background (cf. Gen. 49.19). Certainly their aptitude, not so much for individual prowess as for military leadership, is emphasized: as intent and indomitable as lions and as swift as gazelles even in rugged terrain, v. 8; in v. 14 the least able is capable of commanding a hundred men, the best a thousand.

But even more significant for C's schema is their place of origin: as Gadites they belong to the East Bank tribes. Their arrival in Ziklag, deep in the West Bank, to lend massive (eleven-fold) help alongside the 'Benjaminites' represents the beginning of the new definitive conquest and settlement of all Israel in the land under one new national leader, David. There is an unmistakable verbal reminiscence of the account of the beginning of the original conquest and settlement of the land under Joshua (cf. Josh. 3.15) in v. 15: they 'crossed the Jordan in the first month, when it was overflowing all its banks'. In that original campaign it was the East Bank tribes again who lent decisive military assistance to their West Bank brothers (cf. especially Josh. 4.12). The point is clinched by the note of their sweeping military victories, as in the manner of the original Joshua campaigns: they 'put to flight all those in the valleys, to the east and to the west' (for 'valley' as the place of settlement of the indigenous population, cf., e.g., Josh. 17.16; Judg. 1.19). Under David there is to be realized that which under Joshua was marred by Achar's *ma'al* (Josh. 7; 1 Chron. 2.7).

The arrival of these tribesmen from the north and east marks a moment of critical transition in David's fortunes (vv. 16-18). No longer is he relying only on the unswerving loyalty of his own warriors: the basis of support is ever-widening. Given the previous commitments of these tribesmen to Saul, it is vital that their loyalty is put to the test.

The vulnerability of David is striking as he confronts the newcomers. His sole defence is the intrinsic rightness of his cause as divinely ordained. Therefore, he emerges from his stronghold to meet them (vv. 16-18). His words are direct and rely implicitly on the honesty of their reply: 'have you come to help [*'zr*, as in v. 1b] or to betray?' If they have come to help, then let their commitment be absolute. If they betray, then their injustice is underlined: 'I have done no harm'. But David reminds them that they, too, are implicated in the intrinsic rightness of his cause: God, who is the sole power behind his power, is the one who will vindicate his own cause. Thus David appeals not only to their sense of shared destiny, but also to their shared tradition: if they betray him, 'may the God of *our* fathers [cf. 1 Chron. 5.25] see and punish' (v. 17).

The response (v. 18) is given on behalf of all by Amasai, chief of 'the thirty' (*kethib*; or of 'the chariot warriors', *qere*; cf. 1 Chron. 11.11). Mandelkern identifies him with Amasa, the son of David's sister, Abigail (1 Chron. 2.17), but in the context one might have expected the figure presented in v. 4, Ishmaiah, the consonantal outline of whose name is not dissimilar to that of Amasai, to be the individual concerned. If so, the fact that he is from Gibeon, Saul's home town, makes his utterance the more significant. He is seized with ecstatic possession by the divine spirit ('the spirit clothed him': the same formulation is used again in C of Zechariah, 2 Chron. 24.20; outside C, it is used of Gideon in Judg. 6.34; for similar expressions of divine inspiration, cf. 1 Chron. 5.26): God himself is indeed controlling the response and vindicating David.

Nonetheless, the words of the opening line of Amasai's speech, 'To you, O David, and with you, O son of Jesse' are strangely indirect: the NRSV rendering, 'We are yours, O David, and with you...' is possible, but there is, in fact, no use of the first person plural personal pronoun 'we' in the entire utterance, by which their spokesman binds them: the emphasis is on the repeated word 'peace' and that may be what is intended in the first line as well, 'Peace to you...' 'Peace', from the root for wholeness, implies the maintenance of relations in their full integrity; if that is done, all else follows. Amasai picks up the theological terms of David's address and adds the recognition, using again the key root *'zr*, 'For your God has helped you'. The change from David's 'our God' to Amasai's 'your God' is a significant acknowledgment of David's unique status as agent for God in the world.

This is the oath of loyalty which inaugurates the decisive phase in

David's ascent to the throne. It is based on the fundamental perception that David's emergence is no chance human contrivance, but rests on the action of God: the helper behind the helpers is none other than the ancestral God of Israel, yet once more, and this time decisively, intervening in the destiny of his people. It is with help like this in accord with the underlying divine help that David can organize his forces.

Section B probably refers to David's early days at Ziklag: the 'troops' at the end of v. 18 in the Samuel version would be those whom he sent out on expedition against the Negev (1 Sam. 27.8-9).

C. *1 Chronicles 12.19-22: Supporters from Manasseh*

This section, with its explicit reference to the battle of Mt Gilboa (cf. 1 Chron. 10), must refer to David's last days at Ziklag (for the chronology, see 1 Sam. 27.7; 29.3). The seven army commanders of Manasseh desert to David when Saul's power is clearly at its eclipse. As Judah and Benjamin have earlier represented the south and Gad the East Bank, so Manasseh represents the north in this phase. The Philistines feared that David and his followers would change sides in the middle of their campaign against Saul with disastrous results for themselves. David was, therefore, not permitted to join in the battle. This is an implicit recognition by the Philistines of David's now formidable power. The Manassites with seeming opportunism choose this moment to join David: Saul is powerless to help them; David is in good standing with the Philistines; yet spared from implication in the death of Saul. Yet, without grudging, these Manassites too are welcomed as 'helpers'.

Given the distance of C from the detail of the text of Samuel, the 'band' with which the Manassites assisted (v. 21) is more likely to be the same as that mentioned at the end of v. 18 (the same word *g*ᵉ*dûd* is again used; so NRSV footnote), than the raiding band of the Amalekites referred to in 1 Sam. 30.8 (so NRSV text).

Once again the thematic term *'zr* recurs throughout this section, reaching the climax in v. 22 (cf. vv. 19, 21): 'Thus daily they were coming to David *to help* him until the camp grew as large as the camp of God'. C penetrates to the heart of the matter with the use of the emotive word 'camp', redolent of the period of Israel's sojourn in the wilderness and of the great military campaigns of the early period (e.g. 1 Chron. 9.19; Exod. 14.19; Josh. 6.11). But more, yet once again sacramental thinking is in evidence: the campaigns of David are wholly in consonance with the campaigns of God himself with his people; the camp of David *is* none other than the camp of God (for the phrase cf. Gen. 32.2; for the identification of the camp of Israel with the camp of the LORD, 2 Chron. 14.13, Ps. 78.28; compare the meaning of the phrase 'LORD of hosts', 1 Chron. 11.9).

D. *1 Chronicles 12.23-40: David's Supporters at Hebron*

In the final section of the retrospective account of the growth of David's support among the Israelites, C reaches the climactic moment when David receives at Hebron the allegiance of the entire twelve tribe system of Israel, both officers and men (v. 38, 'all these...came to Hebron', is resumptive of 1 Chron. 11.1, 3).

The support is now so massive that names of individuals can scarcely any longer be given (only Jehoiada and Zadok in connection with the priesthood in vv. 27-28). Instead, gross statistics of the groups involved must suffice. But even the total of 1220 officers and 339,600 men is hardly complete: officers are only given for Zadok, Issachar and Naphtali; Issachar lacks a number for the ordinary foot-soldiers. Even when given, the number does not represent Israel as a whole: these were only the delegates (cf. the 18,000 from Manasseh in v. 31b); there were others in the landward areas who were able to supply the delegates (v. 38b).

As before, while C presupposes material in Samuel–Kings, he makes no overt use of it. Instead, he resumes his own earlier adaptation of it in v. 23: 'who came to David in Hebron [cf. 1 Chron. 11.1] to turn the kingdom of Saul over to him, according to the word of the LORD [cf. 1 Chron. 10.14]'.

MT divides the section into fourteen paragraphs, essentially an introduction followed by a paragraph for each tribe, but with some variation: Judah, Simeon, Levi, Zadok, Benjamin, Ephraim, Half-Manasseh (West Bank), Issachar, Zebulun, Naphtali, Dan, Asher, Reuben/Gad/Half-Manasseh (East Bank).

The sequence in which C lists the twelve tribes of Israel in this passage is without exact parallel anywhere else in the Hebrew Bible (cf. 1 Chron. 2.1-2; Gen. 46; Exod. 1; Num. 1; 7; 13; 26; 34; Deut. 27; Josh. 15-19; 21; Judg. 1; Ezek. 48 [twice]). The nearest is, perhaps significantly, the account of tribal conquests in Judges 1 (though that list includes only eight of the twelve): the order is a logical geographical one beginning in the South of the West Bank and continuing to the north and then turning to the East Bank. Dan (now included in the complete people of Israel; contrast 1 Chron. 2–8) is in its later, northern, position.

The dry statistics of the representatives (vv. 23-38; cf. table of comparative statistics at 1 Chron. 5.18) are enlivened by C with a great variety of descriptive phrases, many of them synonyms.

> The difficulty of distinguishing meanings may illustrated in the first verse: 'These are the numbers of the heads of the troops of the army', where 'heads' could mean 'army divisions' (e.g. 1 Sam. 13.17-18), 'leaders' (as v. 32), or even, 'sum totals' (so similarly NRSV, though not at 1 Chron. 11.10), all of which could suitably fit the context. The high-ranking warriors are variously known as 'prince', 'chief', 'commander' (vv. 28, 32, 34); the ordinary combatants as 'armed troops, lancers, warriors, men of renown, who sally forth [1 Chron. 1.12] with the army, and fall into battle line' (e.g. vv. 23, 24, 25, 30, 33, 36).

Of particular note is the specification of the Levites (v. 26) and priests under military leadership (vv. 27-28: Jehoiada is otherwise known only through his son Benaiah, cf. 1 Chron. 11.22-25; presumably it is that Jehoiada that is meant and not the high priest in the time of Joash, 2 Chron. 22.11–24.25). The clergy, too, have their place in the camp of the LORD of hosts (cf. the warrior priests in the time of Uzziah, 2 Chron. 26.17). So Zadok, presumably the chief priest to be (1 Chron. 6.8, etc.), is here described as a 'young warrior' (NRSV, v. 28).

The representatives of Issachar ideally fulfil their role as 'elders': they are described here as 'men who had understanding of the times, to know what Israel ought to do' (v. 32). This perception of the right time for a particular action is one of the gifts and responsibilities of the 'wise' (cf. Isa. 28.23-29; Eccles. 3.1-11) among whose number the elders were especially to be found (cf. the parallel texts Jer. 18.18 and Ezek. 7.26 for the identification of the wise man with the elder).

Verse 38b emphasizes that all Israel was unanimously and wholeheartedly in support of these actions of their leaders and representatives (cf. the phrase at the end of v. 33, literally, 'without a heart and a heart', that is, without divided mind and feelings, the opposite of the 'double heart' of Ps. 12.2). While the tenacious loyalty of the Benjaminites to their kinsman Saul is emphasized, v. 29, even their complement of representatives is not lacking.

Verses 39-40 set the covenant and anointing ceremony that took place at Hebron (1 Chron. 11.3) within the wider context of the universal rejoicing of all Israel. The people at large have the opportunity to give tangible expression to their support. The coronation and covenant are set within three days of feasting by this huge assembly at Hebron. To supply this celebration the resources of the kindred (so, rather than NRSV 'neighbours', v. 40) of the representatives even to the far northern reaches of the country (though Dan is again omitted, cf. 1 Chron. 7!) have to be brought by every available animal train. All, whether physically present or not, have a share in the great act whereby national unity is now focused on the person of David.

The emotional response to the ideal at least provisionally or even partially realized is 'joy', *śimḥâ* now to become a recurrent theme in C: 1 Chron. 15.16*, 25; 16.10, 31; 29.9*, 17*, 22*; 2 Chron. 6.41*; 7.10; 15.15*; 20.27*; 23.13, 18*, 21; 24.10*; 29.30*, 36*; 30.21*, 23*, 25*, 26* [* = C material].

1 CHRONICLES 13: DAVID'S INITIATIVE TO FETCH THE ARK OF GOD IS CUT SHORT

In the retrospect of 1 Chron. 11.10–12.40, C has detailed the four phases in which all Israel has rallied to David's support. The narrative now resumes at the point where it was broken off in 1 Chron. 11.9: Jerusalem has been captured, and the citadel built; David has taken up residence in the 'city of David' and reigns with ever-growing power, because 'the LORD of Hosts is with him' (1 Chron. 11.4-9).

The ultimate task of the house of David is, however, to enable Israel at last to fulfil its duty towards God amid the nations of humanity. That task has been expounded in terms of the negative example of Saul in 1 Chron. 10.13-14, explicitly now referred to in v. 3. Saul failed to live a life of complete devotion to the LORD; he did not resort to him and to him alone in all things for guidance. If David's sole recourse is to be to the LORD, then his obvious next move is to bring into direct association with his throne the ark of God, the supreme traditional symbol of the presence and dynamic power of God, neglect of which was Saul's specific failure.

This chapter emphasizes the sacramental character of the ark: to be in the presence of the ark is to be in the very presence of God himself (vv. 8, 10). Symbol and reality are one; to resort to the ark is indeed to resort to the sovereign of the universe. The chapter thus also expounds a significant consequence of this close identification between God and ark: as God's holiness is not to be infringed by those who would approach him (e.g. Lev. 10.3), so too the ark must be treated as holy. Holiness, an idea fundamental to C's work (see the discussion of the Levites in 1 Chron. 6), is present here by implication even if the word itself is not actually used.

> Both MT paragraphing and traditional chapter division agree in treating 1 Chronicles 13 as a single unit.

The chapter opens with another expression of unanimity of purpose (cf. 1 Chron. 11.1): 'David took counsel together' collectively and individually with the commanders of the people, now identified from the preceding chapters (v. 1). 'Taking counsel' (*y'ṣ*), as an expression of national unity of purpose and commitment, is another of C's key terms: cf. Jehoshaphat (2 Chron. 20.21), Hezekiah (2 Chron. 30.2, 23; 32.3); there are negative examples in 2 Chron. 10.6, 8 (Rehoboam); 25.17 (Amaziah).

It is these leading representatives of the people, who constitute 'the *assembly* of Israel' (v. 2). Here C uses a word, *qāhāl*, which belongs to that cluster of words expressing 'gathering' already noted at 1 Chron. 11.1. *qāhāl* also belongs to the traditional terminology applied to the Israel of the wilderness wandering period (e.g. Exod. 12.6; Num. 10.7): the language of the time of the original formation of the people under Moses is now reapplied to the community in renewal under David (C uses the root thirty-seven times, the Pentateuch forty-eight).

In Deuteronomy *qāhāl* is especially used of Israel as constituted as the people of God by the revelation and covenant at Horeb (5.22; 9.10; 10.4; 18.16) and of the exclusiveness of that community (23.1-3, 8). Elsewhere in the Pentateuch, it is used typically of Israel as rebellious (Exod. 16.3; Num. 14.5; 16.3; 20.2-12) and of its constant need of sin offering and atonement (so in the only two contexts in Leviticus, Lev. 4.13-21; 16.17, 33; cf. Num. 16.47; 19.20). In both of these aspects, the word is redolent of ideas that are central to C's purpose.

For the understanding of the sequel of this narrative it is important, in the light of the failure to follow the Mosaic prescriptions as to the correct procedure for bearing the ark (1 Chron. 15.12-15), to appreciate that the *qāhāl* is made up of the representatives of the *laity*. Despite 1 Chron. 12.26-28, the priests and Levites are still 'in the cities of their pasture-lands' (there is a circumstantial clause at the end of v. 2a, 'Now the priests and Levites were with them in the cities...'; see 1 Chron. 15.3-4, where the gathering of the *qāhāl* and of the priests and Levites is done in two separate actions; cf. 1 Chron. 28.1).

David's words to the *qāhāl* (vv. 2-3) again stress unanimity: the emphasis on the first person plural is striking, 'our God...our brethren...together to us...let us...to us...for we'. Also striking are the pains to involve every individual even to the remotest corners of the land (the use of the plural, '*lands* of Israel', v. 2, implies the separation of the different elements that require reunification; the phrase is unique to C and recurs in 2 Chron. 34.33). This is not simply wise political action at the moment of transition from the old decentralized order of all Israel living in their holdings (1 Chron. 9.2) to the new regime, with its central focus, Jerusalem. It is the moment of the reconstitution of all Israel as the LORD's people under the LORD's anointed representative; the commitment of all is essential. Therefore, advisedly, David challenges the *qāhāl*, 'If it seems good to you'. But even more essential is the proviso that the impulse for the whole development comes from the LORD himself, 'if it is of the LORD our God'. But how could they know?

The Hebrew uses an unexpectedly violent verb in this context for the dynamic nature of the proposal of Israel (v. 2): *nipr^{e}ṣâ*, literally, 'let us *burst forth* and send to our brothers...' (cf. 2 Chron. 31.5, where it is again used of 'the word').

NRSV's 'if it is the will of the LORD our God' relates the verb to the previous phrase against the MT punctuation, and tacitly emends the reading to *nirṣ^{e}tâ*.

One may assume that the word has been deliberately chosen to express the hot-headed and unconsidered way in which David sets about an action that is perfectly laudable in itself (cf. his proposal to build a Temple in Jerusalem in 1 Chronicles 17: in principle, acceptable; in practice, unacceptable). The point of the narrative is to stress that the ark can only be handled in the way laid down in the Mosaic tradition (1 Chron. 15.15). Thus, the word is counterpoised in v. 11 and in 1 Chron. 15.13, where the action of God is described by the same drastic term: the LORD 'bursts forth' upon the perpetrator of an act that is not pleasing to him (cf. 1 Chron. 13.11; 14.11, where again the same root is used). David explains the need for the new order by explicit reference to Saul's failure. The verb (v. 3) 'let us bring again', better 'transfer', picks up the 'transfer' of kingship to David as already expressed in 1 Chron. 10.14; 12.23.

In this chapter, C uses a title, 'the ark of God', which is found elsewhere only in 1 and 2 Samuel (e.g. 1 Sam. 3.3), indeed, a title unique to himself, 'the ark of *our* God' (v. 3). In this context, the stress is on the cosmic nature of the Deity; therefore the term 'God' is employed rather than the domestic Israelite, 'the LORD' (cf. vv. 8, 12 [twice], 14, where C has changed the term from that in Samuel–Kings; see below on 'the Name', in v. 6). In more domestic contexts, C will later use the title for the ark particularly current in Deuteronomy, 'the ark of the covenant' (e.g., 1 Chron. 15.25; see above on 'the presence of the LORD' in 1 Chron. 11.3).

The *qāhāl* readily responds to David's proposal (v. 4). The new order commences. The unanimous commitment thus given is put into effect with concerted action: 'David assembled all Israel' (v. 5; C deliberately now uses the verb derived from *qāhāl*). The totality of the people is indicated by giving the widest possible definition of the land 'from the Shihor of Egypt, [i.e. the eastern branch of the Nile; cf. Isa. 23.3] to the entrance to Hamath [i.e. the northern Beqa' of Lebanon]'.

The phrase recurs in reversed form in 2 Chron. 7.8 = 1 Kgs 8.65. For this as a traditional definition of the limits of the land of Canaan, cf. Josh. 13.3-5.

The specification of Hamath is congenial to C's purpose; Hamath is Israel's immediate northern neighbour, the point at which Israel meets the outside world of the nations from which she herself took her origins. The gratitude of the king of Hamath for David's military might against their common foe, the Aramaeans of Damascus, belongs to C's scheme of not only the national, but also the now dawning international recognition of David (1 Chron. 18.9-10).

C hastens on in his narrative to make the main point (vv. 6-14): the ark betokens nothing less than the fearsome presence of the LORD. However great the artless joy of the people, however well-motivated their intention, God and his ark retain their awesome otherness, unapproachable to all except those whom God has designated himself (cf. 1 Chron. 15.2; cf. also the 2000 cubits—about 1 km—between the ark and the people in Josh. 3.4).

Many incidents of the story of the ark in 1 Sam. 4.1–7.2 are presupposed. These narratives explain how the ark had once been in the sanctuary at Shiloh, how it was later captured by the Philistines, and—the specific background of this narrative—how it came to be in Kiriath-jearim (v. 6), and who Abinadab was (v. 7).

From v. 6b the narrative runs closely parallel to 2 Sam. 6.2b-11, but even from it C omits the circumstantial detail that Uzza (C maintains this form of the name throughout) and Ahio were the sons of Abinadab.

Baalah (v. 6) is again identified with Kiriath-jearim in Josh. 15.9. The inappropriate resonance of the name of the place with that of the rival deity, Baal, may be a reason for C to retain it: this was no place for the ark of the LORD to be.

The awesome significance of the ark is already indicated by the title of God which C retains here from 2 Sam. 6.2: 'the LORD enthroned on the cherubim, as the Name is called' (v. 6).

The text may not be altogether sound; the Samuel text is fuller: 'the ark of God, over which the Name is called, the Name of the LORD of Hosts enthroned on the cherubim' ('to have one's name called over something' means 'to claim ownership of it', e.g. 2 Sam. 12.28). The emphasis in C's somewhat rearranged text as it now stands is no longer on the beneficent intervention of 'the LORD of Hosts' on behalf of his people (that point has already been made in 1 Chron. 11.9).

The title, 'enthroned on the cherubim', stresses the unapproachableness of God (cf. the cherubim protecting the way to the garden of Eden and the tree of life in Gen. 3.24) and his terrifying, free, transcendent power (the cherubim propel the throne-chariot of God, cf. 1 Chron. 28.18 and especially Ezekiel 1, 10; Pss. 18.10; 80.1; 99.1). It is by this title that God is to be known henceforth in his universal dominion exercised from Jerusalem (2 Kgs 19.15).

'Enthroned' (*yôšēb*) as the term of God's cosmic reign, and also of the human king's status as the representative and agent of that reign, is to be a recurrent theme in C (e.g., 1 Chron. 17.1).

The 'Name' of God, another of C's recurrent themes, implies both the transcendence (as here) and the immanence of God ('my Name can be *there*' e.g. 2 Chron. 6.5-6, and can be *known*, e.g. 2 Chron. 6.33). God cannot be known in himself but only in his relationship. But because he relates himself, he can be invoked by name, addressed in worship (e.g. 1 Chron. 16.8). In relationship, further, God reveals something of himself and this revelation provides authority for those who speak in his name (e.g. 1 Chron. 21.19) or bless in his name (e.g. 1 Chron. 16.2). The name of God is thus the spur to action: it is his revealed nature that is to be vindicated on earth, the fame by which the acknowledgment of all is to be won (e.g. 1 Chron. 17.24), the honour that is to be safeguarded and reverenced (e.g. 1 Chron. 16.29).

David and all Israel are aware of the sanctity of the ark: they place it upon a new cart so that no contamination may pollute it (v. 7, though the repetition of the adjective at the end of the verse in 2 Sam. 6.3 is omitted). But there is no hint that they observe—one must assume that they do not—the restrictions that it is only the Levites who may lift the ark (referred to in 1 Chron. 15.15 as a command of Moses of which they ought, thus, to have been aware; cf. Deut. 10.8; Num. 3.31; and so at the original entry into the land, Josh. 3.3, etc.). Its ascent towards Jerusalem is, indeed, accompanied by vocal and instrumental music typical in C of the Levites and priests (cf. the Levites already in 1 Chron. 6.31; for the priests, cf. 1 Chron. 15, 24); but, again, there is no statement that it was the priests and Levites who actually performed the music on this occasion. The very fact that song and instrumental accompaniment have still to be ordained by David as specific functions of the Levites in 1 Chronicles 15 (cf. 1 Chron. 6.31), when the ark is finally with all ordered seemliness brought into Jerusalem, suggest that here there is yet another false start (cf. 1 Chron. 1.1): Israel's rejoicing is at best a disorganized, over-exuberant tumult, a cacophony of raucous chant and blaring fanfare (v. 8).

> Lyres, lutes and cymbals are to be the instruments of the Levites, trumpets of the priests. Tambourines are specified here for the only time in C (but cf. Ps. 68.25).

In an instant (v. 9), the throng is silenced at 'the threshing floor of Chidon ["the javelin"]', a suitable place indeed for the sudden intervention of God.

> The site is otherwise unknown and differently named in 2 Sam. 6.6. It may be mere chance that the other awesome encounter David has with God is at another threshing floor in 1 Chronicles 21.

In a crowning act of populist piety Uzza, in misguided zeal, 'reaches out' to the ark (v. 9; C does not say that he even manages to touch it, as in Samuel–Kings), to steady it or save it from falling. The cattle should be left to know best (1 Sam. 6.12)! At once, at this very threat of infringement of the holy, impulsive and inadvertent though it be, the guilty individual is destroyed. The basic themes of C, presumptuous intrusion into the sphere of the Divine, and the penalty for even involuntary infringement of the holy, once more appear.

David's elation turns first to anger (v. 11) and then to terror (v. 12): anger that the celebrations conducted with the highest of motives and the most laudable of aims—to recreate the people of God around the symbol of the presence of God—has been blighted and spurned. The grim event David commemorates for all time by naming the spot Perez-Uzza, 'the breaking forth upon Uzza'. But David's profounder reaction is fear. An unreflective, carefree relationship, motivated even with the best of intentions, is impossible with such a God. He cannot be presumed upon; the initiative is always his; his demands have been declared and are absolute. To resort to the LORD does indeed mean total obedience and unreserved commitment. As the ark symbolizes God's presence, so one's duties towards the ark must be met with the same punctiliousness as one's duties towards God. David, chastened, needs time for reflection: is this God wholly arbitrary in his otherness, or are there appropriate actions whereby one may safely associate with this God?

> Already the element of the uncanny and the irrational is being reduced by C. Samuel's, 'How shall the ark...come to me?', that is to say, David was unwilling to take the ark home, as though the ark possessed by itself powers of blind destruction, is replaced by C's, 'How shall I bring...to me?', that is, David did not in fact take the ark home (v. 12). The focus has changed from blind fear of the irrational to the necessary preparations which David knows he must make to receive the token of the very presence of God within his own residence.

C emphasizes David's initiative in the whole matter. With due circumspection, David diverts the ark for a trial period into the household of Obed-edom. Will he too, like Uzza, be slain?

C retains the striking note that Obed-edom was a Gittite, that is, from the Philistine town of Gath. But, more significantly, in the sequel, C identifies Obed-edom as a Levite with responsibilities as 'gatekeeper to the ark' (1 Chron. 15.24), a lute-player among the temple musicians (1 Chron. 16.5), son, indeed, of Jeduthun (1 Chron. 16.38), and keeper of the Temple storehouses (2 Chron. 25.24). Obed-edom is not a conveniently expendable alien (cf. 1 Chron. 8.13, where the original population were driven out by Benjamin), but a Levite, one of the approved personnel. It is by such a one, himself consecrated to the services of the sanctuary, guardian of the sanctity of the ark and custodian of the people's paying of all their dues (cf. 1 Chron. 9.26), that the ark may be tended and brought into association with the Davidic house.

It is the experiences of this chapter that form the basis of the definitive act of bringing the ark into Jerusalem, as recorded in 1 Chronicles 15. David hereafter ensures that it is only under the leadership of those duly consecrated, as defined by the Law of Moses, that such an act can be performed.

Meantime, in ch. 14, C picks up 1 Chron. 11.9: he shows how David in the interim of waiting 'grew progressively greater' in the eyes of the neighbouring states (in Samuel this material in ch. 14 continues from 11.9). He too, like Obed-edom, is continuing to be blessed in all he does.

1 CHRONICLES 14.1–16.43: THE INSTALLATION OF THE ARK IN JERUSALEM

C has been expounding the statement in 1 Chron. 11.9 that 'David grew progressively greater because the LORD of Hosts was with him'. The human endorsement of David as king within Israel has been given with the unanimous support of the people (1 Chron. 11.10–12.40). David's plan has been to clinch theologically his status as the LORD's anointed by bringing into his new capital, Jerusalem, the ark of God, the visible symbol of God's dominion, with which that title 'LORD of hosts' is primarily associated. But in 1 Chronicles 13 the first attempt to fetch the ark has been abruptly cut short, invalidated because the instructions of Moses were not followed to the letter. David's plan seems to be no further forward.

1 Chronicles 14 opens the definitive stage in the bringing in of the ark, this time because it is done in full accord with the will of God. This accord is shown not just because it is done in conformity with the Law of Moses; more fundamentally, it is done because of David's total compliance with the way in which God is ordering events.

Given the volume and variety of the materials in the next three chapters (1 Chron. 14–16), it is perhaps as well at the outset to outline the closely interrelated argument that C is presenting (the analysis follows the MT paragraph markers).

David's advance continues in fact unchecked: God as the effective power behind David's reign disposes events in David's favour. Thus, international recognition now begins:

1 Chronicles

14.1-2	Tyre first, willingly, sends gifts to enable David to build his palace as the visible expression to all the world that he is indeed king of Israel.
14.3-12	David's status as king is evident from the number of wives he now takes. The Philistines are provoked into conflict with this upstart neighbour and begin to have to acknowledge against their will, after their defeat at Baal-

	perazim, that David is indeed the invincible king of Israel.
14.13–15.15	After the second defeat of the Philistines, the fame and fear of David spread through all lands and nations. The time has come to prepare the tent for the ark in Jerusalem: once again the assembly of all Israel is called but this time, in conformity with the Law of Moses, the ark is borne by the Levites.

The preparations for the appropriate liturgies to accompany the ark are now made:

1 Chronicles	
15.16	David commands the Levites to install their musicians in office (cf. 1 Chron. 6.31-47);
15.17-29	the musicians are installed and the ark is brought up from the house of Obed-edom to Jerusalem;
16.1-4	David concludes the ceremony with sacrifice and blessing;
16.5-7	David appoints Asaph as head of leader of praise;
16.8-22; 23-36	Asaph's psalm, in two sections;
16.37-43	David appoints Asaph and others to minister at the ark in Jerusalem and the remainder to minister in the tabernacle in Gibeon.

(The motif of 'building a house', whether as palace, Temple, or dynasty, will then link 1 Chron. 17 to the foregoing [cf. especially, 'house/houses', 1 Chron. 14.1; 15.1; 16.43]. The themes of international recognition will be resumed in 1 Chron. 18–20, and Temple-building from 1 Chron. 21–2 Chron. 7. 2 Chron. 8–9 again deals with the international recognition of the Davidic House: the climax of its fortunes are reached with Solomon's reign.)

It is appropriate, then, to consider this immediate material in two main sections: 1 Chron. 14.1–15.15, international recognition and preparations for installing the ark of God; and 1 Chron. 15.16–16.43, the installation of the ark of the covenant of the LORD in Jerusalem.

In these sections there are both substantial parallels to other biblical passages and substantial blocks of independent materials:

1 Chronicles	
14.1-16	cf. 2 Sam. 5.11-25;
14.17–15.2	independent;
15.3	cf. 2 Sam. 6.15;
15.4-24	independent;
15.25–16.3	cf. 2 Sam. 6.12b-19a;
16.4-7	independent;

16.8-22	cf. Ps. 105.1-15;
16.23-36	cf. Pss. 96.1b-13a; 106.1, 47-48;
16.37-42	independent;
16.43	cf. 2 Sam. 6.19b-20a.

2 Samuel 5–6 thus clearly provides C with the main framework for his argument, but is being used with great freedom.

1 Chronicles 14.1–15.15: International Recognition and Preparations for Installing the Ark of God

Whether the ark is physically present with David in Jerusalem or not does not affect the rule of God's vicegerent on earth: the power is available even if the symbol is lacking. God continues to control the destinies of nations.

The first of the nations of the world to accord David recognition is Israel's immediate neighbour on the northern coast, Tyre (v. 1). C's form of the name of the king of Tyre is Huram (*qere*; cf. 2 Chron. 2.3; Hiram in Samuel–Kings and English versions). The natural way for C's readers to interpret the name would be to understand it as related to the root of *ḥērem*, 'devoted thing' (1 Chron. 2.7), and thus to understand it to mean, 'the devoted one' (for form, cf. GKC §52s).

Technically, the name is an abbreviation of the name 'Ahiram', 'my brother is exalted/brother of the exalted one', known from Phoenician inscriptions, from quite different roots (cf. KBS). Such scientific knowledge is of relevance only in highlighting the distinctive character of C's presentation.

If so, there is a link here to C's central theme. 1 Chronicles 2.7 has introduced the point, precisely in relation to *ḥērem*, that the absolute requirement on Israel is to devote to God everything that is due to him. Huram, the 'righteous Gentile', does just that. He is to be a staunch ally to David in the supply of building materials—the famed cedars of Lebanon—and of skilled craftsmen for his palace. That support he is to continue in greatly intensified manner to Solomon in relation to the building of the Temple in Jerusalem (2 Chron. 2.3-16) and in the supply and manning of a trading fleet in the Red Sea (2 Chron. 8.18) and in the Mediterranean (2 Chron. 9.21).

The dependence of David on Tyrian masons and carpenters is slightly played down in C: 'to build a house for him' as contrasted with 2 Sam. 5.11, 'and they built...'

For David this recognition is confirmation ('Then David *knew*', cf. 1 Chron. 17.18) that the LORD of Hosts has indeed '*established* him as king over Israel' (v. 2).

Here C introduces what is to be a key term, *kûn*: as God 'establishes' David, so David 'establishes/prepares' the site for the ark (1 Chron. 15.1, 3, 12). Cf. 1 Chron. 17.11; 22.3, 10, 14; 28.2, 7; 29.2, 3, 16, 19; 2 Chron. 1.4; 2.7; 3.1; 6.2. It is also used of the inner disposition, 'to determine', 2 Chron. 12.14; 27.6; 30.19; 35.20.

It is God's purpose that David's kingship should be recognized, not merely for its own sake, but for the fulfilling of God's purpose through Israel: 'his kingdom was highly exalted for the sake of his people Israel' (v. 2; cf. 1 Chron. 11.2). Beyond the monarchy lies the destiny of the people; the monarchy is of utility when it enables the people to attain that destiny.

It may be that there is a deliberate pun in the adverb 'highly', which C adds to the Samuel text here: the Hebrew *(l*^{e}*)ma'lâ* echoes and presumably deliberately contrasts with the key word, *ma'al* (1 Chron. 2.7). There are a number of occasions later in the work, notably 2 Chron. 16.12, where such a play on words seems to be made (cf. 1 Chron. 22.5; 29.3, 25; 2 Chron. 1.1; 17.12; 20.19; 26.8), though sometimes the word is merely adverbial (1 Chron. 23.3, 24; 2 Chron. 4.4).

As in the parallel in 2 Sam. 5.13-16, there now follows a list of the 'sons and daughters' (though only sons are actually named here) born to David in Jerusalem (vv. 3-7). C's presentation is not constrained by mere chronological considerations: the birth of these children patently cannot fit into the three-month period while the ark is in the house of Obed-edom. The point of their introduction here, as in Samuel, is to interrelate the consolidation of David's position inside Israel and his growing international recognition. The verses relate back to 1 Chron. 11.4-9: Jerusalem has been captured, settled and consolidated. Its status is now further enhanced by the growth of the royal house of David. This enhanced status of Jerusalem is placed within the context of international recognition, voluntary in the case of the Tyrians (vv. 1-2), enforced in the case of the Philistines (vv. 8-16).

C has already used the material in vv. 4-7, with the same two sons additional to the Samuel version, within the context of the genealogy of the house of David, 1 Chron. 3.5-8: there are a few changes in wording and in the form of the names. Perhaps most interesting is the case of the second last son who is called here Beeliada ('Baal knows'), compare Eliada ('El knows') in 1 Chron. 3.8. A potential flaw in the devotion of the Davidic house is hereby announced (but cf. the place-name Baal-perazim retained in v. 11).

C adds in v. 3 the material from 2 Sam. 5.13, which he had omitted in 1 Chronicles 3. C, typically, abbreviates and smooths, omitting the reference to Hebron and, especially, the information in Samuel–Kings that David took to himself not only wives but also concubines (contrast Rehoboam, 2 Chron. 11.21). C's emphasis is on the equal status of all the sons born to David in Jerusalem. C also employs the more emphatic 'David begot' to the 'were born to David' of Samuel.

After the locking-piece of vv. 3-7, which connects the present chapter to the theme of the consolidation of David's position within Israel begun in 1 Chron. 11.1-9, C resumes in vv. 8-17 the impact David is making on the international scene.

The Philistines (for their key role in C as emblematic of the lurking power of the world of the nations, cf. 1 Chron. 1.12) are now thoroughly alarmed by the threatening turn of events. He who had formerly been their ally against Saul, the weak king of Israel (1 Chron. 12.19), has now himself 'been anointed king over *all* Israel' (v. 8).

C strengthens his underlying text in 2 Sam. 5.17 by adding 'all' (Samuel already has 'all the Philistines') and focuses more sharply on David by making him the subject of the verb rather than Samuel's 'they anointed David...'

A strong Israel under David is now in a position to engulf the favoured lands of the Philistines on the coastal plain. Accordingly, the Philistines launch two successive campaigns (vv. 8-12; 13-16), advancing on both occasions on Jerusalem by way of the valley of Rephaim (cf. 1 Chron. 11.15), which runs up from the west between Bethlehem and Jerusalem.

Both times C uses the verb *pšṭ* for the assonance with 'Philistines' as in 1 Chron. 10.8. No doubt they were hoping to repeat their successful tactics against Saul.

The military objective was presumably to threaten the new capital, while cutting it off from support from David's tribal power-base in Judah.

The main point of the narrative, in both C and Samuel, is that, before each engagement, 'David inquired of God' (vv. 10, 14). The verb used here (*š'l*) is the same as that used in connection with Saul in

1 Chron. 10.13 (there in addition to the synonym, *drš*). The contrast is made plain between the scrupulous faithfulness of David and the catastrophic faithlessness of Saul. At this moment of conflict with the world of the nations as represented by the Philistines, the Deity is referred to by his universal title 'God' (v. 10; Samuel uses the Israelite title 'the LORD'; so in vv. 11, 14, 15, 16, though not fully consistently. Cf. the title of the ark in 1 Chron. 13.3; 15.1, 'the ark of God').

David's reliance upon God is underlined in different ways in the two episodes. In the first he sallies boldly forth (the thematic term *yṣ'*, 1 Chron. 1.12, is used in v. 8; contrast 2 Sam. 5.17, where David beats a strategic retreat). But it is in no confidence in mere human strength that he goes: his question to God is not, 'If I advance on the Philistines, shall I be successful', but 'Shall I advance and will you deliver them into my power?' Battles are won not by the relative physical strengths of the opposing forces but by the determining will of God. (Cf. 2 Chron. 14.11; C again abbreviates the underlying Samuel text. For the motif of the LORD fighting for Israel, cf. 2 Chron. 13.15; 17.10; 20.15, 17, 29; 25.8; 32.8.)

On the successful outcome of the battle, David makes appropriate confession: 'God has burst through my enemies by my hand [human instrumentality in the approved service of God, rather than the 'before me' of Samuel] like a bursting flood' (v. 11). The root 'bursting out' (*prṣ*) is the same as that used in 1 Chron. 13.2, 11 of the dynamic irruption of the divine will. Because of this first signal success of David against the traditional foe, the Philistines, the place was known thereafter by a name reflecting that root, Baal-perazim, 'lord, or owner, of irruptive powers' (C retains the name despite the possibility of misunderstanding through association with Baal).

> This demonstration of divine power, perpetuated by the place name, was to become a ground of appeal for such divine intervention for later generations (if Mount Perazim in Isa. 28.21 is to be identified with the present place name).

C makes significant changes from the parent text in v. 12. The powerlessness of the opposing deities of the Philistines is made still clearer by him: it is not 'their idols' (so Samuel) that the Philistines abandon in their headlong rout, but 'their gods'. In Samuel David and his men carried these idols away; here, in scrupulous avoidance of contamination from the pollution of these pagan objects, David commands them to be burned.

On the occasion of the second attack by the Philistines (vv. 13-16), David again provides the model of obedient submission to God. The Philistines repeat their tactics (*pšṭ*) and their line of attack (v. 13, 'the valley'; Samuel adds 'of Rephaim'). David, flushed with success from the first engagement, might well have proceeded forthwith to repeat the manoeuvre which had brought him victory before. But, on the contrary, with a due sense of the primacy of God's continuing disposal of events, he submits the situation to God's control. This time the guidance is the opposite: the 'go up' of v. 10 is countered by, 'you shall not go up' (v. 14), followed by a tactical withdrawal and a feint to a clump of balsam trees. 'A sound of marching in the tops of the...trees' (v. 15) will then be the sign for the attack, for it will be the sound of the sallying forth of the cosmic powers mustered by the LORD of hosts, himself determining the outcome of the battle. Led by such a force, David sweeps the Philistines out of the hill country and the lowlands from Gibeon (the home-town of the powerless Saul, 1 Chron. 9.39) to Gezer.

2 Sam. 5.25 has 'Geba' for 'Gibeon' (cf. 1 Chron. 6.60; 8.6) and reads more cautiously, 'as far as the approaches to Gezer' (cf. 1 Chron. 20.4 for the location of Gezer on the Philistine frontier).

C's own climactic verse (v. 17) sums up David's progress to date and the realities of the situation. Among the world of nations, the primary sphere of God's activity (1 Chron. 1), David's repute grows as the leader of the nation realizing its destiny as the true people of God. But this progress in fame and respect could not be achieved but for the underlying reality of the action of God (for this respect, 'fear', *paḥad*, cf. Asa, 2 Chron. 14.14; Jehoshaphat, 2 Chron. 17.10; 19.7; 20.29).

After presenting the evidence of continuing divine favour shown by David's international prestige in 1 Chronicles 14, C returns in 1 Chronicles 15–16 to the theme of the central role of Jerusalem already begun in 1 Chronicles 11–13. Jerusalem's position at the heart of David's kingdom and nascent empire was to have been confirmed by the bringing in of the ark (1 Chron. 13). That action had, however, been marred by a presumptuous act whereby the holiness of the ark had been infringed. David had abandoned the enterprise for three months. In C's account the reason for the delay is not so much to test by the fate of its custodian whether the reasons for the LORD's displeasure had been correctly determined (C omits from his account

2 Sam. 6.12a, the news of the blessing of the house of Obed-edom, which was surely proof that the LORD's disposition towards his people was benign). Rather, the delay provides David with the opportunity to organize the appropriate procedures for the reception and care of the ark.

C's especial interest in the correct procedures for the installation of the ark is indicated by the very substantial addition of material that he makes to his base text in Samuel: only 15.25-29; 16.1-3, 43 have direct parallels in 2 Sam. 6.12b-20a. In the process, the Samuel material is radically transformed from the description of an impassioned display of religious fervour on David's part, compounded of eager desire to please and dread fear of divine displeasure, to one of stately, well-ordered ceremonial, its confidence in its approach to the holy based on its assurance that all is being carried out in accordance with the will of God revealed in the Torah.

David's arrangements for the installation of the ark proceed step by step in logical progression. Amid the bustle of the repair and extension of Jerusalem (1 Chron. 11.8), David 'prepared a place for the ark of God' (1 Chron. 15.1). This phrase virtually provides a title for the next two chapters: it includes not only the structure, indicated in the next phrase, 'and pitched a tent for it', but also the organization of the personnel and their functions as ministrants. The 'tent' is a special one for the purpose and is not to be confused with the Tent of Meeting, which is about to be pitched at Gibeon (1 Chron. 16.39). It reflects the long-standing tradition of the appropriate shelter for the ark as a movable object capable of being carried into battle, of the years of wandering in the wilderness (cf. 1 Chron. 17.5; Num. 10.35-36).

Strict adherence to the law that only the Levites may bear the ark, explicitly referred to in v. 13, and of which the Uzza incident had been a sharp reminder, is then enjoined (contrast 1 Chron. 13.7-10). With that stipulation, the attempt to fetch the ark, at first aborted, can be resumed, this time successfully: v. 3, 'David assembled (*qhl* again) all Israel', deliberately echoes 1 Chron. 13.5; it is also an anticipation of v. 28. Though it is only the Levites who may bear the ark, it is still in principle 'all Israel' who are involved in this act of unification around the central focus of the nation's life.

Having enunciated the general principle in v. 2, David now takes the appropriate action of gathering (*'sp*, another of the cluster of verbs for 'collecting', etc., noted at 1 Chron. 11.1) the priests and Levites

(vv. 4-10). The three branches of the Levites, Kohath, Gershom and Merari (1 Chron. 6.16-30: for the sequence here, 2 Chron. 29.12-14) are represented by their contemporary leaders: Uriel (v. 5) is of the ninth generation of Kohath according to the genealogy of 1 Chron. 6.24, and Asaiah of the eighth of Merari according to 1 Chron. 6.30. One would have expected to find the otherwise unnamed Joel (v. 7, though cf. 1 Chron. 23.8; 26.22 [BDB]) in the genealogy of Gershom in 1 Chron. 6.20-21, but, as noted there, that genealogy is incomplete. The relative numerical strengths of the three branches is striking: Kohath is the smallest despite the fact that it is the most privileged of the three, Merari the largest, though the lowest in status (see 1 Chron. 6.29-30).

At first sight it is puzzling that, having cited all three levitical branches by their leaders, C should then proceed to list an additional three (vv. 8-10), especially when, according to Exod. 6.16-24 and Num. 3.14-30, all of these three belong to the already mentioned branch of Kohath (Hebron, v. 9, and Uzziel, v. 10, are the third and fourth sons of Kohath; Elizaphan, v. 8, the second son of Uzziel). Num. 3.31 makes the reason for the specification of these three clear: they are the families responsible for the transportation and care of the 'holy things', including the ark. Their presence is, thus, essential for the due installation of the ark in David's Jerusalem.

It may be noted that in the list of Levites in 1 Chronicles 6 no mention had been made of these branches of the Levites beyond the names of their progenitors Hebron and Uzziel (1 Chron. 6.18), the interest in that chapter being concentrated on the Levites who function as priests and as Temple musicians. C takes the opportunity here to record these names for the first and only time in the Hebrew Bible.

When the whole body of priests and Levites has been assembled, David summons their responsible representatives—the two chief priests Zadok and Abiathar (C is not interested in suggesting any rivalry between these two, such as comes to a head in 1 Kings 1–2; the unity of the nation is his concern), and the leaders of the three main branches of the Levites and of the three houses with particular responsibility for the 'holy' (Num. 3.28)—for the transportation of the ark into Jerusalem (vv. 11-15).

The basic theme of C is touched upon once again. The whole of Israel's life is to be sanctified by being disposed around the ark in the centre in great concentric rings of ever heightened holiness as that centre is approached. Into the innermost circle, where the ark itself stands, where the LORD of hosts is enthroned above the cherubim, only those who have been specially set apart can presume to enter. For this awesome moment, those sanctified representatives of the people must again 'sanctify themselves' (by ablution, abstinence, Exod. 19.10, 15, and sacrifice, cf. Exod. 29): the root *qdš*, so typical of C's vocabulary, is here used for the first time in the narrative section (v. 12; cf. 1 Chron. 6.49; 9.29). With the verb *prṣ*, 'broke forth', v. 13, the grim reminder of the Perez-uzza incident of ch. 13 is made. For the ultimate purpose is that, in contradistinction to previous practice, the LORD may be resorted to (the verb *drš* in v. 13 picks up the key term already used in 1 Chron. 10.13; NRSV, 'we did not give it proper care', is a possible translation in the light of 1 Chron. 13.3, but does not penetrate so deeply into the heart of the matter). Only by the punctilious observance of the procedures as revealed by God to Moses can the ark be properly handled and God fitly consulted: in obedience to the king, it is these procedures that the Levites now fulfil to the letter. For the carrying of the ark by poles on the shoulders of the Levites, see Exod. 25.12-14, Num. 4.6, 15; 7.9, Deut. 10.8; 31.9, 25; 2 Chron. 35.3.

1 Chronicles 15.16–16.43: The Installation of the Ark of the Covenant of the Lord

MT places 1 Chron. 15.16 as a paragraph by itself to underline the momentous significance of the institution about to be created. The ark, borne into Jerusalem by Levites, must continue to be served by Levites. The ark is not an inert symbol, a mere talisman; its significance has constantly to be realized through the liturgy, both when it is carried in procession and when it is at rest in its sanctuary. It is through the power of the liturgy associated with the ark that the community is drawn into the significance of what the ark stands for—the dominion of God. Levites have, accordingly, to be set in office: as musicians to conduct the liturgy and as gatekeepers to protect the ark's sanctity. 1 Chronicles 15.16 thus functions as an introduction to the next sections of the presentation down to 1 Chron. 16.43: the identification of the musicians, the work they have to perform and the message they have to proclaim (thematic terms 'to proclaim', *hišmîa‘* [concealed in NRSV's translation, 'loud'], and 'joy' [*śimhâ* cf. 1 Chron.

12.40], which capture the spirit of celebration that pervades the whole, link introduction and following sections together, 1 Chron. 15.16, 19, 25, 28; 16.5, 10, 31, 42).

The initiative comes again from David. Already in 1 Chron. 6.31-47 David's designation of those who are to be singers in the liturgy 'from the time the ark came to rest...until Solomon built the Temple', that is, precisely the period inaugurated by the present chapter, has been recorded. David now commands that these appointments be put into effect by the chief Levites (those specified as chiefs in vv. 5-7?).

NRSV suggests that the chief Levites undertake the appointing of the singers. While the verb *he'ᵉmîd*, one of C's key terms, as indicated at 1 Chron. 6.31, can mean 'to appoint', it can also mean 'to put into operation', 'reinstate' a previous established institution, e.g. 2 Chron. 20.21. Here the sense is that the levitical leaders should 'present, install' those already designated (cf. the intransitive use of the same root, *'md*, in 2 Chron. 5.12 and the related noun of place in 2 Chron. 35.15).

1 Chronicles 15.17-25: The Levites Attending the Ark as Singers and Gatekeepers

In contrast to the free exuberance of the abortive first attempt to bring in the ark (1 Chron. 13), C now stipulates that only Levites duly consecrated for the task can appropriately conduct the procession.

The organization of the music appears to be as follows. There is a chief musician appointed from each of the three families of Levi: Heman from Kohath, Asaph from Gershom and Ethan from Merari (cf. table at 1 Chron. 9.12-32).

MT divides the section into two paragraphs of very unequal length, v. 17a and vv. 17b-25. The effect is once again to list the levitical families in descending order of importance and to separate Kohath and Gershom (v. 17a) from Merari, who is brought directly into association with the musicians and gatekeepers (vv. 17b-25; for the separation of Merari, cf. 1 Chron. 6.29, 44-47; 9.14-16).

These three leaders sound the cymbals (v. 19). Along with them are their fourteen instrumentalists of the 'second rank', also termed 'gatekeepers' (v. 18), eight playing lutes and six playing lyres.

The lists in vv. 18 and 20-21 do not quite correspond—v. 21 adds the fourteenth name. None of the players (except Obed-edom, especially, cf. 1 Chron. 13.14, Mattithiah, 1 Chron. 16.5; 25.3, 21, and Jeiel, 2 Chron. 20.14) occurs elsewhere in the Hebrew Bible.

The precise significance of the musical (?) directions in vv. 20-21 is unclear (cf. KBS): 'According to Alamoth' occurs in the title of Ps. 46.1 and is perhaps to be restored to the title of Psalm 49 from 48.14, 'for ever'; one would expect it to mean 'according to maidens', cf. Ps. 68.25, 'between them maidens playing timbrels'. 'According to the Sheminith' (literally, 'the eighth'—the eighth string? the [lower] octave?) recurs in the title to Psalms 6 and 12.

The three-fold reference to 'gatekeepers' (vv. 18, 23, 24; cf. 1 Chron. 9.17-26) emphasizes the absolute necessity for preserving the sanctity of the ark and supervising all the rites associated with it.

The role of the official in v. 22 is unclear: 'Chenaniah, the leader of the Levites in lifting; he instructed in lifting because he had or imparted understanding (*mēbîn*)'. The word 'lifting' (*maśśā'*) has several possible meanings. NRSV translates it as 'music', that is, the lifting of the voice (cf. its frequent use of prophetic utterance, e.g. 2 Chron. 24.27; Isa. 13.1–23.1). If so, the specific sense may be the actual words sung to the accompaniment of the music, the liturgy itself (cf. 1 Chron. 16.8-36). Alternatively, since the word *maśśā'* is used specifically in the context of bearing the ark in 2 Chron. 35.3 (in which context the word *mēbîn*, 'have or impart understanding', recurs), that is a very likely meaning for it here: the actual lifting of the ark itself is under the supervision of the chief porter (again otherwise unknown; cf. v. 27, where, however, the text is problematical).

It is striking, in view of the reconstruction of C's view of the history of the sanctuary before the founding of the Temple offered above (1 Chron. 11.3; 15.1), to note the great concentration of occurrences of the word *maśśā'* in Numbers 4 (vv. 15, 19, 24, 27 [twice], 31, 32, 47, 49), precisely in connection with the transportation of the Tabernacle by the three levitical families.

Yet a third possible meaning of *maśśā'* has to be seriously entertained—'contribution' (cf. the related noun *maś'ēt* in 2 Chron. 24.6, 9, a context central to elucidating the reason for the disapproval of David's census in 1 Chronicles 21; cf. also the use of the related verb *nś'* [BDB, s.v., *qal* 2(e), 'bring (an offering)']). If this Chenaniah is the same as the individual mentioned in 1 Chron. 26.29 (cf. 2 Chron. 31.12-13), who was in charge of overseeing the contributions of the laity country-wide, then the reference here is to this levy. It would be appropriate at this solemn moment of the muster of the people to accompany the bearing of the ark into Jerusalem that the capitation tax for atonement should be levied to avoid a recurrence of the breaking out of the LORD as in 1 Chronicles 13 (the key term for the muster, *pqd*, occurs both in the context of the Chenaniah of 1 Chron. 26.30, 32 and in the legislation on the muster in Exod. 30.12; see further on 1 Chron. 21.2).

The stationing of the appropriate Levites is completed by the specification of the seven priests (otherwise unknown). It is the prerogative of the priests alone to sound the trumpets (e.g. 1 Chron. 16.6; cf. Num.10.8 and contrast the improper use implied in the first, abortive attempt to fetch the ark in 1 Chron. 13.8). In shattering sound that is beyond the expression of words, the blaring trumpets announce the theophany (Num. 10.9-10; 31.1-12), the arrival of God the victor in battle, now ritualized by the arrival of his ark in his sanctuary. The Levites with their psalms sing the ordered verbal response of the community to this self-manifestation of God.

It is only when such designated personnel are duly in place and carrying out their appointed duties—they and no-one else—that David and the representatives and leaders of Israel can proceed with the bringing in of the ark of the victorious cosmic God. It has been to make that point that C has inserted all the material in vv. 4-24. Having made that clear, C is now in a position to rejoin the Samuel source (v. 25). But C points up the underlying Samuel text: whereas 2 Sam. 6.12b reads in matter-of-fact way, 'David went and brought up the ark of God...', C now makes it an act of all Israel, in order to expunge the failure of 1 Chronicles 13: 'So it was David and the elders of Israel and the leaders...who were the ones who went to bring up the ark....'

The ark is now designated by C with the title, 'the ark of the covenant of the LORD' (v. 25). While in the preceding chapter in the context of the international recognition of David, and in the previous verse in celebration of God's cosmic victory, it had been the universal term for Deity that had been used ('the ark of *God*'; so Samuel still here), C is now concerned about the inner-Israel significance of the ark: at this formal moment of the final integration of symbol and reality at the centre of the nation's life, it is Israel in relation to the LORD, the name by which Deity has been made known to Israel alone, as the people of the LORD that stands now in the forefront of interest (C adds the term 'covenant' to the Samuel text also in vv. 26, 28; 1 Chron. 17.1; cf. 1 Chron. 11.3).

1 Chronicles 15.26-29: The Triumphal Procession

The narrative of the entry of the ark into Jerusalem now follows (vv. 26-29). It is an event of harmony and immediacy between God and his people under David. The ideal character of the moment is indicated by a number of features.

The complete oneness of David's action with the will of God is indicated by the fact that he fulfils the role of chief priest: there is no bar of unworthiness excluding him from this supreme function. Here is monarchy at its fullest potential: Israel under David can realize that perfect bond with God that is God's own desire and design. The approval of God is evidenced by his supplying of favourable assistance (key term, *'zr*, 1 Chron. 5.20) to the Levites, the official bearers of the ark. C's version, with this strong emphasis on the prevenient grace of God, is in contrast to that of Samuel, where, after six fearful paces, ox and fatling are sacrificed to avert any possible displeasure on the part of God.

Oneness between God and people is further evidenced by the holocausts of 'seven bulls and seven rams' (v. 26). (C's plural 'they' to the 'he' of Samuel, namely, David, continues to stress the unanimity of the whole people just expressed in v. 25.) The question that immediately occurs to one about the location of the altar at which this sacrifice was offered is immediately answered on the assumption that the tabernacle, including the portable brazen altar of holocaust (Exod. 27.1-8), is being borne by the three families of Levites (cf. one of the possible meanings of *maśśā'*, v. 22).

The harmony of the occasion is made the more striking by a comparison of this ceremony under David with the ceremony of the rededication of the Temple under Hezekiah in 2 Chron. 29.21-24, where the consciousness of alienation from God and the need for atonement in consequence of the long series of acts of *ma'al*, culminating in his father Ahaz's closing down of the Temple, requires the addition of the seven goats as sin offering, of which there is no mention here.

It is perhaps further witness to the freedom and naturalness of the relationship between God and people ('theonomy') at this time that the sacrifice offered corresponds to none of the sacrifices detailed as proper to any particular occasion in the legal prescriptions in the Pentateuch (as in Num. 28–29). The only similar instances belong to other exceptional occasions that are equally 'outside the law', and, indeed, involving, non-Israelites: Balaam (Num. 23.1, 29) and Job's friends (Job 42.8). Ezekiel's equally free vision of the future order of festivals, includes, nonetheless, the goat of the sin offering (Ezek. 45.23).

Even further testimony is the role played by David himself (v. 27): David is here the chief priest, the intermediary between his people and God. He is clad in the priestly garment of linen (the robe *m*^{e}*'îl*, in which it is tempting to see a deliberate pun on *ma'al*—one derivation of *ma'al* being from *m*^{e}*'îl*, 'cloak', that is, 'covering, masking true motives', just as a synonym, *beged*, means both 'garment' and 'treachery'). While the robe elsewhere in the Hebrew Bible is recognized as being worn principally by members of royal families (1 Sam. 18.4; 24.5; 2 Sam. 13.18; Ezek. 26.16), it is one of the 'holy garments' (Exod. 28.2) worn by the priesthood, to set them apart (Exod. 28.3), described in Exod. 28.31-34.

That David is indeed dressed as a priest is made unambiguous by the reference at the close of the verse to his wearing an ephod, a vestment worn above the *m*^{e}*'îl* by the priest, again described in Exodus 28 (vv. 4-14). The wearing of the ephod expresses clearly the mediatorial role of the wearer: on the two stones attached to the ephod as described in Exod. 28.9-12 were engraved the names of the twelve tribes of Israel, which were thus carried on his very garments by the priest as he approached God. Equally, the ephod, through its association with the sacred lots of *'ûrîm* and *tūmmîm*, was part of the essential means whereby God communicated his divine guidance to his people (e.g. 1 Sam. 23.9-12). Both by bringing in the ark and by wearing the ephod, David was 'resorting to the LORD' for guidance, in the most complete ways possible (contrast Saul, 1 Chron. 10.13-14): only through such a figure, with direct and immediate access to God, can the ideal of Israel's vocation to be the people of God be realized.

As a foil, C retains the unfavourable reaction of Saul's daughter Michal in v. 29, to reinforce the contrast between David's joyous fulfilment of his kingly role as the one who resorts to the LORD, and the sour, dismissive intransigence of the deposed royal house, who maintain their disdain of such vehicles of resorting to the LORD as the ark (cf. their neglect, cited in 1 Chron. 13.3) and the ephod.

Suitably to his presentation of the occasion in v. 26, where the divine gracious initiative is stressed and the fear-ridden placation of a potentially angry deity is omitted, C describes the comportment of David in more restrained and dignified terms than Samuel: his is no longer the wild frenzy of the dervish in ecstatic possession, but measured celebration in dance and song to the accompaniment of the levitical singers and musicians (vv. 27-29).

The text of C's added phrase in v. 27aβγ, 'and all the Levites....the singers', is uncertain. The NRSV has, in fact, emended the text in the phrase 'leader of the music of the singers'. MT reads, 'and all the Levites, who were bearing the ark, and the singers, and Chenaniah the leader as regards the lifting, the singers'.

Verse 28, 'So all Israel were bringing up [*ma'ᵃlîm*; another play on *ma'al*?] the ark...' rounds off v. 3. Their 'shouting' (*tᵉrû'â*) is no mere baying of a rabble, but the organized festal acclamation of the coming of God into their midst, awesome in his holiness, majesty and power. (For other occasions on which the festal shout [*tᵉrû'â*] was raised, see, for example, New Year's Day, Lev. 23.24, Num. 29.1; acclaiming the dynamic advent of God as king in the liturgy of the cult, Ps. 47.5; celebrating his feats of deliverance in the fields of creation and of battle, Ps. 33.3, cf. Josh. 6.5, 20; 1 Sam. 4.5, 6; cf. use below at 2 Chron. 13.12; 15.14.) The association with the jubilee is particularly appropriate (Lev. 25.9), the announcement of the definitive restoration of the community to its ideal state: here Israel under David is in the condition that C can only look forward to in the end time (cf. 2 Chron. 36.22-23). The jubilee is also inaugurated with the sounding of the 'horn' (*šôpār*, Lev. 25.9), the public announcement and summons to the community at large to respond to a decisive moment (cf. other associations of the *šôpār* with a new reign [e.g. 1 Kgs 1.34], mobilization for war [e.g. Judg. 3.27] or demobilization [e.g. 2 Sam. 2.28], the Day of the LORD [Joel 2.1], cf. use in the liturgy, Pss. 47.5; 81.3; 98.6; 150.3).

1 Chronicles 16.1-4: The Installation of the Ark in the Tent which David Has Prepared for It (1 Chronicles 15.1)

Again, the joyous spontaneity of the new order is expressed by whole burnt offerings and communion sacrifices (v. 1) offered on the brazen altar as in 1 Chron. 15.26. C again emphasizes the all-Israel aspect by reading 'they offered' for the 'David offered' of 2 Sam. 6.17. David's supreme mediatorial role as priest is extended (v. 2) by his blessing of the people at the conclusion of the sacrifice (cf. Num. 6.23-26; Ecclus.

50.20-21). David's subsequent act of distributing provisions to every individual, recorded also in Samuel, is without parallel in the Hebrew Bible (even the meaning of the terms 'a portion of meat, and a cake of raisins' is uncertain). It may be understood as an act of royal hospitality and table fellowship confirming the bond between king and people and the solidarity of their action. But also striking is that the root of the verb 'to distribute' (*ḥlq*) is to be highly typical of C's presentation of David's reign: David is the one who apportions not only supplies to his people as here but also rosters of duties to the priests and Levites (1 Chron. 23.6).

There is a certain similarity between the role filled by David here, as cult founder, and that of Moses. Moses, too, was *ad hoc* officiant at the altar (Exod. 24.7, 8; necessarily so at the institution of the Aaronic priesthood in Lev. 8); summoner (*qhl*) of the people (Exod. 35.1; Num. 20.10); pitcher of tent for the ark (Exod. 33.7); and blesser of the people (Deut. 33.1). As David has already been presented as a new Joshua (1 Chron. 12.15), so, in fact more typically, here he is portrayed as the new Moses, uniquely favoured with intimacy with God, above and beyond the forms and institutions of worship that he is to bequeath to be observed after him (cf. 1 Chron. 22.13; 2 Chron. 23.18).

C at this point breaks off from his parent Samuel text, to resume it virtually without omission at v. 43 with the note of the departure of the people to their homes. For C, however, this is the critical moment of the bifurcation of the sanctuary. The ark now stays in David's capital, Jerusalem; the altar and the tabernacle, meanwhile, go to Gibeon (1 Chron. 16.39). It is Solomon, the builder of the Temple, who will achieve the definitive integration of the sanctuary (2 Chron. 5–7).

The account of the installation of the ark would not be complete were no mention made of arrangements appropriate to the maintenance of the relations between God and people through the intermediacy of the ark, the proper form, that is, of 'resorting to the LORD'. The climax of the installation is, accordingly, the appointment of Levites to undertake the perpetual service of the ark (v. 4).

The functions of these Levites are defined in three terms, all concerned with liturgical worship: 'to invoke, to thank, and to praise the LORD'. The last two are clear enough: the Levites appointed have the task of expressing the thanks on particular occasions, especially in the life of the community, perhaps also of the individual, for special benefit received (such as victory gained, recovery from sickness); they have also the responsibility of raising the hymn in praise of God's mighty works in creation and redemption (there are numerous psalms that fit either category, for example, Ps. 66 for the thanksgiving, Ps. 8 for the hymn).

The nature of the first task of the Levites is less clear: the verb (*lehazkîr*) is used with the noun 'name' in the sense of 'to invoke' (e.g. Exod. 20.24), as NRSV translates, though 'name' is not actually mentioned here. It can also, however, mean, when used by itself, as here, 'to recall', especially 'to bring to light' past offences (Num. 5.15, 1 Kgs 17.18), hence, virtually, 'to confess'. Given that there are so many Psalms of lament in the Psalter, one might expect reference to be made to them here alongside the thanksgiving and the hymn. That this may be the case here is suggested by the fact that *lehazkîr* appears in the title of two Psalms (38 and 70), both of which are laments, and the first of which is a penitential psalm. The source of the material in vv. 34-36 and the implication of v. 35 clearly suggests such an element (see below).

1 Chronicles 16.5-7: The Personnel at the Ark under Asaph

The list of the names of the Levites and priests appointed by David 'for the first time' (v. 7) for this work is given in vv. 5-6. The individuals mentioned are largely drawn from those listed in 1 Chron. 15.17-18, with some omissions and changes in form of name or sequence. Of the three chief musicians, only Asaph of the line of Gershom is now retained, as are nine of the fourteen musicians of the second rank and one of the priests, plus one new one, making twelve in all. They, with their prayers and praises set to music, are to be in perpetual attendance before the ark. This association of Asaph with the ark is to be of significance in the later narrative in connection with victories on the battlefield still to be won (2 Chron. 20.14-22; cf. 29.13; 35.15).

1 Chronicles 16.8-36: The Psalms of Asaph

There now follows in vv. 8-36 the thanksgiving and confession appointed by David.

> Given the other Psalms of Asaph noted already at 1 Chron. 6.31-42, and the fact that the present passage is made up of only parts of three different Psalms (vv. 8-22 = Ps. 105.1-15; vv. 23-33 = Ps. 96.1b-13a; vv. 34-36

= Ps. 106.1, 47-48, all with minor variations), all without ascription in the Psalter, it is likely that these verses are only a small sample of Asaph's repertoire.

The three parent Psalms, from which vv. 8-36 are derived, each belong to a distinctive category of Psalm: Psalm 105 is a great song of national thanksgiving for the mighty acts of God in bringing his people into being through the deliverance from Egypt and their safe conduct through the wilderness; the Psalm ends with the significant comment on the reason for this deliverance and safekeeping: 'that they [Israel] might keep his statutes and observe his laws' (Ps. 105.45), that is, that God's ideal commonwealth might be realized. Psalm 96 is a pure hymn celebrating the universal dominion of the LORD as creator. Psalm 106, by contrast, is a long confession of historic national sin. By combining material from these three Psalms, each of a different category, C is exploiting the resources of Israel's liturgical heritage in the fullest possible way within the limited space of these verses. His selection is a distillation of the material most relevant to his theme of Israel's vocation to realize God's purposes among the nations of the world, their abject and repeated failure to do so, and their continuing dependence on new acts of God's pardon and restoration.

The features in these Psalm passages quoted by C that are most apposite for his purpose may now be noted. C's composite Psalm begins, naturally enough, with a summons to Israel (vv. 8-13), 'offspring of Israel' (RSV, 'Abraham', emends the text in the light of Ps. 105.6: but for C the point is the role of *Israel* within the descendants of Abraham [so now NRSV]; cf. the parallel, 'sons of Jacob' [v. 13]) to give thanks to God and to invoke his name (1 Chron. 4.10). It is notable that this thanksgiving is no mere giving vent to private devotion in the intimacy of the Temple liturgy, but is the active proclamation 'among the peoples' (v. 8), the very world of the nations from which Israel took its origin in order to fulfil God's purpose (1 Chron. 1). But the mainspring of such a proclamation is the vivid bringing to mind ('remember' v. 12) of the 'wonderful works that he has done' and Israel's total surrender in full joyous commitment to celebrate them and to realize them as the source and basis of their true being. This is expressed in v. 10, 'glory in his holy name' (cf. 1 Chron. 13.6): their authentic being can be affirmed only in the name, that is, the revealed nature of Israel's God as holy, his nature as the awesome, transcendent one, whose purpose none dare infringe or thwart. In the word, 'holy' (*qdš*, 1 Chron. 6.49), the basic theme of the whole of C's work is thus touched on already at the beginning of the psalm. The objective physical expression of this devotion to God and commitment to his will is also noted: 'seek the LORD and his strength' (with the key term 'seek', *drš*, 1 Chron. 10.13-14, signifying the exclusive resorting to God). Under the figure of 'his strength', the ark as the focus and symbol of the divine presence is meant (JPSV notes this point with reference to 'strength' as a title of the ark in Pss. 78.61; 132.8). The psalm thus relates directly to the immediately preceding narrative of the bringing of the ark to Jerusalem.

The reference to the ark in v. 11 provides the bridge to the immediately following section (vv. 14-22; so also 'judgments', vv. 12, 14). The ark as container of the tablets of the Decalogue (Deut. 10.1-5) testifies (cf. Exod. 25.16, etc.) to the covenant relationship between God and Israel. It is this covenant that specifies the basic character of the God, whom Israel has been summoned to thank in vv. 8-13. Once again the universal context of God's dealing with his people is stated at the outset (v. 14): the covenant with Israel has the widest implications for Israel's role amid the nations (1 Chron. 1). In the MT, v. 15 actually begins with an imperative, 'Remember', and admonition to Israel, as in v. 12, to bear constantly in mind, and live continually by, the fact that God has bound his people to himself 'for a thousand generations'. The obligation on Israel as well as the grace of God are stressed.

In v. 16 C now retains the reference to Abraham (cf. the location of the Temple-to-be on Abraham's Mount Moriah, 2 Chron. 3.1). It is a psalm recalling the covenant with the founding patriarch of the people (Gen. 12; 15; 17), rather than the formal covenant with the people itself as a whole at Sinai (Exod. 19–24), that C finds it most apposite to cite. The content of this most basic covenant is the oath sworn by God to the patriarchs: 'To you I will give the land of Canaan' (v. 18). C also cites the Psalmist's confession that in the interim of waiting for the fulfilment of the covenant promise, God allowed no-one (in v. 21 the underlying text is changed from 'humankind' to 'any individual'), no matter how exalted in rank in human terms, to molest his tiny vagabond people, who are, nonetheless, God's kingdom of anointed priests, the inspired bearers of his word. There is pathos and point in this: for C, Israel is still 'in exile', still the homeless wanderer on the face of the earth at the mercy of the great powers. For the Israel in this unchanged predicament it is the promises to the original founding father, himself in still greater weakness and vulnerability than his latest descendants, that are of especial meaning and benefit. But Abraham has a still wider significance: as the 'father of a multitude of nations' in the twentieth generation after creation (1 Chron. 1) he binds together the fate of Israel and the wider circle of the human race.

The third section of C's composite psalm (vv. 23-33) corresponds to the first (vv. 8-13); they are linked thematically by the words 'wonderful works' (vv. 9, 12, 24), 'strength' (vv. 11, 28) and 'judge' (vv. 12, 33). Like the first, so the second is a summons to praise God, only this time those summoned are not Israel, the recipients of special favour, but the whole world, its inhabitants, the nations and peoples (vv. 23-30a), and creation as a whole, heavens, earth, sea and land, and the trees of the forest (vv. 30b-33). For this wider company, the appropriate response is the hymn in praise of God's universally and perpetually recognizable glory and might in the created universe (e.g. v. 26b) and also his universal dominion over the destinies of the nations (e.g. v. 31b), rather than the thanksgiving for the particular gift of the covenant, as in the summons to Israel in vv. 8-22).

This universal summons corresponds to C's purpose: his work begins with Adam, the father of humankind, created for immediacy of fellowship with God. All Adam's children are now summoned to acknowledge God's purpose portrayed in Israel's history, his sole deity and transcendent power declared in creation and to 'ascribe to the LORD the glory due to his name' (v. 29; thus the cosmic dimensions of the tradition of Jerusalemite royal theology as in v. 26b are affirmed not only by kings Solomon, 2 Chron. 6.14, 18, and Jehoshaphat, 2 Chron. 20.6, but acknowledged by foreign kings Huram, 2 Chron. 2.12, and Cyrus, 2 Chron. 36.23). It is difficult in this phrase not to find an echo of the appeal of Joshua to the convicted Achan in Josh.7.19 (cf. 1 Chron. 2.7), 'to give glory to the LORD', that is, to confess, God's knowledge of the infringement of the holy things which has been committed, and his justice in exercising his rule among humankind. The nations are called, accordingly, to make confession of their submission, to acknowledge with dread God's sovereignty, and, clad in fitting garb ('holy array', root *qdš*), to bring their tribute (*minḥâ* now to become the technical term for the recognition of God and of David as his vicegerent, 1 Chron. 18.2, 6; 2 Chron. 9.24; 17.5, 11; 26.8; 32.23).

C does not say, 'to his sanctuary', or, 'to his courts', as in Ps. 96.6, 8, for, on his scheme of things, the Temple has not yet been constructed. Rather, he reads, 'in his place', v. 27; cf. 'place' in 1 Chron. 15.1, and, 'before him', v. 29.

Thus the nations recognize that in Israel God has fulfilled his salvation, the destiny intended for humankind. It is in this glorious consummation of the purpose of God that all created nature is summoned to rejoice, the universe which finds itself restored to harmony in the reconciliation of the human race, through the universal acknowledgment of the reign of God (vv. 30-33).

C makes the interconnection of the rejoicing of nature and the acknowledgment of God by humankind tighter by transposing v. 31b from its position in the Psalm between v. 30a and 30b by changing the verb from the imperative 'say' to the jussive 'let them say'.

Using the opening of Psalm 106, 'O give thanks to the LORD, for he is good' (the epithet of God to be appealed to in 2 Chron. 30.18), C's composite Psalm resumes the summons of its beginning as if to round the whole composition off (v. 34). But immediately a note of sombre realism is struck: the picture of the previous section of nature rejoicing in unison, with the universal acknowledgment of the sovereignty of God, is an ideal that awaits its consummation in the future. Israel, indeed, is still 'in exile'. The mood of the Psalm therefore changes to petition: 'Deliver us, O God of our salvation', both 'deliver' and 'salvation' being words derived from the same root, which has already been used in v. 23 (*yš'*, 1 Chron. 11.14). C intensifies the appeal of the Psalm by adding 'salvation' and, in the next phrase, 'rescue us' (*nṣl*, 1 Chron. 11.14). God's wonderful deeds of deliverance have been made manifest in the past; the final marvellous work awaits its time, when Israel will be gathered 'from among the nations', those same corrupting powers from among which it was called at the beginning. This ultimate act will be performed in the final inscrutability of the divine purpose, when God acts for his name's sake and when, in response, Israel will give thanks to that same holy name (again the root *qdš*). The Psalm therefore closes with an expression of pure, objective worship, 'Blessed be the LORD, the God of Israel', wrung from the heart of Israel 'in exile' awaiting in humble patience that glorious future deliverance whose dawning lies concealed in the unfathomable mystery of the divine will. The words are, in fact, part of the closing doxology of the entire fourth book of the Psalter (Pss. 90–106), the contents of which C has thus freely used for his composite psalm. The final phrase of the doxology, 'And let all the people say, "Amen!" Praise the LORD' (Ps. 106.48), C has actually incorporated into his narrative, changing the verbs from the jussive to the indicative: 'Then all the people said, "Amen", and praised the LORD'. The model of devotion provided by the Psalm is translated into the actualities of life.

1 Chronicles 16.37-43: The Bifurcation of the Sanctuary

Verses 37-38 pick up 1 Chron. 16.4-6 and repeat their substance. The role of Merarites is again significant. Jeduthun is a Merarite (cf. 1 Chron. 6.44); Hosah recurs in 1 Chron. 26.10-19, where he too is identified as a Merarite. This appointment of Merarites to care for the tent within which the ark is now placed links with the wider duties of the Merarites in connection with the tabernacle (Num. 4.29-33). The presence of Merarites in both parts of the institutions thus affirms the ideal unity of the one sanctuary now temporarily divided.

The task of Asaph is 'to minister before the ark': what this involves has already been defined in 1 Chron. 16.4 as 'to confess, to give thanks and to praise', that is, through the words of the liturgy as reflected in the Psalter. 'As each day requires' presumably means that the psalms proper to each day whether ordinary weekday, Sabbath or festival, are to be sung by Asaph and his brethren.

Verses 39-42, which concern the tent of meeting and the altar of burnt-offering at Gibeon, do not strictly belong to the narrative of events concerning the ark in Jerusalem, but are added, nonetheless, because these two institutions, the tent and the ark, remain in the meantime the foci of Israel's worship until David constructs the altar in Jerusalem (1 Chron. 22.1) and Solomon has completed the building of the Temple (2 Chron. 2–7).

The 'tabernacle of the LORD' is the tabernacle associated with the period of the wandering in the wilderness (Exod. 25.9, etc.), which now ends up at Gibeon. Notably, when C specifies the priest who functions at Gibeon, he mentions only Zadok, omitting Abiathar (contrast 1 Chron. 15.11), whose line is destined to be supplanted in the intrigues surrounding Solomon's accession in 1 Kings 1–2. The duties of the Zadokite priesthood are there defined as the offering of the continual burnt offering in punctilious observance of the revealed law of God (cf. Num. 28–29).

As C has already stated in 1 Chron. 6.31-47, David was responsible for the organization of the levitical singers. This passage now makes clear that they are in the meantime divided as to location: whereas Asaph and his brethren of the line of Gershon officiate before the ark in Jerusalem, Heman and Jeduthun of the lines of Kohath and Merari function in Gibeon (v. 41). Their duties are, like those of Asaph, 'to give thanks to the LORD', singing to the accompaniment of the same types of musical instrument. A snatch of their typical thanksgiving is reproduced, 'for his steadfast love endures for ever', a frequent refrain in the Psalter (Pss. 100.5; 106.1; 107.1; 118.1-4, 29; 136.1-26), which has already occurred in Asaph's psalm in 1 Chron. 16.34, and which C is to make use of again in 2 Chron. 5.13; 7.3, 6; 20.21.

With v. 43, C resumes the narrative as in 2 Sam. 6.19. The Davidic organization of priest and Levite before ark and altar being now carried out, the populace as a whole, who have given their total assent and support, are now free to depart. The next phase in the consolidation of David's power is about to begin: David, having as chief priest blessed his people (1 Chron. 16.2), now 'turns' [Samuel, 'returns'] to bless his house. The word 'house', with which the chapter ends, forms the link to the next chapter: David, having glorified his own house, desires to build a fitting house for God. God's reply, through the prophetic word of Nathan, is that it is God who will build for David a house, not David for God. C makes this transition from 'house' to 'dynasty' the clearer by omitting the distracting material on David's wife, Michal, daughter of Saul (2 Sam. 6.20b-23), useful foil though it might have provided.

1 CHRONICLES 17: DAVID'S PROPOSAL TO BUILD A TEMPLE IS REJECTED

For the second of three occasions (cf. 1 Chron. 13; 21) David rushes into an action on his own terms. Once again the action is, with qualifications, intrinsically acceptable; but David has to learn once more hard lessons about reliance upon God. Even acceptable proposals offered with the best of intentions are unacceptable if not taken on God's initiative and on God's terms.

The argument of the chapter has a number of layers, which only become fully apparent if the chapter is set within the wider context of David's reign. A preliminary review of the argument is in order.

1 Chronicles 17 is closely parallel to 2 Samuel 7. Significant variations will be noted below.

David is assailed by a sense of the absurd inappropriateness of his position. He, the agent, is enjoying the ultimate in luxury and status, a palace panelled in cedar-wood, an expression of his position among the world of the nations endorsed by God himself (1 Chron. 14.1-2), while the ark, the symbol of the cosmic power of the LORD of hosts which upholds his throne, is installed in a tent (1 Chron. 15.1). David proposes to remedy the gross imbalance by constructing a new Temple for the ark in Jerusalem.

God's responds to David's proposal at a number of levels. First, a Temple is not necessary as the symbol of God's dominion. The original significance of the ark was as the symbol of the all-prevailing power of the LORD of hosts on the field of battle (cf. especially 1 Sam. 4.1–7.1). The ark in its tent has been and can remain a most adequate portrayal of the nature of God's sovereignty on earth—his dynamic readiness to intervene at any place or time (vv. 4-6).

A second objection is that the expression of God's sovereignty is already in being in the person and house of David. David *cannot* build a house for the LORD, because the LORD has already built his own house, and that house, could David but see it, is David himself (vv. 7-11, 12b-14).

These two objections in principle are going to be paralleled in the account of David's census in 1 Chronicles 21.

Nonetheless, in practice David's proposal is acceptable, but premature. God is going to allow the Temple to be built for the ark. The intended meaning of that house is to be made explicitly clear in two later chapters—1 Chron. 22.9 and 1 Chron. 28.2: the Temple is the 'resting place' of the ark. The fact that the ark can now 'rest' expresses the truth that it is no longer needed as of old on active service in war: Israel's foes have been conquered; Israel's dominion has been extended to its farthest limits; there is no further need for battle. The resting of the ark is thus the symbol of victory won, of peace achieved, of the universal reign of God inaugurated and acknowledged by the nations of the world. The Temple, thus, as 'resting place' for the ark, will symbolize the universal pacification wrought by the LORD through David. But David's wars of pacification of the world in the LORD's name are by no means yet over (cf. 1 Chron. 18–20 for campaigns still to come).

At the end of 1 Chron. 17.1a, C omits the crucial phrase from his source text in 2 Sam. 7.1b, 'now the LORD had given him [David] rest on all sides from all his enemies'.

Only when these wars are over and the world is at peace can there be talk of the construction of the Temple. But, by that time, David, with blood on his hands, will, by the very process of the pacification, have debarred himself from constructing the symbol of that peace (1 Chron. 22.8; 28.3). David thus once again becomes a new Moses, this time the vicarious sufferer, who, like Moses, is incapacitated by the process from participating in the realization (compare Deut. 1.37; Num. 20.12), and is disqualified by the necessity of the means by which God's purpose is to be accomplished from creating the symbol of the accomplishment of that purpose. It can only be his son Solomon (*šᵉlōmô*, 'his peace'), the man of peace (*šālôm*; 1 Chron. 22.9), who will be able to construct that Temple (1 Chron. 17.12a).

But, by a double irony, David, by his next headstrong action (the census in 1 Chron. 21), is going to have to raise at least the altar in Jerusalem. This will be in accord with neither his own present intention nor the LORD's: it will be at the site marking his failure, not his success; but that very failure is to be the way in which he is to force the issue and begin at least to plan the construction of the Temple.

1 Chronicles 17 falls into three clearly defined sections:

1. vv. 1-2: David's immediate plan to build a Temple;
2. vv. 3-15: Nathan the prophet receives a two-fold oracle (MT subdivides the section between the two parts of the oracle);
3. vv. 16-27: David's response in prayer.

1. *Verses 1-2: David's Immediate Plan to Build a Temple*

The point at issue in the chapter is focused on the word 'house', which occurs no fewer than fourteen times (e.g. David's palace, v. 1; the Temple which he proposes to build, v. 4; the dynasty which the LORD will provide, v. 10; the Temple which Solomon will build, v. 12, and which God will acknowledge, v. 14).

The chapter opens with David's laudable sense of outrage at the gross imbalance between the splendour of the 'house' in which he is enthroned and the miserable inadequacy of the goats' hair tent as of the poorest bedouin in which the ark, where the LORD of hosts is enthroned, is lodged (1 Chron. 13.6).

C heightens the contrast in dwellings. Whereas 2 Sam. 7.2b reads 'while the ark of God dwells inside tent-curtains', C renders '... under tent-curtains', as though the tent were a mere awning.

C, in contrast to Samuel–Kings, allows David here to use the familiar, Israelite, intimate term 'the LORD', to underline further David's unwitting presumptuousness. He assumes he is acting all for the best for the sake of his God.

With the forcefulness of understatement—David does not even say that he intends to build a Temple—David shares his thoughts with Nathan the prophet, now introduced for the first time. Nathan's ready response gives the initial impression that he is but a standard Near Eastern court prophet who, in the pay of his king, is expected to provide the theological sanction for a royal enterprise. His reply, 'Do as you plan because God is with you', is based on the assumptions of the divine endorsement of David's rule affirmed from the beginning and shared by all (for the preposition 'with' cf. 1 Chron. 11.9, and, again, v. 8). Nathan's use not of the domestic 'the LORD' (as in 2 Sam. 7.3) but of the supra-national, transcendent term, 'God', heightens still further David's assumed absolute authority.

2. *Verses 3-15: Nathan the Prophet Receives a Two-fold Oracle*

It is that same God who responds, with designs of a different order. That very night his word comes to Nathan. The reply is in two parts, vv. 4-7aα and 7aβ-14, the first negative, the second positive.

The MT paragraph marker after v. 7aα points up the correspondence between vv. 4aα and 7aα: v. 7aα, 'Now thus you will say to my servant, to David', resumes v. 4aα. The specific reply to David that follows in the second part from v. 7aβ is clearly marked off against the first part. The difference in content between the two parts is thus emphasized. The first part gives the reason for God's negative response in terms of a retrospect on the nature of the sanctuary hitherto: 'I have not needed a Temple'. The second part, the oracle to David proper, gives the reason for the refusal in terms of David's own experience. For the formula , 'Now, therefore...', which links the two parts, the message to the prior reasoning, cf. 1 Chron. 21.8, 12; 28.8; 2 Chron. 6.16, 17, 41; 19.7.

Nathan is first sharply reminded of David's true status, 'my servant' (v. 4; the word occurs an unprecedented twelve times in this chapter): he is not the free potentate, who can dream up grandiose plans; he is but the slave of the LORD. The message is authenticated with the 'messenger formula', 'thus says the LORD' (cf. the analogous use in the secular sphere in international diplomacy, 2 Chron. 32.10). The emphatic personal pronoun with the negative 'not you' in this first reply is about to be contrasted with the emphatic personal pronoun 'I' in the second (v. 7).

The reply is subtly changed in C. 2 Sam. 7.5, 'Shall you build me a house for my dwelling?' seems to imply that a Temple in principle is a suspect concept; C's, 'It is not you that shall build me the dwelling house' seems to imply that while David will not be permitted to build the Temple, the concept as such is acceptable.

The first part reminds David in historical terms that a Temple is not necessary. The effective power of the LORD symbolized by the ark has been manifested all through Israel's history: from the time it was brought into being as a people, to its entry into the land and during the leadership of the judges thereafter, the ark has never needed a temple for its validation. God's dynamic accompanying presence is better represented by a nomad's movable tent than by the permanent structure of a temple. The term *miškān* ('place of dwelling', v. 5, as, for example, in Exod. 25–40 for the tabernacle) alludes to the character of that presence as the indwelling, encountering, guiding glory of the LORD.

> C changes the 'I have been going about in tent and in tabernacle' of 2 Sam. 7.6 to the somewhat ungrammatical, 'I have been from tent to tent and from tabernacle': it is just possible that the last phrase of this formulation reflects the separation of the ark from the tabernacle now at Gibeon, as recounted in 1 Chronicles 16.
>
> C emphasizes also the perpetual unity and destiny of the people by using the term 'Israel' rather than the 'descendants of Israel' of Samuel (so again in v. 6). Equally, the perennial significance of the action of God is underlined by the omission of the explicit reference in Samuel to 'Egypt', that is, to any limited event in the past, even an event of the towering significance of the exodus from Egypt.

If not one of the previous national leaders appointed by God to shepherd his people has ever received an injunction to build a Temple for this God who roams at large through place and time with his people, why should it be necessary now? The pastoral figure of speech, 'shepherd', is deliberately chosen to refer to Israel's essentially nomadic character in the theological sense as wanderers in place and time. It also picks up David's own pastoral background and experience, no doubt in terms of reproof. He, if anyone, should understand what is involved in caring for a flock of free wanderers and the lifestyle the shepherd should adopt. The emphasis in this chapter on the people as the ultimate concern of the leaders is striking (vv. 7, 9, 10, 21, 22; cf. 1 Chron. 11.2).

Equally deliberate is the picking up of the phrase 'house of cedar' at the end of v. 6 from David's description of his own circumstances in v. 1. Here, reproof turns to sarcasm: what has God to do with confinement in a life of settled luxury?

> The chapter deals with a number of religious paradoxes. It is a natural human reaction to wish to show gratitude by returning gifts to the giver. But there is an element of the absurd in that reaction. How can mere human beings provide for the provider of all?
>
> It is natural that human beings should seek some place where they can be in touch with the power of the unseen world of the divine. But how can the universal divine power be appropriately symbolized, let alone confined, in local, physical terms?

The second part of the message is contained in vv. 7aβ-14. It might have been expected that, since Nathan had been commissioned with the first version of the message, this second version would have recounted the actual delivery of the message by Nathan to David. Instead, this second version is again couched in the form of the commissioning of the prophet. No version of the message as actually given to David is recorded; v. 15 only states that the message, with its injunctions and in its glorious vision, was indeed delivered in full accord with this double commissioning of Nathan. This double commissioning with the very words of the LORD, especially with the positive words now following the negative, adds trenchancy to the message.

The second version of the message opens again (v. 7aβ) with the 'messenger formula', 'thus says the LORD'. It is now extended to include the emphatically transcendent form of the title, 'the LORD of hosts', the power underpinning David's rule (cf. 1 Chron. 11.9).

The message begins with another historical retrospect—the LORD's personal dealings with David in the past. The opening emphatic personal pronoun, 'I', contrasts with the 'you' of v. 4. David owes everything to the LORD. Again the point is made that, as himself once a shepherd, David more than anyone should be aware of the fundamental character of God and of his relation with his people, for which the nomadic imagery is so appropriate (cf. v. 5; for the terminology, cf. 1 Chron. 11.2. C presupposes the narrative of 1 Sam. 16.1-13).

Verse 8 looks back and forward. The character of God described in v. 6 has been made known to David in his personal experience ('wherever you have walked', v. 8a, picks up 'wherever I have walked', v. 6). In v. 8b the promise for the future is given: David will rank in status with the greatest on earth.

> It is notable that in this half-verse C has retained from 2 Sam. 7.9 a statement merely of David's equality with the greatest rulers of the world. An acknowledgment of David's supreme status, such as follows in 1 Chronicles 18–20, might have been expected here. Not all things have yet been put under his feet: the project of Temple-building is premature.

The promise to David is resumed at the end of v. 10a. But C pauses for a moment to consider the implications of these promises for Israel as a whole. The ideal for Israel is now set for realization through David. The ideal is expressed first in its own terms: God will give his people 'a place' , where he will 'plant' them and where they can 'dwell in their location with no more anxiety'. That internal condition is then expressed in terms of the cessation of any external threat. None of 'the agents of unrighteousness' (as Lev. 19.35-36 makes clear, the Hebrew term used, *'awlâ*, is the opposite of 'righteousness', *ṣedeq*, which is defined there as the disposing of affairs in accordance with the standards laid down by God) will any longer ‘wear out’ God’s people.

C reads ‘wear out’ for the ‘afflict’ of 2 Sam. 7.10. NRSV (and other English versions) link the first phrase of v. 10 with v. 9, making the judges period also part of the time of ‘wearing out’. The present verse division in MT between vv. 9 and 10 separates Israel’s maltreatment at the hands of others—unspecified—at the beginning of its history from what began to happen thereafter in the time of the judges. The judges period thus marks the beginning of the process of subjugation of David’s enemies. C thus changes the verb in 2 Sam. 7.11 from ‘give rest’ (root *nûaḥ*, cf. the omission of the same verb in v. 1), to ‘subdue’: the ‘rest’ after the wars of pacification is still awaited in C’s presentation. ‘Subdue’ (root *kn‘*) may contain within it a pun on the name ‘Canaanite’ (*k*^{e}*na‘*^{a}*nî*).

In the context of C (as indeed already in Samuel), this hope for the future is eschatological. The ideal announced to David awaits its realization in the end time across the shambles of actual historical experience. For people not yet in possession of the promise, the pathos of the highly emotive terms used (‘I will give a place to my people Israel; I will plant them and they will dwell in their place with no more anxiety’, v. 9) is profound.

The focus of attention switches back again to David. The unbroken success of the conquests to be recounted in 1 Chronicles 18–20 is promised.

The true climax of the divine message to David is now reached (v. 10b): far from David constructing a house for the LORD, the LORD is going to construct a house for David. At the moment of solemn declaration, the statement is put into the third person, with ‘house’ in the emphatic position.

In Samuel the formulation looks like a lapse into the reported speech by Nathan to David: ‘the LORD will declare to you, that a house will the LORD make for you’. C modifies the verb ‘make’ to ‘build’ in order to make clear the contrast with v. 4, ‘*you* will not build the house for me’ and v. 12, ‘he shall build a house for me’.

The nature of this house is now revealed. It is not to be built in stone and lime but in the living fabric of an unbroken succession of descendants. The actual identity of the son to whom and through whom David’s rule will be handed down after his death is not divulged at this point (nor was it in Samuel): the fundamental promise is to David’s progeny (‘seed’). The word includes the immediate heir but also implies the line of heirs (‘sons’) in perpetuity (v. 11).

There is a certain vitality in C's euphemism for the death of David: 'when his days have been completed' he will 'walk with' his forefathers, rather than the static 'lie' with them of 2 Sam. 7.12. The continuity of succession is stressed by C's use of 'your seed...which proceeds from your sons'; Samuel lays greater emphasis on David's paternity: 'your seed...which proceeds from your loins'.

The rule of this line of descendants will be as firmly established as David's own: the key term, *kûn*, used of the confirmation of David in 1 Chron. 14.2, is now applied to his lineal descendants (the same verb is used again in v. 12b, this time in the intensive conjugation). 'Raise up', *qûm* (v. 11), becomes another thematic term, cf. 2 Chron. 6.10; 7.18. The names of Josiah's son, Jehoiakim (*qûm*), and grandson Jehoiachin (*kûn*), use these two roots, no doubt as statements of hope of the continuation of the dynasty.

It is this line of descent (again the expression is general rather than personalized) that will build the 'house' for the LORD (v. 12). That is, it will inherit without further bloodshed that universal pacification brought about through the agency of David, which will enable the ark of the covenant to be installed in a permanent building. The formulation in v. 12a thus parallels v. 4b in order to mark the contrast between the prohibition to David and the permission to his descendant.

One may assume the phrasing is deliberate: C has modified the 'for my name' of 2 Sam. 7.13 to 'for me' in order to make the formulation (emphatic personal pronoun 'he'—the 'descendant' of v. 11—before the verb, 'shall build', and the prepositional phrase, 'for me') completely parallel.

The formulation of v. 12a also parallels v. 10b. Here is the other contrast: although God is to build the house for David, David's successor can build the house for God. It is only then that Temple and palace, the institutional counterparts of the relation between God and king, will be brought into being.

The nature of the relationship between God and Davidic king can only be expressed in the closest familial terms, 'father' and 'son' (v. 13; cf. the Jerusalem tradition of theology in Psalms, e.g. Ps. 2.7). Here is a solemn act of adoption, with, again, the use of emphatic personal pronouns: '*I* shall become father to him; and *he* shall become son to me'. The bond thus transcends even that of covenant: it goes beyond the voluntary, contractual status of a mere agreement between two parties and has become the necessary and inescapable tie as between members of the same family. It is a relationship that is irrevocable; the loyalty within it is unconditional.

C omits even the possibility, noted in 2 Sam. 7.14, that the king may be backsliding and require discipline. C heightens the direct divine instrumentality: 'I will not remove my steadfast love from with him [with emphatic double preposition]' for the 'my steadfast love will not depart from him' of Samuel. The continuation, 'as I removed it from the one who was before you', gives the defunct regime of Saul less prominence than the Samuel version, 'as I removed it from with Saul whom I removed out of your way'. Nonetheless, the conditionality of the status of the Davidic king is to be stated in David's own version of Nathan's oracle in 1 Chron. 22.10-13; cf. 2 Chron. 7.17-22.

The relationship between God and the Davidic king is developed in a still more far-reaching way in v. 14. The Davidic house is God's house; the Davidic kingdom is God's kingdom (these are ideas to be repeated in 1 Chron. 28.5: the throne of David is God's throne). With these ideas the most fundamental reason why David cannot build the Temple is stated in profoundest theological terms. David cannot build the LORD a house for, in a way that surpasses David's utmost imaginings, the LORD's house is already in being in his own person and descendants. It is through this house of human flesh and blood that the LORD is going to actualize his presence among his people and through them in the world. Here the sacramental role of Israel as earthly counterpart to the cosmic forces of the LORD of hosts finds its sharpest focus in the sacramental role of the Davidic king whose rule and status are the living expression of God's own reign.

Verse 14a shows the most startling variation from Samuel in this chapter. Whereas in 2 Sam. 7.16 the promise was 'your house and your kingdom shall be established for ever in succession to you', C reads, 'I will appoint (the key term *he'ᵉmîd*, 1 Chron. 6.31) [your descendants] in my house and in my kingdom for ever'.

3. *Verses 16-27: David's Response in Prayer*

David's prayer in response to Nathan's message falls into three parts:

vv. 16-22, in the past tense, are a confession, acknowledging the mighty acts of God;
vv. 23-24, mostly in the jussive ('let it be... '), are a petition for the continuation of these mighty acts;
vv. 25-27 are a summary of the first two sections, again in the past tense.

Verses 16-22 contain David's confession.

Nathan's message has opened David's eyes to his status as the LORD's slave and to its full implications. Overwhelmed, David reviews God's unimagined dealings with him, his family, his descendants and his people—and, by implication, humanity. The breathless six-fold repetition of the divine names in these verses—ten-fold in the prayer as a whole—in the fervent vocative, 'O LORD, my God', etc., well conveys David's wonderment ('who am I?', cf. 1 Chron. 29.14; and Moses, again, Exod. 3.11) at the sudden transformation of even his highest aspiration.

David is called 'king' only by virtue of the LORD's kingship (v. 16). He 'sat before' the LORD, that is, as a member of the divine council in the presence of the ark of the covenant, in the tent that he had himself introduced into Jerusalem (1 Chron. 16.1). His use of both the intimate 'the LORD' and the transcendent 'God' expresses a proper awareness both of his station and of the power that has led him. There is perhaps a hint in the use of the double 'the LORD God' of the resumption of the divine titles in the primeval narratives of Genesis 2–3 (so again, 1 Chron. 28.20; 29.1 [David]; 2 Chron. 1.9; 6.41-42. [Solomon]; 26.18 [condemnation of Uzziah], all in C's own material; oddly enough the use in 2 Sam. 7.25 is not reproduced by C here in v. 23, nor 2 Kgs 19.19 in Hezekiah's prayer in 2 Chron. 32.20). What is happening in David is of cosmic significance and concerns the creation and goal of humanity.

> C is more emphatic on this point than 2 Sam. 7.18, which simply uses 'my Lord, the LORD'.

This cosmic significance is made explicit in v. 17. David acknowledges the grace still more abounding in the elevation of his 'house' into a dynasty stretching into the remotest future. Verse 17b is, unfortunately, obscure (as is Samuel): 'you will regard me as the turning of man upwards' (??); it might suggest that, in David, the prototype order for Adam, humankind, is tending towards fulfilment. But the dealing of God with David is not only in acts (v. 18): David has been brought into a living relationship, with one who knows with the most intimate knowledge (cf. 1 Chron. 14.2). This knowledge made known to him takes David beyond the limits of utterance.

However, this display of the mighty acts of God is not only made known to David but is openly declared to the world (v. 19; the text and verse division of 2 Sam. 7.20-22 differ at this point). In the light of this personal experience and of the manifestation of it to humanity, David is led from the confession of the incomparability of the LORD to the affirmation of his sole deity: no other power is worthy of the name 'God' (v. 20).

If this is true on the basis of personal experience, how much more must it be validated when it is extended to the national experience of Israel (v. 21)? As the LORD is unique, so Israel is unique. But this uniqueness arises because of the incomparability of the LORD and because of the uniqueness of the acts he has performed on Israel's behalf in the freeing of them from slavery in Egypt, in driving out the nations of Canaan (cf. 1 Chron. 11.4) and (v. 22) in binding himself to them in perpetual covenant. These demonstrations of the LORD's power are public knowledge, bringing him recognition and renown throughout the earth.

The mood changes at v. 23. David turns from acknowledgment to petition. Four more times the LORD is addressed, three of them by name, as though, suitably chastened, the David who had presumptuously used the divine name at the beginning of the chapter had now learned its true significance (2 Sam. 7.25, by contrast, uses here the compound 'the LORD, God'). Logically, in view of the confession that the LORD acts in a way far beyond the utmost human imagination, there is no need or, even, possibility for such a petition. But in terms of the needs of human psychology David seeks reassurance that the great affirmations will be reaffirmed in continuing experience (have 'Amen' pronounced on them, vv. 23-24).

The petition corresponds to the confession: for David as slave and for his dynasty (v. 23); for the perpetual universal recognition of the LORD in the fundamental theological terms, 'the LORD of hosts is the God of Israel, the God for Israel'; for the consequent recognition of the implications of the divine title 'the LORD of hosts' for the Davidic house—that it is confirmed (the key term, *kûn*, 1 Chron. 14.2, is again used) by the LORD as sacramental, the earthly counterpart of the cosmic forces (v. 24).

Verses 25-27 round off the chapter. Whereas 2 Sam. 7.28-29 continues the petition in this section with imperatives and jussives, C resumes the past tense of the first section and includes the petition under that past tense. C thus solves the tension between the confession and petition of the first two parts. The LORD has acted and has revealed the significance of the action; it is his act that has enabled the petition which has thus been taken up into the act of the LORD. The difference between Samuel and C is well expressed in the last verse. Whereas Samuel reads, 'And now continue to bless...; by your blessing may the house of your slave be blessed for ever', C reads, 'And now you have continued to bless...; you have blessed and are to be blessed for ever'.

1 CHRONICLES 18–20: THE FULFILMENT OF THE LORD'S PROMISE TO SUBDUE DAVID'S ENEMIES

C groups David's foreign conquests together in order to show in one concerted presentation how the LORD's promise in 1 Chron. 17.10 ('I will subdue all your enemies') was totally fulfilled. This grouping is made clear by a comparison with the order of the materials in 2 Samuel (almost all the materials in 1 Chronicles 18–20 are paralleled in 2 Samuel, with some significant omissions and rearrangement):

1 Chronicles	*2 Samuel*
18	8
19.1–20.1	10.1–11.1
20.2-3	12.30-31
20.4-8	21.18-22

But the narrative is also underlining the unfitness of David, as the man who has shed 'much blood' (1 Chron. 22.8), to be the builder of the Temple in Jerusalem. The broadly annalistic tone of his source in Samuel–Kings suits this purpose admirably. (For comparative statistics, see table at 1 Chron. 5.21.)

1 Chronicles 18: The Pacification of Israel's Neighbours

The sequence of the narratives of conquest (or recognition) in 1 Chronicles 18 is west, east, north and south.

1. The campaign resumes against the emblematic foe, the Philistines (1 Chron. 18.1; cf. 1 Chron. 1.12; 14.8-16), the immediate neighbours to the west. They now lose the border territory of Gath.

2. Moab (1 Chron. 18.2), the immediate neighbours to the east, become David's slaves and pay tribute (for *minḥâ*, the key term for the acknowledgment of the LORD's sovereignty through David, cf. 1 Chron. 16.29; C omits the gruesome slaughter of half the population recorded in Samuel–Kings).

3(a). Zobah (1 Chron. 18.3-4), the immediate Aramaean neighbours to the north, lose many prisoners of war to David: 7000 of their cavalry (Samuel–Kings reads 1700); 20,000 of their infantry; nine-tenths of their chariot forces are disabled, the remaining hundred appropriated. This conflict provides a dramatic example of what is involved in these campaigns. It is not simply a matter of the subjugation of a threatening neighbouring power: Zobah are defeated as they presumptuously seek to set up a monument to commemorate their victories at the Euphrates, which is the goal of David's own imperial expansion in fulfilment of the promises to the patriarchs in Gen. 15.18 (cf. 1 Chron. 5.9). They are also the champions of a rival system. Their king bears the programmatic name, Hadadezer, 'Hadad [the proper name of the Canaanite deity, Baal (KBS)] is help', which contains within it the key term, *'zr* (1 Chron. 5.20; it recurs in v. 5, no doubt with a certain grim humour: Hadad the help needs help). Here are counter-claims to the affirmation that the LORD alone, as sole disposer of events, is the source of help.

The word *yād*, translated 'monument' in NRSV (v. 3), is ambiguous: it means basically 'hand' and from that physical sense a number of metaphorical senses are derived. It does indeed gain the meaning 'monument' in, for example, 1 Sam. 15.12 (BDB, s.v., 4a); but it might also mean 'power' (BDB, s.v., 2), that is, 'imperial expansion', as is suggested by the sequel in 1 Chron. 19.16.

In that case the verb 'set up' should be understood in the sense of 'impose' (cf. BDB, s.v., *hiphil* 4). 2 Sam. 8.3 reads a different verb, 'restore', implying previous action or possession; but C is envisaging the campaign as a once for all engagement between the champion of the LORD and the champion of Hadad.

3(b). The threat to one Aramaean state draws in another—Damascus, the great Aramaean power to the north east (1 Chron. 18.5-8). David inflicts 22,000 casualties, imposes garrisons (the missing term is supplied by 2 Sam. 8.6) and levies tribute. From the spoils of Zobah Jerusalem is enriched with gold and bronze; from the latter, C adds to his source, Solomon is eventually to make the bronze furnishings of the temple (cf. 2 Chron. 3.15–4.6, 11-18). Unlike Achar (1 Chron. 2.7), that is, David dedicates the spoils of victory to the LORD, the bestower of victory: in exemplary fashion he avoids any taint of *ma'al*.

4. Zobah's northern neighbour, the king of Hamath, is delighted at David's success against his ancient enemy (1 Chron. 18.9-11; MT

opens a new paragraph, vv. 9-17). In recognition he sends gifts of gold, silver and bronze, likewise dedicated to the LORD, as with all the spoils and tribute from all the nations round about.

Some of these conquests have yet to be recounted. The lands of Edom, Moab and Ammon, to which Israel has no right (Deut. 2.16-22), send tokens of recognition which David 'levies' (literally, 'lifts', v. 11) upon them.

5. The slaughter of 18,000 Edomites, Israel's southern neighbours, (1 Chron. 18.12-13a), by David's nephew, Abshai (cf. 1 Chron. 2.16; Samuel is silent on Abshai's role), at the Valley of Salt (= the Arabah [Grollenberg]; cf. 2 Chron. 25.11) virtually completes the circuit of Israel's immediately bordering nations. Garrisons are imposed as an expression of Israelite hegemony. Relations with the remaining nation, Ammon, and the punitive expedition they provoked is to be the subject of 1 Chron. 19.1–20.3.

The completion of the subjugation of the neighbouring nations in all directions prompts the theological reflection in 1 Chron. 18.13b, 14 (already anticipated in 1 Chron. 18.6b): all David's success is due to the fact that it is the LORD who has given him the victory (key root *yš'*, 1 Chron. 11.14). In consequence of the LORD's all-prevailing power, David is enabled to rule 'all Israel', now the greater Israel from Nile to Euphrates, in *mišpāṭ* and *ṣᵉdāqâ*. *mišpāṭ* (conventionally, 'justice') is a key term in the theology of the Hebrew Bible: it expresses the divine order imposed by God on creation as creator and sustainer (cf. already 1 Chron. 16.12, 14). There is again a sacramental dimension: the laws which uphold the universe in the macrocosm have their counterpart in the laws which uphold every aspect of human life in the microcosm of God's people and in their dealings with the world of the nations. It is David's role, by virtue of his status as slave of the creator, to uphold that divine order within God's people and in their relations with the nations (it is because the discharge of law is one of the chief aspects of the maintenance of order within a community that *mišpāṭ* often has the narrower meaning of 'justice'). *ṣᵉdāqâ* (cf. its opposite in 1 Chron. 17.9), conventionally rendered 'righteousness', means the actual vindication of *mišpāṭ* within society and the world at large in conformity with the norms of the divine order (for the further application of the idea, cf. 2 Chron. 6.23; 9.8; 12.6; 36.11, the programmatic name of the last king of Judah, Zedekiah, 'The LORD is my righteousness').

The practical means whereby David vindicates order within society is through his appointees as his deputies in the various spheres of national life (1 Chron. 18.15-17)—army, court and cult. In principle, however, in this ideal period of his rule David remains supreme ruler in all these spheres, even in priestly matters. Abshai has just been mentioned (1 Chron. 18.12). His brother, Joab, commander of the citizen army and destined to play a significant role in the three following chapters, is now reintroduced (cf. 1 Chron. 11.6). The remaining officials are transcribed from 2 Sam. 8.16-18, though with some variation.

Jehoshaphat, 'the recorder', is mentioned here for the only time in C; Zadok and Abiathar, the priests, have already appeared in 1 Chron. 15.11; for the only time in the Hebrew Bible Abiathar's son is called Abimelech—in Samuel–Kings he is called Ahimelech, as in 1 Chron. 24.6; Shavsha, 'the secretary', appears in the form of 'Seraiah' in 2 Sam. 8.17, 'Sheva' in 2 Sam. 20.25, and 'Shishah' in 1 Kgs 4.3; Benaiah, the commander of the foreign mercenaries, has been mentioned in 1 Chron. 11.24. The most interesting modification concerns David's sons: whereas in Samuel–Kings they are called 'priests', here, in order not to dilute David's role, only the oldest of them are mentioned and these are termed merely his 'attendants'.

It may be that, for C, both the recorder and the secretary are Levites. The office of recorder (*mazkîr*) is mentioned in C again only in 2 Chron. 34.8 in connection with Temple repairs—but only those duly consecrated could attend to such affairs. The father of the holder of the office of the day in 2 Kgs 18.18, 37 is called Asaph, otherwise only a levitical name (except Neh. 2.8?—and even there the individual is concerned with materials for Temple as well as city). The title *mazkîr* is from the same verb, (*l*^{e})*hazkîr*, by which part of the duties of the Asaphites is defined in 1 Chron. 16.4

Even more significant in the light of the sequel is the office of secretary–scribe (cf. already 1 Chron. 2.55 for its position immediately alongside the house of David). While in 1 Chron. 27.32 (if the reference is to the position and not just a descriptive term) the holder was an uncle of David, another holder of the office is termed a Levite in 1 Chron. 24.6. The connection of the scribe with the Temple is further confirmation (cf. 2 Chron. 24.11; 34.13) and especially his entitlement to handle the book of the Law (2 Chron. 34.15-16, 18). For the understanding of the nature of the guilt which David is about to incur by embarking on his census of the people (1 Chron. 21), it is crucial to note that the muster of Israel for service in the LORD's host is a sacral task that ought to lie within the responsibilities of the scribe (2 Chron. 26.11; cf. 2 Kgs 25.19), not those of the army commander, Joab.

1 Chronicles 19.1–20.3: Conflict with Ammon

1 Chronicles 19–20 uses two specific incidents—conflicts with the Ammonites on the East Bank (19.1–20.3) and with the Philistines on the West (20.4-8)—to amplify the account of David's relations with the neighbouring peoples begun in ch. 18. These incidents have already been obliquely referred to in 1 Chron. 18.11b.

The conflict with Ammon also explains the specific factors which had brought David into the conflict with the Aramaeans, recounted in 1 Chron. 18.3-8.

> The opening phrase of both sections, 'After this...' (19.1; 20.4), is vague chronologically and serves merely to introduce these signal instances of David's foreign relations. It is unlikely that 1 Chronicles 19 recounts a *second* campaign of David against Hadadezer of Zobah, who figures prominently in vv. 16-18: if David had already subdued Hadadezer so comprehensively in 1 Chronicles 18, how could he have revived to pose such a threat in 1 Chronicles 19? The statistics between the two chapters tolerably match: 7000 cavalry in 18.4 and 19.18; 42,000 infantry in 18.4-5, 40,000 in 19.18. This chapter also, then, makes clear what Hadadezer was doing on the Euphrates in 1 Chron. 18.3: he was seeking to impose his leadership on the pan-Aramaean confederation in order to mobilize all their forces against Israel.

This section presents the longest account of the confrontations between David and the nations. It thus functions well as the signal example of the threat of incursion by the nations of the world, not only because it is posed by some of those most strategically placed to menace Israel, but also because it comes from that point in the compass whence, traditionally, that threat has been greatest (see, for example, Jeremiah's 'Foe from the North', Jer. 1.13-16, etc.). These representative nations of the foe from the north, despite all their wiles, are powerless against the purpose of the LORD discharged through his anointed servant, David.

The incident begins with the notice of the accession of a new king of the Ammonites (v. 1).

In v. 1 C adds in the name of the former Ammonite king, 'Nahash', 'snake' (he had shown himself a monster of cruelty in connection with the rise of Saul, 1 Sam.11.1-2, an incident concerning Saul that C excludes as irrelevant to his account, but which is presupposed in 1 Chron. 10.11-12). Contrariwise, he omits the name of the new king of Ammon, 'Hanun', 'shown grace'. It is the maintenance of the existing order that is uppermost in C's presentation.

David hopes for the continuation of the friendly relations he has enjoyed with the former king. He expresses this relationship in the language of covenant and international treaty: he wishes 'to deal loyally with' the son as he had with the father (v. 2). This hope for the continuation of the former treaty relationship is couched as a message of condolence on the death of the old king. But the desire to maintain the treaty relationship has within it an implicit claim to suzerainty on David's part.

C very subtly indicates the question of status in his reformulation of the Samuel narrative: whereas 2 Sam. 10.2 says, '*as* his father showed me...', stressing the reciprocity of the action as between equals, C downgrades that occasion by making it merely an appropriate response: '*because* his father showed me...' (the incident to which David refers is not recorded in either Samuel–Kings or C). David's 'messengers' have also been downgraded from the 'officials' in Samuel; they are mere deliverers of a communication from a superior to an inferior.

But, given the ideology of kingship in the ancient Near East, where kings were regarded as representatives and agents of deity on earth, the accession of a new king was a moment charged with far-reaching theological implications and expectations. Hanun's advisers see the opportunity for a redefinition of status (v. 3). They suggest David has a more sinister motive: he has sent spies so that he can overthrow the Ammonite state.

C heightens 2 Sam. 10.3 by reading 'land' for 'city'. In so doing, he introduces the illogical sequence, 'search out, overthrow and spy'; Samuel has the last two verbs in reverse order. The final phrase, 'they have come', instead of the repetition in Samuel, 'David has sent', implies that the invasion has already in principle begun.

MT opens a new paragraph at v. 4. Israel's neighbours are not prepared to give them the recognition their status as the people of God requires, nor are they content to accept their place in God's order of things. David's emissaries are subjected to gross humiliation: like slaves or prisoners of war, they are shaved and their clothes are cut to expose their nakedness.

> C resumes the 'officials' of Samuel to retain the flagrant violation of etiquette, but reads 'shaved them', rather than 'shaved half of their beards', perhaps implying bodily besides facial hair, and uses an alternative word for 'buttocks'.

Verse 5 adds a sympathetic human touch: Israel's unfortunate returning emissaries are allowed to recover from their humiliation before they have to present themselves again at court. They stay in Jericho, the first city back across the Jordan from Ammon, until their beards have regrown.

> C adds explanatory phrases to make it clear that it was not the abused messengers who reported in person to David, but others on their behalf.

The glee of the Ammonites in humiliating David through his emissaries is short-lived (vv. 6-7). They soon realize that Israel will avenge the insult and seek to reassert its appropriate status. Accordingly, they summon support from their powerful neighbours to the north, the Aramaean confederation stretching from the Hermon region (Maacah), through the Beqa' in Lebanon (Zobah) to the Euphrates (Aram-naharaim). The prized contribution of the Aramaeans is cavalry, the élite fighting force of the ancient world. But the immediate consequence of the refusal of the Ammonites to recognize the role of Israel is loss of sovereignty and impoverishment as they pay a large inducement to the Aramaeans.

> C, even where it remains the same in substance as Samuel, shows a number of variations: 'They had put themselves in bad odour with David', rather than merely 'were in bad odour...'; Hanun himself is singled out for mention besides his Ammonite subjects, to stress the theological dimension of the rival divine champions; the sum paid by the Ammonites to the Aramaeans is specified.
>
> C lists three Armaean peoples: Aram-naharaim features only here in C and is best known in the Hebrew Bible as the area from which Balaam, the prophet summoned by Moab to curse Israel, came (Deut. 23.3-5, where, significantly, the Ammonites are coupled with the Moabites); Maacah is a name used on several occasions by C to indicate the lurking threat of the nations (e.g., 1 Chron. 2.48; 7.15-16; 8.29 and 9.35); Zobah has already figured in 1 Chron. 18.3-8 as suffering a punitive invasion from David with heavy losses.
>
> 2 Sam. 10.6, by contrast, omits the remoter Aram-naharaim and lists

four nearer neighbours, Zobah, Maacah, Beth-rehob, which lay between them in southern Lebanon, and Tob, to the south of Maacah.

C uses the equivalent of an entire verse not present in Samuel to give statistics to emphasize the enormous numbers and the threat this onslaught of the nations posed to Israel. 32,000 chariots are thrown into the conflict, the largest chariot squadron in the Hebrew Bible (the next largest is the equally improbable 30,000 of the Philistines, 1 Sam. 13.5; cf. 1000 in 1 Chron. 18.4; Solmon's 1400 in 2 Chron. 1.14, 4000 in 2 Chron. 9.25; Shishak's 1200 in 2 Chron. 12.3; 300 in the Egyptian invading force in 2 Chron. 14.9). Significantly, the king of Maacah, another potential rival as divinely designated leader, is mentioned along with his people. By contrast, the statistics in Samuel make no mention of chariots but only of infantry—20,000 from Zobah (and Beth-rehob?), 1000 from Maacah and 12,000 from Tob. For comparative statistics on the cost, cf. 1 Chron. 29.4.

The place where this seemingly invincible coalition gathered was Medeba, on the eastern frontier of the East Bank tribe, Reuben (Josh. 13.9, 16). This city, being on the Israelite–Moabite frontier, again implies Moabite complicity in the affair.

It is presumably a sign of confidence in the invincibility of his cause on David's part that he does not take the field in person, but sends Joab, his military deputy as commander of the citizen army and chief warrior (see, especially, 1 Chron. 2.16; 11.6, 8, 39; 18.15), to lead the hosts of Israel in battle (v. 8): the champions (*gibbôrîm*) of Israel are now arrayed against the champions of the world (cf. 1 Chron. 1.10; 11.10). No statistics are given for the Israelites; but they were surely heavily outnumbered and, in comparison with their adversaries, grossly under-equipped.

The text in both and Samuel and C is slightly obscure. 2 Sam. 10.7 reads, 'all the host, the warriors'. C's text is unlikely to be sound: 'a whole host, the warriors'; the first noun is indefinite irregularly construed with the object marker.

The tactics of the nations are clear (v. 9): Ammon leads the defence of the city (the programmatic word *yṣ'*, 1 Chron. 1.12, underlines the collision between the rival systems of Israel and the nations, cf. the causative from the same root, 'brought out', in v. 16; cf. 1 Chron. 20.1), while the Aramaeans are deployed separately in the open country. In contrast to 2 Sam. 10.8, C stresses the presence of the Aramaean *kings*, thus implying the cosmic struggle going on behind the scenes.

Samuel repeats its list of four Aramaean states; C, mentioning simply 'the kings', goes straight to the cosmic point. C reads 'at the entrance to the city', where Samuel reads, 'at the entrance to the gate'.

Israel is caught between the two forces (vv. 10-12). Joab selects the pick of the army to take on the Aramaeans, now quite clearly identified as the major threat, leaving his brother Abshai (for whose recent successful campaign against Edom see 1 Chron. 18.12-13) to engage the Ammonites. A prudential note, perhaps out of character for a pure Yahwist, is struck: if either gets into difficulty, the other will help. What is not entertained is that both might be worsted.

MT adds a paragraph marker between the two 'if' clauses in v. 12, in the middle of Joab's speech: 'If the Aramaeans are too strong for me, then you will become my rescue'; 'If the Ammonites are too strong for you, then I will rescue you'. This arresting of the flow of the narrative lays stress on two key terms, 'be strong' (*ḥzq*, 1 Chron. 11.10) and 'rescue' (*yš'*, 1 Chron. 11.14).

Joab leaves his brother on a higher theological note (v. 13). He exhorts him to be resolute, using the same vocabulary as Moses and Joshua at the time of the original conquest of the land (e.g. Josh. 1.6-9; cf. 1 Chron. 11.10) and affirms that their fight is not only on behalf of their people but also for the very cities of their God. With due submission, he commits the outcome of the battle to Yahweh: the LORD of the cosmic hosts will surely aid their earthly counterpart (cf. 1 Chron. 14.15).

Joab apparently effortlessly puts the Aramaeans to flight (vv. 14-15). The Ammonites, seeing their powerful allies routed, take refuge in Medeba. Joab returns to Jerusalem to report the victory to David.

In v. 14, C, true to the ideology of the wars of the LORD, stresses that it was the mere threat of battle rather than an actual engagement that sufficed, by reading, 'drew near before Aram for battle', rather than 'drew near for battle with Aram' as in 2 Sam. 10.13.

C makes a number of adjustments in v. 15. Joab's higher rank than Abshai's is stressed: it was Joab's success against Aram that caused Ammon, 'they too', to flee from Joab's brother. The fact that it was the Aramaeans behind the Ammonites who were the true threat is made clear by the omission of 'Joab returned from against the Ammonites' in 2 Sam. 10.14.

MT opens a new paragraph at v. 16 to signal the greatly heightened significance of the renewed hostilities with the Aramaeans. The reverse has goaded the Aramaeans into attempting an even more comprehensive assault on Israel. Their related peoples in the Euphrates valley are now summoned to lend their weight to the coalition. Once again, the cosmic implications are made clear: their 'host' is now engaged in battle with Israel's host. The leadership has passed back to Zobah, identified as David's direct adversary in 1 Chron. 18.3-8 Hadadezer now shows his disdain for David by fielding merely his commander-in-chief (cf. Joab in v. 8), rather than personally leading his troops.

2 Sam. 10.16 makes it clear that Hadadezer was already involved in the summoning and mustering of these eastern Aramaeans.

At this moment of comprehensive showdown, David musters (cf. the cluster of verbs noted in 1 Chron. 11.1) *all* Israel and comes out in person (v. 17). Without waiting this time for the Aramaeans to advance, he takes the battle to them in their own territory.

C's text is somewhat repetitive: 'he came to them and drew up his forces against them. David drew up his forces to confront the Aramaeans in battle...' The repetition is caused by C's reading 'to them' instead of 'to Helam', as in 2 Sam. 10.17, this being the name of the place in the territory of Zobah to which David advanced, already mentioned in the Samuel–Kings parallel to v. 16 as the meeting point of the Aramaeans, and also by his insistence that it was David, not the 'Aramaeans' of Samuel–Kings, who took the initiative in the encounter.

The Aramaeans are routed (v. 18): their forces are cut to pieces and their commander-in-chief is executed.

C exaggerates the figures for the Aramaean losses: for the '700 chariots' of 2 Sam. 10.18 it reads '7000'. On the other hand, it reads more plausibly '40,000 infantry' for the '40,000 cavalry' in Samuel.

Samuel implies that the Aramaean commander was slain in battle rather than executed as a criminal.

The outcome is entirely satisfactory for God's cause (v. 19): the subjects and vassals of Hadadezer go over his head and 'make peace' (root of *šālôm*) with David, the true suzerain, and become his subjects on the terms that they will never again assist the Ammonites. Relations between Israel and Aram as far as the Euphrates are restored to equilibrium.

C suppresses the note in 2 Sam. 10.19 that the 'subjects of Hadadezer' were 'kings', in order not to impair in any way the status of the LORD's anointed. Compare how in Samuel 'they made peace with Israel and served them' rather than C's 'made peace with David and served him'. In Samuel the Aramaeans hereafter are 'afraid' to assist Ammon 'again', whereas in C they are now 'unwilling ever'.

The subjugation of the Ammonites, those initially responsible for the whole crisis, is dealt with in a separate paragraph, 1 Chron. 20.1-3. It is only a matter of time before the Ammonites, now left defenceless by the double defeat of the Aramaeans and their subsequent peace treaty, are themselves subdued by Israel. For such a mopping up operation David's military deputy Joab, the commander of the citizen army, suffices—he does not even need to be commissioned for the job (though 2 Sam. 11.1 adds that detail); David can himself again remain in Jerusalem.

When the normal campaigning season arrives, Joab leads out 'the host': he invades the territory of the Ammonites, devastates it (the verb *hišḥît*, which echoes the vocabulary of the Passover in Exod. 12.13, 23, here used for the first time, is to become an important thematic term, cf. 1 Chron. 21.12, where it is turned against Israel) and, after a siege of unspecified length, captures Rabbah, 'the great one', and turns it into a heap of ruins.

The echo of Exod. 12.13 may account for C's addition of 'land of' before 'Ammonites' and of the verb '*smote* [NRSV, 'attacked'] Rabbah'.

'Spring' (literally 'the return of the year'), with better weather conditions and ripening harvests to feed the army on the march, marks the season for invasion (for other kings 'advancing'—the key term, *yṣ'*—at this season, cf. Benhadad, 1 Kgs 20.22, 26; Nebuchadnezzar, 2 Chron. 36.10).

The phrase, with its theological emphasis, describing Israel's army as 'the strength of the host', recurs in connection with Uzziah in 2 Chron. 26.13 (Samuel reads here 'his officials... and all Israel').

In Samuel the narrative continues after the parallel to 1 Chron. 20.1a with the story of David's adultery with Bathsheba—the hinge of the presentation of David's reign in Samuel–Kings. Of this there is not a word in C: for him the equally catastrophic hinge of David's reign is to follow in 1 Chronicles 21.

The parallels in Samuel–Kings now follow in 2 Sam. 12.26, 30-31. 2 Sam. 12.26 is less drastic than 1 Chron. 20.1: Joab merely 'fought against Rabbah... and captured the royal city'.

C also omits 2 Sam. 12.27-29—Joab's message from Rabbah to David, to gather the remainder of the host and come to take the city in person, and David's acting upon it. In C's presentation such a message to the LORD's anointed from an underling would be entirely inappropriate.

David removes the weighty jewel-encrusted gold crown from the head of the king of the Ammonites and crowns himself king in his place (vv. 2-3). How the spoils of Ammon referred to in 1 Chron. 18.11 were acquired is now made explicit. 'Spoils', *šālāl*, as symbol of the imposed recognition of the Davidic house as the leaders of the LORD's host on earth, is now to be a recurring theme (cf. 1 Chron. 26.27; 2 Chron. 15.11; 20.25; contrast 2 Chron. 24.23; 28.8, 15).

C now includes grisly details of the torture and mass execution of the inhabitants of Ammon (so JPSV contra NRSV). If voluntary recognition of the sovereignty of LORD's anointed is not forthcoming, then acknowledgment must be extracted by force. A people misled by its leaders has to pay a terrible price (cf. 2 Chron. 25.11-12). But before the conclusion is drawn that C endorses acts of barbarity in the LORD's name, the evidence to follow in 1 Chronicles 21–22 must be weighed up: the reader has now been given ample evidence that David is indeed the one who has 'shed much blood' and has thereby disqualified himself from building the Temple (1 Chron. 22.8); there is also the question whether David has fully appreciated the sacral nature of these wars, precisely the point at issue in his census in 1 Chronicles 21.

1 Chronicles 20.4-8: Conflict with the Philistines

As the narratives of David's wars began with the Philistines (1 Chron. 18.1; even 1 Chron. 14.8), the emblematic power breaking in from the world of the nations (1 Chron. 1.12), so they now conclude.

Three incidents are recorded. All involve single combat between an Israelite hero and one of the indigenous local population, here termed 'Rephaim', the legendary race of giants (e.g. Deut. 3.11, significantly associating them also with the Ammonites with whom C has just dealt). These incidents take place in the borderland between Israel and the Philistines in the lowlands to the west of Jerusalem (C specifies Gezer and Gath).

C reads, 'War broke out', implying that this was the definitive series of engagements, which solved the question once and for all, for the 'There was war again' of 2 Sam. 21.18, as though this were another incident in a continuing sequence. See C's addition at the end of this verse: 'they were subdued' (root *kn'*, with perhaps, again, a play on 'Canaanite', cf. 1 Chron. 17.10).

The Samuel parallels are now to be found in 2 Sam. 21.18-22. The intervening chapters in 2 Samuel (13.1–21.17) contain material irrelevant or uncongenial to C's purpose and have been omitted: for example, the deadly rivalries between David's sons, arising in part at least out of David's indecision about who should succeed him; residual pretenders to the throne among the Benjaminites. Even the immediately preceding passage, 2 Sam. 21.15-17, which records another incident against the Philistines, has been suppressed, because it speaks of physical weakness on David's part and such a threat to his life that he is debarred by his warriors from taking further personal part in the campaigns. In C's presentation of this as the period of David's ascendancy, none of this is appropriate. Accordingly, he records only the last three incidents (contrast 2 Sam. 21.22: 'these *four* were born to the Rephaim...').

The first incident is at Gezer (v. 4). Although Gezer is listed among the towns subjugated by Joshua and is designated as a city of refuge in the territory of Ephraim, it was recognized that the indigenous population continued to survive there (e.g. Judg. 1.29; cf. 1 Chron. 6.67). It was as much a frontier town on the West Bank as Medeba was on the East (2 Sam. 5.25).

Samuel reads the place-name as 'Gob' (location unknown [Grollenberg]), in both this and the following verse.

The Philistine champion is otherwise unknown, but he is described by a term that is used in the Hebrew Bible either of house-born slaves or of the offspring of the indigenous population who are regarded as menials (Josh. 16.10). He was overcome by the Israelite hero already encountered in 1 Chron. 11.29 (cf. 1 Chron. 27.11; for Hushah, his place of origin, cf. 1 Chron. 4.4).

The next incident (v. 5) is unlocated by C but the place of origin of the giant involved implies Gath (so v. 8). Israel's hero, Elhanan, has also been met already (1 Chron. 11.26). The 'weavers' beam' is the conventional description for the shaft of a spear which only such a huge man could wield (cf. 1 Chron. 11.23; 1 Sam. 17.7)

The text between C and 2 Sam.21.19 seems particularly confused:

C: Elhanan son of Jau/ir kills Lahmi the brother of Goliath.

Samuel: Elhanan son of Jaare-oregim the Bethlehemite kills Goliath.

Both texts may be partly sound, partly corrupt. At the beginning, C's 'Elhanan son of Jau/ir', though the name Jau/ir is otherwise unknown, looks preferable to the '...son of Jaare-oregim' of Samuel, which has probably been corrupted by attraction with 'the weavers' beam [*m*ᵉ*nôr 'ōr*ᵉ*gîm*]' at the end of the verse. But C has then probably suppressed the sensational statement in Samuel that it was not David who slew Goliath (as in 1 Sam. 17), but Elhanan. 'Lahmi' is then a corruption of

'Beth*lehemi*te', presumably introduced to provide a second Philistine giant from Gath.

Yet another freakish local giant is introduced (vv. 6-7). Like Goliath (1 Sam. 17.10), he delivers a taunting, derisive challenge to Israel—presumably about their inability to match such a warrior—and, by implication, to Israel's God. C notes laconically that he is dealt with by the son of one of David's brothers (for whom cf. 1 Chron. 2.13). Verse 8 sums up these Philistine encounters: Philistia, despite all the giants of its indigenous population, is now firmly in the control of David and his people.

C's presentation of David's reign to date is of an ideal on the brink of realization. As the LORD's anointed he is perfectly fitted to be God's agent on earth; under his leadership Israel is equipped to be the LORD's host. Through his campaigns David has brought about the pacification of the world round about and the recognition, through their spoils or tribute, of the nations. The oneness between God and the human race, already lost in Adam, is in process of restoration. There has been no hint of personal human shortcoming in God's chosen king, David. But twice over, in relation to the ark in 1 Chronicles 13 and the Temple in 1 Chronicles 17, doubts have arisen about David's understanding of the sacral. A question hangs over his conduct of the wars of pacification as the wars of the LORD. These doubts are about to grow into the crisis of David's attempt to hold a census of his people in 1 Chronicles 21. Failure in the realm of the sacral, the holiness which lies at the heart of Israel's vocation among the nations of the world, shatters the ideal of oneness and immediacy between God and king and opens the way to the necessary substitute form of the relationship through rites of retrospective atonement.

1 Chronicles 21.1–22.4: The Census, Pivotal Event of David's Reign

The destiny of Israel is to realize on behalf of the nations of the world that relationship with God which was God's purpose in Adam. That relationship with God requires a life of holiness as defined in the Torah. C is dealing with the question of how far the monarchy at its most ideal—the sacramental Jerusalemite tradition whereby David as the representative of God on earth leads the host of Israel which is the earthly counterpart of the cosmic forces at the LORD's disposal for the direction of the life of the universe—enables Israel's attainment of that holiness. If not, how can Israel be fitted to play its role among the nations of the world?

David has succeeded brilliantly on the plane of human events in establishing his throne within Israel in the most ideal possible manner with the unanimous support of the people, 1 Chronicles 11–12, and in gaining recognition of his rule from the nations round about, by force or by acknowledgment, 1 Chronicles 14; 18–20. In relation to the pursuit of holiness as laid down in the Torah, however, David has already faltered twice through impulsive action. In 1 Chronicles 13 the Torah legislation on the bearers of the ark (cf. 1 Chron. 15.15) has been flouted; in 1 Chronicles 17 David's proposal to build a Temple is premature and invalidated by his bloody wars of subjugation. Now, as will be argued below, the third and decisive infringement of the sphere of the holy takes place: David incurs guilt particularly by his violation of the legislation on the muster of the people as laid down in Exod. 30.11-16.

These repeated failures on David's part now make it obvious that, however valid the affirmations of royal sacramental theology may be, Israel's attainment of holiness can only be through the ministry of the Levites, beginning with the rites of the altar.

The parallels to this section of Chronicles (but only as far as v. 26) are to be found in 2 Samuel 24. There are some highly significant differences, which will be noted below.

Once again there comes a trial of David's oneness with the purpose of God (the opening paragraph runs in MT from vv. 1-7). The catalyst in the situation is now Satan (v. 1). In the Hebrew Bible, Satan is not the principle of evil over against the principle of good; there is no such dualism, for God himself remains the arbiter of good and evil. 'Satan' is, in this context, a proper name, but it is derived from the common noun 'satan', meaning 'opponent, adversary', used in the Hebrew Bible in the realm of ordinary inter-human relations (e.g. 1 Kgs 5.4). It may then be used theologically of the role of an angel sent to confront a wayward human being (e.g. Num. 22.22-23). As is especially clear from Job 1–2, 'the satan' is the technical term for that particular officer in the heavenly court, the 'counsel for the prosecution' (cf. Ps. 109.6 for the equivalent in the human lawcourt), whose task it is to argue the case against human beings, even to tempt and afflict them in order to check their sincerity and establish that all is as it appears to be: in Job's case, that piety and obedience are utterly genuine and disinterested and will survive all trial and adversity (the verb in Job 2.3 of the satan provoking God against Job is also used here of Satan's provoking David). In 1 Chron. 21.1 the word is used without the definite article; it has now become a proper name: the holder of the office of *śāṭān* is now identified with his role and is given that title as his proper name. Satan is, precisely, the tempter, in the sense not merely of enticing a human being to a specific act against God, but, through that act, of testing the genuineness of that individual's relationship to God. The responsibility for succumbing to the provocation of Satan remains, however, with David.

The differences in the presentation from 2 Sam. 24.1 are striking. There the Satan does not figure; it is the anger of the LORD that is 'again' kindled against Israel; it is the LORD himself who incites, indeed commands, David to act against them; in the census Israel and Judah are separately specified. There is no room for these concepts in C: the exploration in C thus far is on the potentiality of the monarchy, not on its failure; the people of God are one and are not to be divided between 'Israel' and 'Judah' (though the separate statistics are, in fact, given in v. 5).

The gravity of the situation is, however, compounded. It is against *Israel* that Satan's probing is directed. David's office as king is not merely a matter of his own status; beyond David the individual lies David in his role as incorporation of Israel as God's people. The fall of the leader is the fall of the people.

Satan awakens in David's mind the idea of counting the people. David (v. 2), identified personally by name for responsibility (Samuel just 'the king'), commands Joab (1 Chron. 11; 18–20), the commander-in-chief of the Israelite citizen army, and the other commanders (cf., e.g., 1 Chron. 13.1), to make a census of Israel from the southernmost town, Beer-sheba, to the northernmost, Dan.

The formulation of David's command to Joab (who is initially addressed alone) in 2 Sam. 24.2, 'rove [*šûṭ*] through all the tribes of Israel' uses the same verb that the satan has used of his own roving up and down in the world in Job 1.7; 2.2 and may have aided the reformulation in 1 Chron. 21.1 in terms of *Satan*'s activities. In Samuel the census takes place in the opposite direction, from Dan to Beer-sheba (the standard sequence in the Hebrew Bible). Presumably C, conscious of the political realities for the post-exilic community of the circumscribed territory around Jerusalem, has to begin from the south (cf. 2 Chron. 30.5). In Samuel the fiscal and military objective of the census of Israel as a civil entity is more clearly brought out by the choice of vocabulary: '*review the people* that I may know the number of *the people*'. C stresses the theological factors: the *counting* of *Israel*.

To the modern reader, accustomed to the census as an instrument of governmental planning even for beneficial purposes such as welfare or education, David's proposal seems not only unexceptionable but positively laudable. What, then, is so wrong with David's census, particularly when 'counting' the people dominates so much of the book (cf., e.g., 1 Chron. 11.11; 23.3)?

As in the discussion of why David's proposal to build a Temple was unacceptable (1 Chron. 17), so here a number of passages beyond the immediate context have to be taken into account. Joab's own explanation of what is so wrong with David's proposal requires considerable filling out. He begins with two points of principle. First, the proposed census *cannot* be undertaken (v. 3; cf. 1 Chron. 17: a house *cannot* be built for God, since God has already built his house—the house of David): the number of the people is a matter of the blessing of the LORD; as the blessings of the LORD are unnumbered, so the people blessed by him, potentially a hundred-fold, are innumerable. Joab's words, 'May the LORD increase his people a hundredfold', amount to a refusal on grounds of impossibility. They echo a similar protest, about an equally impossible commission, by Moses (Deut. 1.11): as it is, the people are uncountable; all the more so, when God's promises about the increase of the people are fulfiilled. Joab's point is made clearer in the cross-reference in 1 Chron. 27.23-24: the people could not be counted because God had promised to Abraham precisely that his descendants would be beyond counting (Gen. 15.5; 22.17; cf. Gen. 13.16). For David to count the people is, thus, to fly in the face of God's promise; it is to check up on the fulfilment of the promise and amounts to doubting it. Note David's stated purpose in holding the census: that he may 'know their number' (v. 2). It is not enough for him to trust the promise of God about the uncountability of Israel as the people of God: as in the story of the tree of knowledge in Gen. 2–3, he seeks humanly to know, in order to supplement, if not supplant, unquestioning reliance upon God (contrast 1 Chron. 14.2).

C's emphasis on the fact that they are *God's* people is notable (v. 3; cf. 1 Chron. 11.2): 2 Sam. 24.3 reads simply 'the people'.

Joab's second point of principle is that the census is unnecessary (v. 3; cf. 1 Chron. 17: a Temple is unnecessary): David already has all Israel as his submissive slaves; what more can he want?

C adds this second reason by reading, 'Are they not, O Lord, the king, all your subjects?', for the 'while the eyes of my Lord, the king, see it [i.e., the hundred-fold increase of the people]' of Samuel.

But, as v. 5 is to make clear, there is a further dimension: the census is designed as a muster to establish the military capability of Israel. This is tantamount to checking up on the ability of Israel to be the LORD's host, to carry out LORD's purpose, and on the ability of the LORD to work through and to defend his own people. It is this military purpose of David that leads into the heart of his offence.

The objection to David's proposed census is now no longer one of principle (that the census is impossible or unnecessary) but one of practice. A census is, in fact, legitimate (cf. 1 Chron. 17, a Temple can, in fact, be built), but it must be carried out in the approved manner—and that is certainly not by the commander-in-chief of the citizen army acting with the other army commanders at the king's behest.

The way of conducting a census of the people that is theologically appropriate is laid down in Exod. 30.11-16. The root *pqd* in the word 'muster' (*mipqād*, v. 5; NRSV obscures the point by rendering '*total* number'), now to become a key term in C, links C and Exod. 30.11-16 together.

The root *pqd* recurs in C in v. 6; 1 Chron. 23.11, 24; 24.3, 19; 26.30, 32; 2 Chron. 12.10; 17.14; 23.14, 18; 24.11; 25.5; 26.11; 31.13; 34.10, 12, 17; 36.23.

Exod. 30.11-16 outlines the appropriate practice of the census:

> 12When you [Moses] take a census of the Israelites to register them (*p^e^qudîm*), at registration (*p^e^qōd*) all of them shall give a ransom for their lives to the LORD, so that no plague (*negep*) may come upon them for being registered (*p^e^qōd*). 13This is what each one who is registered (*p^e^qudîm*) shall give: half a shekel... as an offering to the LORD. 14Each one who is registered (*p^e^qudîm*), from twenty years old and upward, shall give the LORD's offering15... to make atonement for your lives. 16You shall take the atonement money from the Israelites and designate it for the service of the tent of meeting; before the LORD it will be a reminder to [better: 'for', cf. Num. 31.54] the Israelites of the ransom given for your lives [NRSV].

C both illuminates and applies this legislation (see especially, 2 Chron. 24.6; 25.5; 26.11). The Israelite males from twenty and upward are registered for military service. War is not being glorified: military service is only legitimate within the context of fighting the LORD's battles as the LORD's host. Killing on the field of battle is an inevitable consequence of war: but taking the life of another human being immediately warrants the payment of life for life (cf. Gen. 9.5-6; Num. 35.33, for the full horror at bloodshed and the seriousness of the consequences of shedding blood). The sequence of 1 Chronicles 21 after the account of David's bloody wars in 1 Chronicles 18–20 now takes on an ominous note. Only the necessary sacral preparation for war as the LORD's war can avert that inevitable forfeiture of life by those who take life. It is that sacral preparation that the legislation in Exod. 30.11-16 provides: the half-shekel given by all is the indemnity laid up as a perpetual reminder before the LORD for the life of '*you* all', that is, not just of the combatants, but of the community at large, on whose behalf the host sallies forth and which might suffer because of the blood shed by the host.

This legislation in Exodus is concerned precisely with atonement, the maintenance of the oneness between community and God, which will otherwise be broken even by acts of necessary bloodshed. These rites of atonement are not, thus, in response to actions already committed; they are not retrospective to restore what has already been disturbed. They are, rather, precautionary, prospective measures, which anticipate the possibility of bloodshed. They are rites of prophylactic atonement that have to be observed, as the people set out to war, in order to maintain the existing oneness of Israel with God.

It is David's neglect of these necessary preliminaries to the muster of the host of Israel, with the involvement of the Levites, that lies at the heart of his offence (*'ašmâ*, as Joab call it, v. 3), which will bring the penalty not just on himself but on Israel. The sequel is about to show the catastrophic consequences of the neglect of this legislation, the 'plague' (*maggēpâ*, vv. 17, 22, is from the same root as *negep* in Exod. 30.12) that befalls the people. Because these rites of prospective, prophylactic atonement have been ignored, rites of retroactive atonement—therepairing of the relationship damaged through that failure—have now to be brought into operation, as 1 Chron. 22.1 makes clear.

'ašmâ, 'incurring guilt', now becomes one of the key terms of C's theology (so, again, 2 Chron. 24.18; 28.10, 13; 33.23, all in independent C material). It links David's failure with the basic legislation on holiness, the guilt incurred through *ma'al*, the infringement of holiness, and the possibility of atonement in Lev. 5.14–6.7, which C is expounding at length in narrative form in his book: 'so shall one be forgiven for committing any of the acts by which one may *incur guilt*' (Lev. 6.7; cf. Lev. 6.5; 22.14-16).

Joab is overruled (v. 4). As the agent of the representative of the divine king, he must do his bidding. In one terse sentence, C records that Joab passed through the whole of Israel and returned to Jerusalem. It can hardly be mere coincidence that C—unlike Samuel uses the other verb of the Satan in Job 1.7; 2.2: 'passed through'.

> C omits 2 Sam. 24.4bαii-8a, the itinerary Joab followed through the East Bank from south to north then down the West Bank from Dan to Beersheba, and the length of time, 'nine months and twenty days', which, according to 2 Sam. 24.8b, the census took. He also now omits any mention of the other army commanders who assisted Joab.

Joab brings the statistics of the muster of the people to David (v. 5; C again uses the name to emphasize the personal responsibility, while Samuel keeps the title, 'the king'). The count is now broken down with the number for the united kingdom as a whole and separate statistics for Judah—a portent of divisions and disasters to come: 1,100,000 swordsmen all told, of whom 470,000 are in Judah.

2 Sam. 24.9 gives slightly different statistics in a different format: 800,000 from the north and 500,000 from the south. For comparative statistics cf. 1 Chron. 5.18.

C now adds a verse of his own about Joab's scruples (v. 6). Subordinate officer though he is, he refuses to muster Levi, the sacral tribe, and Benjamin, within whose territories Jerusalem is placed.

The term, *tô'ēbâ*, with which C denotes Joab's revulsion (2 Chron. 28.3; 33.2; 34.33; 36.8, 14) expresses that which is cultically and morally abhorrent (see, for example, Deut. 14.3 in connection with the list of dietary prescriptions that render Israel holy, Deut. 14.2-21). *tô'ēbâ* characterizes the nations of the world as represented by the pre-Israelite population of the land (2 Chron. 33.2; cf., e.g., Deut. 12.28-31) and is thus that which it should be precisely Israel's destiny to avoid.

Joab's scruples have two advantages: they leave unsullied Jerusalem, which, as the sequel relates, is to become the site of altar; and they leave imprecise the exact number of Israelites.

The addition of this verse thus explains the difference in statistics between C and Samuel in v. 5.

Verse 7 is the climax of the paragraph (contra NRSV). The LORD immediately inflicts disaster on Israel: in sacramental thinking, to lapse is by that act to bring disaster.

C fundamentally modifies a fragment of 2 Sam. 24.10a, 'David's heart smote him', to 'the LORD smote Israel'; thus, whereas in Samuel David's remorse anticipates the punitive act, in C it is caused by it. As C stands this punitive act, which is unspecified, is separate from the penalty which is to follow in vv. 14-15.

David now confesses the enormity of his failure (v. 8; to lend weight, MT places this verse in a paragraph by itself). At this pivotal confession in this pivotal chapter C introduces for the first time the word 'sin', *ḥṭ'* (cf. v. 17 and references at 2 Chron. 6.22). It is notable that at this point the familiar intimacy implied by the use of the Divine name, 'the LORD', is now abandoned. The rupture of the immediate relationship which David has enjoyed hitherto is expressed by the address in the formal, objective terms, 'O God'.

Samuel at this point still retains 'the LORD'. That the change to 'God' in C is no mere textual accident is confirmed by the omission of the 'the LORD' of Samuel in the second half of the verse.

David asks for the removal of the consequences of his error and folly: for the only time in his work C uses the term *'āwôn*, 'error', and the penalty that follows (e.g. Lev. 5.17). But now comes the next phase in C's unfolding of his doctrine of atonement. Even to an abject confession of failure and ineptitude, there can be no cheap grace extended. Sin affects not simply the sinner, but the fabric of the community around him. It brings with it long-term consequences; there are changes in the situation that can only be reversed in the end time. David has fundamentally assailed God's promise; he has sought to supplant trust by knowledge; he has compromised his status as God's representative and has implicated God's people, who are the instruments of the implementation of that promise; he has infringed the sphere of the holy. The relationship can be repaired, but not restored to what it was before; and in the process of repair much distress must result.

The response of God is mediated through Gad, David's court seer (vv. 9-12).

> Gad's message is structured with the utmost economy to keep up the pace of the account. In the transmission of a prophetic message there are in principle two main phases:[1] the commissioning of the messenger and the delivery of the message to the recipient. The message itself is classically structured in two parts: the review of the situation which has provoked the message (introduced in principle by some such phrase as, 'Because you have done such and such a thing'); and the message proper, announcing the impending action the sender is about to take (beginning in principle with a phrase like, 'Therefore, I am about to do the following'). At the beginning of the second part of the message, after the 'Therefore', comes, again in principle, the 'messenger formula', 'thus says the LORD' (cf. 1 Chron. 17.3-15). Here, the situation is taken as read; only the message proper, prefaced by the 'messenger formula', is given. To maintain suspense, that message is split between the commissioning of the prophet in v. 10 and the delivery in vv. 11-12: one has to wait for the delivery of the message before one knows what the 'three things' are that Gad is commissioned to offer.

Gad's normally expected role was, as his name ('good fortune') implies, to foretell auspicious outcomes to the royal activities; now he has the inauspicious task of announcing the terms of the repair of the relationship.

1. Cf. C. Westermann, *Basic Forms of Prophetic Speech* (trans. Hugh Clayton White; London: Lutterworth, 1967), p. 130.

C pares down 2 Sam. 24.11 in v. 9, omitting the temporal note at the beginning of the verse, 'David arose in the morning', and the title of Gad, 'prophet'.

Gad offers David the choice of one of the three standard instruments of divine chastisement: famine, war or plague.

C reads 'directing towards' rather than the 'holding over' you (v. 10) of Samuel.

The choice of only one of three is a measure of the divine leniency, but is still an agonising one. C adds a firm, 'Thus says the LORD, choose' at the end of v. 11.

The choices are presumably held to be equivalent, but are dramatically graded, with length and intensity in inverse proportions: three years of famine, three months of flight, slaughter and pursuit in war, or three days of plague (v. 12).

To the third choice C adds the phrase, 'and the angel of the LORD as destroyer (*mašḥît*) throughout all the borders of Israel': the destroying angel, the *mašḥît*, occurs in Exod. 12.13, 23 as the slayer of the Egyptian first-born, while sparing those of Israel. Here is a horrifying reversal of the Passover, Israel's foundational act of deliverance (compare the Passover celebrations under Hezekiah and Josiah in 2 Chron. 30; 35): the force of destruction is now turned against Israel itself.

This motif of the destroyer C is to use a number of times: v. 15 (twice* + once); 2 Chron. 12.7*, 12*; 20.23*; 21.7; 22.4*; 24.23*; 25.16*; 26.16*; 27.2*; 34.11*; 35.21*; 36.19*; and see already 1 Chron. 20.1 (* = C's own material).

Samuel reads 'seven years' for the first choice and, more directly, 'flight from your adversaries' in the second. The balancing phrases 'the sword of your enemies' and 'the sword of the LORD' in the second and third choices have been added by C.

Gad leaves David in desolate isolation as he makes the grim choice: 'now choose what answer I am to take back to him who sent me'.

C significantly omits the first element of 'knowledge' in the 'Now *know* and see what answer I am to take back' of Samuel (v. 12; cf. v. 2)

MT subdivides the outcome (vv. 13-26) into three sections, culminating in the building of the altar.

Verses 13-15 record David's choice, the unleashing of the plague, but the sparing of Jerusalem, the proposed site of the altar. David's choice can only be a submission to the direct punishment of the merciful LORD rather than to punishment indirectly mediated through unpredictable human agency (v. 13).

C makes David take personal responsibility 'that I should fall', rather than '...we...', as in 2 Sam. 24.14.

David's choice is interpreted to be plague (v. 14). C concisely notes the casualties for the whole community—70,000.

Samuel adds further detail about time and about the inclusiveness of the plague for the whole community from Dan to Beer-sheba.

C stresses the instrumentality of God in sending the angel of destruction (v. 15; in Samuel the angel is at this point a free agent; 'send', *šlḥ*, as the reaction provoked by a situation, e.g. 2 Chron. 24.19; 25.15; 30.1; 34.29). The angel is sent to destroy even Jerusalem. But, when the angel reaches Jerusalem, the LORD relents and stops the spread of the plague at the threshing-floor of Ornan the Jebusite. Jerusalem itself has been spared. From the narrative itself it is clear that the location is the site of the Temple courtyard on the exposed ridge to the north of the city where one would expect a threshing-floor to be located.

Nothing is known of Ornan outside this narrative (and the cross-reference in 2 Chron. 3.1). The consonantal outline of the name in C (*'rnn*) is close to that of the word for 'ark' (*'rwn*): is a pun intended? Araunah, is thought to be related to a Hittite noun meaning 'noble' [cf. KBS, s.v.].

In vv. 16-17, David's confession and petition, David is overwhelmed at the awesome apparition embodying the cosmic forces, which once he had represented and are now turned to destruction against his people because of his actions (v. 16; though the title does not occur here, it is tempting to relate this figure to the 'captain of the LORD's host', Josh. 5.13-14, especially when the phrases, 'he lifted up his eyes and saw...standing...with his sword drawn in his hand...and he fell down [on his] face...and said', occur in both; for David as the new Joshua, cf. 1 Chron. 12.15). He and the elders with him, clad in sackcloth as a rite of national lamentation, throw themselves prostrate to the ground in an act of powerless supplication.

C has developed this action of self-abasement before the apparition from a single phrase in 2 Sam. 24.17, 'when he saw the angel who was smiting the people'.

David now, in confession, seeks to draw all the blame to himself (v. 17): with emphatic personal pronouns he declares that he was the one who thought of the census in the first place. He intercedes for his innocent people and prays that the penalty of plague should fall on himself and on his house.

As he approaches the heart of his subject, C has again expanded the underlying Samuel text, adding especially the phrase about David's origination of the idea of the census, the urgency of the appeal, 'O LORD my God', and the closing phrase, 'let no plague strike your people'. The change 'I have erred' to 'I have done evil' matches the use of the same root (*r*")at the beginning of v. 7, 'it was evil in the sight of the LORD'; apart from 1 Chron. 16.22, these are the only uses of the verb from the root in C (cf. 1 Chron. 2.3).

In vv. 18-26, which concern the building of the altar, the instruction to David to build an altar on the threshing-floor is relayed from angel to prophet to David (v. 18; contrast David's confident initiative in 1 Chron. 17.1).

C emphasizes the indirectness of David's decision to build an altar by adding the tier of the angel of the LORD. At the beginning of the verse 2 Sam. 24.18 has simply, 'On that day Gad came to David and said to him, "Go up to erect an altar..."'

There is a remoteness from God in the formulation in C: 'David went up by the word of Gad, which he had spoken in the name of the LORD' (v. 19). David, the once headstrong initiator, can now only comply with Gad's instructions. There is a chilling doubt about whether what David does is, or can be, immediately directed by the LORD.

Samuel has more confident immediacy: '... according to the word of Gad, as the LORD had commanded'.

Verse 20 switches the scene to Ornan and his threshing-floor. He too had seen the angel of destruction. But, while his four sons had hidden themselves, he continued threshing wheat. The time of year indicated is high summer. David's census must have been in anticipation of yet further campaigns in the following spring (cf. 1 Chron. 20.1).

This vivid little sketch has no counterpart in Samuel.

David approaches Ornan (v. 21). He has to adopt the humiliating role of suppliant. But, as soon as Ornan catches sight of him, he leaves the threshing-floor and prostrates himself before David in respect and submission.

C shears David of the title 'king' and of the attendants he is given in 2 Sam. 24.20.

David seeks to buy the threshing-floor from Ornan so that he may build an altar there to Yahweh (v. 22). He will pay the full market value: he hopes that if it is at personal cost, reparation may be made for his guilt and the plague may be stemmed and removed from his people (cf. the link between reparation and atonement in Lev. 5.14–6.7).

C omits the honorific address by Araunah to David, 'Why is my lord, the king, coming to his servant?' that appears in Samuel. C's addition 'the *place* of the theshing-floor' has within it the overtone already of 'sanctuary' (cf. v. 25 and, e.g., Josh. 5.15). Hardly surprisingly, C has added the link between the purchase price and the averting of the plague.

With exemplary piety, this foreigner, Ornan, is ready (v. 23) to give his threshing-floor for nothing and to furnish the necessary materials for the cultus: for victims, his cattle treading out the grain; for wood-offering, his threshing-sledges; for cereal offering, his threshed wheat. Ornan the Jebusite thus contributes to C's overall theological pattern: as representative of the world of the nations, oneness with whom God has sought from Adam, he stands ready, at this crisis of restart at the heart of Israel's own life, to supply the necessary outward furnishings of the atonement cult.

C allows David here his title in the mouth of Ornan. For the 'let my lord the king *offer* what is best in his eyes' found in 2 Sam. 24.22, C reads with a change of one consonant, '...*do*...'

C, with greater regard for the minutiae of the cultus, has added the cereal offering (e.g. Exod. 29.2), keeping the rhetorical balance by omitting 'the harness of the oxen' under the wood-offering that appears in Samuel.

The last phrase, 'all I hereby give', has been adapted by C from the beginning of 2 Sam. 24.23, the rest of which C omits: 'The whole Araunah, the king, gave to the king. Araunah said to the king, "May Yahweh, your God, accept you"'. One can see why, on grounds of the coherence of the story, the sensational attribution to Araunah of the title 'king' (assuming the text of Samuel is sound) and the unacceptability of the foreigner using the divine name, C has omitted this material.

Verse 24 indicates that atonement must be made in Israel for Israel, so that Israel may realize in itself on behalf of the world that quality of life which is human destiny. That atonement can be legitimized only by purchase. David cannot offer to God what belongs to another person; Israel cannot have atonement made for it at the cost of a foreigner. As in the priestly practice of sacrifice in Lev. 5.14–6.7, the victim must be a costly part of the very life-support system of the offerers themselves. Atonement is not offered *gratis*. David must, therefore, make the purchase at full cost price.

> C emphasizes that it is 'at full value' (Samuel: 'for a price'). The reason is given rather more fully: 'I will not offer what is yours to the LORD nor sacrifice burnt-offering at no cost'; Samuel reads simply, 'I will not sacrifice burnt offerings to the LORD, my God, at no cost'.

The purchase cost is, indeed, vast (v. 25): David pays Ornan 600 shekels of gold for the site of the sanctuary. Significantly, he does not buy the cattle and other items, which are part of Ornan's own life-support system and possibly invalid, therefore, even by purchase, as David's offering.

> The figure in 2 Sam. 24.24 is much less: 50 shekels of silver—and that includes the cattle as well as the threshing-floor.
>
> The value of ancient units of money is notoriously difficult to determine, given such variables as historical period, whether coinage or weights are used, region, official and unofficial rates, sacred and secular rates, conversion rate between gold and silver and between different units, value for money, genre of narrative. It is perhaps best to give some comparative data for mainly secular transactions from the Hebrew Bible itself (for further comparative date cf. table at 1 Chron. 29.4):
>
> quarter shekel of silver for an oracle from a seer, 1 Sam. 9.8;
> 17 shekels of silver for a field at Anathoth, Jer. 32.9;
> 30 shekels of silver for a gored manservant or maidservant, Exod. 21.32;
> 50 shekels of silver as indemnity for each Israelite warrior paid by Menahem, 2 Kgs 15.20;
> 200 shekels of silver for goodly 'garment of Shinar' taken by Achan, and gold bar of 50 shekels, Josh. 7.21;
> 400 shekels of silver for cave of Machpelah, Gen. 23.15.

David builds his altar and offers whole burnt offerings, to express complete devotion, and communion sacrifices, to express the longing for the restoration of relationships between God and worshippers (v. 26). He invokes the LORD by name (cf. 1 Chron. 4.10), in the hope that the sacrifices will be acceptable and the personal relationship restored. The LORD answers him by fire: as the means by which the physical sacrifice is transformed into smoke ascending into the heavens, fire sent by God is the symbol for the acceptance by God of the worshipper and of the statement implied by the sacrifice (cf. 2 Chron. 7.1; Lev. 9.24; 1 Kgs 18.24, 38).

> Samuel takes the matter in a much more local and immediate way. There is no mention of the invocation of the LORD by name and of the answering by fire. Rather, the LORD is besought successfully for the land and the plague is removed. At that point Samuel terminates the narrative.

The final section (1 Chron. 21.27–22.4), on the founding of the sanctuary in Jerusalem, MT again subdivides into three.

Verses 27-30 deal with the immediate and long-term consequences of the incident. The immediate consequence is that the relationship has been repaired; the LORD commands the destroying angel to sheathe his sword (v. 27). But there are long-term effects as well (v. 28). David, having once successfully sacrificed at the new altar on the former threshing-floor of Ornan, continues to sacrifice there (the vocabulary implies the communion sacrifices of the repaired relationship).

Indeed, he has to (vv. 29-30). For the sanctuary at Gibeon, whither he has diverted the tabernacle of the LORD and the altar of burnt offerings (1 Chron. 16.39), which were made long ago in the wilderness in the time of Moses, is now debarred to David by the self-same destroying angel (just as the way back to Eden was permanently blocked to the first generation of humanity, Gen. 3.24). The implication is that David once enjoyed immediate access to the altar (cf. 1 Chron. 16.2); but that old relationship of immediacy which David once enjoyed with the LORD is definitively and irreparably ruptured.

1 Chronicles 22.1, which MT places for emphasis in a paragraph by itself, now gives the formal proclamation that David makes to his people. This new altar in Jerusalem is henceforth to be the substitute place, the definitive restart, where oneness between God and people is to be realized. As a consequence of David's guilt (1 Chron. 21.3), a paradigm shift has taken place in the mode of Israel's realization of itself as the people of God; a new balance in the respective roles of king and priesthood has been established. This is where the new house of God, with all its new specifications, rites and clergy, is to be built. It is with this new Temple that most of the remainder of the account

of David's reign and of that of Solomon is concerned down to 2 Chronicles 7.

Verses 2-4 clinch the point of the founding of the new sanctuary. With characteristic exuberance, David forthwith begins the preliminary planning for the construction of the Temple in Jerusalem. The first task is to collect the necessary materials, the stone, the metal and the wood.

David gathers (cf. 1 Chron. 11.1) the resident foreigners to begin the preparations for the most basic of all the materials: he 'appoints' (cf. 1 Chron. 6.31) them to act as quarrymen to produce dressed stone (v. 2; cf. the role of the Gibeonites as hewers of wood for the Temple noted at 1 Chron. 8.29-40). They figure again under Solomon in 2 Chron. 2.17-18, where their numbers and jobs are more closely defined (cf. 2 Chron. 30.25). As Israel finds its role, the nations of the world, from whom Israel took its origins, find among God's people their place in the construction of the new order.

Iron and bronze in amounts beyond computation are prepared (v. 3; for the key root, *kûn*, for the reciprocal actions of David and the LORD, cf. 1 Chron. 14.2): the iron for nails for the doors and for tie-bands, the bronze presumably for the chief furnishings and vessels (cf. 1 Chron. 18.8; 2 Chron. 3.15-17; 4.1-6; 6.13) and for musical instruments (1 Chron. 15.19) though the purpose is not specified here.

> 'Tie-bands' occurs again in C in 2 Chron. 34.11, where it is used of wood.

For the amounts of cedar acquired from Lebanon (v. 4), cf. 1 Chron. 14.1; 2 Chron. 2.2-3. The materials in ascending order of value (stone–iron–bronze–cedarwood) are to be resumed in v. 14 in descending order (gold–silver–bronze–iron–wood–stone), just as v. 15 corresponds to v. 2.

1 CHRONICLES 22.5-19: DAVID COMMISSIONS SOLOMON TO BUILD THE TEMPLE

This section begins the cycle of David's farewell speeches (cf. v. 5) in chs. 22, 28–29, which enfolds his organization of the personnel of the Temple and of supervision of the laity (chs. 23–27).

MT subdivides the section into two subsections:

- vv. 5-6: David's resolve to assist his son Solomon to build the Temple and his appointment of Solomon as builder;
- vv. 7-19: David's address to Solomon (vv. 7-16) and the leaders of the community (vv. 17-19).

In vv. 5-6 David's actions resume the topic of Nathan's oracle in 1 Chronicles 17. It is to be the son of David who succeeds him who will carry out the task of building the Temple. It is notable how it is Temple-building and not kingly rule as such that stands in the foreground: the role of king, that is, of representative of the LORD on earth, is now, with the pacification of the earth, expressed through, and subordinated to, his function as builder of the Temple where the ark of God will be at rest and where at the altar, after the debacle of the previous chapter, the atonement cult will be practised (cf. 1 Chron. 22.1).

> It is simply assumed in C that it is Solomon who succeeds David and not any of David's other sons (cf. the bald statements already in 1 Chron. 6.10, 32; but for his succession as a matter of divine election cf. 1 Chron. 28.6; 29.1): the murky intrigues in 2 Samuel 13–1 Kings 2 concerning the succession to the throne find no echo here (Solomon's chief rivals, such as Absalom and Adonijah, are missing in the narrative sections of C).

The magnitude of the task of Temple-building now confronts David. As a sacramental building dedicated to the LORD as sovereign of the universe, it must share the attributes of God himself (cf., e.g., 1 Chron. 29.11); it must be itself of surpassing glory and fame ('name', 1 Chron. 13.6; so again vv. 7, 8, 10, 19; for the possible pun on 'surpassing', cf. 1 Chron. 14.2). The masterful old king feels acutely the inexperience of Solomon as a raw youth (1 Chron. 29.1; cf. 2 Chron. 13.7; 2 Chron. 34.27). David consequently recognizes the obligation that rests upon himself to make all the necessary arrangements (the key term, *kûn*, 1 Chron. 14.2, is used twice) for the building of the Temple before he dies (v. 5). The centrality and significance of what is done in Jerusalem 'for all lands' is stressed: here continues the exploration of the potentiality of the monarchy to realize God's dominion on earth and thus realize the destiny of Israel at the heart of all humanity—but now through the Temple.

Having willed the means, David now ordains the ends: he formally summons Solomon (v. 6) and instructs him to build the Temple for 'the LORD, the God of Israel', a title that combines both the intimate Israelite and the universal attributes of deity.

Verses 7-16: David's Address to Solomon

David's address is in two parts: a retrospect (vv. 7-10) and an exhortation based on that retrospect (vv. 11-16). The link is formed by the opening word of v. 11, 'now' (cf. 1 Chron. 21.12b).

David begins by referring to the terms of the LORD's promise to his house through Nathan in 1 Chronicles 17. The wording in vv. 7-8aα (and v. 10) is tolerably close (cf. 1 Chron. 17.2-4, 12-14): David's ambition, now long-standing, to honour the LORD by building him a house (the formal expression, 'it has been in my mind', is used in C only in connection with moments of high resolve, usually with reference building or refurbishment of the Temple; cf. 1 Chron. 28.2; 2 Chron. 24.4; 29.10). But, when it comes to giving the reason why David cannot build the Temple (v. 8aβb), the account diverges. It is no longer, as in 1 Chronicles 17, that the idea is unnecessary (since the beginning of the history of his people, the LORD has never desired such a thing) or impossible (the LORD's house is already in being in the house of David). Rather, the reason is ritual (as in 1 Chron. 28.3): David as the shedder of much human blood (1 Chron. 18–20; unatoned, 1 Chron. 21) is not a fit person build a house in honour of the LORD. Here, at least, Solomon's inexperience is an advantage.

The characterization of Solomon as 'a man of rest' (v. 9) is unique. It implies the end of hostilities under the LORD's blessing: 'rest', *m^e^nûḥâ*, is one of the epithets of the land as a place of peace after the turmoil of the settlement struggles (cf. 1 Chron. 6.31; Num. 10.33; Deut. 12.9, and, especially, Solomon's dedicatory prayer, 1 Kgs 8.56) and of the Temple as the resting place of the ark (1 Chron. 22.18; 28.2; Ps. 132.8, 14). This is the fundamental point here: the Temple can be built because it is the 'resting place' of the ark; but the ark can only have a resting place when the LORD, whose symbol in war the ark is, has given to his people the rest which arises from the pacification of the world. The verb from the same root, 'to give rest', thus follows in the next phrase. 'The giver of rest' is a stock conception for the LORD, especially in Deuteronomic passages, such as Exod. 33.14; Deut. 12.10; 25.19; Josh. 1.13; 23.1; 2 Sam. 7.1, 11; 1 Kgs 5.4; cf. 1 Chron. 23.25; 2 Chron. 14.5-6; 15.15; 20.30.

The particular word play on 'Solomon' [*š^e^lōmô*, 'his peace'] and 'peace' [*šālôm*; cf. 1 Chron. 12.18], reflecting the theory that the name conveys the nature, is also unique (though the association is to be found in 1 Kgs 4.24-25). The following word, 'quiet', is particularly associated in C with cessation of war or communal strife (1 Chron. 4.40; 2 Chron. 14.1, 5-6; 20.30; 23.21).

Verse 10, the climactic statement about Solomon as worthy builder of Temple because of his status as adopted son, echoes closely the phraseology of the Nathan oracle of 1 Chron. 17.12-14. The keynote root, *kûn* (1 Chron. 14.2) is yet again used (cf. v. 5), this time in connection the LORD'S establishment of Solomon's throne.

David now turns to exhort Solomon (v. 11). The warrant has been given; the implications can now be drawn. The prayer that the LORD will be 'with' Solomon sounds the messianic expectation (so vv. 16, 18; cf. 1 Chron. 5.20; 11.9). Only on this basis can he 'succeed' (*hiṣlîaḥ*, now to become another thematic term).

The verb *hiṣlîaḥ*, 'to succeed, prosper', occurs usually in material unique to C (but 2 Chron. 18.11, 14 is paralleled in 1 Kgs 22.12, 15). Success is a divine gift, which is conditional upon seeking the LORD, defined here expressly in terms of obedience to the commandments of the Torah (vv. 12-13). The verb becomes a thematic term for the reign of Solomon (1 Chron. 29.23; 2 Chron. 7.11) and for subsequent kings (2 Chron. 14.4-7; 20.20; contrast 13.12; 24.20; 26.5; 31.21; 32.30).

Appropriately for the dawning status of Solomon, David has switched from 'the LORD, *my* God' (v. 7) to 'the LORD, *your* God' (v. 11).

David prays for the divine gifts of prudence and understanding (the same pairing of attributes as in 2 Chron. 2.12) and of guidance so that the law may be put into effect (vv. 12-13). That will be the assurance of success. There is a deliberate incorporation of the primary system of Israel's life, the law of Moses with its statutes and ordinances, into the new order. But this association with the Law introduces an important qualification to the relationship between God and the house of David: whereas from 1 Chronicles 17 it might appear that the relationship is unconditional, here it is made unambiguous that the relationship and the blessings that flow from it are dependent upon the obedience and commitment of the Davidic king as measured by the Torah (cf. 1 Chron. 28.7-8; 2 Chron. 6.16; 23.18; every promise is conditional, for example, the promise to Josiah, 2 Chron. 34.28, as contrasted with 35.23-24).

David's exhortation to Solomon, 'be strong [*ḥzq*, 1 Chron. 11.10] and courageous' is, therefore, reminiscent of that of Moses to his successor, Joshua (e.g. Deut. 31.7-8; cf. Deut. 1.21; Josh. 8.1, to be repeated by David to Solomon in similar terms in 1 Chron. 28.20; cf. 2 Chron. 20.15, 17; 32.7; for David as the new Moses, cf. 1 Chron. 16.1-4).

David refers to the immediate task (vv. 14-15 correspond in part in reverse order to vv. 2-4): at the cost of much personal exertion (for David's 'affliction' cf. Ps. 132.1), he has made ready (again the key-note root, *kûn*, v. 5) vast quantities of the materials for the construction of the Temple, the 100,000 talents of gold and the 1,000,000 talents of silver (for the sums, cf. tables at 1 Chron. 21.25; 29.4), besides untold bronze and the iron. In the light of 1 Chron. 29.2, the 'stone' that he has prepared includes both jewels and fine building-materials. Teams of the necessary labourers and craftsmen have equally been organized. Verse 16 now goes beyond what was begun in vv. 2-4.

In vv. 17-19, David turns in a concluding exhortation to all the leaders of the community 'to help' (1 Chron. 5.20) his son. This section anticipates 1 Chronicles 28–29.

David's speech is again divided into two parts, with the hinge-word 'now' at the beginning of the second part in v. 19 (cf. v. 11). Verse 18 thus provides the ground for the action they are exhorted to take. It is a retrospect couched in the form of a rhetorical question in order to constrain still greater assent and commitment. They can see that the LORD their God (1 Chron. 11.2) has been with them (cf. v. 11), and that, therefore, the world round about has been pacified (the same root for 'rest' as in v. 9) and the land and its inhabitants (1 Chron. 11.4) have been subdued (2 Chron. 28.10) before David as the LORD's vicegerent and themselves as his host.

The appropriate response is, therefore, demanded (v. 19). The commitment required is one of 'heart and soul', the whole-hearted application of mind and emotion (1 Chron. 28.9; 2 Chron. 15.12; 34.31). The task is defined by the key term, 'seeking the LORD' (*drš*, 1 Chron. 10.13-14), with the double designation of deity. The way so to seek the LORD, to resort to him in all things, is the new order of the Temple. The building of the Temple will complete the affirmation of the universal sovereignty of God and will bring together every means of consulting and relying upon his will: the ark of the covenant representing the immediacy of the tie between Israel and the LORD, presently in its tent in Jerusalem (1 Chron. 16.1), and the whole ritual system of the objective worship of the cosmic God, presently located in the Tabernacle at Gibeon (1 Chron. 16.39). The fulfilment of this exhortation is in 2 Chron. 5.5.

1 Chronicles 23–27: The Personnel of Temple and Community

In 1 Chron. 22.5-16, David has designated Solomon as builder of the Temple. Now in 1 Chron. 23.1 David 'makes Solomon king'. But, despite David's address to the leaders of the community (1 Chron. 22.17-19), there is, as yet, no response or assent from these leaders. That has to wait until 1 Chron. 29.22, when 'they make Solomon... king a second time'. In preparation for that public acknowledgment, the aged David now (v. 2) turns to organize the personnel, clerical and lay, who will serve the Temple and community. This organization is part of the blueprint that David will pass to Solomon in 1 Chron. 28.11-19. David's inappropriate census of 1 Chronicles 21 is now followed in 1 Chronicles 23–27 by the appropriate numbering of the people (1 Chron. 23.3; 27.1) and assignment of their duties.

> The verb 'to gather' has been used at a similarly decisive moment of organization for change in 1 Chron. 15.4 and of concerted action in 1 Chron. 19.17; compare 1 Chron. 11.1.

The following chapters spell out the various groups referred to in v. 2, to which it thus acts as title:

1. the Levites (1 Chron. 23);
    2. the priests and non-Aaronic Levites (1 Chron. 24);
    3. the musicians (1 Chron. 25);
    4. the gatekeepers and treasurers (1 Chron. 26);
5. the lay supervisors (1 Chron. 27).

'Levite' is the comprehensive term for the clerical personnel serving the Temple; it thus includes the specialized roles listed in the following groups 2–4. Some of the names given in 1 Chronicles 23, indeed, recur in 1 Chronicles 24 and 26.

> There is a series of resumptions and interconnections between these chapters:

1 Chron. 23.3	defines the age at which the Levites are eligible for service as thirty and is resumed by 1 Chron. 23.24, which redefines it as twenty, and is then followed by a résumé of their duties in 1 Chron. 23.25-32;
1 Chron. 23.13	lists Aaron and is resumed by 1 Chron. 24.1-19, which gives a breakdown of the twenty-four divisions of the Aaronic priesthood;
1 Chron. 23.16-24aα	lists the non-Aaronic Levites of Kohath and Merari and is resumed in 1 Chron. 24.20-31;
1 Chron. 24.1-19	introduces the casting of lots for priestly service; the divisions by lot of non-priestly Levites and of the levitical musicians and gatekeepers follows in 1 Chron. 24.20–26.

The major paragraph markers of MT throw the priesthood in 1 Chron. 24.1-19, with its three subdivisions, into prominence. 1 Chronicles 23 is dealt with in one major section (with considerable subdivision); 1 Chron. 24.20–25.8 links the remainder of the Levites with the musicians; the divisions of the musicians is dealt with in a separate section in 1 Chron. 25.9-31; the gatekeepers and treasurers are given great prominence in four paragraphs in 1 Chronicles 26; the laity in two paragraphs in 1 Chronicles 27.

The laity, mentioned first in 1 Chron. 23.2, are treated last in 1 Chronicles 27. They open and close the system and thus form the framework for the whole. This is appropriate: while the system of holiness managed and maintained by the Levites is the means, it is the role of Israel that is the end.

1. *The Levites (1 Chronicles 23.3-32)*

Sensationally, now it is legitimate to count the Levites (v. 3; contrast 1 Chron. 21.2, 5, where words from the same root are used). One must assume that the proper procedures as laid down in Numbers 4 are being followed (the key term of the sacral muster, *pqd*, cf. 1 Chron. 21.4, occurs in vv. 11, 24). The age at which the Levites can officiate is initially given here as thirty (v. 3). This corresponds to the legislation in Num. 4.3-49 and contrasts with twenty-five in Num. 8.24 and the subsequent modification to twenty later in this chapter (vv. 24-27; so Ezra 3.8).

The 38,000 (easily accommodated within the statistical discrepancy noted in 1 Chron. 21.5-6; the clergy thus amount to about one in thirty of the adult male population) are divided as follows (vv. 4-5):

24,000 to superintend all the 'work', that is, rites and activities, in the Temple, rather than its construction (cf. vv. 28-32 for a full account). The number is obviously determined by the 12 months of the year (cf. 1 Chron. 27).

6000 supervisors and arbiters

4000 gatekeepers

4000 musicians—'hymning the LORD on the instruments I have appointed for the purpose' (for the first-person interjection, cf. 1 Chron. 28.19)

These round figures suggest the ideological nature of the writing.

David divides these into their 'divisions', their duty-rosters, a term that will now recur frequently in connection not only with David in chs. 23–28 and Solomon (2 Chron. 8.14; contrast 2 Chron. 5.11), but also with reforming priests and kings (2 Chron. 23.8; 31.2, 15-17; 35.4, 10). The genealogical connections of the Levites in vv. 6-23 are best appreciated in tabular form (see opposite).

MT divides the genealogical material into nine paragraphs, no doubt for similar purposes: broadly, each generation is given a different paragraph, except in paras. 7 (vv. 13-18, where the descendants of Moses are included) and 9 (again Merari is not separated but heads the final section, vv. 21-32; cf. 1 Chron. 9.12-32).

A number of points may be made about this table.

C has already given many of these names in connection with the central role assigned to the Levites by David in 1 Chronicles 6 in the pre-Temple period (1 Chron. 6.32). These arrangements are now brought up to date for the Temple itself.

The names of the first two generations of Levi and his three sons follow the standard form (as in, for example, Gen. 46.11). As far as the third generation is concerned, the only deviation is the name of the elder son of Gershon, which is given as Libni in 1 Chron. 6.17 (so Exod. 6.17, Num. 3.18, 21; cf. Num. 26.58). Ladan reappears in 1 Chron. 26.21.

Apart from Aaron and Moses, the names of the fourth generation are not so familiar and occasion some difficulties. Some are markedly divergent from other lists. In Exod. 6.21-22 the sons of Izhar are Korah (so Num. 16.1, cf. Num. 26.58), Nepheg and Zichri, while the sons of Uzziel are Mishael, Elzaphan and Sithri. Jehiel reappears in 1 Chron. 29.8 in charge of the treasuries (so along with Zetham and Joel in 1 Chron. 26.20-25 where they are his sons). Joel has perhaps already figured at the bringing up of the ark of the covenant into Jerusalem in 1 Chron. 15.7, 11, along with the sons of Hebron and Uzziel (but not those listed here).

The Levites (1 Chronicles 23.6-23)

<table>
<tr><td colspan="10">Levi</td></tr>
<tr><td colspan="2">Gershon</td><td colspan="6">Kohath</td><td colspan="2">Merari</td></tr>
<tr><td>Ladan</td><td>Shimei</td><td colspan="3">Amram</td><td>Izhar</td><td>Hebron</td><td>Uzziel</td><td>Mahli</td><td>Mushi</td></tr>
<tr><td>Jehiel</td><td>Jahath Zin/za Jeush+Beriah</td><td>Aaron</td><td colspan="2">Moses</td><td>Shelomith</td><td>Jeriah Amariah Jahaziel Jekameam</td><td>Micah Isshiah</td><td>Eleazar Kish</td><td>Mahli Eder Jeremoth</td></tr>
<tr><td>Zetham Joel</td><td></td><td></td><td colspan="2"></td><td></td><td></td><td></td><td></td><td></td></tr>
<tr><td>?Shelomoth Haziel Haran</td><td></td><td></td><td>Gershom</td><td>Eliezer</td><td></td><td></td><td></td><td></td><td></td></tr>
<tr><td></td><td></td><td></td><td>Shebuel</td><td>Rehabiah</td><td></td><td></td><td></td><td></td><td></td></tr>
</table>

The precise affiliation of Shelomoth, Haziel and Haran is not clear (the first two show a passing resemblance to sons of Izhar and Hebron in vv. 18-19; the name Haziel is not otherwise known in the Hebrew Bible nor is Haran elsewhere used of a Levite): in v. 9 they are said to be heads of household, yet in vv. 10-11 four (other?) sons of Shimei are given, two of whom are considered as forming a single household for a shared assignment of duty. Jahath has already figured in the pre-Temple organization in 1 Chron. 6.43. Zina (or Zizah, as he appears in v. 11), Jeush and Beriah are otherwise unknown.

The names of Moses' sons, Gershom and Eliezer, are recorded together only in Exod. 18.3-4 (Exod. 2.22 for Gershon alone) and again in C at 1 Chron. 26.24-25 in connection with responsibilities for the treasuries. So similarly Shebuel and Rehabiah (1 Chron. 24.20-21; 26.24-25).

Izhar has already been encountered in the pre-Temple arrangements in 1 Chron. 6.2-47. He also will reappear in 1 Chron. 24.22 with Shelomith. Hebron's sons are repeated in 1 Chron. 24.23, the first also in 1 Chron. 26.31. Uzziel's, Mahli's and Mushi's sons also are repeated in 1 Chron. 24.24-30.

Within the lists of names there are a few discursive items. Verse 13 gives a preview of the exceptional status of Aaron, which is to be the subject of 1 Chronicles 24. Aaron and his descendants, as the priests, are those who are in charge of the 'most holy' (cf. 1 Chron. 6.49; 2 Chron. 3.8, 10; 4.22; 5.7).

The term 'most holy' is applied in the Hebrew Bible to the altar and the furnishings of the Temple as a whole (e.g. Exod. 30.29), the incense (Exod. 30.36) and certain offerings (the cereal offering, the sin offering and the guilt offering, e.g. Num. 18.9; the showbread, Lev. 24.9; devoted objects, Lev. 27.28).

It is also their task to officiate at the altar of burnt offerings and to pronounce the 'Aaronic' blessing (Num. 6.24-26).

Moses, as 'man of God', is the prophetic figure *par excellence* (v. 14; for the title see, for example, 1 Sam. 9.6; 1 Kgs 17.24). But the subordination of the prophet to the function of the Levite is indicated by the way in which his descendants are firmly located among the Levites (cf. 1 Chron. 25.1 for the role of prophecy within the liturgy).

C provides a summary of the duties of the Levites (vv. 24-32). The hierarchy is firmly in place, family by family, with the responsible heads within each clearly designated to ensure the execution of the tasks assigned.

Verses 24-27 describe the modification in counting the Levites that David now introduces. Whereas in v. 3 the age for enrolment in service is thirty, here it is reduced to twenty. This reduction in age is directly connected with the new era of peace that the construction of the Temple as resting place for the ark symbolizes (cf. 1 Chron. 22.9). The construction of the Temple now also makes redundant the movable shrine of the Tabernacle, which it was the duty of the Levites to transport (Num. 4; the verb in the phrase 'the LORD *has taken up residence* in Jerusalem', v. 25, is from the same root as 'tabernacle'). The Levites can now devote all their attention from the age of twenty to the practice of the system of holiness.

The connection between the reduction of the age of enrolment of the Levites and the era of peace is not clear. If the duty of transportation has been removed, one would have thought that fewer, not more, Levites should be brought into service. Does the previous age of thirty imply that hitherto the Levites were also liable to military service between the ages of twenty and thirty (for twenty as the age for the enrolment of the rest of the community in the army, cf. Num. 1.3; twenty is also defined as the age of attaining adulthood, for example in Exod. 30.14; Lev. 27.3)? Levites as bearers of arms have already figured in C, 1 Chron. 12.26-28. Num. 1.47-51, reflecting conditions here superseded, expressly forbids such an enrolment of the Levites.

The specific duties of the Levites (other than those who were priests) are given in some detail in vv. 28-32. These verses give as complete a picture of the activities of the Levites in the Temple as can be found anywhere in the Hebrew Bible.

Their 'appointment' (literally, 'place of standing', from the root *'md*, 1 Chron. 6.31) is to assist the priests in maintaining the rites of the Temple; the goal of all that they do is the maintenance of 'the purity of all holy things' (v. 28; see, for example, 2 Chron. 29.15-18; 34.3-8 for the conjunction of purification and holiness). For this purpose, they supervise access to the two courts of the Temple (2 Chron. 33.5; cf., e.g., 1 Kgs 6.36; 2 Kgs 21.5; 23.12). The outer court was that to which the laity were admitted (Jer. 26.2; Ezek. 10.5, cf. sketch at 2 Chron. 23.5). The inner court was the 'court of the priests' (2 Chron. 4.9). For an indication of the difference in holiness between the two courts, including the danger of 'infecting' the outer court with the holiness of the inner, see Ezek. 42.14; 44.17, 19, 21; 2 Chron. 29.16.

There were side chambers in each court and the Levites were also responsible for good practice in them. The chambers in the outside court were the rooms where the meals associated with the communion sacrifice were eaten by the representatives of the laity (cf. 1 Sam. 9.22). Such chambers continued to be associated with prominent families (cf., e.g., Jer. 35.2, 4; 36.10, 12). There were thus appropriate arrangements for sacrificial slaughter associated with them (Ezek. 40.38). In the inner court were the chambers of the Levites, both priestly and non-priestly. There the priests guarded the sacred vessels of the cultus (Ezra 8.29) and ate 'the most holy things' relating to the cereal, sin and guilt offerings (Ezek. 42.13), and stored the first-fruits and the tithes, which the Levites were instrumental in collecting (Neh. 10.35-39; cf. Neh. 13.5, 9).

Among the rites of the Temple themselves ('the practice of the service of the house of God', v. 28), they were responsible for preparing and arranging the showbread (v. 29; cf. 1 Chron. 9.32). The grain offering (already 1 Chron. 9.29) was presented at the altar of burnt offerings as an integral part of the morning and evening sacrifice, as well as on other stated and *ad hoc* occasions (cf. Lev. 7.12; 14.10, 21; Num. 6.15; 15.4; 28–29). A number of its special features are mentioned here: it was in the form of fine flour (of which also the bread of the presence was made, Lev. 24.5), mixed with oil, and of wafers of unleavened bread which had had oil poured over them. As a substitute for the holocaust offered by an individual, the grain offering could be in form of flour mixed with oil, or oven-baked or griddle-baked (cf. Lev. 2.5). Significantly for their responsibilities in this connection, the grain offering featured in the rites by which the priesthood were themselves consecrated (Exod. 29.2; Lev. 6.20-23; cf. Num. 8.8 for Levites); as 'most holy things' they figured as part of their emoluments from the offerings of Israel that they had to consecrate (e.g. Lev. 2.3; 5.11-13).

Their responsibility for absolute standards of measure of volume and length (v. 29; cf. Lev. 19.35-36) is understandable: the Levites in their network of levitical cities were responsible for the ingathering of the tithes, that is, the tokens of the sanctity of Israel's life as a whole. It is precisely short-changing in such offerings in kind that constitutes *ma'al* (Lev. 5.15). The singers and instrumentalists among them had to be present at the time of the daily morning and evening sacrifices to raise the thanksgivings and the hymns (v. 30; cf. 1 Chron. 16.4). For the tariff of sacrifices at the stated weekly, monthly and annual festivals, v. 31, cf. again Numbers 28–29.

In sum, the supervision of the whole system of sanctification, all the activities in the Temple and of all engaged in them, falls to the Levites (v. 32; so already, 1 Chron. 9.27; cf., e.g., Num. 3.6-9; yet they in turn are under the direction of the priests, Num. 18.1-6). The terms 'tent of meeting', meaning the nave of the Temple, and 'sanctuary', meaning the inner sanctuary of the Temple, are traditional terms retained from the account of the tabernacle, as in, for example, Lev. 16.17.

2. *The Priests (1 Chronicles 24.1-19) and Non-priestly Levites of Kohath and Merari (1 Chronicles 24.20-31)*

The Priests (1 Chronicles 24.1-19)

Verse 1 picks up the list of descendants of Aaron left undeveloped at 1 Chron. 23.13. The resumption of the list of non-priestly Levites from 1 Chron. 23.16-24aα in 1 Chron. 24.20-30 has the effect of throwing this section on the Aaronic priesthood into greater prominence.

The MT division into three sections also adds weight to this account of the priesthood: vv. 1-6 (subdivided vv. 1-5, v. 6), the two major families of the Aaronic priesthood and their twenty-four divisions; vv. 7-18, their duty-roster assigned by lot; v. 19, formal summary.

Once again the interrelationship of the names in vv. 1-19 can be grasped more readily by means of a table (see following page).

The right-hand column of this table lists the twenty-four divisions of the duty roster of the two surviving priestly families, Eleazar and Ithamar. This column is not genealogical, but lists the priestly families in the order which they were assigned by lot (v. 5): thus the first sixteen do not belong exclusively to Eleazar, nor the last eight to Ithamar (for example, on the argument of 1 Chron. 9.10, 12, nos. 1, 2 and 21 belong to Eleazar and 5 and 16 to Ithamar).

It may be presumed that the number of divisions relates to the twelve months of the year, and thus points to a roster of duties in the Temple (cf. 1 Chron. 27.1). The proportion 2 Eleazar:1 Ithamar suggests the ideological nature of the composition; organizational realities are here cast in the form of family relationship.

Numbers 4 gives a rare insight into the respective supervisory duties of the priests: Eleazar in connection with Kohath, and Ithamar in connection with Gershon and Merari. This supervisory role makes it appropriate that the non-priestly Levites of the families of Kohath and Merari follow in vv. 20-31 and the musicians and gatekeepers in chs. 25–26.

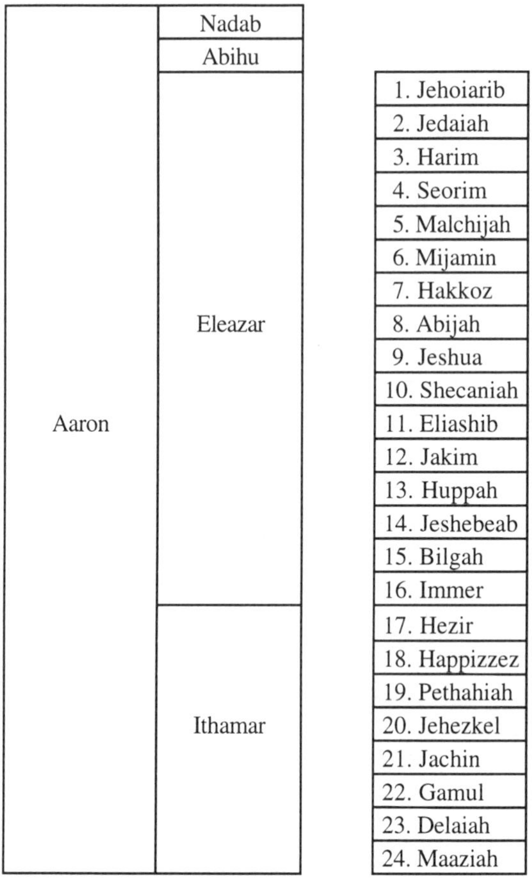
Aaron
Nadab
Abihu
Eleazar
Ithamar
1. Jehoiarib
2. Jedaiah
3. Harim
4. Seorim
5. Malchijah
6. Mijamin
7. Hakkoz
8. Abijah
9. Jeshua
10. Shecaniah
11. Eliashib
12. Jakim
13. Huppah
14. Jeshebeab
15. Bilgah
16. Immer
17. Hezir
18. Happizzez
19. Pethahiah
20. Jehezkel
21. Jachin
22. Gamul
23. Delaiah
24. Maaziah

Verse 1a acts as a title. There is a sense that the abrupt opening is a continuation of 1 Chron. 23.6, which is then modified by v. 3: David is organizing the personnel of the sanctuary, but at the heart of the cultus it is no longer David alone, who has now forfeited his immediacy of access to God as high priest (1 Chron. 16.3), who has sole right of organizing the priesthood. Associated with David's authority, which is, in truth, a supervisory authority, since the actual allocation of duties is to be made by lot, are now the leaders of the two priestly families: the singular verb, 'he divided', becomes the plural, 'they divided' in v. 4. Indeed, by v. 19, authority to assign duties has passed directly to Aaron alone under direct command of God (the last phrase of v. 3, 'their assignment by their duties', is resumed at the beginning of v. 19).

In v. 1, as elsewhere in the Hebrew Bible, the two older sons of

Aaron, destroyed because of liturgical malpractice (Lev. 10.1-7, Num. 3.2-4; 26.60-61), though not a word of that is breathed here, retain their place even if without function in the ideal presentation (cf. Exod. 24.1, 9). They provide C with yet another example of false start and restart (cf. 1 Chron. 6.3).

David is assisted in the task of assigning duties by the contemporary representatives of the two main surviving branches, Zadok of the Eleazar branch and Ahimelech of the Ithamar (v. 3). C records none of the intrigues, recorded in Samuel–Kings, of Zadok and Ahimelech's father, Abiathar, surrounding the accession of Solomon (1 Kgs 1–2). His theory of the affiliation of Zadok places him firmly within a unitary Israelite tradition (see especially, already, 1 Chron. 6.8, 12; 15.11; 16.39; Ezra 7.2; Neh. 11.11). Ahimelech, son of Ahitub, priest of Nob (1 Sam. 21.2ff.), has been mentioned already (as Abimelech in MT) in 1 Chron. 18.16.

Fair dealing is assured (v. 5), not only by the presence of these leaders of their respective branches, but also by assigning the duties among these divisions by lot. Their equal status is indicated by the unique title, 'leaders of holy things, leaders of God' (cf. Isa. 43.28), which they all share. For the use of lots on such occasions, see also the apportioning of the promised land among the twelve tribes of Israel (e.g. Josh. 19.51) or the allocation of levitical cities (Josh. 21.1-40; cf. 1 Chron. 6.54-81; 25.9; 26.14). By this means the direct guidance of God is sought (cf. 1 Sam. 14.38-45).

In v. 6 (a sub-paragraph in MT), a levitical scribe, otherwise unknown (but cf. 1 Chron. 18.16), formally registers the roster before the king and the officials of the community, Zadok (now elevated here as '*the* priest'), Ahimelech, and the heads of the families of priests and Levites. The last phrase of v. 6 is obscure but it seems to indicate the 2:1 ratio of Eleazar over Ithamar (cf. JPSV: 'one clan more taken for Eleazar for each one taken of Ithamar').

In vv. 7-18, of the twenty-four names, only nos. 1, 2, 5, 16 and 21 have figured in the list of the inhabitants of Jerusalem in 1 Chron. 9.10-12, while nos. 1-3, 6, 8 (9?), 10, 15, 16 and 24 figure in one or other of the lists of priests in Ezra 2.36-39 // Neh. 7.39-42; Ezra 10.21-22; Neh. 10.2-8; 12.1-7, 12-21. No. 5 may be represented by his 'son', Pashhur, who figures in some of these lists (cf. Jer. 21.1). No.7 was one of the priestly families that had difficulty in establishing its credentials in the post-exilic period (Ezra 2.61 // Neh. 7.63).

The formal summary in v. 19 picks up v. 3. The omission of David now is notable: the authority for the drawing up of the duty roster is now attributed to Aaron. The reference 'in accordance with their practice as directed by Aaron...as the Lord the God of Israel commanded him' must be to Numbers 3–4, despite the supersession of tabernacle by Temple (cf. 1 Chron. 23.24). Whatever the variations in practice, the principles remain and there is continuity between the institutions. A sense of 'timeless contemporaneity' is again evident (cf. 1 Chron. 9.3-34).

The Non-Aaronic Levites of Kohath and Merari (1 Chronicles 24.20-31)

The MT paragraphing links this section with the musicians in 1 Chronicles 25.

Verses 20-31 pick up 1 Chron. 23.16-24aα, resuming the question of the families of the non-priestly Levites. Once again, tabulation makes C's presentation more readily appreciated (see opposite).

The differences from 1 Chronicles 23 are apparent. The line of Gershon has been omitted (other names omitted are placed in brackets in the table); that is, the discussion resumes from, essentially, 1 Chron. 23.16: the family of Amram of the line of Kohath, from the point immediately after Aaron, who, as the father of the priesthood, has just been the subject of the substantial discussion in 1 Chron. 24.1-19. Again, C throws the theological point he is making into relief by the literary formulation: the Aaronic priesthood stands centrally, girt around by the Levites.

> Some of the names show presumably trivial difference—Shubael, Shelomoth and Jerimoth. A more substantial difficulty is presented in vv. 26-27, where it is uncertain how Jaaziah and his sons fit in under the line of Merari.

These verses add eleven names to the later generations of the various levitical lines. Of these none is otherwise identifiable with certainty. Nor are their roles more closely defined. However, it is striking that if 'Beno' is understood as 'his son' rather than a proper name, the names of 24 Levites of the fourth and subsequent generations are here listed, a number which would indeed correspond with the 24 divisions of the priesthood detailed earlier in the chapter, as v. 31 suggests. These Levites, who are neither musicians (1 Chron. 25) nor gatekeepers (1 Chron. 26), are presumably the direct assistants in cultic

The Non-Aaronic Levites of Kohath and Merari (1 Chronicles 24.20-31)

<table>
<tr><td colspan="10">(Levi)</td></tr>
<tr><td colspan="7">(Kohath)</td><td colspan="3">Merari</td></tr>
<tr><td colspan="3">Amram</td><td>Izhar</td><td>Hebron</td><td colspan="2">Uzziel</td><td colspan="2">Mahli</td><td>Mushi</td></tr>
<tr><td>(Aaron)</td><td colspan="2">(Moses)</td><td>Shelomoth</td><td>Jeriah Amariah Jahaziel Jekameam</td><td>Micah</td><td>Isshiah</td><td>Eleazar</td><td>Kish</td><td>Mahli Eder Jerimoth</td></tr>
<tr><td></td><td>(Gershom)</td><td>(Eliezer)</td><td>Jahath</td><td></td><td>Shamir</td><td>Zechariah</td><td></td><td>Jerahmeel</td><td></td></tr>
<tr><td></td><td>Shubael</td><td>Rehabiah</td><td></td><td></td><td></td><td></td><td colspan="3">?Jaaziah</td></tr>
<tr><td></td><td>Jehdeiah</td><td>Isshiah</td><td></td><td></td><td></td><td></td><td colspan="3">Beno Shoham Zaccur Ibri</td></tr>
</table>

matters to the priests ('side by side', v. 31 [NEB]; for omnibus portrayal, see 1 Chron. 6.48; 2 Chron. 8.14; 31.2, 35.14). Again, the strict supervision by the highest personages in the community to ensure non-preferential treatment by the assigning of the duties by lot is stressed.

3. *The Musicians (1 Chronicles 25)*

Verse 1 shows how the three families of musicians, Asaph, Heman and Jeduthun, each represent one of the main families of the Levites: Gershon, Kohath and Merari respectively (cf. 1 Chron. 6.31-47; 15.16–16.42). The opening verb, 'David...*separated*...' is thus carefully chosen: the musicians are designated from the main body of the Levites to fulfil a particular levitical task.

> MT thus treats vv. 1-8 as the continuation of 1 Chron. 24.20-31 with good reason: out of the bulk of the non-priestly Levites of 1 Chron. 23.6-23; 24.20-30, 288 (v. 7; = 12 × 24) specialist musicians are appointed to represent all three families.
>
> MT further subdivides: vv. 1-3; 4-6bα; 6bβ-7. Verses 1-3 give the general introduction, with the families of Asaph and Jeduthun and their four plus six members; vv. 4-6bα the family of Heman with its fourteen members; plus the matching conclusion to v. 1 in v. 6abα. The apparent eccentricity of MT's division of vv. 6bβ from 6bα is not without its rationale: it is a *casus pendens*, 'As for Asaph...' introducing the final note on the skill and numbers of the musicians, and the impartiality of their placing in the roster.

The terms used here for Israel as a participatory worshipping community are astonishingly elevated. Israel itself are called the 'host', the sacramental term generally reserved for the people as mobilized for military action in the service of the LORD, as the earthly counterpart of his cosmic forces (1 Chron. 5.18). Their leaders are, therefore, 'officers' (1 Chron. 11.6). As in other passages in the Hebrew Bible (e.g. Josh. 6; Isa. 30.29-33), however, war has here been transposed into the liturgy of the cult: by dynamic intervention in war symbolized by the ark, now laid up in the Temple, the 'LORD of hosts' has given rest to his people; the intervention to secure that rest is now to be appropriated through the liturgy. It is Israel as a whole acting concertedly through their military leaders who set apart the leaders of their praise.

The function of music, equally, could not be stated more loftily: it is nothing less than 'prophesying' (v. 1; cf. vv. 2, 3, 5, where the ancestors of the musicians are said to 'prophesy' or are called 'seer'). Through the medium of the liturgy, the word of God is imparted to the worshipping community. In this ideal presentation, those who are set apart are thereby empowered to be direct channels of communication between God and people. It is in response to the actions of the LORD now expressed in word and appropriated in liturgical action that the thanksgiving and hymn of the congregation are raised.

Strings (lyre and lute) and percussion (cymbals) are the standard musical instruments identified (so already 1 Chron. 13.8; 15.16, 28; 16.5).

The three divisions of the musicians are now given (vv. 2-5) under their eponymous ancestors, in the order Asaph (Gershon), Jeduthun (Merari), and Heman (Kohath). It is unlikely that each group played a separate instrument, despite the fact that in v. 3 Jeduthun appears to be identified as the lyre players (compare 1 Chron. 15.19, where all three leaders sound the cymbals, or 2 Chron. 5.12, where the leaders, but not the instruments, are in the same sequence; the particular task 'to raise the hymn and thanksgiving' [1 Chron. 16.4] is associated in Ezra 3.10-11 with the cymbals). In v. 5 there is an obscure reference to Heman 'raising a horn (*qeren*)', but that is a metaphorical expression, meaning 'to triumph' (cf. Lam. 2.17), and has nothing to do with sounding the horn (*šôpār*, or *yôbēl*) as a musical instrument (in a similar context in 1 Chron. 15.16 the text runs, 'to raise loud sound *with voice* [*b*ᵉ*qôl*]'). Equally, the summary in v. 6 lumps all the musicians together without distinction of role or competence, while the statistics in these and the following verses, with their very uneven distribution among the three families and the random way in which the families are associated by lot, require that competence in all aspects of music-making was shared by each family.

The expression, 'at the hands of the king', in v. 2 does not seem to imply special status or function for Asaph (despite 1 Chron. 16.37), since it is applied to all three in v. 6.

Like the priesthood, they are allotted twenty-four divisions, but, unlike the priesthood, not all are descended from the central family of Kohath. Nonetheless, the centrality of Kohath is recognized in that it provides the major share of the musicians: Heman has fourteen divisions, while Asaph has only four and Jeduthun six.

Once again, in order to secure perfect fairness and consonance with the LORD's will, no matter the age, status, experience and skill of those concerned, the order in which the divisions serve is determined by lot (v. 8; cf. 1 Chron. 24.5-31). The sequence in which these twenty-four descendants of Asaph, Jeduthun and Heman officiate is given in vv. 9-31: Asaph's four descendants take up positions 3, 1, 5, and 7 in the sequence; Jeduthun's six, 2, 4, 8, 10 (the name 'Shimei' is restored in v. 3 from v. 17), 12 and 14; Heman's fourteen in the order 6, 9, 11(?), 13, 15, 16, 18, 20, 22, 24, 17, 19, 21 and 23.

The names of some of Heman's descendants in particular throw up some obscurities (there are minor variations in the names of some of the others): he is credited with 14 sons, but 15 are listed; Uzziel and Ezer (v. 4) correspond to none of the names in the list in vv. 9-31, the nearest being Azarel (v. 18), with whom one or other must be equated; NRSV gets the right number by assuming that Romamti-ezer is one name. In addition, some of the names in v. 4 are in anomalous forms as proper names, especially, Giddalti, 'I have magnified', Romamti, 'I have exalted', Joshbekashah, 'one dwelling in hardship', Mallothi, 'I have languished'.

Only some of the 24 individuals seem to recur in the Hebrew Bible: Zaccur in Neh. 12.35; Mattithiah in 1 Chron. 15.18, 21; 16.5; Mattaniah in 1 Chron. 9.15; Neh. 11.17 (perhaps an example of C's way of making different generations contemporaneous, cf. Hanani here and Neh. 12.36).

In vv. 9-31, twelve members of family, 'sons and brothers', are assigned to each of the 24 'sons' of Asaph, Jeduthun and Heman, producing the grand total of 288 noted in v. 7 (a phrase similar to those at the end of all these verse has to be added at the end of v. 9a to make the sums come right). Again, the ideological character of these figures is clear: the fixed number of musicians needed at any one time to lead the worship in the Temple determines the number of 'sons' and 'brothers'. A similar artificiality is no doubt to be seen in the perfect numbers of Heman's family in v. 5: 2 × 7 sons + 3 daughters.

4. *The Gatekeepers and Treasurers (1 Chronicles 26)*

For material on the gatekeepers and treasurers, cf. especially 1 Chron. 9.12-32.

There is an initial temptation to divide the chapter into two sections by topic (*BHK* and *BHS*): vv. 1-19 on the gatekeepers; vv. 20-32 on the treasurers (especially since v. 19 is a summary of what has gone before; but then so is v. 12). But, as in 1 Chron. 9.12-32, both groups of officials are dealt with by MT together (though here in a more complex subdivision): the delivery of materials to the treasuries (the key external indicator of the practice of holiness by the community) is obviously dependent on the work of the gatekeepers. This is made clear in v. 15: the reception point for the people's offerings in kind is at the south gate, whence it is transmitted by the gatekeepers to the treasurers.

Thus the MT divisions cut across these groups:

vv. 1-5:	the two main families of gatekeepers, Meshelemiah and Obed-edom;
vv. 6-13:	subdivided between the next generations of Obed-edom (vv. 6-9) and Hosah (vv. 10-13);
vv. 14-28:	subdivided between casting of lots for duty at the east and north gates (Meshelemiah; v. 14) and at the south (Obed-edom) and west (Hosah) gates, followed by the treasurers who work in the Temple (vv. 15-28);
vv. 29-32:	the Levites who work outside the Temple, supervising the contributions of the laity in the landward areas.

The gatekeepers of the Temple are derived from the two Levitical families of Kohath (specifically, Korah, vv. 1-3, 9) and Merari (vv. 4-8, 10-11). The treasurers are only from Gershon and Kohath. A table, partly already given in 1 Chronicles 23 (the names bracketed do not recur here), will provide an overview of the relationships (see following page).

The line of Kohath is here represented by the family of Korah, who, in 1 Chron. 6.37-38 is identified as another son of Izhar. Korah's descendant, Meshelemiah (already mentioned in 1 Chron. 9.19, 21), is the leading figure of this group of gatekeepers.

The genealogical sequence given in v. 1 is:

Korah → Asaph → Kore → Meshelemiah/Shelemiah;

contrast 1 Chron. 9.19, 21:

Korah → Ebiasaph → Kore → Meshelemiah/Shelemiah;

The contracted form 'Asaph', unique to this context, arises presumably by contamination from the name of the entirely different Gershonite line of musicians of 1 Chronicles 25.

The family of Merari is divided into two groups: Obed-edom (vv. 4-8) and Hosah (vv. 10-11). C, having introduced statistics about Obed-edom in v. 8, interrupts his account of Merari to give in v. 9 statistics about the Kohathite–Korahite gatekeepers, thus locking the two groups

The Gatekeeper and Treasurers (1 Chronicles 26)

<table>
<tr><td colspan="12">(Levi)</td></tr>
<tr><td colspan="2">Gershon (v.21)</td><td colspan="7">(Kohath)</td><td colspan="3">Merari (v. 10)</td></tr>
<tr><td rowspan="5">Ladan
(v. 21)
Jehiel
(v. 21)
Zetham Joel
(v. 22)

(Shelomoth
etc.?)</td><td rowspan="5">(Shimei)

(Jahath
etc.)</td><td colspan="3">Amram
(v. 23)</td><td colspan="2">Izhar
(v. 23)</td><td rowspan="5">Hebron
(v. 23)
Jeriah
(v. 31)
?

?
?
Hashabiah
(v. 30)</td><td rowspan="5">Uzziel
(v. 23)
(Micah
etc.)</td><td rowspan="5">(Mahli)

(Eleazar
etc.)</td><td colspan="2">(Mushi)</td></tr>
<tr><td rowspan="4">(Aaron)</td><td colspan="2">Moses
(v. 24)</td><td>(Shelomith)</td><td>Korah
(v. 1)</td><td>(Mahli)</td><td>(Eder etc.)</td></tr>
<tr><td>Gershom
(v. 24)</td><td>Eliezer
(v. 25)</td><td>?</td><td>Asaph
(v. 1)</td><td>(11 generations
1 Chron. 6.44-47)</td><td>?</td></tr>
<tr><td>Shebuel
(v. 24)</td><td>Rehabiah
(v. 25)</td><td>?
?</td><td>Kore
(v. 1)</td><td>Obed-edom
(vv. 4, 15)</td><td>?
?</td></tr>
<tr><td></td><td>3 generations
Shelomith
(vv. 25f.)</td><td>Chenaniah
(v. 29)</td><td>Meshelemiah
(vv. 2, 9, 14)
Zechariah etc.
(vv. 2, 14)</td><td>Shemaiah etc.
(vv. 4, 6f.)</td><td>Hosah,
etc.
(vv. 10, 16)
Shuppim?
(v. 16)</td></tr>
</table>

together. They then have their duties apportioned by lot (v. 13). Obed-edom has already been introduced as the caretaker of the ark in 1 Chron. 13.13-14 and as a musician–gatekeeper of the family of Merari at the installation of the ark in 1 Chron. 15.18-24; 16.5; in 1 Chron. 16.38, along with Hosah, he is in charge of the ark in its tent in Jerusalem.

The statistics show that the Merarites, though (or because?) they are the cadet branch of Levites, are by far the dominant group among the gatekeepers: 62 'sons and brothers' of Obed-edom (contrast 68 'brothers' in 1 Chron. 16.38), plus 13 to Hosah, as opposed to the mere 18 of the Korahites. The special blessing of God on Obed-edom, evident in the period of the stay of the ark in his house (1 Chron. 13.14), is further shown by the growth of his family to include eight sons (Meshelemiah has but seven). To prove the point, the line of Obed-edom's first-born is traced into the six (?; the text of v. 7 may be disturbed) sons of the next generation. All are given the designation 'mighty hero' (vv. 6-9, 30-32): the physical prowess once necessary on the field of battle with the LORD's army is now required—and is fully in evidence (cf. 1 Chron. 9.13)—to bear their responsibilities (the key word, *mišmeret*, is used in v. 12, cf. 1 Chron. 9.27) in the service of the sanctuary where the LORD's victories are re-enacted.

> Apart from the leading members of these families, Meshelemiah, Obed-edom and Hosah, none of their 25 descendants named here recurs in the Hebrew Bible.

Verses 14-19 record the apportioning by lot (as was the case for the priests and the singers, cf. 1 Chron. 24.5-31; 25.8-31) of duties at the four gates of the Temple. Zechariah, his first-born, is introduced alongside (Me)Shelemiah of the Kohathite family to cover for the fourth gate along with Obed-edom and Hosah. He is called here 'a prudent counsellor' (cf. 1 Chron. 22.12) on grounds that are not divulged, but presumably to justify his elevation to the position of being a suitable candidate to be put in charge of a gate. Though smaller in overall numbers, Kohath thus retains equality of status as responsible for two out of the four gates. (Me)Shelemiah of the Kohathite family is assigned the east (cf. 1 Chron. 9.18); Zechariah, the north (contrast 1 Chron. 9.21); Obed-edom, the south; and the remainder of the Merarites (under Hosah and, one hitherto unmentioned, Shuppim), to the west.

> This disposition of gatekeepers by lot round the Temple contrasts with the appointed arrangement of the Levites round the Tabernacle in the wilderness in Numbers 3, where Merari is to the north, Kohath to the south and Gershon to the west, while Aaron and Moses were encamped to the east.

This distribution may explain the disproportionate way in which the numbers of Merarites had to grow in comparison with those of the Kohathites. For, allied to the duties at the southern gate, was the oversight of the 'house of gathering' (v. 15), presumably the collection point to which the people's offerings in kind were brought to the Temple (cf. 2 Chron. 25.24; Neh. 12.25). From the southern gate, between the outer and inner courts (cf. sketch at 2 Chron. 23.5), these offerings would be transmitted by the Levites in suitable preservation of the degrees of holiness to the appropriate chambers in the inner court of the Temple (cf. 1 Chron. 23.28). Thus, in contrast to the north, where there were but four, there were at the south not only four gatekeepers daily, but also two Levites working as a pair (NIV, 'two at a time'; NRSV, 'two and two', does not translate the distributive idiom and leaves the meaning unclear) in attendance at this collection point (v. 17); compare the six at the major access point at the east (cf. 2 Chron. 24.8).

There were also (v. 16) at the western gate added responsibilities—the charge of the 'Shallecheth gate' at the 'ascending road' (to the Temple mount, presumably, rather than running northwards, as Judg. 21.19 might suggest). The name of this gate is otherwise unknown, but it is tempting to deduce from it (it is related to the verb 'to throw out') that it was the gate from which the refuse of the Temple, such as the ashes of the altar, was removed (unfortunately, such a passage as Lev. 6.10-11, where the action envisaged is described, is not in explicit enough terms; the verb 'to throw out' is used of the removal of rubbish in, or from, the Temple precinct in such contexts as 2 Chron. 30.14; 33.15; Neh. 13.8, but again without the necessary precision).

> The further details on the western gate in v. 18 are uncertain: there were four gatekeepers at the highway and two at 'the colonnade' (a variant of this uncertain word ['vestibule', KBS] occurs in an equally obscure passage in 2 Kgs 23.11).

The account of the Levites is completed by the list of the treasurers in 1 Chron. 26.20-32. This part, concerned with the contributions of the laity, prepares for the details of the organization of the laity in 1 Chronicles 27.

The names here, for the most part, pick up the data of 1 Chron. 23.6-20 (see table above), so that this section rounds off the discussion of the Levites in 1 Chronicles 23–26 neatly with an inclusio: it ends as it began. As in 1 Chronicles 9, the section comes to its climax with the role of the Levites as monitors of Israel's holiness.

In contrast to their dominance among the gatekeepers, the most obvious difference is the complete absence of Merari among the treasurers. The climactic role of the treasurers is indicated by the fact that chief responsibility is vested in the family of Moses, the most senior non-priestly Levitical family (specifically in Shebuel, v. 24).

Some of the names in this section pose problems. Ahijah in v. 20 is otherwise unknown and there is a strong case for regarding it as a corruption of *'ᵃḥêhem*, 'their brothers'. In v. 25, between Rehabiah and Shelomith, the three individuals named are otherwise unidentified. The Shelomith mentioned may be another otherwise unknown descendant of Eliezer; on the other hand, the text may be imperfect (it needs some marginal adjustment at the beginning of the verse) and this Shelomith may be the already attested son of Izhar of that name (1 Chron. 23.18; 24.22, though in Exod. 6.21 there is no mention of a son of that name to Izhar). In v. 29 Izhar has a descendant Chenaniah and in v. 30 Hebron a descendant Hashabiah, both of whose lines of descent are otherwise unknown.

The chief duties of these Levites are to collect and store the 'holy things', the offerings of the people which are the tokens of their sanctification (see discussion under 1 Chron. 6.49). David is especially careful to deposit all the goods once dedicated to the LORD as spoils of the LORD's wars of conquest; it was failure in this matter that had occasioned the archetypal infringement of the LORD's prerogatives, the *ma'al* of Achar, with which Israel's whole settlement of the land had been marred from the start (1 Chron. 2.7). Accordingly, David lodges all the spoils that he and Joab his commander of the Israelite host and all their captains and heads of households had taken, specifically for the purpose of consolidating the Temple. He also lodges those dedicated by Samuel the seer, as well as those of Saul, the first king, who had eventually disgraced himself by his *ma'al* (1 Chron. 10), and of his army-commander, Abner (1 Sam. 14.50).

The element of the theoretical is evident from these verses. Everything that has been dedicated is entrusted to the charge of these treasurers—but the Temple has not yet been built and thus is not there to receive the goods nor be 'strengthened' (v. 27; the same verb will be used in 2 Chron. 24.5, 12; 34.8, 10 [cf. 29.3], of repairs to the Temple). None of Samuel's deposits nor any of Abner's exploits is actually recorded in C; they have to be understood from Samuel–Kings.

The same punctilious care is shown by David for the work of the Levites not just in the Temple but in their levitical cities throughout the community at large (vv. 29-32). There they act as 'supervisors and arbiters' (1 Chron. 23.4). The key term, *pqd*, is used twice in this section (vv. 29, 32; cf. 1 Chron. 21.5): it is the mobilization of the laity of Israel for their tasks in peace and in war ('the work of the LORD and the service of the king' [v. 30, cf. v. 32], the latter the sacramental sign of the former), the payment of the half-shekel capitation tax for atonement, the instruction of the people and the monitoring their exact payment of tithes and other sacred dues and their adjudication on questions of clean and unclean (cf. 1 Chron. 23.28-29), that are the primary tasks of these Levites. It is by this role that the Levites ensure those precise observances by the whole community, that are the outward expression of their dedication as God's people.

Stress is laid on the fact that it is the whole people, first on the West Bank (vv. 29-30) and then on the East (vv. 31-32), who are laid under this levitical discipline.

The number of Levites involved on the West Bank (1700) as opposed to those on the more sparsely populated East Bank (2700) perhaps indicates the comparative neglect this area had suffered. The note that it was in David's last year that this organization on the East Bank was checked over, also suggests the more marginal position of that area. Yet the impression is that faithful work has been going on for all these years, despite that fact that no audit (the key term, *drš*, 1 Chron. 10.13-14, now used of inquiry as to human practice, v. 31) had been made (cf. the positive elements in the evaluation of the East Bank tribes in 1 Chron. 5.18-22). The centre on the East Bank from which these operations were launched was Jazer in the territory of Gad, which has already featured as a levitical city in 1 Chron. 6.81.

This sequence, West Bank–East Bank, corresponds to the accounts of the *ma'al* of the people first on West Bank and then on East in 1 Chronicles 2–5. It suggests that C is concerned to show how, through David's actions, the sorry tale of *ma'al* can be arrested, and the primal ideal of the sanctification of the people can be attained through the system of monarchy and Temple.

5. *The Lay Supervisors (1 Chronicles 27)*

1 Chronicles 27 completes the rosters of duty that David decreed for the organization of the Temple and of his kingdom. The lists end as they began in 1 Chron. 23.2—with the laity. All this organization first and last concerns the people of God as a whole: their holiness and their ability to be the LORD's host (vv. 3, 5) on earth under the leadership of his house of David.

C returns to the question of the census (cf. 1 Chron. 21). For the maintenance of Israel's status David has to carry out his legitimate activities as king and for that he requires the support of his people. To ensure that support he has to organize them and to organize them he has to know their number. How is this legitimate organization to be carried out?

The chapter is divided into two main sections. The first (vv. 1-15) describes the roster of duties as regards the organization of the laity. The second section (vv. 16-32) lists the tribal leaders and the royal officials.

Verses 1-15: The Organization of the People

For each of the twelve months of the year there is a matching 'division' of 24,000 civil and military leaders and supervisors (cf. 1 Chron. 23.4, 6 for the 'divisions' and 'supervisors' of the Levites). Over each division is a high official or, in the case of the first three, his assistant or deputy.

Oddly enough, while MT has twelve subdivisions in this section, they do not altogether coincide with the twelve months of the year: the first is introductory (v. 1); months one and two are then combined in the second subsection (vv. 2-4).

The coincidence of the figure of 24,000 between the divisions of these officials and the Levites in 1 Chron. 23.4 is striking: the officials here must be regarded as, so to speak, 'lay Levites', working in the service of the king in parallel to the sacral work of the Levites. The number functions differently, however, in the two contexts: here it is determined by the twelve tribes of Israel; there by the twelve months of the year.

It must be acknowledged that the topic of the paragraph is slightly elusive. The opening verse is extremely tersely expressed. It seems to mean: 'As for the Israelites with regard to their numbering: the heads of households and the commanders of thousands and hundreds and their supervisors were the ones who were assisting the king with regard to the whole

> matter of the divisions, each of which came on duty and went off duty, a month at a time throughout all the months of the year. Each division had 24,000.' NRSV, 'This is the list of the people of Israel, the heads of families, the commanders... and their officers who served the king in all matters concerning the divisions... each division numbering twenty-four thousand', is, I think, misleading: it seems to imply that the whole people are in twelve divisions of 24,000: but the resulting figure of 288,000 is far too small (cf. 1 Chron. 21.5). Rather, the point at issue is that the people are counted (but the number is not specified, cf. v. 23) by teams of their heads of families and army commanders, that is, the civil and military leaders, under supervisors: it is each of these teams that amounts to 24,000 (cf. NEB). NRSV [and other English versions] is obliged to translate '*in* his division' in the subsequent verses (vv. 2, 4-5, 7-15) where the Hebrew consistently says 'over'. The total population of Israel served by this vast array of supervisors can only be surmised (cf. 1 Chron. 21 and the third section of this chapter, vv. 23-24, for the ban on such information; 1,300,000 males [cf. 1 Chron. 21.5] over twenty could well imply a total population four times that number).

The precise manner of organization is not made clear; nor is the purpose of the roster of duties made explicit (NIV makes it 'the *army* divisions', cf. vv. 3, 5, but that may generalize too far from these verses; 'host' in the broadest sense is what Israel as a whole is). In a similar organization under Solomon in 1 Kgs 4.7-19 (not used by C), Israel (as opposed to Judah) is divided into twelve districts, each with the responsibility of maintaining the royal court for one month. Here, too, the supervisors are only in office for one month in the year, so that it might be assumed that the district they represented had responsibility only for that month. But in C no districts are specified. Thus it may be that the whole country was responsible for making regular contributions for the whole year. Presumably, month by month each was responsible to the supervisors of the month for supplying labour and materials for the maintenance of all manner of national undertakings as directed by the king. A passage like 2 Chron. 32.27-29 no doubt gives an idea of what C has in mind. That would then account for the huge number of supervisors: 2000 per tribe per month, in order to ensure steady demand from the whole nation throughout the year and steady supply. The exact figures and the scale of social engineering involved speak of a highly theoretical system; C writes at an ideological level and the nightmare of organizing such a civil service in practice does not concern him.

The catalogue of these officials (vv. 2-15) is another example of C's love of the structured list (cf. 1 Chron. 25.9-31). The itemization of each of the twelve divisions usually begins with the phrase, 'the *n*th [leader] of the *n*th month was X...' (cf. v. 5; abbreviated thereafter; an alternative equivalent in vv. 2, 4); it ends with an identically recurring phrase: 'over his division were twenty-four thousand'. Yet there are striking variations within the list in the description of the leader.

There are no fewer than seven patterns on which these leaders are described: the commonest is 'X, the such-and-such, of such-and-such a place' (nos. 8, 9, 10, 12), with its variant, 'X, the such-and-such, from such-and-such a place' (nos. 7, 11); but there are also 'X, the such-and-such' (nos 2 and, probably, 5); 'X, the son of Y, the such-and-such' (no. 6); 'X, the son of Y, from such-and-such a place' (no. 1); 'X, the brother of Y' (no.4); 'X, the son of Y, the such-and-such' (no. 3). In the list the anecdotal gradually gives way to the annalistic.

In the case of the first five there are additional comments about the status of the leadership. The chief position is termed simply 'over the division' (vv. 2, 4); alternatively, 'head' (v. 3) or 'commander' (vv. 5, 8). The chief subordinate is termed 'chief officer' (more usually translated, 'leader') in v. 4 (if the text is sound).

Some of these commanders are known from other texts, particularly 1 Chron. 11.11-47:

A Jashobeam occurs as David's leading hero in 1 Chron. 11.11, but he is given a different father here. As a descendant of Perez (v. 3), he is a Judaean (cf. 1 Chron. 2.4).

Dodai the Ahohite (v. 4a) is the father of David's second hero, according to 1 Chron. 11.12. He is a Benjaminite. If the text of v. 4b is right, another Benjaminite, Mikloth (cf. 1 Chron. 8.32), may be mentioned as his subordinate.

Benaiah, a familiar figure in the intrigues surrounding the succession of Solomon in 1 Kings 1–2, has already appeared in 1 Chron. 11.22-25; 18.17. It is not elsewhere stated that he (or his father, Jehoiada; is there confusion here with the figure in 2 Chron. 22.11–24.25) was chief priest (unless 2 Sam. 8.18 implies as much). He came from Kabzeel in southern Judah. Ironically, in 1 Kings 1–2, he functions as Solomon's agent, who was responsible for the death of Joab, among others, and succeeded him as commander of the hosts of Israel (1 Kgs 2.34-35). Once again, C is not interested in such sordid details, though the fact that his son, Ammizabad (v. 6; otherwise unknown), is mentioned as his successor as commander of the second division may reflect these incidents and his taking higher office.

Asahel (v. 7), Joab's brother, has been mentioned at 1 Chron. 2.16 and 11.26. His violent death, recorded in 2 Samuel 2—long before the fortieth year of David's reign—but ignored by C, may account for Zebadiah, his son and successor (again otherwise unknown), being mentioned here. As David's nephew and grand-nephew, respectively, they were Judaeans.

Shamhuth (v. 8) does not figure elsewhere, nor does his gentilic, 'the Izrah' (which is, in any case, a dubious reading: it should have the ending '-ite' and should probably be emended to 'Zerahite', as in vv. 11, 13; that is, as a descendant of Zerah, Perez's brother [1 Chron. 2.4], he was yet another Judaean).

Ira (v. 9) has been listed in 1 Chron. 11.28. From Tekoa, he too is a Judaean.

Helez (v. 10) is listed in 1 Chron. 11.27. Through him Ephraim is now represented.

Sibbecai (v. 11) has already appeared in 1 Chron. 20.4 as well as 1 Chron. 11.29. As a Zerahite from Hushah (cf. 1 Chron. 4.4), he also is a Judaean.

Abiezer (v. 12; cf. 1 Chron. 11.28) from Anathoth is overtly identified as a Benjaminite.

Maharai (v. 13; cf. 1 Chron. 11.30), from Netophah which is associated with Bethlehem in Neh.7.26, is yet another Judaean.

The second Benaiah of the list (v. 14; cf. 1 Chron. 11.31) is explicitly termed an Ephraimite.

Heldai (v. 15), presumably to be equated with the Heled of 1 Chron. 11.30, comes from the same region of Ephraim as Mahrai. Here he is additionally identified as belonging to Othniel (cf. 1 Chron. 4.13), who is, puzzlingly, a Judaean.

The very restricted range of tribes from which these supervisors are drawn is striking: seven, if not eight, from Judah, two from Benjamin and two or three from Ephraim. All come from central West Bank tribes with the centre of gravity emphatically placed in David's home town of Bethlehem and its environs.

The Leaders of the Twelve Tribes and the Royal Officials (vv. 16-34)
The second section begins with the list of the leaders in charge of the various tribes of Israel. The tribes are laid out for the most part in pairs. These chiefs are called 'leader' (v. 16) or 'commander' (v. 22). They must have been included among the 'heads of households' and 'commanders' of v. 1. Over against vv. 1-15, however, they represent the traditional tribal framework into which David's new structured system is now introduced. The old order is thus flanked on each side

by new officials, those in vv. 2-15 and those about to be listed in vv. 25-34.

For the first half-dozen tribes of Israel the list follows tolerably close to the traditional models of Gen. 46.8-25, Exod. 1.2-4 (cf. 1 Chron. 2.1): Reuben, Simeon, Levi (but C here adds Aaron), Judah, Issachar, Zebulun. For the second part, the sequence Naphtali–Ephraim–Manasseh–Benjamin–Dan is unique.

While the sequence Joseph–Benjamin–Dan occurs again in Genesis 46 (and Exod. 1, where, however, for narrative purposes Joseph is excluded), the sequence Naphtali–Joseph is only found in Ezekiel 48.3-5 (where Joseph is also divided between Ephraim and Manasseh, but the placing of Benjamin and Dan is different). In 1 Chron. 2.2 the order is Dan–Joseph–Benjamin–Naphtali.

This list has, thus, some anomalies: the number 12 is gained by splitting Aaron off from Levi, and representing Joseph doubly by Ephraim and Manasseh; but the 'concubine Zilpah' tribes of Gad, on the East Bank between Reuben and Manasseh, and Asher, in the far north-west, have been omitted (are they subsumed under their neighbours, the major branch of the 'Leah' tribes?). One of the dominant motives must have been to emphasize the crucial importance in the new order of things of the sacrificial cult as offered by Aaron, alongside the teaching and monitoring role of the Levites. As in the traditional scheme of 1 Chron. 2.2 (but in contradistinction to C's own presentation in 1 Chron. 2.3–8.40), Dan is present (associated with Benjamin, perhaps implying the traditional geographical location of Dan in the central part of the country to the west of Benjamin before the 'Danite migration' of Judg. 18).

The various leaders of the twelve tribes itemized here are for the most part unknown from other parts of the Hebrew Bible. Only a few call for note:

Hashabiah, the Levite (v. 17), may be the son of Levi's grandson Hebron, mentioned in 1 Chron. 26.30.

Zadok retains his position as the chief of the Aaronic priests as in 1 Chronicles 24.

It is not surprising to find one of the brothers of king David, himself a Judahite, specified as leader in Judah, but none of David's brothers bears the name Elihu, given here (cf. 1 Chron. 2.13-15; the closest in form is that of the oldest brother, Eliab).

The name Abner, the father of the Benjaminite leader (v. 21), is notable: it is the same as that of Saul's cousin and leader of the Benjaminite host under Saul (1 Sam. 14.50). If it is the same individual, then David has indeed accomplished a remarkable feat of integrating his people, including even the most powerful leaders of his erstwhile opponents.

Verses 23-24 add a note on the numbering of the people referred to in v. 1 (as well as the noun, 'number', the verb at the beginning of v. 23, *nś'*, picks up the vocabulary of census [cf. the note on the related noun *maśśā'* in 1 Chron. 15.22]). There is no repetition of the mistakes of the past census (1 Chron. 21). The objection in principle that the people *cannot* be counted because of the promised blessing of God (Gen. 15.5, etc.; cf. note on 1 Chron. 21.3) is met here by the note that David makes no attempt to include in his muster for service those who are twenty years of age and under (for twenty as the age of attaining adulthood and its full responsibilities, cf. 1 Chron. 23.27).

Verse 24 alludes to the aborted census of 1 Chronicles 21 associated with Joab. Despite his efforts to dissuade his royal master, he is implicated in the guilt of the offence. For the association of divine anger in connection with infringement of the sphere of the divine, see, for example, Num. 1.53; 16.46; 18.5, and, especially, Josh. 22.20, where Achan's archetypal *ma'al* is brought into association with divine anger (cf. 2 Chron. 19.2 [where it is contrasted with the LORD's love], 10; 24.18 [in both of which it is associated with *'ašmâ*, 'guilt', cf 1 Chron. 21.3]; 29.8; 32.25-26).

The aborted census, incomplete and unacceptable in principle as it is, finds no place in the annals of David's reign. No such annals are referred to for David in Samuel–Kings (Solomon is the first king for whom such records exist, 1 Kgs 11.41): this raises the question of whether what C has in mind here is not the prophetic account of David's reign referred to in 1 Chron. 29.29 (see introduction to 2 Chron. 10–36).

The curious fact is noted in the margin of the Hebrew Bible, that 1 Chron. 27.25 stands, at least from the point of view of the number of verses, precisely at the centre of C's work: 1 Chron. 27.25a completes $882\frac{1}{2}$ verses out of a total of 1765. That is to say, at the mid-point of his work C portrays, in as ideal terms as is now possible, the restoration of Israel's life under David's rule, after the disaster of the first census. (In terms of bulk of material, the mid-point, mechanically speaking, actually falls—no less appropriately—around 2 Chronicles 5: Solomon's completion of the Temple.)

Given the systems of contribution now in place, the goods thus elicited must be stored. The final subsections list the number of officials in charge of the royal treasuries and of other royal enterprises and conclude with the names of the chief officials (vv. 25-34).

First, the twelve administrators are listed who are responsible for the management of the range of the royal economic interests (vv. 25-31). Agriculture is the major industry and requires seven officials. The exploitation of the renewable resources of the land, its three staple products of corn, wine and oil, is a potent symbol of the people's obligation to God for the gift of the land, their dependence upon him and the blessing which they receive at his hand. The two officials in charge of storage are mentioned first; they must have been the secular equivalent of the Levites as monitors of the people's offerings in the sacral realm (cf. 1 Chron. 26). 'The controller of the king's warehouses' (v. 25a) presumably functions in Jerusalem itself. The second official is in charge of all the regional depots: every settlement is involved from the largest towns, through the villages to the outlying security posts (v. 25b).

Five officials are in charge of agricultural production. The first must be for the grain (v. 26). The importance of wine is indicated by there being not only one official in charge of the vineyards, but another for the canteens (v. 27). The production of olive oil also requires two officials, one in charge of the olive groves (and also the groves of sycamores in the Shephelah), the other supervising the storage (v. 28).

Finally, for the exploitation of the pastoral resources, there are five further officials over the royal estates: two for the cattle in the favoured flat lands of the plain of Sharon and the valleys, presumably especially the Valley of Jezreel; and one each for the camels, the donkeys (the females are specified to emphasize the breeding aspect) and the sheep and goats.

A lively picture of the integrating role of the monarchy through its widespread economic interests is suggested by this list. The term used for David's wealth (*rᵉkûš*, v. 31) is the old comprehensive term used of Abraham, among others, in Gen. 12.5 and elsewhere of patriarchal prosperity, especially in livestock, under the hand of God. In 2 Chron. 31.3; 35.7, however, the word will be used of the resources of the king that enable him to make provision for the people's sacrifices. This suggests a sacramental sense in the word: the king's estates are not private property held for personal gain; they are expressions of the king's standing. The levies on the people are not so much taxation to support the royal court as an expression of their commitment to their role as the LORD's host under his representative on earth. This sense of economic solidarity with the king, God's agent, matches the obligations towards God in the material terms of the payment of holy dues through the Levites, failure in which underlies the whole of C's presentation (cf. 'divisions', v. 1).

The officials named are not certainly found elsewhere (the first, Azmaveth [v. 25], may have already appeared in 1 Chron. 11.33 as one of David's early warrior supporters).

Six of them are given places of origin. Those which can be identified are highly appropriate: the superintendent of the vineyards (v. 27) comes from Ramah in the hill country suitable for vines to the north of Jerusalem; the superintendent of the cattle in Sharon (v. 29) from Sharon; the superintendent of the camel caravaneers (v. 30), from the Ishmaelites (cf. Gen. 37.25-36; his name is also reminiscent of *'ibil*, one of the Arabic words for 'camels'); a descendant of Hagar, Ishmael's mother (Gen. 16.15), is the chief shepherd (cf. 1 Chron. 5.10, 19-21).

The list of officials ends with David's chief officers of state: the counsellors, the commander of the professional army, the priest and the commander of the citizen army (vv. 32-34).

Pride of place is given to an otherwise unknown uncle of David, Jonathan: he is not only a trusted adviser but, as 'secretary', must have occupied high, if not the highest, office (though in 1 Chron. 18.16 that is held by Shavsha). An equally unknown Jehiel (a brother of the leader of David's early warrior-band?—cf. 1 Chron. 11.11) has the responsibility for (the control of? education of?) (or ranks alongside?) David's sons.

A curious omission is the recorder (1 Chron. 18.15).

In Samuel–Kings there are enormous tensions between some of these figures. Ahithophel and Hushai (v. 33) were advisers locked in deadly rivalry (2 Sam. 15–17). C totally ignores their machinations; they are, indeed, only mentioned in this passage in C. Rather, it would seem, C is concerned to present the harmony of an ideal system; the members of David's entourage by definition cannot be in dispute with one another. Similarly, irreconcilable differences are to be manifested between the old pre-monarchic order represented by Abiathar, the priest, and Joab, the captain of the citizen army, on the one hand, and the representatives of the new order, on the other, of which only Benaiah the son of Jehoiada is mentioned here (v. 34; cf. 1 Chron. 27.5; oddly, the father and son are interchanged, perhaps precisely to avoid identifying these generations with the notorious feuding that came to a head at the accession of Solomon, 1 Kgs 1–2). Abiathar's rival, Zadok, is not even mentioned here.

With the completion of all these preparations for the system whereby ideal conditions can be restored and maintained within the people of Israel, David now summons the leaders of the people in order to begin the handing over of power to Solomon.

1 CHRONICLES 28–29: DAVID'S REIGN FULFILLED

1 Chronicles 23–27 have defined the agencies organized by David through which the system of holiness is to be put in place whereby Israel may attain its destiny as the host on earth of the LORD of hosts. With the necessary institutions now defined, this concluding section on David's reign resumes the discussion of 1 Chronicles 22: what remains to be achieved is the building of the Temple, but that is a task which has to be completed by David's successor.

This concluding section on David's reign may be divided as follows (so MT, except that it combines paragraphs 5 and 6):

1. David summons the whole leadership to Jerusalem as a *qāhāl* and publicly announces that Solomon has been chosen by the LORD as successor to the Davidic throne (1 Chron. 28.1-8).
2. David's address to Solomon (1 Chron. 28.9-10).
3. David hands over to Solomon the divinely revealed plans of the Temple, its personnel and equipment (1 Chron. 28.11-19).
4. Resumption of address to Solomon (1 Chron. 28.20-21)
5. Resumption of address to the *qāhāl*: David gives an account of his preparations of materials for the Temple and invites free-will offerings from these representatives of the people (1 Chron. 29.1-5).
6. The giving of free-will offerings (1 Chron. 29.6-9).
7. David's praising of the LORD and prayer in the presence of the *qāhāl* (1 Chron. 29.10-19).
8. David's exhortation to the *qāhāl* to bless; the sacrifice on the following day; the coronation of Solomon and the appointment of Zadok (1 Chron. 29.20-25).

   The entire narrative of these farewell addresses by David is rounded off by the resumption in 1 Chron. 29.24 of the first and last named in the list of those summoned in 1 Chron. 28.1 (the commanders and the warriors).

9. Annalistic summary on David's reign (1 Chron. 29.26-30).

1. *David's Address to the* qāhāl *(1 Chronicles 28.1-8)*

David summons the lay leadership of the community to Jerusalem as a *qāhāl* ('sacral assembly'; cf. v. 8, where it is called, 'the assembly of the LORD'; cf. 1 Chron. 13.2; the verb from the root is used in v. 1; the noun in v. 8; cf. 1 Chron. 29.1, 10, 20).

The officers and officials specified in 1 Chronicles 27 are now listed in a rather different order: first the traditional tribal leaders (cf. 1 Chron. 27.16-22); then the royal appointees—the leaders of the new divisions (cf. 1 Chron. 27.1-15), the superintendents of the royal estates (cf. 1 Chron. 27.25-31); finally, David's immediate entourage, his courtiers (here appearing for the first and only time of the Davidic House in C [cf. 2 Chron. 18.8 of the north]) and warriors (cf. 1 Chron. 11.10).

As in 1 Chronicles 13; 15, the separation of laity and clergy is striking. The Levites are not yet mentioned here because they belong to the blueprint of the Temple and its personnel and worship about to be handed over by David to Solomon to be brought into effect by him (1 Chron. 28.13, 21). Compare the institution of Zadok as priest only in 1 Chron. 29.22.

David's speech opens with the authoritative, 'Hear me' (v. 2a), to be found again in speeches of Davidic kings and prophets (cf. 2 Chron. 13.4). He addresses the gathering as 'his brothers and his people': in the one phrase their traditional solidarity as a tribal system and the new monarchical leadership are deftly combined.

As so often (cf. 1 Chron. 17.7), David's speech falls into two parts hinged around the 'And now' (v. 8). The first part (vv. 2b-7) provides the reason for the action introduced by 'And now' and enjoined by imperatives (v. 8).

Verses 2b-7 state the grounds for Solomon's succession to the throne. As in his address to Solomon in 1 Chron. 22.7-10, David first explains in the light of 1 Chronicles 17 why he has to leave unfinished to his successor the project of building the Temple.

Verse 3 begins with the same strong contrastive pronoun: '*I* intended..., *but God* said...' as in 1 Chron. 17.4, 7: 'Not *you*..., *I*...'; cf. 1 Chron. 22.7, where again the solemn vocabulary for 'intended' recurs.

David's plans to build the Temple have been premature: for, since the Temple will be the resting place of the ark, the symbol of the LORD's dynamic presence on the field of battle, it can only be built once the wars of pacification have been completed. Only then can the ark be installed in its 'house of rest' (v. 2; cf. 1 Chron. 22.9). Only in that state of rest can the ark be called 'our God's footstool' (v. 2, for the only time in C; cf. Pss. 99.5; 132.7; Lam. 2.1), a title which safeguards the transcendence of God (it is only his footstool) while at the same time affirming his presence amidst his people (it is at least his footstool; for 'God' with C's characteristic pronominal suffix, cf. 1 Chron. 11.2 and, in this chapter, vv. 8 [twice], 20; cf. 1 Chron. 29.2, 3 [twice], 13, 16, 17, 20).

But there is a further reason why David himself cannot build the Temple (v. 3). Through these very wars, he has shed much blood and has thus disqualified himself for the task: 1 Chronicles 21 shows the awesome consequences of undertaking military action without the necessary preliminary rights of expiation. He has, accordingly, done the most that can be permitted him: if he himself cannot build, at least he can undertake the task of preparing all the materials necessary for the construction (the keynote root, *kûn*, 1 Chron. 14.2, is used at the end of v. 2).

> There may be another dimension in the postponement of the building of the Temple till after the death of David. If, as in Num. 35.28, it is necessary for the death of the high priest before there can be expiation for blood shed by accidental homicide, how much more must this be the case for deliberate slaughter in war (cf. David's role as high priest in 1 Chron. 16.2)? The distinction between the inadvertent and the deliberate is fundamental to C's use of the concept *ma'al*: it, too, concerns accidental violation of the laws of holiness and it is that violation for which the law of Lev. 5.14–6.7 is designed to compensate; Israel's predicament, by contrast, is that she has been guilty of the deliberate defrauding of God. This is the major theme in the second part of C's work in 2 Chron. 10–36.

But this correction of David's plan about the house of God serves to underline the consistency of God's purpose as regards the house of David. This purpose is expressed now in terms of election, used here for the first time in C in connection with the house of David (vv. 4-5; cf. already the election of the Levites in 1 Chron. 15.2). God has already determined who will be the builder of the Temple and it is that decision of God that David now brings before the *qāhāl* as the warrant for Solomon's succession. 'Election' implies that there is a free choice available among a variety of options (compare David's being given the offer of choice—the same verb—of one among three in 1 Chron. 21.10). Whatever intrinsic qualities David and his house possess—all in any case endowments gifted by God—these do not form the basis of their claim to the throne. Their claim is based solely on God's choice. The unfettered freedom of God to choose is established by the four-stage process: out of the twelve tribes of Israel, he has chosen the one tribe of Judah; out of that tribe, the one family of Jesse; out of Jesse's seven sons (1 Chron. 2.13-15), David; and out of the David's nineteen sons (1 Chron. 3.1-8), the chosen one, Solomon.

Yet further confirmation of the status of the Davidic king is provided by the sacramental principle: the throne of David is none other than the throne of God (v. 5; cf. 2 Chron. 9.8). By divine appointment it is but the visible manifestation of the dominion of God himself.

The validity of Solomon's status is confirmed yet further by the fact that this election is sealed by a covenant of adoption expressed in the most intimate terms possible: Solomon becomes God's son, God his father (v. 6; cf. 1 Chron. 22.10). Because this kingship is, in principle, divinely decreed and sustained and is transparent to rule of God himself, it is everlasting. Yet there is an element of contingency (v. 7): the maintenance of the covenant depends upon the continued faithfulness of the Davidic house.

The conditions laid down here are not just a matter of the punishment that will follow violation of the covenant. Rather, the sacramental principle is again in full play: only so long as the Davidic king adheres with total loyalty to the Torah can he be the human agent of God; to be disloyal is by that act to forfeit status. The sacramental principle is illustrated here by the key term, *kûn*: it is *as* the human monarch commits himself to the establishment of the Temple (v. 2) that he is himself established by God (v. 7; cf. 1 Chron. 14.2; 15.1 and the similar play on the verb 'build' in 1 Chron. 17.4, 10).

The action being enjoined, 'and now', in v. 8 on the basis of these arguments and in the light of the solemn opening, 'in the presence of all Israel, the *qāhāl* of the LORD and in the hearing of our God', is surprising: the natural upshot of the argument would be, 'therefore, I declare Solomon to be my successor'. Instead, C, no doubt presupposing that, turns to even more fundamental matters: 'keep and enquire after all the commandments of the LORD, your God'. Nothing could more clearly indicate that monarchy is not an end in itself: it is, rather, the means whereby the whole community fulfils its destiny by undertaking that most basic of responsibilities—resorting to the LORD in all things (cf. 1 Chron. 10.13-14). Nor are all these elaborate arrangements of the Temple an end in themselves; the main point is that God's commandments and his statutes will be observed (cf. 1 Chron. 22.13, where the Law of Moses was stressed).

The address comes to its climax in v. 8 with a statement of the fundamentally gracious purpose of God for his people. Their ideal state of existence is, 'that you may possess the good land and pass it on as an inheritance to your descendants after you in perpetuity' (v. 8). Israel, in fulfilling its role in the world, enjoys security and prosperity in 'the good land'. 'Good things' will later be the general expression for Israel's ideal condition (cf., e.g., 2 Chron. 10.7), which conforms to the nature of God himself as good (1 Chron. 16.34; 2 Chron. 5.13). It is notable that also for the people (v. 8), as for the house of David (v. 7), a conditional note is struck: 'that you *may* possess the good land'. Even after centuries of occupation, possession is still viewed as future possibility, rather than as assured past achievement. As in Leviticus 26, continued possession of the land is conditional upon observance of the Law (cf. 2 Chron. 33.7-8). The alternative, if Israel fails to be what it is intended to be, is that it loses possession and the land reverts to the world of the nations (cf., e.g., 1 Chron. 11.4; 2 Chron. 20.7).

2. *David's Initial Address to Solomon (1 Chronicles 28.9-10)*

David's initial address to Solomon, now spoken publicly as a direct continuation of the address to the *qāhāl*, renews the commission and encouragement privately communicated in 1 Chron. 22.13. It is constructed in two balanced parts: a general command (v. 9) and the specific command which results from it (v. 10), linked by 'now' (cf. v. 8).

The general command (v. 9) is to maintain undivided loyalty to the LORD. This is expressed in terms of 'knowing' God, the verb which is used of God's relationship with David in 1 Chron. 17.18. The derivative nature of Solomon's kingship is implied: his God is known as 'the God of your father'; the relationship between God and king can only be that which has been inaugurated with David. The unconditional commitment required of Solomon is expressed in terms of 'service' (from the same root as 'slave', 1 Chron. 17.4): the unquestioning devotion as of a slave to his master will recur as the standard obligation of the king in the history of the monarchy about to unfold (cf. 2 Chron. 30.8; 33.16; 34.33; 35.3; contrast 2 Chron. 24.18; 33.3).

That undivided loyalty is described in terms of 'a perfect heart' (again there is a word play [cf. 1 Chron. 22.9], this time between Solomon's name [*š^elōmô*] and the adjective 'perfect' [*šālēm*]; cf. *šālôm*, 'peace', 1 Chron. 12.18) and 'an eager desire'.

There is an ominous underlying note of threat. The reason for complying with David's exhortation is a mixture of conditional promise of divine help and threat of rejection. Another element in the system of correspondence (cf. 1 Chron. 11.9) is now noted: the direct correspondence between God's 'enquiring after' (*drš*) the hidden disposition of every mind and the obligation and rewards of 'enquiring after' (*drš*) him (that again links back to Saul's failures, 1 Chron. 10.13-14). This is an expression of the underlying sacramental principle: it is as Solomon discharges his duty that he is what he is intended to be, the occupant of the LORD's throne (v. 5); to fail in that duty is in that failure to have ceased to enjoy that status. Thus, the verse continues, 'to seek' is 'to find'; 'to forsake' is 'to be rejected'. This is not a matter of retribution, of subsequent payment of penalty, of 'tit for tat'. Rather, the outcome is the immediate expression, not the consequence, of the inner disposition of the individual concerned.

The verb 'to forsake' (*'zb*) is now to become a thematic term in C: cf. especially v. 20*; 2 Chron. 7.19*, 22; 12.1*, 5*; 13.10*, 11*; 15.2*; 21.10*; 24.18*, 20*, 24*; 28.6*; 29.6* (+ *ma'al*); 32.31*; 34.25.

'Reject' (*znḥ*) is much less frequent: 2 Chron. 11.14*; 29.19* (+ *ma'al*).

(* = C's own material.)

In the phrase, 'every inclination of the thoughts', there is a direct cross-reference to the diagnosis of the universal human condition that introduces and concludes the story of the flood (Gen. 6.5; 8.21). The fear of 'rejection' by God or outright experiencing of it is a theme familiar in the Psalms of lamentation on the lips of the Davidic king (e.g. Ps. 44.9). 'Rejection' belongs to C's central vocabulary of failure to accord God his due (e.g. 2 Chron. 12.1; 21.10; 24.20, 24; 32.31; 34.25) and is explanatory of the whole disastrous course of Israel's history under the monarchy.

The argument thus comes to its climax in the specific command (v. 10): by God's own appointment it is Solomon's inescapable destiny to build a house. The specific function of the Temple is made clear by the added phrase, 'the place of holiness': it is to be the means whereby all that is owed to God is fully rendered to him (1 Chron. 6.49). He has no choice but to commit himself to the work: 'be strong' and 'act' have already featured in David's exhortation to Solomon in 1 Chron. 22.13.

3. *David Hands Over to Solomon the Divine Plan of the Temple (1 Chronicles 28.11-19)*

David hands over the plans of the Temple to Solomon, the rosters of duties of the priests and Levites, and the specifications for the Temple's furnishings and equipment.

David's preparation of the materials necessary for the construction of the Temple has been noted in 1 Chron. 22.2-4, 14-16. The organization of the priests and Levites by David has been described in detail in 1 Chronicles 23–26. But nothing in the preceding chapters has dealt with the details of the architectural plans or the specifications of the furnishings, which David now hands on to Solomon (though earlier definitions of the duties of the priests and Levites imply some of these, for example, 1 Chron. 6.48-49; 9.13-34; 23.28-32). The section corresponds to the revelation to Moses in the wilderness of the details of the construction of the Tabernacle (Exod. 25–31; for the figure of Moses in the background of David's conversations with Solomon, cf. 1 Chron. 22.13). David is the new Moses (cf. v. 19). As in Exodus, the whole is constructed in accordance with a heavenly blueprint revealed by God himself ('by the spirit with him', v. 12; cf. 1 Chron. 5.26). The word 'plan', with which the whole section begins and ends (vv. 11, 19), occurs also in Exod. 25.9, 40 (it occurs only 20 times in the whole of the Hebrew Bible). And just as Bezalel is the executor of Moses' blueprint in Exodus 35–40, so in 2 Chronicles 2–4 Solomon is the executor of David's (the correspondence is alluded to in 2 Chron. 1.5).

Many of the following features are unique to C and now occur for the first time in C. The text of v. 11 seems to be disturbed: chambers on two levels and treasuries are nowhere else specified as part of the porch and presumably belong to the Temple as a whole (as NRSV tacitly emends). The Temple proper, but more probably just the holy of holies (cf. Lev. 16.2, 15), is called the 'house of the covering', that is, the covering or lid of the ark, mentioned only here in C (cf. Exod. 25.17-22). Then are listed the Temple courtyards, with their side-chambers and store-chambers (see 1 Chron. 9.26; 23.28; 26.20); thereafter, certain of the furnishings—the lampstands and the lamps (for the first time in C; cf. Exod. 25.31, though

> there there is but one lampstand; the plural, lampstands, is used of the Jerusalem Temple in 1 Kgs 7.49), the tables of the showbread (again for the first time in C; in Exod. 25.23 and 1 Kgs 7.48 there is only one table; the plural occurs only here and again in 2 Chron. 4.19), the forks, basins (both in, e.g., Exod. 27.3), cups (e.g. Exod. 25.29) and bowls (only here and in Ezra 1.10; 8.27; the Ezra passages suggest a considerable number of such bowls—thirty gold, 410 silver—but do not specify their use), and the incense altar (already in 1 Chron. 6.49); the turn of phrase, 'the chariot', that is, 'the cherubim', is unique in the Hebrew Bible (is there a polemical reference here to the 'chariots of the sun' removed from the Temple by Josiah, according to 2 Kgs 23.11, an incident not recorded by C in the parallel passage in 2 Chron. 34.31?). Perhaps, by contrast, the omission of certain features is no less significant, in particular, the dynastic pillars of Jachin and Boaz (cf. 2 Chron. 3.17).

This catalogue well encapsulates the significance of the Temple for C. Right at the outset, the porch emphasizes the holiness of the structure from which all but the duly consecrated are debarred. The treasuries affirm the obligation upon all Israel to render to God all that is due to him before any possibility of access to him can be gained. The ark, with which the whole section begins and ends (vv. 11, 18), provides the appropriate focus for the fundamental meaning of the Temple. The whole structure is referred to not as the 'Temple' but as 'the house of the covering (of the ark)' (v. 11), that is, the sanctuary where the ark of the covenant reposes, on the lid of which atonement is annually effected on the Day of Atonement by the high priest. But, v. 18, the ark is more: its overshadowing cherubim (cf. 1 Chron. 13.6) are the symbol of the irresistible, universal intervention of God, imposing and demanding order in human affairs (for the likening of the dynamic movement of God to a heavenly chariot, compare Ezekiel's 'throne vision' in Ezek. 1, or Isa. 66.15). Again, the reminder is given that the Temple also contains the 'storehouses of the holy things', these offerings in kind dedicated by the people, which are the symbols of the dedication of their whole lives to God (cf. 1 Chron. 23.28). The use of the forks is indicated by the narrative in 1 Sam. 2.13-14: by them the offerings due to the priests were removed from the boiling sacrifices. The basins were the means whereby the sacrificial blood was collected and dashed against the altar of burnt offering (see the use of the associated verb in connection with the burnt offering in, for example, Lev. 1.5, the communion sacrifice in, for example, Lev. 3.2, and, above all, the guilt offering in Lev. 7.2).

The cups were used in connection with the libations of wine associated with the showbread (Num. 4.7) and, no doubt, the daily sacrifices at the altar of burnt-offerings (e.g. Exod. 29.40). The role of the incense altar is indicated in Exod. 30.7-8—to wreathe the nave with smoke night and morning when Aaron trimmed the lamps—and in Lev. 16.12 in rites of atonement (cf. Lev. 4.7 in connection with the sin-offering); the violation of its sanctity is going to be precisely the occasion of Hezekiah's *ma'al* in 2 Chron. 26.16.

The authority of David's blueprint for all Israel's cultic institutions is reinforced by the final verse of the section (v. 19): 'everything was by writing by the hand of the LORD'. The phrase picks up the reference to inspiration in v. 12 (cf., e.g., Ezek. 1–3).

It is followed by a curious interjection in the first person: 'he imparted understanding to me' (cf. 1 Chron. 23.5b, 'by instruments which I made for praising'), in order to emphasize the surpassing authority of the divine revelation of the Temple and its cult to David.

4. *Resumption of Address to Solomon (1 Chronicles 28.20-21)*

The address to Solomon is now resumed in two further short verses (1 Chron. 28.20-21). The imperative of demand (v. 20a) is now supported with the reasons why those demands can be met (vv. 20b, 21).

The same vocabulary of command and encouragement is used as before (the first words of David in v. 20a pick up the end of v. 10). The element of encouragement is strengthened further, as in 1 Chron. 22.13b, with the addition of the phrase, 'do not be afraid or discouraged'.

David now bases his command on an assurance of assistance, both divine (v. 20b) and human (v. 21). He uses the relatively infrequent combination 'the LORD God' to provide the maximum theological impact: the intimacy of the proper name of Israel's God, 'the LORD', coupled with the objectivity of the cosmic term for deity, 'God' (cf. 1 Chron. 17.16-17). But even the intimacy has a note of objectivity within it for Solomon: he only knows this God as the 'God of his father'. It is only by virtue of the pioneering role of David that Solomon is entering upon such a heritage and responsibility. David emphasizes the point in the next phrase, 'My God is with you', using again the preposition 'with' of the messianic name Immanuel (1 Chron. 11.9).

The content of the message of assurance, 'He will not let you go or forsake you', makes a similar point: it too is a formulation familiar from Deuteronomy and the Deuteronomistic History as the encouragement of Moses to Israel and to Joshua as his successor (Deut. 31.6, 8; Josh. 1.5; cf. Deut. 4.31).

But Solomon's reign is hardly considered in and for itself; it is primarily the instrument for the attainment of the fundamental goal, the completion of the Temple, as the last phrase of v. 20 makes plain. Appropriately, therefore, the phrase, 'the work for the service of the LORD's house' (this time in connection with the construction rather than the rites; contrast v. 13 and 1 Chron. 9.13), echoes Moses' preparations in connection with the construction of the tabernacle in Exod. 36.1-7. The human support (v. 21) consists of the 'three estates' of the realm as organized by David: the clergy, the nobles and counsellors, and the laity under their leaders. The whole community could not be in a higher state of readiness of skill and of substance to carry out Solomon's bidding; they stand prepared for every spiritual and temporal service (the repeated word, 'service', picks up Joab's words to David: 'are they not all your servants?', 1 Chron. 21.3).

5. *Resumption of Address to the* qāhāl *(1 Chronicles 29.1-5)*

It is precisely to ensure this readiness on the part of the people that David now turns once more to the *qāhāl*. David's speech is again divided into two sections: vv. 1-5a explain the situation; v. 5b the action required.

The magnitude of the task of building a Temple worthy of the LORD is faced. Solomon is, indeed, the sole one chosen by God; but he is young and inexperienced (cf. 1 Chron. 22.5). The massive nature of the undertaking is suggested by the unusual term for the Temple used (again in v. 19): in Esther (1.2 and many other verses) and Nehemiah (1.1) it refers to the fortress capital of the Persians (a not insignificant observation, given that it is to be Cyrus, the Persian, who is to be charged with the task of reconstructing the Temple, 2 Chron. 36.23). Indeed, it is a superhuman task, for this fortress capital is for no mere human but for God himself (again the double 'the LORD God', as in 1 Chron. 28.20).

David has done all in his power (contrast 1 Chron. 22.14, 'in my poverty'), by virtue of his office, to prepare the necessary materials for the building and furnishings of the Temple (v. 2; the key term, *kûn*, 'to prepare' is again used, 1 Chron. 28.2; 'the house of my God' again affirms the unique status of David; so again v. 3).

The first materials mentioned are listed in descending order of value—gold, silver, bronze, iron, wood (cf. 1 Chron. 22.14). The precise identity of some of the stones listed is uncertain (cf. KBS): both gems (the first two items feature in connection with the High Priest's dress in the tabernacle account in Exod. 25.7) and costly building materials are included.

But now David seeks to lead by personal example (v. 3). Beyond the requirements of office, in his zeal for the house of his God, David has contributed liberally free-will offerings from his own wealth (how that relates to 1 Chron. 27.25 is not clear): gold and silver for the purpose of overlaying the walls of the Temple by the finest craftsmanship (v. 5). These contributions are over and above his other preparations: there may be a deliberately contrastive play on words between 'over and above', *ma'lâ*, and C's thematic term *ma'al*, 'unfaithfulness' (v. 3; cf. 1 Chron. 14.2 and v. 25 below).

The prodigious value of David's gifts of 3000 talents of gold and 7000 talents of silver, and the totals contributed by his people (1 Chron. 29.7), can be appreciated by comparison with other passages in the Hebrew Bible (listing only gold and silver; for an earlier table of comparative values, see at 1 Chron. 21.25).

Half-shekel 'of the sanctuary' of silver is the capitation tax (Exod. 30.13);

1 talent = 3000 shekels (see on 2 Chron. 25.6; cf. Exod. 38.24-28);

100 talents of silver, the hire of an army of 100,000 in 2 Chron. 25.6; an annual national indemnity (2 Chron. 27.5);

100 talents of silver, 1 talent of gold, the fine on Judah by Neco (2 Chron. 36.3);

1000 talents of silver, the hire of the Aramaeans by Ammon against David (1 Chron. 19.6);

29 talents, 730 shekels of gold; 100 talents, 1775 shekels of silver for the construction of the tabernacle (Exod. 38.24-28);

120 talents of gold, brought by the Queen of Sheba to Solomon (2 Chron. 9.9);

450 talents of gold from Ophir, brought by Solomon's fleet (2 Chron. 8.18; 420 in 1 Kgs 9.28);

666 talents of gold, Solomon's annual income (2 Chron. 9.13);

3000 talents of gold of Ophir; 7000 talents of silver, David's free-will offering here (1 Chron. 29.4);

5000 talents of gold; 10,000 talents of silver, the free-will offering of the people (1 Chron. 29.7);

100,000 talents of gold; 1,000,000 talents of silver; David's preparation for the Temple (1 Chron. 22.14).

Verse 5b states the action required in the light of these circumstances. By this example of personal generosity, David invites the free-will offerings of the leaders of his people (cf. 2 Chron. 17.16; 35.8). The challenge is now issued, not as in 1 Chron. 28.8, 9, 20 by imperatives, but dramatically and more searchingly by a question: 'Who is going to offer freely?'

The giving by the community as a whole of free-will offerings for the sanctuary is a feature associated especially with the construction of the Tabernacle (Exod. 35.21–36.7) and with the reconstruction of the Temple (Ezra 1.4, 6; 2.68-69; 7.15-16; 8.28). There is the expectation that such gifts will be brought, and that it is wholly appropriate that they should be brought. They are a yardstick of the zeal, commitment and piety of the community. Yet they are gifts brought freely, without compulsion, as the spontaneous expression of joy and gratitude, in recognition of the blessing of God (e.g., Lev. 23.38; Deut. 16.10; Ps. 54.6; cf. 2 Chron. 17.16; 31.14; 35.8). But more: the turn of phrase that David uses as the invitation to the community leaders has particularly sacral associations: 'who is freely willing to fill his hand today to the LORD?'(so again, 2 Chron. 29.31). One may suspect that this is not just a vivid phrase for open-handed generosity; 'to fill the hand' is the technical term for consecrating a priest or Levite, whether by oneself or by another (e.g. Exod. 28.41; 29.29; 32.29 etc.; cf. 2 Chron. 13.9; 29.31). By their free-will offerings, the leadership and, by extension, the whole community, are dedicating themselves, as it were, by ordination as the priestly people of God. Holiness, as sacramentally focused on the Temple, is the realized ideal for the community as a whole.

6. *The Giving of Free-Will Offerings (1 Chronicles 29.6-9)*

The lay leaders, as identified in 1 Chron. 28.1, respond with the giving of free-will offerings (1 Chron. 29.6-9; MT includes this response in the same section as David's address, as part of one concerted action by king and people).

The same sequence of materials is followed as before (1 Chron. 29.2): the precious metals in declining order of value; then the precious stones. For the scale of their response, see the table above. In addition, they contribute 10,000 darics (a Greek or Persian loan-word [KBS], showing how C is bringing the narrative up to date, presumably gold coins, as opposed to the mere weight represented by the talent; cf. Ezra 2.69; Neh. 7.70-72; also 18,000 talents of bronze; 100,000 talents of iron (the latter not specified for David—it was unworthy that he should have contributed such base metals as bronze and iron).

All these offerings are entrusted to Jehiel, the senior Levite of the branch of Gershon (see 1 Chron. 23.8; 26.21-22), chief guardian of the LORD's treasury in the Temple (v. 8). Only the chief of those clergy ordained for the purpose can fitly transfer these supererogatory expressions of dedication into the service of God. (Quite where these gifts were stored before the Temple was actually built is a practical question that does not trouble C; once again a supratemporal contemporaneity is in evidence, compare the account of the dedication of the Temple in 2 Chron. 5–7.)

This spectacle of responsiveness lifts the whole community to the highest plane of a sense of well-being. The reign of David is brought to its appropriate climax in the infectious joy (the key root, *śmḥ*, is used three times in v. 9, cf. 1 Chron. 12.40) of unreserved giving, of participating in the whole-hearted (the adjective *šālēm* cross-referring to 1 Chron. 28.9) lavishness of according to God the best and the most within the capacity of the people. All possible duty towards God has been fulfilled. The Temple is now acknowledged as the focus of national life: as the resting place of the ark, it is the constant symbol of the LORD's victories won; as the place of atonement, it is the constant statement that holiness is a possibility; as the treasury, it is the constant vehicle of the expression of that holiness.

7. *David's Prayer (1 Chronicles 29.10-19)*

With profoundest satisfaction, David marks this peak of responsiveness of his people with the blessing of the LORD and prayer in the presence of the *qāhāl* (1 Chron. 29.10-19). As supreme representative of his people, he takes the lead in the praise of God (compare Solomon in 2 Chron. 6).

David's prayer falls into three parts (unmarked in MT: these are integrated parts of a single whole): vv. 10-12, affirmation; vv. 13-17, thanksgiving; vv. 18-19, petition.

The prayer begins in vv. 10-12 with the praise of God. David 'blesses' the Lord: in this context, blessing is clearly not invoking favours but acknowledging the source from which they come. Using the objective language of the hymn of praise, David affirms attributes that God has displayed once more in and beyond his dealings with his people. Though he uses the intimate term, 'the LORD', he has a profound sense of the transcendent majesty of God. He does not address God familiarly through the immediacy of his own experience, but through God's long-standing relationship with his people through their founding father, Israel; what has been made known to Israel through a long history is indicative of the eternal nature of God (v. 10).

The supremacy of God over the whole universe is acknowledged and the qualities that go with it (v. 11). One senses that David is struggling with the furthest limits of human speech as he piles up the attributes and the synonyms (cf. the word 'all' used four times already in vv. 11-12): all these affirmations are true; but they can only hint at the inexpressible majesty of God beyond them.

Kingship is one of these attributes: by analogy, the human experience of kingship can convey something of the power and awesome splendour of God. But kingship does not simply provide an analogy. As a sacramental institution, it is itself the vehicle through which these divine qualities manifest themselves on earth: thus in v. 25 God precisely endows Solomon with elements of his own sovereignty over the universe (the 'greatness' and the 'splendour' of kingship; cf. v. 30). The universality of the language used here of God is thus particularly notable: it corresponds to the sense of the universal purpose of God within which the role of Israel is being played out (cf. 1 Chron. 1), and within which the rule of David's own house is set (v. 30; at the end of Solomon's reign in 2 Chron. 8–9 and at the end of the whole work see the equally appropriate universality, 2 Chron. 36.23).

From the universal, David turns to the particular in vv. 13-17. Praise can only modulate into thanksgiving for the specific benefits received (another 'and now' provides the link at the beginning of v. 13; cf. 1 Chron. 28.8, 10). David acknowledges, at this moment of celebration at his own achievement and at the response of his people, that all has in fact been enabled (so again, 2 Chron. 2.6; contrast 2 Chron. 13.20; 20.37) by God himself (v. 14). The thanksgiving can only become a confession in wonderment at human dependence: the so-called free-will offering is only returning to God part of what he has given in the first place. Israel's basic condition before God is acknowledged (v. 15) in the terms of the 'Holiness Code' in Leviticus

25: they are 'aliens and temporary residents' on God's land (significantly, given C's overall chronology, from the chapter on the Jubilee, Lev. 25.23; also Gen. 23.4; Ps. 39.12); Israel's tenure of the land always has been and will in the end be on the LORD's terms as the LORD's tenants. The fleetingness of life—'like a shadow'—is described in terms familiar in Psalms and Wisdom (Pss. 102.11; 144.4; Job 8.9; Eccl. 6.12; 8.13). Accordingly, 'their' power to give 'free-will offerings', specifically, to prepare (the key term *kûn* again, 1 Chron. 28.2) the materials necessary for the construction of the Temple, is simply a reflection of God's power to bestow (v. 16 resumes the point in v. 14; *hāmôn*, 'heap' recurs again in 2 Chron. 31.10). Nonetheless (v. 17), though no-one can give God anything, yet the obligation to acknowledge him remains absolute and it is the sincerity and completeness of that acknowledgment that God requires. Without false modesty, David declares that he and his people have fulfilled his and their obligations ('the upright in heart' is a motif familiar from the Psalms of innocence, cf. Pss. 7.10; 11.2; 32.11; 36.10; 64.10; 94.15; 97.11; 119.7) and that that claim will withstand any investigation. The section thus ends with the reaffirmation of the joy (v. 9) of a celebration with a clear conscience.

The whole prayer ends in vv. 18-19 in petition, first for the people, then for Solomon. The basis of the petition (v. 18) is, as in the first section of the prayer, the immemorial bond between the LORD and his people stretching back to the patriarchal age (to add still greater trenchancy, Abraham and Isaac are now mentioned as well as Israel). David prays that God will maintain (yet another play on the thematic verb, *kûn*) the people's present perfect disposition for ever. Once again, the benefit of Israel's faithfulness for the wider context of humanity is hinted at in the use of the phrase in the flood narrative, 'the imagination of the thoughts of the heart' (Gen. 6.5; cf. 1 Chron. 28.9): this time Israel is to play the key role, so that the attitude of the human mind will be good, not evil.

The petition for Solomon (*šᵉlōmô*, v. 19) is that he too will have a perfect (*šālēm*) mind (for the word play on Solomon's name, cf. 1 Chron. 28.9). That perfection is defined in terms of obedience to all God's commandments, as expressed in the Mosaic law (three standard terms as in 2 Chron. 34.31), and in the carrying out of the building of the fortress–Temple (the term as in v. 1), in accordance with David's preparations (the last word of the prayer is yet another use of the thematic term, *kûn*).

8. *The Celebration (1 Chronicles 29.20-25)*

David marks the realization of his plans with a great celebration (1 Chron. 29.20-25). Once again the priorities are striking (cf. 1 Chron. 28.8): in the first instance it is not the recognition of the new king that the *qāhāl* celebrates, but the completion of the preparations for building the Temple; the coronation has to wait until the next day (v. 22b, if that is the correct understanding; see below). This passage thus illustrates yet again C's fundamental purposes. Solomon's rule is not the goal of the celebration, not an end in itself; the true goal is the building of the Temple as the place of rest of the ark, and thus as symbol of the completion of God's purpose for his people, and through them for the world. Solomon is the necessary but essentially ancillary means whereby this true goal is to be attained.

David invites the people to 'bless' the LORD (v. 20; cf. v. 10). They respond with the same awareness of dependence as he himself has done: the LORD is their God but not by their instrumentality—only by virtue of the revelation to their forefathers (cf.1 Chron. 5.25). Appropriately they 'bow down and prostrate themselves'—sensationally, not only to God but also to the king. Although these two verbs are used elsewhere in the Hebrew Bible of honour being shown by humans to humans, the coupling of God and king with these verbs as the recipients of honour is unique in the Hebrew Bible. It is an entirely appropriate formulation given that it is the LORD's throne on which the king sits (cf. v. 23; 1 Chron. 28.5; but contrast 2 Chron. 24.17, when the king falls away from the Law; for worship of the LORD alone by the king himself and the people, cf. 2 Chron. 20.18; 29.30).

> There may be a further dimension—a covert reference to the Moses story in the Pentateuch: 'worship and bow down' occurs in Exod. 4.31; 12.27, admittedly only to God, but in contexts where the status of Moses is being acknowledged (cf. Exod. 14.31 where the LORD and Moses are coupled as the object of Israel's faith).

Verbal recognition of God passes into the practical (v. 21). The first act is not the anointing of Solomon but one of communal solidarity expressed through communion sacrifices and of corporate commitment to the LORD expressed through whole burnt offerings. These feasts are held again 'with great joy' (v. 22, cf. v. 9).

The colossal scale of the sacrifices offered—1000 bulls, 1000 rams, 1000 lambs—can only be appreciated by comparison, once again, with other lists.

In C:

22,000 cattle and 120,000 sheep (Solomon at the dedication of the Temple in 2 Chron. 7.5; at the installation of the ark in 2 Chron. 5.6 simply uncountable; for the comparable sacrifice under Rehoboam in 2 Chron. 11.16, no statistics are given);

7 bulls, 7 rams, 7 lambs (and 7 goats as a sin offering; Hezekiah at rededication of Temple, 2 Chron. 29.21); plus

70 cattle, 100 rams, 200 lambs as holocaust (as thank offering v. 32); plus

600 cattle, 3000 sheep as thank offering (v. 33); plus

1000 bulls, 7000 sheep (Hezekiah, for additional seven days of unleavened bread 2 Chron. 30.24); plus

1000 bulls, 10,000 sheep (officials, 2 Chron. 30.24);

3000 cattle, 30,000 sheep/goats (Josiah's Passover, 2 Chron. 35.7); plus

300 cattle, 2600 sheep/goats (officials, v. 8); plus

500 cattle, 5000 sheep/goats (Levites, v. 9).

Elsewhere in the Hebrew Bible:

113 bulls, 37 rams and 1067 lambs (not to say a score of goats as sin offerings are the offerings required for the stated yearly cycle, assuming a lunar year of 354 days including 50 sabbaths, Numbers 28–29; Num. 28.5, 7, 14 gives information about the libation of wine.);

12 bulls, 96 rams and 77 lambs (and 12 goats for a sin offering) as whole burnt offerings by the returning exiles (Ezra 8.35);

12 bulls, 12 rams, 12 lambs for burnt offerings (and 12 goats for sin offerings) and 24 bulls, 60 rams, 60 goats, and 60 lambs for communion sacrifices, at the dedication of the altar (Num. 7.87-88).

There may be here two striking differences in comparison with other lists of offerings. (1) The sequence of sacrifices here is communion sacrifices followed by whole burnt offerings. (The text of both vv. 21 and 22 may even imply that the communion sacrifices were celebrated there and then 'on that day', while the whole burnt offerings were delayed until the following day. If so, then only the statistics for the whole burnt offerings are given here. The communion sacrifices 'in accordance with the multitude of all Israel' remain as uncountable as the Israel for whom they are required.) This is the reverse of normal practice, in which the communion sacrifices come last (cf., e.g.,

Lev. 1–7). The sense of solidarity between God and people and among the people expressed through the communion sacrifices is here the dominant mood. Whole burnt offerings to express the unreserved devotion of the people to their God then follow. (2) Matching this sense of unclouded solidarity is the omission of any mention of a sin offering (contrast, for example, 2 Chron. 29.21 in the table above). At this moment of high exaltation, when all duty has been rendered to God and free-will offerings have been given to the utmost of the people's capacity, there is no room for any sense of alienation requiring atonement. (The reason for the omission may be more mundane, however: there are no existing institutions to be purified.)

It is within the context of the communion sacrifices, the celebration of corporate unanimity of purpose, that Solomon is made king (v. 22b). This recognition of Solomon as king is made 'for the second time': David's first designation of Solomon as his successor in 1 Chron. 23.1 is now finally acknowledged by the people. The act of acknowledging Solomon as king is performed by means of anointing (cf. 1 Chron. 11.3: as there, so here the old term 'leader', rather than 'king', is used). Significantly, Solomon is not anointed in his own right but 'for the Lord': it is as the Lord's executive that he holds authority.

The now qualified status of David as king is made clear by the way in which Solomon is not the only figure now to be anointed. Zadok is also now formally installed as High Priest by anointing. Zadok has already been frequently mentioned as priest (cf. 1 Chron. 6.8, 53; 12.28; 15.11; 16.39—where, especially, his role is already well defined; 18.16; 24.3, 6, 31; 27.17), but for the new institution his position has to be reinstituted. Here is the reminder of the changed status even of the Davidic house: ever since the raising of the altar for atonement on the threshing floor of Ornan the Jebusite (1 Chron. 21), the king is disabled from expressing in himself the oneness between God and people. The old priestly role that the king had once discharged (cf. 1 Chron. 15–16) must now, in the wake of the king's own fallibility, be surrendered to the professional priesthood.

Solomon thus takes his place as king, not by virtue of any action which he himself has taken, nor of any conquests accomplished, as on old traditions of ancient Near Eastern monarchy, but, as befits his name, submissively (cf. the Arabic cognate with 'Solomon', *Islam*) and pacifically, dependent on the achievements of his father, whose role he now fills. Nonetheless, he receives full status: it is nothing less than the throne of the LORD that he occupies as the LORD's appointed representative and agent on earth (v. 25; cf. 1 Chron. 28.5).

> 1 Kgs 2.12a, which 1 Chron. 29.23a echoes, omits this high theology, stating merely that 'Solomon sat on the throne of his father'.

C adds the key evaluative term 'he prospered', expressive of the success and welfare that God grants to one who is wholly dutiful towards him (cf. 1 Chron. 22.11-13).

'All Israel' obey him. At this utopian moment, Solomon's authority is unchallenged, indeed, unchallengeable. Those with whom the narrative began, the civil and military leaders, summoned by David for the purpose, and the remainder of the royal house, pledge loyalty (the designation of Solomon before the death of David precludes any sibling rivalry, in contrast to 2 Sam. 13–1 Kgs 2). The act of fealty is as that described in 2 Chron. 30.8.

The vocabulary of the summary verse (v. 25) picks up the first section of David's prayer in 1 Chron. 29.10-12: in sacramental theology Solomon has now ascribed to him attributes of the LORD of whom he is now the representative. The LORD now 'makes Solomon great' (cf. v. 12, and the 'greatness' which belongs to God alone, v. 11); he has conferred upon him the 'splendour of kingship' (cf. v. 11), to a degree unique hitherto (and, one may presume, subsequently) in the annals of the Israelite monarchy. Once again at this climactic point there may be a deliberate contrast between the 'surpassing degree' (*l^ema'lâ*) to which the greatness bestowed upon Solomon is manifested to all Israel and the *ma'al*, 'unfaithfulness', which lies at the heart of Israel's predicament in C's presentation (cf. 1 Chron. 14.2)

9. *Annalistic Summary on David's Reign (1 Chronicles 29.26-30)*

An annalistic summary concludes the account of David's reign (1 Chron. 29.26-30). Verse 27 virtually reproduces 1 Kgs 2.11 with its statistics for the length of the reign of David. The distinctive remainder makes points characteristic of C.

> C typically substitutes 'first and last acts of the king' for the 'all that he did' of Kings (cf. 2 Chron. 9.29).

The commoner origins of David as 'son of Jesse' are again noted: all is due to the gracious election of God (cf. 1 Chron. 28.4-5). The reiterated note that 'David ruled over all Israel' stresses the one destiny of the whole people of God realized in him.

David's life is represented as one of idyllic patriarchal length and prosperity (v. 28; for the formulations, compare Abraham, Gen. 15.15; 25.8, Gideon, Judg. 8.32). 'Wealth and honour' are to become a fixed pair of attributes of the Davidic king (2 Chron. 1.11-12; 17.5; 18.1; 32.27). 'Honour' is an attribute of God as divine king (v. 12, cf. 1 Chron. 16.29) shared by his human representative.

It is noted (v. 29) that all the details of David's life can be found, not in a secular source as in Samuel–Kings, but in the literary works of three generations of prophets, Samuel, Nathan and Gad (each is called by a different title, 'visionary', 'prophet', 'seer', no doubt to include the entire gamut of prophetic activity). Samuel has featured only very tangentially in association with David in C's narrative (1 Chron. 9.22; 11.3; 26.28; cf. 1 Chron. 6.28, 33; 2 Chron. 35.18). Nathan appears only in 1 Chronicles 17 and 2 Chron. 29.25 (cf. 2 Chron. 9.29, where his literary work is referred to again in connection with Solomon's reign). Gad intervenes only in 1 Chronicles 21 (and, like Nathan, his contribution is referred to in 2 Chron. 29.25). The narrative of Samuel–Kings, where further details may be found, may be presupposed by C. The nature of these literary works is not made clear. In view of the reference under Solomon in 2 Chron. 9.29 it seems likely that these are envisaged as prophetic commentaries on the course of events rather than biographies of the individual kings (cf. introduction to 2 Chron. 10–36). Above and beyond the destinies of kings is the destiny of God's people and it is the task of the prophet to bring to bear the absolute standard of the Torah on the reign of the king of the day. The word of God accompanies unfailingly the course of human action and decision and is imparted through the prophets in guidance and warning generation by generation.

The high significance and achievement of David's reign are underlined by the final words of the account (v. 30). All the might of his kingship—again presupposed as divinely ordained and as expressive of the sovereignty of God himself (cf. 1 Chron. 29.10-12)—and the vicissitudes through which it has passed have been recounted not merely because it affects an individual or even his people, but because it is of cardinal importance for 'all the kingdoms of the lands' (cf. their tribute, 1 Chron. 16.29). The problem for humanity as a whole, enunciated in 1 Chronicles 1, has its solution envisaged here in the activities of the house of David in Jerusalem on behalf of the LORD, the God of hosts.

2 CHRONICLES 1–9: THE REIGN OF SOLOMON

The presentation of the reign of Solomon is dominated by the construction of the Temple. This is shown by the fact that, while the reign is divided chronologically into two periods of twenty years, the great preponderance in terms of space (152 verses) is given to the first, the account of the building of the Temple; the second period is not only much shorter (49 verses) but is dated by reference to the first (2 Chron. 8.1, 16). The major MT paragraph markers are followed in the main in the following analysis.

The first twenty years of Solomon's reign—the building of the Temple:

2 Chronicles

1.1-13:	the sacral assembly is convened at the tabernacle at Gibeon: the theological basis of Solomon's rule;
1.14–2.2:	the visible expression of Solomon's rule in military power, wealth, commercial astuteness, and control of the international arms trade, culminating in the arrangements for the work-force to build the Temple;
2.3-10:	Solomon's message to Huram of Tyre to send a master-craftsman, wood and a team of workers for the building of the Temple;
2.11-16:	Huram's gracious reply;
2.17–4.18:	the construction of the Temple, its furnishings and equipment;
4.19–5.1:	the deposit of the golden furnishings in the Temple and the silver and golden objects in the treasuries;
5.2-10:	the installation of the ark in the Temple;
5.11-14:	the glory of the LORD fills the Temple;
6.1-42:	Solomon's prayer of blessing and petition (divided after v. 25 between petitions 2 and 3);
7.1-11:	dedication of the Temple;
7.12-22:	God's gracious response.

The concluding twenty years of Solomon's reign—international recognition:

2 Chronicles

8.1-9:	Solomon's acts of imperial consolidation;
8.10-11:	his personnel and his wife;
8.12-18:	the observances of the Temple; the bringing of the gold of Ophir;
9.1-12:	the visit of the Queen of Sheba;
9.13-16:	Solomon's annual income in gold;
9.17-21:	his ivory throne and golden drinking-vessels;
9.22-24:	universal recognition for Solomon;
9.25-31:	concluding annalistic summary.

Besides this division into two twenty-year periods, there are other features that show how carefully the presentation of the reign of Solomon is constructed. There are a number of corresponding sections, even verbal repetitions, which suggest a 'ring' construction whereby the beginning and the end of the presentation correspond, pivoted about Solomon's prayer in ch. 6:

- the wisdom with which Solomon is endowed by God at Gibeon (1.10) is the reason for the kings of the whole earth seeking out Solomon (9.23);
- 1.14-17, on Solomon's status in Jerusalem, has been brought forward and largely repeated from 9.25-28, its equivalent place in 1 Kgs 10.26-29;
- Solomon's request to Huram of Tyre for building materials for the Temple (2 Chron. 2.3-16) matches the joint activities with Huram (2 Chron. 8.18 and 2 Chron. 9.10, 21).

There are other clear signs of arrangement, especially in the first part:

- the direct revelation to Solomon at the beginning of the first twenty-year period is matched by another at its end (1.2-13; 7.12-22);
- the mission to Huram (2.3-16) is emphatically subordinated to the main task, the building the Temple: it is framed by 2.2 expanded in 2.17-18;
- the sacrifice of dedication in 7.1-3, 6 resumes 5.6, 13, 14, and frames Solomon's prayer in ch. 6.

The deliberateness of the arrangement can be appreciated from the way in which C has selected from and rearranged the underlying Kings text:

2 Chronicles	*1 Kings*
1.1-13	cf. 3.4-15
1.14-17	cf. 10.26-29
2.1-18	cf. 5.2-16
3.1-5.1	cf. 6.1-3, 23-28; 7.23-26, 38a, 39-51
5.2-14	cf. 8.1-11
6.1-42	cf. 8.12-50
7.1-22	cf. 8.54, 62–9.9
8.1-18	cf. 9.10, 17-28
9.1-31	cf. 10.1-28; 11.41-43

One should note the material in 1 Kings *not* used by C. Some of this material passes a negative, even very unfavourable, judgment on Solomon and is, therefore, unsuitable for C's idealized portrait.

Broadly (besides the material on, for instance, the rival claim of Adonijah to the throne in 1 Kgs 1–3.3):

3.16-28	the adjudication of Solomon between the two harlots;
4.1-5.1	a miscellany of materials on Solomon's officials, the bounds of the Solomonic empire, the provisions for the court, and the panegyric on the universal wisdom of Solomon and its international renown (though an echo of 4.21 is used at 2 Chron. 9.26 and of 4.26 at 2 Chron. 9.25);
6.4-22, 29-38	certain of the architectural features of the Temple, a conditional oracle of blessing, the chronology of the construction of the Temple;
7.1-22	Solomon's other construction works (though an echo of 7.13-14 is used at 2 Chron. 2.13-14 and of 7.15-22 at 2 Chron. 3.15-17);
7.27-37	the ten stands (despite the fact that the ten basins to be used with these stands, specified in 7.38-39, are referred to at 2 Chron. 4.6);
8.55-61	Solomon's blessing of his people;
9.11-16	the mortgaging of twenty cities in Galilee to Huram king of Tyre to pay for the timber and the gold required for Solomon's constructions, the need to employ forced labour, the sack of Gezer by Pharaoh and the giving of it as a dowry to his daughter married to Solomon;
11.1-40	Solomon's harem and their influence in introducing religious syncretism during his last years, the forewarning of the division of

> the united kingdom, the emergence of foreign threats to Israel from Edom, Aram, the internal threat from Jeroboam, precipitated by Solomon's use of forced labour, the prophetic oracle in favour of Jeroboam from Ahijah of Shiloh, Jeroboam's asylum in Egypt.

In other words, of the total number of verses in 1 Kings 1–11 (434), C uses about 167 and adds some 34 of his own.

2 Chronicles 1.1-13: The Sacral Assembly Is Convened at the Tabernacle at Gibeon. The Theological Basis of Solomon's Rule

2 Chronicles 1.1 marks the transition into Solomon's reign. The form of reference to the king as 'Solomon, son of David' serves to underline the succession of son to father and the continuity between the two. It will not be used again during the description of Solomon's own reign (though cf. 2 Chron. 9.31): once established, Solomon is endowed with full authority. But it will be used in contexts looking back to the joint achievement of father and son (2 Chron. 30.26; 35.3; cf. 2 Chron. 11.17; 13.6; 33.7; 35.4).

The opening word, Solomon 'became strong', picks up (in the intensive reflexive conjugation of the verb *ḥzq*, 1 Chron. 11.10) the vocabulary of exhortation already used by David to Solomon in 1 Chron. 22.13; 28.10, 20; cf. 29.12. Solomon is about to fulfil every expectation of his father and of his God, specifically in connection with his primary commission to build the Temple.

He is established in authority 'over his kingdom'. As the equation of the throne of the LORD with the throne of David has already made plain (1 Chron. 28.5), Solomon is confirmed as occupant of the divine throne in succession to his father. Thus God is here identified for the first time in relation to Solomon: 'the LORD *his* God is with him' (hitherto the formulation has been in such terms as 'the LORD, the God of Israel' or 'the LORD, *my* God' on the lips of David). Solomon is no longer a merely derivative figure; he is now the LORD's representative in his own right. 'With' again echoes the expectations of Immanuel theology—and their fulfilment in Solomon (1 Chron. 11.9).

As the expression of this relationship, God 'exalts' Solomon: as indicated in 1 Chron. 29.12, 25, God imparts to Solomon sacramentally the quality of his own kingship. Again appropriately at this moment of transition to the new reign, the adverb *lᵉmaʿlâ*, 'to the highest degree', is used (cf. 1 Chron. 14.2), with, no doubt, deliberate play on the contrary term, *ma'al*, the self-willed unfaithfulness of a presumptuous king such as Saul (cf. 1 Chron. 10.13-14).

> The differences between the presentations in C and 1 Kgs 3.1 are striking. Kings is qualified in his assessment of Solomon. Whereas in C Solomon 'makes himself strong', Kings uses the same intensive reflexive conjugation, but of a different verb, to say that Solomon entered into a marriage alliance with the Pharaoh of Egypt. C ignores this marriage at this point in his account, but makes a virtue out of necessity in 2 Chron. 8.11 by noting how Solomon removed the wife of a now chaste alliance from the Jerusalem made holy by the presence of the ark.

For the explanation of how Solomon was thus 'established', the narrative now turns to the gathering of the *qāhāl* with Solomon at the 'Tent of Meeting' at Gibeon (vv. 2-13).

The narrative begins with an imperious note: 'Solomon gave orders'. Solomon assumes full authority over the leaders of his people. The same word introduces the culminating action of the commencement of work on the construction of the Temple in 2 Chron. 2.1.

In the parallel in 1 Kgs 3.4-15, the narrative describes the divine authentication of Solomon's rule in a dream at the 'high place' at Gibeon as a private experience. C puts this experience into a new framework and heavily glosses the Kings presentation. So far from this being a merely private experience, C has turned it into a public act. Solomon's address is to 'all Israel' (v. 2; the new royal organizational terms, 'thousands' and 'hundreds', as well as the traditional term, 'heads of households', are used; cf. 1 Chron. 28.1). Solomon now goes to Gibeon accompanied by the *qāhāl* (1 Chron. 13.2; the term is used in v. 3), the whole sacral assembly of the lay representatives of Israel. Matching this public occasion, therefore, is the affirmation at the end of the section that 'he had become king over Israel' (v. 13; C's addition).

The reason for this public demonstration is made clear by C's long insertion in vv. 3-6: it is all connected with the primary purpose of Solomon's kingship—the building of the Temple. The necessary consequence of the building of the Temple is the integration of the religious institutions, that have prevailed until now, into the new religious centre in Jerusalem. Under David a bifurcation had taken place: the ark had been installed in a special tent in Jerusalem, while the tabernacle had been set up at Gibeon (1 Chron. 16.1, 39). All will be reunited in the new Temple in Jerusalem (2 Chron. 5.5).

Given the notoriety of the high place as a religious institution elsewhere in the Hebrew Bible (not least in the parallel to this passage in 1 Kgs 3.2-3), its theological correctness is carefully indicated by details in the narrative. What signifies is the presence of the tabernacle: this is none other than the tabernacle first constructed in the wilderness (the terminology is that of Exod. 25–31; 35–40), the movable shrine which has been Israel's sole centre of worship since that time (cf. on 1 Chron. 11.3). Its alternative title, 'the Tent of Meeting', is appropriate to its role as the place where, in fulfilment of every duty, Solomon may consult (the key term *drš*, v. 5; cf. 1 Chron. 10.13-14) the LORD. Uniquely in the Hebrew Bible, the 'Tent of Meeting' is here given the epithet '*God's* Tent of Meeting'. The authority of Moses is claimed for it; and even the authority of Moses himself is emphasized by the addition of the title, which stresses his status as God's wholly submissive agent, 'the servant of the LORD' (v. 3b). The altar of burnt offerings is the bronze altar constructed by the master craftsman Bezalel in the wilderness (v. 5; cf. Exod. 27.1-8). Later in the passage (v. 13), Gibeon is closely related to Jerusalem, being termed uniquely in the Hebrew Bible, 'Gibeon of Jerusalem' (if the text is sound [see below]; contrast, for example, Josh. 10.5).

> 1 Kgs 3.3 has noted that, while Solomon 'loved the LORD by walking in the statutes of David', he frequented the high places. The reason for Solomon's going to Gibeon was not because the 'Tent of Meeting' was there but simply because it was the 'greatest' high place. Nor is Kings concerned to stress the theological orthodoxy of the altar at Gibeon or that the sacrifices were offered to the LORD.

Both C and Kings agree on the statistics of the whole burnt offerings—1000 (v. 6; the animals sacrificed are not specified—presumably cattle; for the scale of the offering cf. 1 Chron. 29.21). At this moment when plea before God for recognition of the new king's status stands in the forefront, such an act of utter devotion to the LORD is required: communion sacrifices are not yet appropriate.

It is striking that here Solomon is apparently able to officiate himself at the altar of burnt-offering at Gibeon (cf. 2 Chron. 5.6; 7.4, 5, 7), the action from which David was explicitly debarred in 1 Chron. 21.30. Solomon also later blesses the people (2 Chron. 6.3). Both of these actions characterize the role of high priest and had once been undertaken by David (1 Chron. 16.1-2); in Solomon the ideal status of the king is thus once more restored and realized.

This ideal status is further indicated by the direct revelation Solomon receives from God (v. 7; cf. 2 Chron. 7.12-22). The medium of revelation differs between C and Kings: for C, God (the absolute term is used to denote the finality of the revelation) appeared to Solomon directly 'that night' (v. 7); for Kings the LORD (the name expresses the fraught possibilities of a relationship still to be maintained with all the conditionality that that implies; 'God' is used later in the verse) appeared only in a dream 'by night'. The direct revelation of God without mediation by prophet (contrast 1 Chron. 17.3-15; 21.9-13) to the king untarnished by any shortcoming is remarkable: here is monarchy at its highest potential.

The structure of Solomon's prayer in C is two-fold:

(1) thanksgiving, acknowledging what the LORD has done (v. 8);
(2) petition, introduced by 'Now...' (v. 9, and resumed v. 10; cf. 1 Chron. 17.7).

Kings provides both elements but inserts between them an element of confession by Solomon of his own unworthiness, 'I am a raw youth, who does not know how to go out and come in'. The recognition that Solomon is a callow youth has already been made in C by David (1 Chron. 22.5; 29.1) at the moment of designation. But now that the succession of Solomon as the LORD's chosen appointee has been accomplished, there is no further room for such uncertainty.

Solomon's initial acknowledgment in Kings is more deferential ('my father, David, your servant') and notes the conditional nature of God's faithfulness. Again, C has no need for such tentativeness and can be entirely matter of fact: what God ordained in the first place beyond human volition has now been achieved: 'You have acted with great faithfulness towards my father David and have made me king in his place' (v. 8). The promise of 1 Chron. 17.11, rehearsed in 1 Chron. 22.10, and repeated in 1 Chron. 28.4-5 in terms of the election of Solomon, has been kept. Kings is more this-worldly: the human succession is stressed; the throne is David's throne. True to his theology, C leaves open the recognition that the throne is the LORD's (1 Chron. 28.5).

In the petition in C (v. 9), Solomon addresses God in the more objective terms, 'O LORD God'; Kings is more intimate, 'O LORD, my God'. In content, C is more direct: 'As you have made me king, so let your promise be fulfilled'. But the enormity of the task of ruling over God's people is recognized: terms from the patriarchal covenant in Genesis are used—God's people are as numerous as the dust of the earth (Gen. 13.16; 28.14; Kings is content to say merely that they are too numerous to be counted, with a no doubt deliberate side-glance at David's census [2 Sam. 24.1; 1 Chron. 21]). The specific terms in which Solomon requests that the promise be fulfilled follow in a resumption in v. 10: only the divine gifts of wisdom and knowledge will enable the king 'to go out and come in' (reusing the confession in Kings; for the terms cf. 1 Chron. 1.12; 14.15) and rule God's people.

In Kings the petition about 'discerning between good and evil' is conceived in more specifically juridical terms: compare the narrative of the judgment between the rival claims of the two harlots to an infant which follows in 1 Kgs 3.16-28 in order to demonstrate Solomon's judicial powers.

While Kings pauses for one verse to record how pleasing Solomon's request was to God, C presses straight on into the divine response, which expresses that pleasure (vv. 11-12, opening a new sub-paragraph in MT). Solomon has got his priorities right: the wisdom and knowledge he has requested he shall have from God, for it is God who has made him king and it is God's own people whom he rules. Once again, through the phrase 'my people' (1 Chron. 11.2), the emphasis is on the fact that kingship is not an end in itself but the means whereby Israel is enabled to realize its role in the world.

It is by virtue of the gifts of wisdom and knowledge that the other benefits for which Solomon has not asked will be conferred: wealth and honour (1 Chron. 29.12) unsurpassed by any king before or since, and the long life that evidences the health imparted by the sound relationship with God (cf. 2 Chron. 7.14). The recovery in Solomon of the ideal status of the king leads to the unique manifestation of the benefits which that status bestows.

Kings once more stresses the judicial aptitude and ends on another note of conditionality, again inappropriate for C's presentation of the irresistibility of the success of one divinely designated and endowed.

The narrative concludes with an act of acknowledgment by Solomon: it is in response to this oracle that he goes in worship 'to the high place at Gibeon of Jerusalem, in front of the Tent of Meeting' (as the text seems to say).

As *BHK* and *BHS* note, LXX and Vulgate imply the expected text, '*from* the high place at Gibeon *to* Jerusalem'. But C may want to reinforce the orthodoxy of the high place at Gibeon by this close association with Jerusalem.

Kings in conformity with his presentation records that Solomon awakes from his dream and returns to Jerusalem where he worships before the ark of the covenant—with its implications of the possibility of blessing and curse—and again offers whole burnt offerings and communion sacrifices. The note of anxiety about his status before God and humankind is not lacking in these acts.

2 Chronicles 1.14–2.2: The Material Expression of Solomon's Rule

Solomon's reign marks the perfect realization of the ideal announced through David; in him the full potentiality for the monarchy to enable Israel to fulfil its role in the world is achieved. Everything is in place to enable him to proceed to the main task of his reign—the building of the Temple. He is endowed with every gift of intellect and spirit and with material possessions to match; in crucial contradistinction to his father, he has shed no blood. As this section suggests, a mere show of strength and the shrewd control of the international arms trade by his merchants are all that is required to maintain peace among the nations.

Verses 14-17 are virtually identical with 1 Kgs 10.26-29 (the point of transition in Kings to the negative judgment on Solomon). C has retained a section corresponding to 1 Kgs 10.26-29 at the end of his presentation on Solomon in 2 Chron. 9.25-28, but he has also brought it forward to this point at the beginning of Solomon's reign as part of his 'ring-construction' on Solomon's reign. In its present location it makes a preliminary summary statement on Solomon's wealth and prestige.

2 Chron. 2.1-2 are a collage of materials from 1 Kgs 5.5, 15-16a with additions and adjustments.

The section opens (v. 14) with Solomon's acquisition of the latest in military might—1400 chariots and 12,000 horsemen (the verb, 'gather', is one of the key terms for accession of strength, cf.1 Chron. 11.1). Now for the first time an Israelite king adds such squadrons to his army (in 1 Chron. 18.4 David hamstrung captured horses).

These statistics are difficult to evaluate: cf. 2 Chron. 9.25, where there are '4000 stalls of horses and chariots'; 40,000 in 1 Kgs 4.26.

For statistics for other chariot forces ranging from 300 to 32,000, cf. 1 Chron. 19.7.

As expressions of his might, Solomon stationed them in his capital, Jerusalem, as well as throughout his territory in 'chariot cities', unspecified garrison towns that feature only in connection with Solomon in the Hebrew Bible (cf. 1 Kgs 9.19).

The wealth pouring in to Jerusalem from tribute and trade, and the imports for Solomon's building works, 'make silver (and gold, C adds) as common as stone, and cedar as common as sycamore' (v. 15).

Commerce also flourishes (vv. 16-17; contrast 2 Chron. 15.5; 16.1). Because of the location of Israel on the land-bridge between Africa and Asia, the overland trade route from Egypt to Mesopotamia and Asia Minor has to pass through territory now controlled by Solomon, an advantage his merchants are quick to exploit. Though the text is somewhat obscure, it would appear that Solomon's merchants were acting as importers of horses and chariots from Egypt not just for Solomon but also for export to the kings of the Hittites and the Aramaeans. But the point is not merely commercial: Solomon, as the vicegerent of the LORD of hosts on earth, whose task it is to bring peace to the warring nations, now controls the trade in the most powerful weapons known to the ancient world.

> The sums of money paid—600 shekels of silver for a chariot and 150 for a horse—can again only be appreciated by the price paid for other articles (cf. on 1 Chron. 29.4).

All these advantages are not meant to be enjoyed merely in themselves. They are but the surface manifestation of Solomon's role as the occupant of the LORD's throne. The paragraph therefore comes to its culmination in the prime task of Solomon's reign—the building of the Temple, the supreme sacramental symbol of his rule (1 Chron. 2.1-2).

Solomon issues the order (the verb is the same as in 2 Chron. 1.2, contra NRSV) for the building of the Temple (v. 1). He then 'counts' the labour force required for quarrying the stone (precisely where in the hill country is not said) and in transporting it to Jerusalem (v. 2). This review and organization of the labour force prepares for the next section, the request by Solomon to Huram of Tyre to send him a skilled craftsman and the necessary timber for the work on the interior of the Temple (vv. 3-10). It will be resumed at the beginning of the next but one section in 2 Chron. 2.17, when the building operations themselves begin.

The longer version of this material is in 2 Chron. 2.17. There C makes it clear that, in counting this labour force, Solomon is neither enslaving his own people (contrast 1 Kgs 5.13, though 1 Kgs 9.22 denies that Solomon enslaved his own people) nor repeating the mistake of his father in conducting a census of God's people. This labour force is derived not from native-born Israelites but from the resident aliens whom David had assembled (1 Chron. 22.2)—a point not made by Kings. C slightly alters the statistics: for the reference in Kings to 3300 foremen, C reads 3600.

For 'foremen' C prefers his own technical term for the supervisors of works on the Temple (cf. 2 Chron. 34.12-13, Ezra 3.8-9), though here these supervisors are not levitical but are drawn from among the foreign residents themselves (v. 17). In 2 Chron. 8.10 he uses the term in Kings.

The title in v. 1, 'a house for the name [i.e. renown] of the LORD', uses vocabulary about the revealed character and world-wide reputation of the LORD (cf. 1 Chron. 13.6). The reference to 'a house for his kingship' is presumably to Solomon's palace (though, since, within C's theology, Solomon's kingship is synonymous with the LORD's, the term might, just conceivably be another title for the Temple). It is striking that C suppresses the materials on Solomon's royal palace in 1 Kgs 7.1-12 (Huram had already helped David to build his royal palace, 1 Chron. 14.1), yet there is a direct reference to the palace in 2 Chron. 7.11 (and an implied reference to it in 2 Chron. 9.16-20).

2 CHRONICLES 2.3-16: SOLOMON'S CORRESPONDENCE WITH HURAM OF TYRE

This exchange between friendly powers is tied in integrally to Solomon's preparation of the labour force for the construction of the Temple. The list of resident aliens in Israel who are conscripted for the task immediately precedes it in 2 Chron. 2.2 and is directly resumed and developed in 2 Chron. 2.17-18.

This section is an example of the ideal response of the world of the nations to the sovereignty of God expressed through the rule of the king of the house of David in Jerusalem. It is matched at the other end of the account of Solomon's reign by similar ideal responses in 2 Chronicles 8–9.

The context of the passage thus differs significantly from that of the parent text in 1 Kings 5. For example, there, Solomon's request is in response to an initial overture from Hiram (the form of the king's name in Kings; see on 1 Chron. 14.1) and it is Hiram who largely dictates terms. Here, that initial overture from Hiram is omitted: it is Solomon, the dominant partner in the relationship, who takes the initiative, as befits the divine representative on earth; it is he who offers terms. Many details that serve to point up these differences of emphasis between C and Kings, will be noted in the text below.

MT divides the section into two: vv. 3-10 Solomon's message to Huram; vv. 11-16 Huram's gracious response.

Verses 3-10: Solomon's Message to Huram

The section is structured in an unusually complex way. From previous messages in C, the reader expects a two-part structure, first describing the situation and then drawing the appropriate conclusions, with a hinge, 'And now...', marking the transition (cf. 1 Chron. 17.7).

Here there are, indeed, two parts: vv. 3b-6, and 7-10, introduced by the 'And now'. But both parts have been elaborated with further elements offering explanations or inducements. These are mostly signalled by words and phrases like 'see' (vv. 4, 8b, 10), and 'because' (vv. 5, 6, 8, 9).

The first part, as expected, describes the prevailing situation. But it does not do so merely in a simple statement, 'you treated my father well' (v. 3b); it casts that statement as the first part of a comparative sentence: '*Just as* you treated my father well...' But only the first clause of that comparative sentence is given immediately; the expected, '*so* now continue this favourable treatment with me' (or words to that effect), is suspended until v. 7. There is thus a dramatic interruption of the construction.

The interruption in vv. 4-6 explains Solomon's own proposed course of action in detail (introduced by the particle, 'see'), and lends added weight to the forthcoming request with an *a fortiori* argument: 'you helped David to build a palace for himself with finest cedar wood; *how much more* should you help me, when I am building a Temple to the supreme Deity?'. The whole is clinched with two rhetorical questions: 'who is able to...?' and 'who am I that...?'—least of all, the implication is, Solomon by himself.

The second part deals with the consequences expected, introduced by the hinge, 'And now'. This time there are two requests, introduced by imperatives: v. 7, 'send me a master-craftsman'; v. 8, 'send me timber'. The first has only an implied additional reason ('I have a suitably trained workshop'); the second gives the additional reason overtly, introduced with a formal, 'because' (v. 8aβ: 'because I know that your subjects know how to cut the timber of Lebanon'), with the additional inducement, 'and see there will be co-operation between our work-forces'.

The whole is rounded off by a yet further inducement, v. 10: 'now see [as already in v. 8b], I have prepared provisions for the workmen'.

Solomon has enlisted his resident aliens; he now turns to the 'righteous gentile', Huram, king of Tyre (v. 3). Huram's record for support and recognition of the house of David is already above reproach. As Huram had already helped David to build the royal palace for himself using the finest timber (1 Chron. 14.1; cf. 1 Chron. 22.4), so Solomon seeks his help for the far greater task of building a Temple in honour ('in the name', v. 4; cf. 1 Chron. 13.6) of the supreme cosmic Deity (v. 5).

The immediate reason is, thus, to solicit Huram's help in materials and men: only the best of what the nations of the world have to offer is good enough and that best finds its fulfilment in the service of the God of Israel (cf. already Egyptian horses and chariots in Solomon's army, 2 Chron. 1.14). But there are other levels: as Huram had been the first of the nations of the world to recognize David's rule, so now it is appropriate that Solomon should receive similar recognition at a similar moment in his reign. It is in any case to be expected that on the occasion of a new successor to either throne, previous relations between royal houses should be renewed (cf. 1 Chron. 19.1-2).

Solomon proceeds to state in high theological terms the significance of the projected Temple (v. 4). He speaks again appropriately in terms of 'the LORD, *my* God' (cf. 2 Chron. 1.1). First, the purpose of the Temple is to consecrate to the LORD the offerings by which the Israelites symbolize their duty towards God (cf., e.g., 1 Chron. 23.13). In its nave, the incense is burnt as part of the rites of appeasement and atonement (cf., e.g., Exod. 30.7; Lev. 4.7; 16.12) and the showbread is arranged in symbolical representation of Israel (1 Chron. 9.32); at its altar, sacrifices of whole burnt offerings, statements of the utter devotion of Israel, are offered perpetually twice daily, as well as weekly, monthly and at the three great annual pilgrimage festivals (cf. the tariff of offerings in Num. 28–29).

But Solomon recognizes the merely symbolical nature of the Temple: anticipating his great prayer at the dedication of the Temple in 2 Chron. 6.18, he acknowledges that no human being, not even two co-operating kings able to command the richest resources of earth, can build a 'house' to accommodate such a transcendent God, whom even the highest heavens cannot contain (v. 6; for the vocabulary of powerlessness and wonderment, cf. 1 Chron. 29.14). As a place of 'raising smoke', its altars of incense and of burnt offering can have only adorational and petitionary significance (cf. 1 Chron. 6.49). Yet the Temple will have a sacramental function: as befits the international fame of the LORD, whose 'house' it is, and his supreme status among the gods of the nations, this Temple must be renowned internationally for its size and splendour (v. 5; cf. 1 Chron. 22.5).

It must be assumed that by sending materials for its construction Huram, the foreign king, will by implication be recognizing these claims made on behalf of the LORD (cf. his confessions of faith in vv. 11-12).

> Solomon's approach to Hiram is rather different in Kings: in much less far-reaching theological terms, he merely explains how David had charged him with the building of the Temple which, as a man of bloodshed, David could not undertake himself. With the pacification of the region and no further occasion for bloodshed, Solomon can proceed with the building (C has made the point already in, for example, 1 Chron. 22.8). No claims to the supremacy of the LORD over other gods are made (as in v. 5 here): the LORD is simply 'his'—David's—or 'my'—Solomon's—God (1 Kgs 5.3-5).

Solomon requests first (v. 7) a skilled craftsman who can work in all the metals—again in descending order of value: gold, silver, bronze and iron—fabrics—purple, crimson and blue (representing sea, earth and sky? cf. on 2 Chron. 3.14)—and engraving in the interior of the Temple. The three coloured stuffs are as in the specifications for the Tabernacle in the wilderness (e.g. Exod. 25.4; though the word used here for 'crimson' occurs only in 2 Chron. 2 and 3, while the word for 'purple' is in a slightly different form); continuity between Temple and tabernacle is thus affirmed. It is not that there are no craftsmen in Israel; a team has already been 'brought together' (the word is from the key root, *kûn*, again [see 1 Chron. 14.2]): but native skill is complemented by the expertise and leadership of the acknowledged international authority, who brings the tribute of his craftsmanship to make the Temple of the LORD pre-eminent in the world.

Kings includes no such request by Solomon for a skilled supervisor from Tyre. The nearest equivalent passage is 1 Kgs 7.13-14, where Solomon himself fetches the individual concerned. Once again, C is stressing the contribution of the foreign king. In Kings the skills of the master-craftsman are specified only as working in bronze (cf. 2 Chron. 4.16); C presents him as an all round expert like Bezalel, the master craftsman of the Tabernacle (Exod. 35.30-35).

Solomon's second request (v. 8) is for those materials for which Lebanon is famed—timber; but besides the well-known cedar, Solomon adds cypress and the otherwise unidentified 'algum' [cf. KBS].

Kings gives only cedar (and, later in the narrative, cypress). For the self-deprecating statement by Solomon in Kings, 'For you know that we have no-one who can fell trees as well as the Sidonians', C reads in a more matter of fact way, 'For I know that your workmen are skilled in felling the timber of Lebanon'. C has retained from Kings the phrase, 'My workmen are with your workmen', but, while in Kings that belongs to the scenario, rejected by C, whereby Solomon sends 60,000 Israelites under forced labour to Lebanon, here C seems to be thinking jointly of the works in Lebanon and Israel (cf. the massive totals of the payments in kind envisaged in C over against Kings [2 Chron. 2.10; contrast 1 Kgs 5.11]).

Solomon repeats the reason for his request (v. 9): it is to provide him (again the key root, *kûn*) with the means necessary for constructing a Temple grand enough in size and decoration for honouring the LORD. He offers an appropriate budget (v. 10): 20,000 *kors* of both wheat and barley; 20,000 *baths* of both wine and olive oil to support the labour force.

> In Kings Hiram is invited to set his own terms. The measures of volume can only be appreciated in comparison with the rather random evidence of other passages. For example,
>
> 30 *kors* of fine flour and 60 *kors* of meal was the daily support for Solomon's court (1 Kgs 4.22);
> 10,000 *kors* of both wheat and barley were paid by the Ammonites to Jotham annually for three years (2 Chron. 27.5);
> according to Ezek. 45.11 the *bath* is the same size as the *ephah*. In Zech. 5.6-10 the *ephah* is some kind of container large enough to fit a woman inside.

In the Kings version, it is not clear that these payments were part of the initial offer made by Solomon. Kings mentions only 20,000 *kors* of wheat and 20 *kors* of first-pressing olive oil. The very much larger amounts in C may be explained by the fact that he is including not only the Tyrian woodsmen but also the, presumably Israelite, quarrymen.

Verses 11-16: Huram's Response

> The repeated opening formula in vv. 11 and 12, 'Then Huram said...', alerts the reader to C's editorial activity: v. 11, Huram's warm commendation of Solomon, has no precise parallel in Kings; v. 12 resumes C's edited version of Kings.
>
> These opening formulas nonetheless form the first part of the standard two-part message, hinged together by 'And now' (v. 13; cf. discussion of the structure of vv. 3-10 above). The first part—the recognition of the situation—is here expressed, not in narrative, but in the rhetorical form of acknowledgment of the Divine act (v. 11b) and blessing for it (v. 12), which amount to confession of faith (cf. David's 'blessing' of the Lord in 1 Chron. 29.10). The second part—the drawing of the consequences—is a formal declaration introduced by 'And now': 'I hereby send...' (vv. 13-14). A second 'And now' (v. 15), introduces the second consequence expressed in the imperative: 'send the provisions prepared for the work-force so that the enterprise can begin'.

Huram's reply begins with a warm acknowledgment of Solomon's kingship as evidence of the LORD's love for his people (v. 11; for 'his people', cf. 1 Chron. 11.2). The Queen of Sheba draws a similar conclusion in the matching section at the end of the account of Solomon's reign (2 Chron. 9.8). More sensational is Huram's astonishing confession of faith in the LORD, Israel's God, as the creator of heaven and earth (v. 12; for a similar acknowledgment at the climax of the work, cf. Cyrus, 2 Chron. 36.22-23). In line with the long-standing ancient Near Eastern tradition of building a Temple for the deity who has proved himself supreme (e.g. Baal and Huram texts from Ugarit), Huram's participation in the construction of this Temple to the LORD in Jerusalem contains in itself an implicit acknowledgment of the LORD's status and of the focal role of Jerusalem. What had been achieved under David, Huram now recognizes as being brought to its fulfilment under Solomon. He is the Temple-builder, who by that act will bring universal recognition of the LORD's dominion. To achieve this divinely ordained purpose, Solomon is endowed with the necessary attributes: he is 'wise and knows how to achieve success and be perceptive'. The latter are the very qualities which were the subject of David's prayer for Solomon in 1 Chron. 22.12.

Huram grants the request to send an acknowledged master-craftsman, one Huram-abi by name. In his sphere he has 'wisdom' to match Solomon's. Huram-abi's parentage must be regarded as highly significant: his mother is from Dan and his father from Tyre. Huram-abi bridges the cultures: at this most decisive moment in the history of salvation—the building of the Temple for God in acknowledgment of his recreating through Israel the conditions for his ideal primal relationship with all humanity—a representative, through his mother, of the most outcast part of Israel (cf. the omission of Dan in the genealogies of 1 Chron. 2–8), and, through his father, of the world of the nations beyond, finds a position of honour, indeed, of crucial instrumentality in the work on the sacred structure of the Jerusalem Temple. Though the son of a Tyrian father, Huram-abi bears the programmatic name, 'my father is devoted'.

'Huram-abi' is clearly meant to mean in Hebrew, 'my father [despite being a Phoenician] is a devoted one', rather than, 'my father is the brother of the lofty one', as, strictly speaking, etymologically it should (cf. 1 Chron. 14.1).

Kings omits any reference to a master-craftsman at this point of his presentation—only in 1 Kgs 7.13-14 is such a figure mentioned. There his name is given only as 'Hiram' and his mother comes from Naphtali.

Huram-abi is expert in working in all the mediums Solomon has specified and in more besides: stone, wood, linen. He will be able to execute any commission and to co-operate with the Israelite craftsmen whom David and Solomon have organized.

Huram requests forwarding of the payment in kind that Solomon has promised. While his own men get to work felling the trees and floating them in rafts to Joppa (nearly 150 km), it will be Solomon's responsibility to transport them by land from Joppa to Jerusalem (about 55 km).

> Kings is vaguer about where the logs would be taken ashore. It implies that the payment was left very much to Solomon's unilateral decision. Besides the additional details on the labour force, Kings states that Hiram and Solomon bound themselves by an agreement.

2 CHRONICLES 2.17–5.1: SOLOMON BUILDS THE TEMPLE

2 Chronicles 2.17-18 resumes the matter of the organization of the labour force sketched in at 2 Chron. 2.2, which has formed the framework for Solomon's correspondence with Huram of Tyre. As noted there, fuller details are now given: the total of resident aliens neatly breaks down into porters, quarrymen, and supervisors. Whether as menial conscripts or as wealthy neighbouring monarch, the nations of the world provide essential labour and materials to build a Temple of scale and magnificence worthy of the LORD of heaven and earth.

The Structure of 2 Chronicles 3.1–5.1

2 Chronicles 3.1-2 provides a double heading on the building of the Temple. Verse 1a, 'Solomon began to build the house of the LORD', is matched by the conclusion in 2 Chron. 5.1a, 'Thus was completed all the work which Solomon performed on the house of the LORD'. Verse 1b then provides an important note on the location of the Temple. Verse 2 resumes v. 1a (both verses begin with the same verbs, 'and [he] began to build') and develops it by giving the date: 'on the second day of the second month of the fourth year of his reign'. This date is, however, not matched by another date until 2 Chron. 8.1. The double heading in 2 Chron. 3.1-2, thus, encompasses the whole of Solomon's activities in constructing and dedicating the Temple, which are not to be completed until the end of 2 Chronicles 7. This is wholly appropriate: the meticulous care with which C lists the specifications of the Temple and its furnishings in the following sub-sections down to 5.1 would be meaningless, unless they were brought into association with the following section in chs. 5–7 which infuse life into the whole system.

The main body of material which follows in 2 Chron. 3.3–4.22 is divided into two main parts:

3.3-7 the dimensions and ornamentation of the main building of the Temple;.
3.8–4.22 furnishings of the Temple.

This second part is itself complex, and can be subdivided into three sections:

1. *1 Chronicles 3.8–4.10: A Series of Thirteen Subsections, All Beginning 'And He [Solomon] Made'*

MT marks nine subsections (3.8-13; 14; 15; 16-17; 4.1; 2-5; 6; 7; 8-11a) either coinciding with or combining some of the following.

At the head stands the most important part—the holy of holies:
3.8-9: its construction and specification;
3.10-13: the cherubim within the holy of holies;
3.14: the curtain separating the holy of holies from the nave.

The pillars in front of the Temple:
3.15: their specification;
3.16a: the chains for the capitals of the pillars;
3.16b: the pomegranates on the chains (the pillars erected, 3.17).

The furnishings of the inner courtyard in front of the nave:
4.1: the altar;
4.2-5: the sea;
4.6: the basins.

The furnishings of the nave:
4.7: the lampstands;
4.8a: the tables;
4.8b: and a hundred gold bowls.

Courts:
4.9: the court of the priests; the concourse and its gates (the location of the sea, 4.10).

A fourteenth subsection—but attributed to Huram—is included in 4.11a: the utensils of the altar of burnt offering.

2. *1 Chronicles 4.11b-18: Summary on Huram's Bronze-casting, Introduced by the Phrase, 'So Huram Finished Making' (v. 11b)*

MT places all this material in a single sub-section.

4.12aα: two pillars;
4.12aβ-13: two capitals and their adornments;
4.14: the stands and the basins;

4.15:	the sea;
4.16:	the cultic utensils of the altar of burnt offering.
4.17:	Note on location of bronze-casting.
4.18:	Concluding note: these works are in principle Solomon's.

3. *4.19-22: Summary on Solomon's Gold-working, Introduced by a Single, 'And Solomon Made...'*

MT places 4.19–5.1 in a separate major section with a subdivision at the end of 5.1a.

4.19bα:	the incense altar;
4.19bβ:	the tables for the show bread;
4.20:	the lampstands and the lamps;
4.21-22a:	the utensils for the lamps and the incense altar;
4.22b:	the doors of the holy of holies and the nave.
5.1a:	Concluding note: all Solomon's works 'which he made' for the Temple are completed.

But just as the opening of the whole section in 3.1-2 looks beyond the immediate action of Solomon in the actual construction of the Temple to the wider context of Solomon's reign, so the additional concluding note in 5.1b looks beyond the immediacies of construction and furnishing to the enduring significance of the Temple: it is above all the treasury where Solomon deposits all his father David's dedicated gifts, all the silver and gold and all the utensils. The deposits are the symbol that Israel is rendering to the Lord every duty that they owe to him; the system is now in being whereby Israel is enabled to live the life of holiness. All that remains is to breathe life into that system.

Comment on the Detail of 2 Chronicles 3.1–5.1

2 Chronicles 3.1 provides the general introduction to Solomon's Temple-building operations.

C is more restrained in his presentation of Solomon's activities. Whereas 1 Kgs 6.1 has Solomon move with assurance directly to the task ('he built the Temple in the LORD's honour'), C presents the process: 'Solomon began to build the Temple of the LORD' (so again in v. 2, again in contrast to Samuel–Kings).

C adds a long note in v. 1aβ on a matter of fundamental importance in his presentation—the location of the Temple.

Naturally, the Temple is located in Jerusalem, for that is Solomon's capital city. But in harmony with the presentation of Solomon as the submissive agent who is swept along by a tide of events far beyond his control—instigated by David through the election of God (1 Chron. 28.4-6)—no fewer than four qualifications are made about the location of the Temple; these summarize the argument of C's whole presentation in 1 and 2 Chronicles to date.

1. First, it is noted that the Temple is to be built on the mountain of Moriah. This comment, unique to C, links Solomon's action with the whole destiny of God's people as C has presented it. It was on a mountain in Moriah, that the LORD appeared to Abraham (Gen. 22.2, the only other place where it occurs in the Hebrew Bible). Thus, C is picking up the point he is making at the beginning of his work in 1 Chronicles 1: with Abraham, the definitive restart in the story of human destiny has begun. But Genesis 22 is also concerned with the mountain of Moriah as the place of sacrifice, for it was there that the sacrifice of Isaac was to have taken place and was averted only at the last moment by the substitutionary offering of a ram. Thus, here on the mountain of Moriah when Abraham's latest descendant, David, was about to bring the angel of destruction on his people, God himself interposed to save the remnant (1 Chron. 21.14-15). The Temple marks the spot where the new substitutionary rites of atonement take place and will continue to take place. Thus, theologically speaking, whereas for Kings the Temple is located chronologically by reference to the exodus of Israel from Egypt (1 Kgs 6.1), for C it is located topographically by reference to the theophany to Abraham at the mountain of Moriah.

2. This mountain is the place where the LORD has now appeared to David. The role of David is once again presented as crucial. He is the very one through whose empire the ideal announced in Abraham comes nearest to accomplishment (1 Chron. 11–20) but who in the end shows himself to be most in need of atonement (1 Chron. 21). It is at this location, proven by virtue of the LORD's renewed self-revelation to David at the place where the greatest ideal is expressed and the greatest need met, that the Temple is to be built. Solomon is, once again, the necessarily subordinate agent of 'David his father' (v. 1aγ).

3. The logic of C's presentation of David continues: as in 1 Chronicles 22–29, it can only be David who has the responsibility of making all the preparations for the construction (v. 1bα).

4. The final point, that the Temple is built on the threshing-floor of Ornan the Jebusite (v. 1bβ), restates the point of need. The threshing-floor of Ornan marked the physical limit of the plague; the location of the altar on that threshing-floor continues to mark that boundary. The Temple is the bulwark against the consequences of the guilt of violating God's holiness such as had threatened to engulf David's reign.

2 Chronicles 3.2: The Temporal Framework

Despite the repeated 'Solomon began to build', C gives no indication of how long it actually took to build the Temple. The dates of the dedication of the Temple in 2 Chron. 5.3; 7.10 only give the 'seventh month' but not the year (contrast 1 Kgs 6.37-38, where it is stated that the construction took Solomon seven years). The next matching date is in 2 Chron. 8.1, which introduces the second twenty-year period of Solomon's reign. As far as C is concerned, the matter of chronology is of little interest: the construction of the Temple is the sole focus of the first twenty years of Solomon's reign. He is not concerned to inform the reader whether it took only the seven years of Kings, or, indeed, the remainder of the twenty.

Solomon began to build on the second day of the second month of the fourth year of his reign. The calendar followed here is the 'Babylonian' which began with the spring equinox. The second month is then April or May, that is, well clear of the celebration of Passover–Unleavened Bread in the first month (and towards the end of the harvest period, when labour would be more available, if that is a relevant consideration for C). The building operations begin on the second day of the month, the day after new moon day with its special observances (cf. Num. 28.11-15).

1 Kgs 6.1 does not read 'on the second day': but, while the word in C may be a dittograph with 'the second [month]', it can thus be seen to make perfectly good sense.

As commented above, C omits the dating of the foundation of the Temple by reference to the exodus from Egypt that is found in Kings. C also omits the antiquarian note on the old Canaanite name for the second month found in Kings .

The 'fourth year' will indicate the time necessary for Solomon to ensure that all the arrangements and resources described in 2 Chronicles 2 (the felling and transportation of timber, the quarrying and dressing of stone) are in place. All now follows the blueprint revealed to David (1 Chron. 28.11-19).

2 Chronicles 3.3-7: The Dimensions and Ornamentation of the Temple
The dimensions intended are not fully clear. The Temple is defined as 60 cubits in length and 20 cubits in breadth (v. 3). One might at first sight conclude that these dimensions referred only to the nave of the Temple, for additional specifications are given for the porch (v. 4) and for the holy of holies (v. 8). But a text in Kings, not reproduced by C, specifies that the nave itself was 40 cubits long (1 Kgs 6.17). The holy of holies is thus here included within the 60 cubits. The dimensions of the porch are defective: only its breadth is given in a somewhat obscure phrase, 'twenty cubits across the width of the house abutting the end'. A height is given, 'one hundred and twenty cubits', but it is not made clear whether this refers to the porch or to the main building. One must assume the former in the light of the Kings parallel, where the nave is 30 cubits high.

To avoid confusion with a longer cubit used by Ezekiel (cf. Ezek. 40.5; 43.13, where it is explained that it was longer by a hand-breath), C adds a note that he is using the traditional measure as current in the time of Solomon.

C's Temple is, then, tripartite: the holy of holies, 20 × 20 × 20 cubits; the nave 40 × 20 × 30; the porch 10 × 20 × 120. This indeed corresponds to the rabbinical likening of the Temple to a crouching lion, tall at the front, narrow at the rear (*Mid.* 4.7).

The adornment of the Temple is then described. The porch's interior is inlaid with gold (v. 4b). The nave is panelled with pine overlaid with fine gold from an otherwise unattested exotic location, adorned with palm trees and chains, inlaid with jewels and engraved with cherubim (vv. 5-6). Every rafter, threshold, wall and door is gilded (v. 7). The finest materials that earth can produce, adorned with symbols of life and universal dominion, indeed fulfil David's plan that the Temple would fitly reflect the glory of God: v. 6 uses the word 'glory'—concealed by NRSV in the verb 'adorned'—through which David has expressed his aspirations and prayers for the glorification of the Temple as the appropriate sacramental expression of the nature of God in whose name it is dedicated (1 Chron. 22.5; 29.11, 13).

2 Chronicles 3.8–4.22: The Details of the Furnishings of the Temple

First, there is the long section (2 Chron. 3.8–4.11a) containing the repeated phrase, 'and he made'. The same verbal stem is used over one hundred times in Exodus 25–31 in connection with the construction of the tabernacle, which is now to be integrated into Solomon's Temple (2 Chron. 5.5); Solomon is the new Moses; Huram-abi the new Bezalel (2 Chron. 1.5). But, whoever the craftsman was, it was in principle Solomon himself who was the executor of the task of equipping the Temple to fulfil its role.

2 Chronicles 3.8-9: The Holy of Holies

Whereas 1 Kgs 6.5 includes the descriptive term 'inner area', C, by contrast, and in keeping with his central theme, the sanctification of Israel, prefers in this context the functional term 'the holy of holies'/'the most holy place' (v. 8), for this was the place above all where atonement was effected for Israel.

C reproduces the length and breadth of the holy of holies, but not the height (v. 8a). This may be because of mere abbreviation of the text. But it is striking that C adds here—unless the passage is misplaced—upper chambers (v. 9a; cf. 1 Chron. 28.11).

> Elsewhere in the Hebrew Bible the only additional constructions associated with the outside of the holy of holies (and the nave) are the three storeys of side chambers (e.g. 1 Kgs 6.5-6).

For the comparative value of the enormous weight of gold—600 talents for the overlay (not to mention 50 shekels just for the nails)—used for the adornment of this most sacred place (vv. 8b, 9a), see on 1 Chron. 29.1-5 (e.g. 600 talents is five times the amount the Queen of Sheba brought as a gift to Solomon, 2 Chron. 9.9).

2 Chronicles 3.10–13: The Cherubim

C now turns to the contents of the holy of holies (v. 10; again he uses the term that explains significance, rather than the descriptive term in 1 Kgs 6.23, 'inner area'). This is to be the place where the ark of the covenant is to be installed (2 Chron. 5.2-10). It is to be watched over by two cherubim (for their role as protectors of the unapproachableness of God, as well as the force that propels the divine throne chariot through the universe, cf. 1 Chron. 13.6; 28.18).

Their physical representation is now described. They are constructed from a core (Kings says of wild olive) overlaid with gold (v. 10). They are an identical pair, standing side by side. Each has a pair of wings, spanning ten cubits, touching the wall on one side and meeting the wing of the other in the middle (vv. 11-13). They face into the nave of the Temple (v. 13) to deter unauthorized access to the holy of holies.

C omits the Kings detail that the cherubim were 10 cubits high.

2 Chronicles 3.14: The Curtain

A curtain separates the holy of holies from the nave.

In this, C's Temple is like the tabernacle in the wilderness (e.g. Exod. 26.31), and unlike the Temple in Kings, where there is a double olive-wood door (1 Kgs 6.31-32; so below, 2 Chron. 4.22!).

It is made of the materials as planned in 2 Chron. 2.7, 14. It, too, has cherubim worked upon it to protect the holy of holies from unauthorized entry.

Josephus's comments on the cosmic significance of the flax and colours are instructive:

'The vails, too, which were composed of four things, they declared the four elements; for the fine linen was proper to signify the earth, because the flax grows out of the earth; the purple signified the sea, because that colour is dyed by the blood of the sea shellfish; the blue is fit to signify the air; and the scarlet will naturally be an indication of fire' (*Ant.*, 3.7.7).

'But then this house...the inner part...had golden doors...before these doors there was a veil... It was a Babylonian curtain, embroidered with blue, and fine linen, and scarlet and purple, and of a contexture that was truly wonderful. Nor was this mixture of colours without its mystical interpretation, but was a kind of image of the universe; fire, earth, air, and sea' (*War*, 5.5.4).

2 Chronicles 3.15-17: The Two Pillars, Jachin and Boaz

Two pillars, thirty-five cubits high, are erected in front of the Temple, one on the south called Jachin and one on the north called Boaz. They are decorated with capitals a further five cubits high. The tops of the pillars are swathed with chains from each of which (so 2 Chron. 4.13) are suspended 100 pomegranates.

There are a number of obscurities in these specifications—and variations from those given in Kings.

The height of the pillars is given in 1 Kgs 7.15 as 18 cubits, with a circumference of 12 cubits (cf. Jer. 52.21-23).

It is not clear precisely where these pillars are situated. C reads 'in front of the Temple', 1 Kgs 7.21 vaguely 'at the porch of the Temple'. At all events they must have been freestanding and not integral to the structure of the porch (cf. the great height of the porch of C's Temple); while in 1 Kgs 6.2-3 the height of the porch is not specified, the height of the nave is 30 cubits.

1 Kgs 7.17-20 elaborates much more complicated details about the chains adorning the capitals (cf. 2 Chron. 4.12-13).

There must be a textual problem in 2 Chron. 3.16: the MT reads, 'he made chains in the inner shrine [*badd^{e}bîr*] and put them on top of the pillars'. NRSV follows the closely similar conjectural reading *bārābîd*, 'in chains'. The Kings text is too distant here to be of any service in the restoration of C's text.

The significance of these pillars is nowhere explained in the Hebrew Bible and can only be inferred from the context.

1. The pillars themselves have already been alluded to in passing in 1 Chron. 18.8 as being made from the bronze captured by David from the Aramaeans of Zobah. In the immediate context of C's work, they are thus associated with victory over Israel's immediate rivals in the region. They are monuments commemorating God's carrying out through David, his appointed agent, his will for the pacification of the nations of the world. The spoils of war are dedicated in confession by Israel that it is God who gives victory in battle and that the only battles that Israel can legitimately fight are the Lord's battles.

It is unlikely that there is a reference to one of these pillars in the subsequent narrative, in connection with the restoration of the Davidic monarchy after the attempted coup of Athaliah (2 Chron. 23.13): 'the king's pillar' seems to be located at the eastern gate of the outer court.

It has been conjectured that they have still more fundamental symbolical significance: following a suggestion in Josephus (references above), they represent the pillars on which the earth (symbolized by the nave of the Temple, as heaven is by the holy of holies) is believed to rest (cf., e.g., Ps. 75.3). Such ideas harmoniously cohere: the stability imparted by God at creation to the whole earth is maintained by the activities of the Davidic house, God's representative and agent upon earth. God's victories at creation in the cosmic sphere over the powers of chaos are repeated in the historical realm by the victories of God's vicegerent over the powers of chaos on earth.

2. The names of the pillars, 'Jachin' and 'Boaz', should give some confirmation of their significance. They occur, however, only here (and in the Kings parallel); these single word contexts furthermore make it unclear whether the words are to be read together, or separately as the opening words of some longer expressions. 'Jachin' could mean 'he will establish' or 'may he establish'; that is, it could be a statement or a prayer; the personal subject is most probably God; the unspoken object could be several things, such as the Temple, the Davidic house, or the world, or may be deliberately left unspecified in order to include a wide range. Within the context of C's work, it must be recalled that *kûn*, the root of 'Jachin', is one of the key thematic terms, used both of God's confirmation of David (e.g. 1 Chron. 14.2) and of David's actions in response (e.g. 1 Chron. 15.1). 'Boaz' is usually interpreted as 'in [the] strength', that is, whatever is established is indeed firmly founded or is so in God's strength (though in that case one would expect the form of the word to be 'beoz'). As it stands, the word is identical in form to David's great-grandfather, Boaz (see Ruth 2.1–4.22), who, possibly significantly enough, recurs in the Hebrew Bible only again in C. (1 Chron. 2.11, 12). If the word does not refer directly to David's ancestor, but to 'in [the] strength', then the unexpected form of the word may be due to attraction to the vowelling of the proper name. 'Strength' is also one of the leading themes of C's work, whether of God (e.g. 1 Chron. 16.11) or of human response (e.g. 1 Chron. 13.8). It is one of the traditional epithets of the ark, about to be used at its installation in the Temple (2 Chron. 6.41). Once again, all these elements are appropriate and may be included.

The decoration with pomegranates is also found on the train of the high priest's robe (Exod. 28.34). Pomegranates are associated with the abundance of Egypt (Num. 20.5) and of the promised land (Deut. 8.8); naturally enough, therefore, it occurs with connotations of fertility as the name of a deity (2 Kgs 5.18). Here there is a polemical statement against any such pretensions. None but the God of Israel as creator can lay claim to the bounty of creation; it lies solely within his gift.

2 Chronicles 4.1: The Altar of Burnt Offering

The catalogue now continues out eastwards from the Temple edifice itself into the courtyard. The altar of burnt offerings is described: it is made of bronze, 20 × 20 × 10 cubits. The altar was, naturally, where the full round of sacrificial worship took place, with all its connotations. As the place where the material offerings rose in smoke to the sky, it was the point where the meeting of the physical and spiritual was symbolized. On the symbolical interpretation of the pillars (3.15-17) and the sea (4.2-5), the positioning of the altar standing between sea and pillars is highly significant: it is through the rites of the altar that the powers of chaos are kept in check and the stability of the created order is assured.

There is no equivalent account of the building of this altar in Kings (though cf. 1 Kgs 8.64 where such an altar is presupposed). An analogous altar was constructed for the tabernacle in the wilderness (Exod. 27.1-8).

2 Chronicles 4.2-5: The Sea

Like the pillars, the sea has already been referred to in 1 Chron. 18.8, in connection with the dedication of the spoils of bronze captured from the Aramaeans. It is a large cylindrical basin, 10 cubits in diameter, 5 cubits high, 30 cubits in circumference and a handbreadth in thickness, with a rim like the flower of a lily. It has a capacity of 3000 *baths* (for which see 2 Chron. 2.10). It stood on 12 bulls, three facing in each direction.

In purely utilitarian terms, the function of the sea was for the ablutions of the priests (v. 6). It has been conjectured that it also had symbolical significance, standing for the great deep, the waters of chaos beneath the earth kept in check at creation (compare the possible symbolical significance of the pillars, above). The symbolical significance is heightened by the twelve bulls: as in the case of the pomegranates adorning the pillars, there must be here a polemical statement. The bull is the traditional symbol of fertility in the Near East; the 12 facing in all directions must represent not merely the 12 tribes of Israel but the 12 months of the year, with their zodiacal connotations associated with the Babylonian calendar. Through all space and time, the power of God is transmitted through the purification of the priests to the world.

There is obscurity in the text of v. 3. NRSV tacitly emends. According to C, not only do bulls provide a pedestal for the sea; there are two rows of them measuring ten cubits surrounding it. How is not made clear—though it is stated that they are integrally cast with it—nor to what the measurement 'ten cubits' applies. 1 Kgs 7.24 does not read 'bulls' but some other adornments ('gourds'?) but makes it clear that these are around the side of the sea under the rim; the 'ten cubits' remains obscure.

The capacity of the sea is stated in 1 Kgs 7.26 to be 2000 *baths*, as opposed to C's 3000, thus undermining any attempt to assign an absolute quantity to the *bath*.

2 Chronicles 4.6: The Basins

At this point C introduces large-scale variations from the parent text. 1 Kgs 7.27-37 includes an elaborate description of ten wagons for ten moveable basins to transport water from the sea; at the end of that description it returns to consider the location of the sea. C, however, sharply distinguishes between the sea and the basins: it adds a phrase to explain that the sea has one purpose—it is for the washing of the priests—while the basins have another—the washing of the sacrificial victims. To make the distinction quite clear, C suppresses the account of the construction of the transporting wagons (though they are itemized in the list in 4.14) and keeps only the basins. C also introduces a number of other items not included at this point in the parent text—the lamps, the tables and the courtyard for the priests and the concourse for the laity. Only then does he return to the matter of the location of the sea. The importance of the basins is thus reduced not only by the omission of their elaborate stands, but also by their being listed alongside a number of other items. At the same time, the importance of the sea is heightened by all these elements down to 4.10 being held within the framework of the sea (4.2-6, 10).

The reason for the separation of the sea from the basins can only be surmised. It may be that it is inappropriate that water from the same source should cleanse both the sacrifice and the officiant before and after the sacrifice (for the washing of the priest and the changing of garments before and after sacrifice, see, for example, the rites on the Day of Atonement, Lev. 16.4, 24). It is difficult to avoid here the conclusion that once again it is being firmly stated that the rites of the altar are subsidiary: atonement is made for Israel, not Israel for atonement. The main significance resides in the priests as the central agency through which the bond between God and his people is affirmed. The sacrificial victim is ancillary to this truth. The point is expressed physically: the sea is located between two groups of basins which stand supportively, five on each side.

C uses here rare vocabulary for washing the victim, which is found again in this technical sense only in Ezek. 40.38. Elsewhere, the vocabulary used here for the washing of the priests is used for the washing of the victim (e.g. Lev. 1.9).

The use of the basins for the priests to wash, which C here excludes, is found, by contrast, in the tabernacle text in Exod. 30.18-21.

Two other groups of ten ancillary objects are added, again five each side, now in the nave of the Temple, making, as it were, with the basins, a processional way from the sea to the holy of holies.

2 Chronicles 4.7: The Golden Lampstands

There are to be ten of these in the nave of the Temple (cf. 1 Chron. 28.15), five on the north and five on the south.

Contrast the single seven-branched candlestick familiar from the tabernacle (e.g. Exod. 25.31-39), placed on the south side (Exod. 26.35), which seems to be implied by 2 Chron. 13.11. C's phrase, that they were made 'in the usual way' (so again v. 21), seems, rather, to be justifying an innovation. They have been introduced, with variations, from 1 Kgs 7.49//2 Chron. 4.20, for the reasons suggested above.

2 Chronicles 4.8: The Tables

There is a similar divergence in connection with the tables (already mentioned in 1 Chron. 28.16) as there is with the lamps. Whereas in other texts there is but one (even in 1 Kgs 7.48), here there are ten, again arranged five per side to create the ceremonial way.

For the single table in the tabernacle for the placing of the twelve loaves of the bread of the presence, see, for example, Exod. 25.23-30; Lev. 24.5-9. It was placed on the north side (Exod. 26.35). A single table is implied by C in 2 Chron. 29.18. C does not make clear how the 12 loaves of the bread of the presence are going to be displayed on 10 tables or how the 5 lamps and the 5 tables on each side are to be arranged. Nor does he clarify the relationship between these tables and the incense altar (1 Chron. 28.18; see 2 Chron. 4.19).

The implements that go with the table are described in Exod. 37.16: 'its plates and dishes for incense, and its bowls and flagons with which to pour drink offerings' (cf. Num. 4.7). Here C mentions simply 100 bowls (though the term used here is different from any of those used in Exod. 37.16).

2 Chronicles 4.9: The Courts of the Temple

Having described the processional way from the sea to the holy of holies, C returns to the courts, where he is about to define the location of the sea. C uses terminology here to distinguish clearly between the 'court' of the priests and the great 'concourse' for the people (so again 2 Chron. 6.13, though this is not consistently maintained; see 2 Chron. 33.5). Nothing of the enormous engineering works involved in the construction of such courts is recounted—that hardly lies at the forefront of C's interests. Rather, there is registered the great bronze-clad doors, constructed to protect the area of the sacred (cf. the four gatekeepers, 1 Chron. 9.24; 26.12-19).

There is no equivalent to this verse in the Kings parallel. Elsewhere, Kings speaks merely of the inner and the outer court (cf. 1 Kgs 6.36). The tabernacle has but the one court (e.g. Exod. 27.9-19).

2 Chronicles 4.10: The Location of the Sea

The sea lies immediately within the area of the court of the priests, just to the left on entering. That is, it is here immediately on entry to the area of the sacred that the ablutions of those permitted access can take place, so that there is no possibility of contamination from the world of the profane. The physical space for the rites assuring the atonement and hallowing of the people is secured.

In 1 Kgs 7.39, this verse is the second half of the parallel to v. 6. C has divided it in order to insert the matter on the ten lamps, the ten tables and the courts. In the process, he may have deliberately suppressed the reading in Kings, 'the southerly wall *of the house*', in order to make it quite clear that the sea is located in the court of the priests, not in the Temple building itself.

2 Chronicles 4.11a: The Pots, the Shovels and the Basins

Last in the list of furnishings made for the Temple are the implements for the rites at the altar of burnt offerings: the pots and the shovels for clearing away the fat ashes (Exod. 27.3; alternatively, the pots could be for the boiling of the sacrificial flesh [2 Chron. 35.13]); the basins for receiving the blood of the victims and dashing it against the altar (see 1 Chron. 28.17).

For 'pots' 1 Kgs 7.40 reads 'basins' (the words are visually similar in Hebrew)—surely a case where C provides a better text than Samuel–Kings (cf. v. 16).

In terms of arrangement, it is striking that this verse, then, resumes the discussion on the altar in v. 1. As the sea has provided a framework in vv. 2 and 10 for the intervening objects, so the altar provides a framework for the sea in vv. 1 and 11.

From another point of view it is appropriate that these objects are now mentioned. With these workaday but essential tools made of humble bronze for the discharge of the sacrificial cult, Huram(-abi), the actual artificer of many of these objects, is reintroduced. The summary that now follows on the furnishings of the Temple is all in his name.

2 Chronicles 4.11b-18: Catalogue of Huram-abi's Bronze-castings for the Temple

The catalogue largely reproduces what has already been listed in 3.15–4.11a: the two bronze pillars, with their complicated capitals; the wagons; the basins; the sea with the twelve supporting bulls; the pots, the shovels and the forks. That is to say, Huram-abi is credited with making none of the objects inside the nave of the Temple itself (the 12 gold lampstands and the 12 tables with the 100 gold bowls), let alone the holy of holies (the gilded cherubim and the curtain). His activities begin 'in front of the house' (2 Chron. 3.15): he makes all the objects in the court of the priests—with the exception of the altar. The bronze-clad doors to the Temple courts are not mentioned. Given that the altar was of bronze, it would seem that Huram-abi is denied the construction of certain items of the furnishings of the Temple, not just because of the more precious material of which the object concerned was made, but because of theological propriety: only the native-born king may construct the altar for sacrifice and the furnishings of the Temple building proper. It is the king as representative jointly of God and people who has to be responsible for those parts of the Temple most especially dedicated to the meeting of God and people.

The point of Solomon's ultimate responsibility for manufacture of these objects is reinforced by C's reading in v. 18: whereas 1 Kgs 7.47 reads, 'Solomon *placed* all the objects' (cf. NEB), that is, which Hiram had made, C reads, 'Solomon *made* all these objects'.

Some details call for comment.

The question of the status of the king and his artificer is reaffirmed: even where Huram-abi is credited with the making of the items concerned, it is insisted that 'he made them for the king, Solomon' (vv. 11, 16). Indeed, in principle, Solomon has made them all (v. 18). It may thus be significant that, in v. 11, C omits the 'all' of 1 Kgs 7.40 in the works which Huram-abi made for Solomon.

The Temple is called 'the house of God', using the universal name for the Deity (v. 11), not just the personal name used to express his intimacy with Israel (which Kings uses in this context; so C in v. 16): what is at stake here is a matter of cosmic significance.

The capitals on the two bronze pillars of Jachin and Boaz are described in a more complicated manner. Whereas in 2 Chron. 3.15-16 C contents himself with noting that the capitals were five cubits high and were adorned with chains with 100 pomegranates on them, here the capitals are described as comprising two elements, a spherical shape surmounted by a crown. The spherical parts have networks upon them, with two rows of 100 pomegranates each.

The wagons for the basins, suppressed between vv. 5 and 6, are now included in the inventory, along with the basins themselves.

> Whereas C reads, '*He made* the wagons and *he made* the basins', 1 Kgs 7.43 reads 'ten' (closely similar in form in Hebrew) both times. It is in character for C not to emphasize the wagons by dwelling on their number.

Instead of the 'bowls' of v. 11a, the inventory reads another (aurally similar in Hebrew) cultic implement, 'forks' (for which see 1 Chron. 28.17).

All these items were made of 'polished' bronze. A note is added of the area in the Jordan valley to the north of the Dead Sea, where the ground was of a consistency suitable for making the moulds for bronze-casting. The ability to manufacture these objects, the weight of which was 'beyond calculation', and to organize their transportation, especially the colossal structures of the pillars and the sea, across a distance of some 30 km to Jerusalem, including an ascent of more than 1000 m is impressive (compare the haulage of the great cedar logs from Joppa, 2 Chron. 2.16).

2 Chronicles 4.19–5.1a: The Golden Objects which Solomon Himself Made

Solomon himself makes the objects of gold that are within the nave and the holy of holies of the Temple building proper. The inventory repeats some of the information given earlier in the chapter and adds more: the altar of incense (which was not been mentioned where it was expected in vv. 7-8); the tables for the showbread (v. 8); the lampstands (v. 7), the lampholders and the lamps, with the wick-trimmers and the snuffers; the bowls (v. 8), the pans and the fire-pans; the doors both to the holy of holies and to the nave.

The function of most of the objects not already mentioned in vv. 7-8 is clarified from references elsewhere. The altar of incense (cf. 1 Chron. 28.18) links almost all of the articles listed here. Standing in immediate proximity to the holy of holies, it is the place where incense is burned to wreathe the unapproachable mystery of the divine being as the priest lights the lamps (Exod. 30.7). For the burning of incense a number of implements are required: the pans are for presenting the incense (Num. 7.14) and are associated with the showbread (Exod. 25.29; see Lev. 24.5-9 for the burning of incense with the showbread; cf. 1 Chron. 9.32; 23.29); the fire-pans were used to transport live coals from the altar of burnt offerings in order to burn the incense (Lev. 16.12); they are also associated with the lamps (Exod. 25.38); the lampholders, as their name implies, are shaped like buds and the lamps are placed within them. From context the objects associated with the lamps must be wick-trimmers and snuffers, though the first also occurs as tongs, such as in the vision of Isa. 6.6, of the tongs used to remove a burning coal from the altar of burnt offering. The doors are constructed as the special responsibility of the king to safeguard the rites performed by the approved personnel in both the holy of holies and the nave.

A few points of difference between C and Kings, not already discussed, may be noted. Once again, C uses the term for universal deity (v. 19), whereas 1 Kgs 7.48 uses the specifically Israelite 'Yahweh'. Kings renders 'namely, the golden altar [of incense]' making it the beginning of the specification of 'all the objects which were in the Temple'; C seeks to emphasize Solomon's instrumentality still more exclusively by adding '*and* the golden altar...' (v. 19). In v. 20, C, having already used the material in 1 Kgs 7.49, 'five on the south and five on the north' in v. 7, substitutes, 'and their lamps for burning them as usual'. At the end of v. 21 C adds the phrase, 'they were of pure gold', as a substitute for the omission of 'gold' at the end of v. 19. At the beginning of v. 22 1 Kgs 7.50 had added 'basins' (such as are mentioned in Exod.12.22).

The whole account is concluded with a summary: 'Thus was concluded all the work which Solomon did for the house of the LORD'. There is a play on the verb 'was concluded' (*tišlam*) and Solomon's name (*šᵉlōmô*).

C retains the use of the personal name of the God of Israel from 1 Kgs 7.51, and deprives Solomon of his title, 'king'.

The MT of C rather subtly, and most appropriately, makes of 5.1b a separate paragraph. The whole point of the Temple is not that it is an end in itself: it exists as a statement and enablement of Israel's holiness. Thus the climax of the presentation is that Solomon lodges in the treasury (a key term; cf. 1 Chron. 9.26) all the votive offerings (for which see 1 Chron. 26.26) dedicated by David his father, the agent through whom the whole plan was initiated.

> C again makes sure of comprehensiveness by making the 'silver and gold' not a specification of, but an addition to, 'David's dedicated offerings'. He also adds an 'all' before 'the objects'. At this climactic moment he once again uses the universal term for deity.

The system for the expression of holiness has now been brought into being. All that remains is to infuse that system with life by bringing in the ark and inaugurating the rites and worship of the Temple. It is to that task that Solomon now turns.

2 CHRONICLES 5.2–7.22: THE DEDICATION OF THE TEMPLE

The next scene, the dedication of the Temple, takes place in the seventh month of an unspecified year of Solomon's reign.

1 Kgs 6.38 dates it to Solomon's eleventh year. C's exclusive focus on the Temple makes its construction dominate the entire first twenty years of Solomon's reign (cf. 2 Chron. 3.2).

The account is divided into four major sections (six in MT):

1. the bringing up of the ark from the city of David and its installation in the holy of holies (5.2-14; MT divides also after v. 10);
2. Solomon's acknowledgment, blessing of the people and prayer of petition (6.1-42; MT divides also after v. 25);
3. the festival of dedication of the Temple (7.1-11);
4. the appearing of the LORD to Solomon (7.12-22).

Once more there is some subtlety in the arrangement of these sections. The third section is the resumption of the first (as is clear from the sacrifices at the altar, 5.6 and 7.1; the inability of the priests to endure the manifestation of the glory of God, 5.14 and 7.2; and the praise of the Lord, 5.13 and 7.3) and thus conveys the impression that the long second section was occurring simultaneously with these two. The second section is thus placed prominently between two matching sections. The fourth section has been recast by C as the response to the second section.

For the close relation to 1 Kgs 8.1–9.9, see table in introduction to the Reign of Solomon, 2 Chronicles 1–9.

1. *The Bringing Up of the Ark from the City of David and its Installation in the Holy of Holies (2 Chronicles 5.2–14)*

The story resumes the narrative of 1 Chronicles 15–16—how David fetched the ark from the house of Obed-edom and installed it in a tent that he had prepared for it in the city of David. Solomon now completes the process begun by David by installing the ark in the Temple that David had planned by divine revelation and for the building of which he had made all the preparations (1 Chron. 28.11-19).

There are some striking parallels between the actions of father and son in 1 Chronicles 15–16 and 2 Chronicles 5 and 7: the verbs 'to bring together the congregation' and 'to bring up' the ark; the emphasis on 'all Israel' gathering for the action; the insistence on the Levites as the bearers of the ark; the offering of sacrifice as the ark is borne along in procession; the accompaniment of the proceedings by musicians; the blessing of the people by the king. The chief difference is that there is no unrestrained dancing in front of the ark on the part of Solomon as there had been by David. Solomon is the compliant executor of his father's plans; for him there can be no such experience of the charismatic figure, the exuberant exultation of the immediately empowered and enlightened agent of God. Not least in the light of the three-fold chastening experiences of the mercurial David (1 Chron. 13; 17; 21), Solomon proceeds in measured fashion, with due circumspection, solemnity and dignity.

The passage begins with Solomon's assembling of the leaders of the community (cf. 1 Chron. 11.3) for the purpose of fetching the ark. C uses the thematic verb *qhl*, repeated in v. 3, 'to gather in sacral assembly', as he has already done in 1 Chron. 13.5 in the context of David's plan to fetch the ark into Jerusalem.

Whereas in 1 Kgs 8.1 'elders' is the inclusive term for all the leaders of the community of which the following are the specification, here, in order to stress totality, the conjunction 'and' is added so that they are treated as simply one among a still wider group that also includes the tribal and family heads. The distinction could hardly have been observed in practice.

The phrases 'heads of the tribes' and 'chiefs of the fathers' do not recur in C in quite these forms (but cf. 1 Chron. 4.38; 7.40; 2 Chron. 1.2) and are simply borrowed directly from Kings. Close parallels to these representations of traditional tribal structure are to be found especially in Numbers (e.g. 1.4) and Joshua (e.g. 14.1). All that Israel has ever been is here gathered up and brought to fulfilment.

The subordinate status of Solomon is again marked by the omission of the phrase 'the king, Solomon' before 'Jerusalem' (v. 2). His name is again omitted in v. 3.

For 'Zion' as the pre-Davidic term for Jerusalem, cf. 1 Chron. 11.5, the only other occurrence of 'Zion' in C.

The C formulation emphasizes inclusiveness: all those vested with authority in the traditional tribal structure of the community are brought together with all those duly authorized in the new regime (cf. 1 Chron. 28.1) for this climactic act, this moment of the completion of the new order. A notable feature of this chapter is the recurrent use of the word 'all' to emphasize the participation of the whole community (vv. 2, 3, 4, 6, 11, 12; cf. v. 5, 'all the vessels'). The title, 'ark of the covenant' (v. 2; 1 Chron. 15.25), rather than 'ark of God' (1 Chron. 13.3), emphasizes the communal aspect.

The occasion for the installation of the ark is 'the festival in the seventh month' (v. 3). The seventh month (the designation of the months of the year by means of the ordinal numbers follows the 'Babylonian' calendar; cf. 2 Chron. 3.2) was the first month of the new year on the traditional Canaanite–Hebrew calendar (1 Kgs 8.2 adds the traditional name for the month). It is the time of new beginnings marked religiously by the fact that the Day of Atonement falls on the tenth of the month, when the whole community is solemnly reconsecrated for the coming year (cf. Lev. 16; it is on that day too that the jubilee, that is, the return to ideal conditions, is to be proclaimed, Lev. 25.9-10; both are key texts for C; see 1 Chron. 6.49; 2 Chron. 36.22). It is also marked agriculturally, as well as religiously, by the festival of harvest home (cf. Exod. 23.16b). It is probable that there is also a festival on the first of the month, marking the beginning of the new year (cf. Num. 29.1). It is thus highly appropriate that on this month, traditionally associated with renewal and new beginnings, Solomon should proceed with the inauguration of the new Temple (see, for similar occasions on the same day, Ezra 3, Neh. 8).

The whole community, this time represented merely by the elders (vv. 4-5; cf. 1 Chron. 11.3), go with the priests and the other Levites to bring up the ark, along with the Tent of Meeting and all its cultic furniture, in fulfilment of the injunction of David, 1 Chron. 22.19.

Once again the physical details are not completely clear. The ark and the Tent of Meeting–tabernacle, temporarily separated by David (1 Chron. 16.37-42), are now reunited: the ark is fetched from Zion; the tabernacle and all its furnishings are simultaneously collected from Gibeon. It is not explained how the furnishings of the tabernacle, now incorporated into the Temple (presumably including table for showbread, lamp, incense altar and the related implements, Num. 3.31), and the equivalent furnishings just manufactured by Solomon for the new Temple are to be related.

Whatever the physical questions, the theological point is clear: the old and new dispensations show unbroken continuity.

In v. 5, C abbreviates, replacing the 'ark of the LORD' of Kings with simply, 'the ark'.

C is extremely careful to identify the correct agents for the various acts. In obedience to David's ordaining (1 Chron. 15.2), the Levites carry the ark, while the levitical priests transport the tent and its furnishings (cf. Num. 3.27-32): only those with the requisite degree of sanctity can have contact with particular consecrated areas and their associated sacred objects. Thus, at the climax in v. 7, when the ark is installed in the Temple itself, it is the priests who take over the carrying of the ark in order to bring it through the nave and deposit it in the holy of holies.

This scrupulousness accounts for C's reading in v. 4, where it is now the Levites who carry the ark (in 1 Kgs 8.3 it is the priests). It also accounts for C's change of the construction in v. 5: whereas 1 Kgs 8.4 reads, 'They [the priests] brought up the ark of the LORD and the Tent of Meeting and all the holy vessels which were in the Tent. The priests and the Levites bought them up', C runs, 'They [the Levites] brought up the ark; and as for the Tent of Meeting and all the holy vessels, these the levitical priests brought up'.

The authorized sacral bearers of the ark are accompanied by the king and the whole congregation (v. 6): C here uses for the only time in his work a term for Israel in religious assembly (*'ēdâ*) that is rich in association. It is the traditional term for Israel as the travelling 'congregation' in the wilderness (most frequently in Numbers, e.g. 1.2). It is particularly appropriate since it is associated with the word for 'meeting' in the standard designation of the Tabernacle as the 'Tent of Meeting', which C uses several times (e.g. 1 Chron. 6.32; 2 Chron. 1.3, 6, 13; cf., e.g., Lev. 1.1, where the Tent of Meeting is precisely the place of revelation of the sacrificial system). 'Meeting' is, furthermore, the technical term for 'festival [as a fixed time and place for meeting for religious purpose]' that C also often uses (e.g. 1 Chron. 23.31; 2 Chron. 2.4). Equally unique is C's use here of the related verb 'to assemble' (cf., e.g., Num. 10.3-4). This choice of vocabulary (retained from Kings) underlines the commitment and common purpose of the whole community formalized by religious ritual at this moment of historic fulfilment.

This community of action is emphasized by the associated rites. The transfer of the ark is accompanied by uncountable sacrifices (v. 6). The vocabulary for 'sacrifice' employed (confirmed by the sequel, 2 Chron. 7.1, 4) implies that the sacrifices offered are not just whole burnt offerings, but include communion sacrifices, that is, those shared among the people with the priests, with the due portions being offered to God (so already 1 Chron. 15.26; 21.28; 29.21; cf., e.g., Lev. 3.1-17). The vocabulary also implies the lavish scale of the sacrifices, so that those who share them have more than enough and to spare. The expression of solidarity among the people and with their God could not be more clearly put. What would have been in any case a festival is turned into an event of unsurpassable celebration.

In 1 Chron. 15.26 these sacrifices were offered *en route*, presumably at Bezalel's portable altar (2 Chron. 1.5). That is presumably what is implied here: the note in v. 6, that 'the king and all the congregation...were sacrificing' comes before the account in v. 7 that the ark was deposited in the holy of holies. The dedication of the new altar of burnt offering is not spoken about until 2 Chron. 7.9.

With the mention that the priests have deposited the ark in the holy of holies, C pauses in vv. 7-10, in material largely retained from Kings, to register the significance of the ark. The opening and closing comments underlining the fundamental significance of the ark thus frame the whole section.

- As already in v. 2, the ark's full title is given: it is 'the ark of the covenant of the LORD'. It is the supreme symbol and effective channel of the relationship between God, his people and the world (for the ideas and associations of the title, see, for example, the Psalm in 1 Chron. 16, especially vv. 8-22).
- It is deposited in the holiest place of all: it is the focus for Israel's vocation to holiness in the world.
- It is under the protection of the cherubim, who guard the access to it and preserve it from all contamination (cf. 1 Chron. 13.6; 28.18; 2 Chron. 3.10-13).

C is more matter-of-fact than Kings. It merely states *that* the cherubim were covering the ark (v. 8); 1 Kgs 8.7 says, 'because...'.

C reads that the cherubim were *covering* the ark; Kings that they were *sheltering* it. The two verbs have identical consonants, two being interchanged. C has used the verb which occurs here in Kings in 1 Chron. 28.18.

- The bars by which the ark was transported call for special mention (v. 9). They are now no longer visible to the nave, let alone the outside world.

The Hebrew—and, possibly, the text—is a little obscure at this point: 'the bars were long and the heads of the bars were visible from the ark matching the inner shrine but they were not visible outside'. This would appear to indicate that the bars fitted exactly into the inner shrine and did not protrude outside (how could they, when there was a door between the inner shrine and the nave [2 Chron. 4.22] and a curtain [2 Chron. 3.14]?). 1 Kgs 8.8 reads, 'The bars were long and [so long that?] the heads of the bars were visible from the nave in front of the inner shrine but they were not visible outside [the whole Temple building?]'. NRSV emends the C reading from Kings (without acknowledgment).

- The ark, the symbol in war of the LORD's prevailing presence, has now reached its place of rest; it need no longer be carried out into battle. The world is, in principle, pacified. To the statement that the ark is now in the inner sanctuary, the text adds the poignant phrase, 'to this day'. That is, from the moment of the foundation of Solomon's Temple the purpose of God has been realized. Given C's overall eschatological presentation, and in the light of the cold realities of history, not least the destruction of the Temple itself in the reign of Zedekiah (2 Chron. 36.19), this can only be so proleptically and in principle (contrast 2 Chron. 35.3).

Kings links the phrase 'to this day' to the bars. Again C's reading fits perfectly into his presentation.

- The text concludes by picking up the central significance of the ark of the covenant: it is the focus of Israel's life because it contains the two tablets of the Decalogue revealed to Moses at Mt Horeb. These are the irreducible digest of the terms of the covenant, indeed are here equated with the covenant (cf. Deut. 4.13), through which Israel will realize its destiny both for itself and, through itself, for the rest of humanity. Though C has not reproduced any of the narratives of the Pentateuch, Moses is presupposed as the key mediator of revelation throughout C's work (so already in, for example, 1 Chron. 6.49; 22.13), just as the exodus from Egypt is only alluded to in passing, yet is clearly the signal event of God's activity (so already in 1 Chron. 17.21; cf. 2 Chron. 6.5; 7.22;

20.10). David is the agent through whom the destiny of Israel announced in Moses is reaffirmed and fulfilled.

Moses figures in C 20 times; only three with parallels in Samuel–Kings (here, 2 Chron. 25.4 and 33.8). 'Horeb' occurs only here in C (no doubt because of the dependency on Samuel–Kings); 'Sinai', not at all.

While C reads merely, 'the two tablets which Moses gave in Horeb', 1 Kgs 8.9, with greater interest in antiquarian details, reads, 'the two tablets of stone which Moses put there [i.e., in the ark] in Horeb'. C again condenses at the end of v. 10 by omitting 'land' before 'Egypt'.

C now moves to the climax of the narrative of the installation of the ark in the Temple (vv. 11-14, a separate section in MT). Just as all the lay *qāhāl* of Israel are present, so too are all the priests. The usual roster of twenty-four divisions, into which they are divided for service (1 Chron. 24), is suspended; all the priests must share in the moment of dedication of the Temple as the definitive means of realizing their role among their people from this time forward.

Once again, how this could physically have been accomplished is of little concern to C. All 24 divisions of the priests must have amounted to many thousands (all the levites over 30 years of age amounted to 38,000, according to 1 Chron. 23.4-5, but how many of them were priests is not made clear; see the inhibition expressed in 1 Chron. 27.24; for some priestly statistics see Ezra 2.36-39). It would have been impossible for the number implied to participate directly in the conveying of the ark or even to be in the procession in the narrow nave of the Temple. The theological point is paramount: none could be lacking at this climactic moment.

Equally, the 288 members of the three families of levitical musicians (for which see 1 Chron. 15.16–16.43; 25.1-31) must be in attendance: Asaph, who had been before the ark in Zion, and Heman and Jeduthun, who had been with the Tent of Meeting at Gibeon. These play on the harp and lute with the cymbals in order to declare the praise of God in the words laid down by David (1 Chron. 16.8-36; 'praising the LORD because he is good; because his steadfast love endures for ever' in v. 13 echoes 1 Chron. 16.34 and is about to be repeated symmetrically on the other side of Solomon's prayer of dedication in 2 Chron. 7.3; cf. Pss. 106.1; 107.1; 118.1, 29; 136.1; see Ezra 3.11 for a similar moment of dedication). They are accompanied by the 120 priests who sound the trumpets (cf. 1 Chron. 15.24).

At this climactic moment the response of God in self-disclosure to his people takes place. This is expressed in traditional terms reminiscent of the self-disclosure of God at Sinai/Horeb (Exod. 19) and in the tabernacle (Exod. 40.34-38). The act of depositing the ark in the holy of holies to the accompaniment of the fervent music of the levites is accepted by God by the descent of the cloud (as in 2 Chron. 7.1 he is about to express his acceptance of sacrifice by the descent of fire). The choir of Asaph, Heman and Jeduthun express in song this gracious purpose of God for his people. But at the same time, the cloud as symbol of theophany declares the overwhelming majesty of God. So unbearable to mere human capacity is the searing glare of the divine self-manifestation that it must be veiled. Even the priests, despite their sanctification for the approach to God, are driven back from the nave of the Temple. Just so, Israel at Sinai were overwhelmed by the terror of the divine self-disclosure and retired awestruck to the safety of the camp; then too, the priests were not allowed access to the mountain (Exod. 19.24). It is to herald that awesome theophany that the priests with their blaring trumpets sound their clarion (compare the rolls of thunder that accompanied the theophany at Sinai).

The overwhelming experience of God's self-manifestation is summed up in the word, 'glory' (*kbd*, cf. already of God in 1 Chron. 16.24, 28-29). In a physical sense, the related verb (and adjective) means 'to be heavy' (1 Chron. 10.3; 2 Chron. 10.4, etc.); hence, of humans, 'weighty', in the moral and social sense, 'respect-worthy', 'renowned' (1 Chron. 4.9; 11.21, 25) for what they are in themselves and what their deeds disclose.

The material in vv. 11b-13a on the musical accompaniment by the Levites and priests has been added by C, thus heightening the ritualistic character of the presentation (vv. 11a and 13b—or equivalent—are continuous in 1 Kgs 8.10). NRSV's failure to translate v. 11a with a sentence is a reflection of the disturbance caused by C at this point.

Verse 13b, 'the house was filled with smoke, the house of the LORD', replacing the 'smoke was filling the house of the LORD' of Kings, lays the emphasis on the Temple with its ritual rather than on the smoke.

In v. 14, C reads 'the house of God', thus universalizing 'the house of the LORD' in Kings.

2. *Solomon's Acknowledgment, Blessing of the People and Prayer of Petition (2 Chronicles 6.1-42)*

Solomon's Acknowledgment (Verses 1-2)

The descent of God in the cloud just witnessed is a statement by God himself of the fitness and acceptability of the Temple. Solomon's first words are of grateful acknowledgment before God: he has carried out the task, for which he was commissioned (1 Chron. 22.6); he has built the Temple and has sought to fulfil every requirement in so doing; his work has been graciously accepted.

To make this acknowledgment, Solomon speaks facing the Temple itself (cf. v. 3). One of the requirements he had to meet in building the Temple is stated in the fundamental principle (not hitherto encountered in C): 'The LORD has commanded that he must dwell in darkness' (v. 1). The absoluteness of this requirement is indicated by the fact that, though Solomon is addressing God (v. 2), he cites that requirement in objective terms, with God spoken of in the third person. The descent of God to this dark space which he has created is objective evidence that God has been pleased to accept the Temple and to take up residence in the midst of his people.

The requirement that God should dwell in darkness goes back to the Mosaic age. At Sinai, God preserved the full mystery of his glory in the obscurity of the thick cloud as he descended upon the mountain (Exod. 20.21; Deut. 4.11; 5.22; cf., e.g., Pss. 18.9; 97.2). That mystery was preserved uninfringed within the windowless Tabernacle (Exod. 40.34). Within the new idiom of the Temple, Solomon has preserved that darkness in the windowless holy of holies.

Solomon is then emboldened to address God directly (v. 2). He declares that he, Solomon, has built a house for God. He gives two additional grounds for its acceptability:

- it is 'a lofty house': Solomon has built it of fitting splendour to represent sacramentally God's majesty in material terms on earth;
- 'it is a place for you to reign for ever.' 'Place' comes from the same root as the key thematic term, *kûn*, introduced in 1 Chron. 14.2;15.1: this house represents the culmination of all the ordaining by God, and the planning and preparation by David in response, since the beginning of the dynasty. 'Reign' is from the same root as the title of God '*seated* on the cherubim' associated with the ark (e.g. 1 Chron. 13.6): this Temple by virtue of its housing the ark is henceforth enabled to become the channel through which the power and majesty of God associated with the ark are now expressed.

These verses almost exactly reproduce Kings; the only difference of substance is at the beginning of v. 2, where C emphasizes the identity of the builder, '*I* have built...' rather than, as in 1 Kgs 8.13, the act of building, 'I have *indeed* built...' C's emphatic pronoun 'I (have built)' matches the emphatic pronoun of the divine promise 'he (shall build)' in 1 Chron. 17.12; 22.10.

Solomon's Blessing of the People (Verses 3-11)

Solomon now turns round (v. 3) to 'bless' the *qāhāl*, the whole company of the laity (1 Chron. 13.2). It is notable that Solomon exercises a full priestly role: it is the king who blesses the people, just as he offers sacrifice (2 Chron. 5.6), as David had done in the time of his acceptance (1 Chron. 16.2); there is no mention of the priest as in 1 Chron. 23.13.

The 'blessing' is again untypical in form (cf. 1 Chron. 29.10). It is, rather, a declaration, this time before the people, that Solomon has fulfilled all his responsibilities. The declaration in v. 10, 'I have built the house for the name of the LORD, the God of Israel', picks up the declaration to the LORD in v. 2. As Solomon has presented his warrant to God, so he now formally presents his credentials to the people.

The blessing thus begins rather oddly (v. 4): it is not the people whom Solomon blesses but the LORD's actions that he acknowledges. The basis for all these achievements is the great acts of God for David (C is here using materials already drawn upon in 1 Chron. 17.1-15; 22.7-11; 28.2-3).

The divine endorsement of David's action is indicated by its unprecedented nature (v. 5): never before in the history of God's people has God 'chosen' (for 'election', cf. 1 Chron. 28.4) a particular city in a particular tribe 'for my name [1 Chron. 13.6] to be there', nor a particular individual to carry out the function of leadership over the tribes (C adds 'leader'; cf.1 Chron. 11.2). What had been a proof of the objection in principle to the construction of the Temple (1 Chron. 17.5-6) is now turned into a proof of its unsurpassed significance.

In contrast to the notorious refusal in Deuteronomy to identify Jerusalem as the actual site of the Temple (presumably a reaction of writers during the Babylonian exile reflecting unwillingness to localize the name of God in a place of now uncertain, even discredited, standing), C (in independent material in v. 6) with his eschatological Zionism can transcend the miserable actualities of history and find in Jerusalem and its associated Davidic dynasty the necessary focus for his expectation: 'I have chosen Jerusalem so that my name may be there; I have chosen David to be over my people Israel'.

Solomon continues his explanations by citing David's purpose in v. 7 (the solemn formulation is used as in 1 Chron. 22.7; 28.2) and God's response to it in vv. 8-9: David's plan to build a Temple for the name of God is endorsed by God as good but, without repeating the reason, God's promise that that plan will be carried out by a son of David is recounted.

Solomon affirms that God has now kept that promise (v. 10). With a play on the verb *qûm* (1 Chron. 17.11), Solomon states that as God has 'confirmed' his word, so he, Solomon, is 'confirmed' as successor to David. The same root that is used of the LORD's reigning in v. 2, is now used by Solomon in reference to his own reigning on the throne of Israel: as for David, so now for Solomon, the reign of the Davidic king is the sacramental expression of the reign of the divine king.

All this provides Solomon with his warrant before the people for his building of the Temple and his inclusion within it of the ark of the covenant (vv. 10-11).

In v. 11 C omits 'a place for' before 'the ark', and simplifies the last phrase, reading only 'with the children of Israel' for 'with our fathers when he brought them out from the land of Egypt': C is bringing the destiny of Israel up to date, linking it with the destiny of the Davidic royal house.

Solomon's Prayer of Petition (Verses 12-42)

C finds in the great prayer of Solomon presented in 1 Kgs 8.22-53 an almost completely congenial expression of his theology of the significance of the Temple. There are only a few, but very significant, modifications of the parent text.

C begins in vv. 12-13 with a more elaborate setting of the scene than is to be found in Kings. In 1 Kgs 8.22 it is the mediatorial role of Solomon that is plainly in evidence: Solomon stands between altar and people to make his petition. C, with greater concern for degrees of holiness, adds almost a complete verse (v. 13) in order to point out that this petition in the presence of the people cannot take place in the inner court of the Temple where the altar of burnt offering is, but must be in the outer concourse (cf. 2 Chron. 4.9). There Solomon has constructed a massive platform of bronze, five cubits square and three cubits high.

Nothing is said about this platform anywhere else in the Hebrew Bible, not even in the earlier specifications of the furnishings of the Temple in C.

The same word is used of the bronze basins in 2 Chron. 4.6 and presumably implies that the platform was like an upturned hollow vessel.

On this eminence the king kneels humbly before God with his empty hands stretched upwards, a gesture of petition eloquent enough in itself to express unconditional dependence on the gracious response of God.

Verse 13b repeats almost word for word v. 12, but is a virtual commentary on, indeed correction of, it: 'he stood in the presence of all the *qāhāl* of Israel...—rather, he stood *on the platform and fell on his knees* in the presence of all the *qāhāl* of Israel...' (cf. 1 Kgs 8.54).

Solomon's prayer itself is constructed with careful symmetry: the opening in vv. 16-17, 20 matches the conclusion in vv. 40-41.

- It is fundamentally a prayer of petition: compare the formula 'so now' (cf. 1 Chron. 17.7) that introduces the petition proper (vv. 16-17, 40-41).
- The petition that 'God's eyes (and ears also, on the second occurrence) may be open to attend to prayers in this Temple', is repeated at the end (vv. 20, 40).

The formula in v. 40, matching vv. 16, 17, most of the rest of v. 40 and all of vv. 41-42 have been added by C to the parent Kings text.

In between, there are seven instances of the particular circumstances that will lead people to direct their prayers towards the Temple:

1. wrong-doing between members of the community (vv. 22-23);
2. national humiliation at the hands of their enemies (vv. 24-25);
3. drought (vv. 26-27);
4. distress of whatever kind, international, national or individual (vv. 28-31);
   including in a subsection, 5. (vv. 32-33), the plight of the foreigner;
6. Israel going out to battle on a God-given mission (vv. 34-35); including the sub-case, 7, the inevitable situation when Israel is disloyal to God (vv. 36-39).

MT breaks up the prayer into sections by inserting a major paragraph marker after no. 2 (this draws attention to the fact that the first two cases are introduced by the hypothetical conjunction, 'if', whereas the remainder speak in terms of greater certainty, 'when') and subsidiary paragraph markers after nos.1, 3, and 4, and between the two petitions in vv. 40-41 (for the effect of that, see below).

Solomon begins his prayer with a hymn affirming the characteristics of God (vv. 14-15); these provide the basis for the petition which follows. God is extolled first in his incomparability throughout the whole universe (v. 14a). But then also in his particularity (v. 14b): his incomparability is expressed in terms of the distinctiveness of the relationship he has formed in covenant with one people, Israel, to whom he has revealed his own name, 'the LORD'. He has made them his servants; he can be relied upon to maintain his side of the relationship with them unfailingly. But, as Solomon is acutely aware, there is a conditional element in the quality of this relationship: he acknowledges, these servants must 'walk before you with complete devotion of mind and will'.

The evidence for the steadfastness of God is his fulfilment of his promise to David (v. 15; cf. v. 4). God has promised that the Davidic king will be his servant *par excellence*: for this purpose there will be an unending succession of David's physical descendants to sit on the throne. As David's son, Solomon acknowledges with gratitude that what God has promised God has himself fulfilled. That fulfilment Solomon now makes the basis for his petition that through all time the promises will continue to be fulfilled. But Solomon is equally aware of the conditional element within the relationship: those who are called 'God's servants' have also had laid upon them an awesome responsibility. If God is to *keep* his promise, David's descendants have to *keep* his Law (v. 16; the formulation is reproduced from 1 Kgs 8.25 where it is derived, with variation in order of the promise and the condition attached, from 1 Kgs 2.4; cf. the oracle through Nathan in 1 Chron. 17.14).

This play on words is only part of the extensive play on words in this section. Tight correspondence, between the warrant for affirming the character of God in the constancy he has shown to the house of David, the content of the petition and the conditions for the fulfilment of the petition, extends to the language used: variations on the formulation 'keeping covenant/loyalty/promise to his servant[s]' recur in each of vv. 14-17.

In v. 14 C abbreviates: 'heaven and earth' are enough to indicate universality for the greater distinctiveness of 1 Kgs 8.23: 'heaven above and earth beneath'.

More significant is the change in v. 16, 'to walk in my *Torah*', rather than the 'to walk before me' of 1 Kgs 8.25: C is more insistent on the objectively codified statement of the conditions of God's covenant in the Law of Moses. 'Walk', as the metaphor for giving God the obedience due to him, is about be much used: 2 Chron. 6.27, 31; 7.17; 11.17; 17.3, 4; 20.32; 21.6, 12, 13, 20; 22.3, 5; 28.2; 34.2, 31.

It is to be noted that, as in the conception of C's work as a whole, especially with regard to the role of the Levites, the prayer of petition is concerned not with failure, but with the possibility of maintenance of an ideal in the full awareness of the possibility of failure. This becomes particularly clear from the matching section in vv. 40-41, which is peculiar to C: the petition is not in response to some crisis that has befallen the community, but is connected primarily with the ideal role the Temple might fulfil by which help will be available for the petitioner in any crisis which may then befall. Compare the ideas of prospective, prophylactic atonement noted in connection with 1 Chron. 21.5.

In the next section (vv. 18-21) Solomon expresses wonderment at the gracious condescension of God. If the highest heavens (v. 18; cf. already 2 Chron. 2.6) cannot contain God—Solomon deliberately uses the transcendental, universal term for deity—how can he be expected to be accessible at one mere spot on earth? And how can he be expected at that spot to be interested in the prayers and petitions of Solomon, one mere human individual (Solomon now uses the intimate name of deity, 'the LORD', as well as 'my God', v. 19)? The wonderment is focused in the verb 'to dwell', which has already been used as key term to express God's cosmic rule (e.g. 1 Chron. 13.6; 17.5; 28.5). The paradox is resolved in sacramental terms by acknowledging that God's dwelling is indeed in the cosmic realm but that he has 'placed his name' in the Temple (v. 20), that is, has permitted himself to be invoked there in prayer at the place where he has revealed his nature through both ark and altar. The 'name' is thus the link between the macrocosmic realm of the heavens and the microcosm of the Jerusalem Temple at the centre of the earth (the ark as the footstool of God is another means of expressing this interconnection of the two realms, 1 Chron. 28.2).

In v. 18 C amplifies his parent text with a phrase essential to his whole presentation: to the 'will God indeed dwell on earth?' of 1 Kgs 8.27 C adds 'with Adam/humankind'. As in the thesis of the whole work presented in 1 Chronicles 1, C is concerned with the destiny of the entire human race, within which Israel with its vocation to holiness, related not least to the new Temple, has a vital function.

In content the petition now comes very close to C's concerns throughout his work. The prayers that God will hear are specified as lamentations, pleas for mercy and cries for help (v. 19). That is, it is in response to the agonized cries of humanity, arising for the most part out of their recognition of the consequences of their sin and folly, that Solomon intercedes. Correspondingly, what Solomon requests is forgiveness (v. 21). The Temple, as the place where the sin offering is presented, is thus even more fundamentally the place where God unceasingly hears and answers the prayers of the penitent and, above all, forgives.

In v. 19 C generalizes the LORD's willingness to hear prayer at all times by omitting the specific 'today' found in 1 Kgs 8.28, which is concerned with the day of the dedication of the Temple. In v. 20 more familiar quotation of the LORD's direct speech of 1 Kgs 8.29, 'of which you have said, 'My name shall be there'', is replaced by a more respectful reported speech, 'where you have commanded to place your name'. C's 'you will hear *from* your dwelling place, the heavens' in v. 21 stresses God's cosmic rule, while the '...*unto* your dwelling-place...' in 1 Kgs 8.30 emphasizes the accessibility of God to the prayer of the suppliant even in the heavens (compare C's reading throughout the chapter '*from* heaven', rather than '*in* heaven' as in Kings, vv. 23, 25, 30, 33, 35, 39, though not v. 27, presumably by oversight).

This section introduces the vocabulary of the petitions that are to be the recurrent themes of the following sections:

- the root from which the noun 'lament' and the related verb 'intercede' are derived occurs in vv. 19 (3×), 20 (2×), 21; so again vv. 24, 26, 29, 32, 34, 35, 38, 39, 40;
- 'plea for mercy', vv. 19, 21; so again vv. 24, 29, 35, 37, 39 ('the ringing cry' is only in v. 19);
- the plea to 'hear' (especially from the heavens, the realm of God's cosmic rule), vv. 19, 21 (3×); so again vv. 23, 25, 27, 30, 33, 35, 39;
- the root from which the verb of God's 'paying heed' and the preposition 'before [God's presence, and the like]' are derived, v. 19 (2×); so again vv. 22, 24;
- the verb 'to forgive', v. 21; so again vv. 25, 27, 30, 39;
- 'sin' is highly characteristic of the section, vv. 22, 24, 25, 26 (2×), 27, 36 (2×), 37, 39;
- the ideal which God intends for his people is expressed with great poignancy in the phrase 'the land which you have given to them and their fathers', or the like, in vv. 25, 27, 31, 38.

It is at once evident how relevant all these petitions are to C's central theme. The distribution of the root 'to sin' (*ḥṭ'*) in C is highly significant: it has occurred for the first time in 1 Chron. 21.8, 17, the chapter about David's sin that is instrumental in the choice of the site of the altar in Jerusalem. Apart from the ten occurrences in this chapter and its resumption in 2 Chron. 7.14, the root reappears only in 2 Chron. 25.4; 28.13; 29.21, 23, 24 (2×); 33.19, all of them, except 2 Chron. 25.4, in material peculiar to C. Sin and the eradication of its consequences is what lies precisely at the centre of the rites on the day of atonement (cf. Lev. 16).

Solomon now cites a number of specific occasions when the divinely willed ideal of tranquil possession of the land has been disturbed, which will give rise to invoking God's intervention. These show that forgiveness for sin is not just a matter of a penalty incurred that can be set aside by gracious divine decision so that life resumes its even tenor as though nothing untoward had happened. Rather, sin concerns grievous dislocations of life and these require costly reinstatement. The petitions envisage a progressively worsening situation for Israel. In the first two, prayer is possible *within the Temple* itself, beginning from in front of the very altar. In the next two it is a matter of prayer *towards the Temple*: it is as though Israel, while still allowed access to Jerusalem, is debarred from the Temple itself—and in this Israel is no better off than the fifth case considered, that of the Gentiles. In the second last case, Israel seems to be debarred from Jerusalem and can only pray *towards the city and the Temple*. Last of all, Israel is in exile and can only pray *towards the land, the city and the Temple*.

The structure of these seven petitions is uniformly of two parts. A situation of crisis is introduced, usually with variations on the conjunctions, 'if' or 'when'. This is followed by the petition proper, usually introduced by the emphatic personal pronoun: 'so do *you* listen from the heavens...'

1. The instances begin in the immediacy of personal human relations (vv. 22-23). One member of the community sins against another by plotting his downfall through misuse of sworn evidence in lawsuits. The circumstances are not explained, but one may compare the situation of settling property disputes by oath as in Lev. 6.1-5, the key text on *ma'al*, or of attempting to dispossess a fellow Israelite by perjury, as is guarded against in the Decalogue (Exod. 20.16) (though in both passages the vocabulary concerning oaths is different from that used here). Such legal processes conducted under oath involve the invocation of God's name. But God is the impartial judge, who scrupulously

rewards those who are in the right and requites the wrong-doer with his own wrong—in this case, the intending dispossessor will be himself dispossessed.

C is slightly stronger about the divine requital, not just *condemning* the culprit, as in 1 Kgs 8.32, but in making the evil planned *redound* on himself. Again there is a correspondence between act and status.

Later in C, the root used here for 'wicked' (*rš'*) is defined specifically in terms of following the ways of Ahab as a direct negation of the ways of the LORD (2 Chron. 19.2*; 20.35*; 22.3*; 24.7*, the only other passages in C, apart from the present context and v. 37, where the root occurs). By contrast, 'righteousness' (*ṣdq*), used here of the wronged innocent party, is otherwise used in C only of the sacramental rule of David (1 Chron. 18.14; cf. of Solomon, 2 Chron. 9.8; the name 'Zedekiah', 2 Chron. 36.11; and of the LORD himself, 2 Chron. 12.6*). Such a specific application would not be inappropriate for C's argument.

(* = C's own material.)

Loss of land, falling as penalty for wrong-doing, through the immediate intervention of God, may thus already be present in this opening section of the petition proper. It is certainly the dominant theme in the following sections.

2. The next case is altogether more grave (vv. 24-25). Israel as a whole has now sinned against God himself (how is left unexplained here—that is about to be unfolded in the rest of 2 Chronicles). The consequence of their sin is that they have lost land through conquest by their enemies (again these await specification in the following narrative). But the petition is that, in response to their repentance, acknowledgment of God's nature (the verb *ydh* here is reminiscent of the explanation for the name Judah–Jew in Gen. 29.35; cf. Gen. 49.8; the force of the phraseology is not dissimilar to 'giving God glory' in the context of a criminal charge; cf. the Achan narrative, Josh. 7.19; 1 Chron. 16.4), lament and plea for mercy, God will forgive and restore them to their land. Strikingly, 'repent' (v. 24) and 'restore' (v. 25) come from the same root, *šûb* (cf. vv. 37-38): in sacramental theology, if they return, they shall be granted a return (2 Chron. 30.9). But within the context of C as a whole, that petition can only be answered in the end-time.

C is more immanentist than 1 Kgs 8.33 in v. 24, reading 'and they plead for mercy *before you* in this house' rather than '...*to you*...'. In 1 Kgs 8.34 the land was given 'to their ancestors'; C makes it more personal by adding 'to them' as well as 'to their ancestors'.

3. Once again (vv. 26-27) it is against God himself that Israel has sinned (a generic singular noun is used in this context to indicate sin as a condition, rather than as a series of acts). This time the agency of retribution is not human but in the realm of creation—the rains fail. Thus, while Israel is not actually dispossessed of its land, it is deprived of its use. But, yet once more, God will be gracious to his repentant people. He will supply them not only with water as the basic physical necessity of life, but with instruction, by which he will guide them (the verb comes from the root of Torah, the Law of Moses) into a creative way of living. The construction is notable: it is not their own land which they possess; God restores to them *his* land, which they can possess as his hereditary tenants (cf. Lev. 25.23). There they will be sustained by his natural and spiritual gifts.

C reads 'you will guide them *unto* the good path in which they should walk'; 1 Kgs 8.36 reads the otherwise regular construction of a straightforward direct object, 'the good path'.

4. The disasters multiply (vv. 28-31): famine, plague, two kinds of crop failure, two kinds of locusts, all intensified by enemy invasion and disease of every imaginable kind. The last two items in v. 28 relate to the vocabulary of the plagues of Egypt (Exod. 11.1; 15.26; compare the 'negative Passover', 1 Chron. 21.12 and the use of the contrast sickness...health, 1 Chron. 10.3). Human responsibility in provoking these disasters is given full scope: God in responding to the petition will reward all according to their deserts (v. 30, reproduced virtually intact from 1 Kgs 8.39, reflects a retributive concept of punishment rather than the sacramental one characteristic of C; cf. 2 Chron. 30.9).

The petition proper in this section is the longest in the whole composition. God's universal sovereignty is stressed. In the phrase, 'so will you hear from heaven, the established foundation of your sovereignty', C reproduces vocabulary from Kings that is central to his preoccupations: 'established foundation (*mākôn*)' picks up the key thematic term, *kûn*, announced in such passages as 1 Chron. 14.2. God's response to the petitionary prayer is inseparably bound up with the universal order of the divine plan, at the centre of which stands the role of his people and of the Davidic king. As a consequence of that universal rule, it is with 'the heart of all humankind' that God is concerned.

As in v. 18, C makes a slight but significant adjustment to his parent text: whereas 1 Kgs 8.38 in soliciting the LORD's response might be understood to limit it in this section to Israel (he uses an apposition, which would naturally be translated, 'any person, *even* all your people Israel'), C, in line with his argument about Israel's role in human destiny as a whole, makes the universalist note explicit by adding a conjunction, 'any person *and* all your people...' [v. 29]).

This demonstration of the divine acquaintance with human concerns world-wide is designed to have an effect on Israel as well. They must be awed by this knowledge into a profounder grasp of their vocation in the midst of the nations of humanity. The purpose of their living 'upon the face of the ground which you gave to their fathers' is that they have been placed centrally in the world to realize on behalf of humanity as a whole the particular quality of life which stems from obedience to God.

To stress the point of obedience, C adds in v. 31 the phrase, 'to walk in your ways' (cf. v. 16), to the 'in order that they may fear you' of 1 Kgs 8.40. Other changes from Samuel–Kings are more minor: for example, in v. 30 Kings reads, 'You will forgive *and act* and give...' and adds 'all' before 'humankind'.

5. These universalist ideas prepare for the next section (vv. 32-33) in which the foreigner's petition can also be accepted. Notable in this section is the omission of any mention of sin. As far as Israel is concerned, the stress is on their sin and the consequent forfeiture of the land on which their status depends. Here, by contrast, the foreigner, who has been attracted by God's fame—the language used, 'the mighty hand and the outstretched arm', is reminiscent of the description of the exodus from Egypt as the signal demonstration of God's power, for example in Deut. 4.34—and turns to God in sincerity, is simply the object of God's gracious acceptance (for 'invoke', cf. 1 Chron. 4.10). God's house, where atonement is worked for Israel, is indeed the focus for the petitions of all nations. Appropriately enough in connection with foreign nations, the seat of God's universal dominion in the heavens is again mentioned as in v. 30. As in the previous section, a motive is given for God's gracious acceptance. This is nothing less than the denouement of God's purposes: it is so that all nations of the earth may hear and come to acknowledge him, as Israel does, and recognize the role that the Jerusalem Temple plays within that purpose.

C slightly abbreviates the text of 1 Kgs 8.42 in v. 32 (or may omit a phrase by *homoioteleuton*), at the end of which it also changes the verbs into the plural.

6. For the sole time in the series Israel themselves are blameless (vv. 34-35). They are on a military expedition at the behest of God (the key term, *yṣ'*, 1 Chron. 1.12). As God's faithful executors, their petition even on some foreign field of battle will be heard and their right vindicated by victory.

C is more direct in address: 'they pray to *you*', where 1 Kgs 8.44 reads, 'to the LORD'. C also adds the demonstrative adjective, 'this', to 'the city which you have chosen'.

7. But the last, climactic, case is the more typical, indeed inevitable (vv. 36-39). It begins and ends with a similar phrase, 'when they sin/they have sinned against you'. In his anger God has handed them over to their enemies and they languish as captives in enemy territory. Yet if they return to their senses (there is a constant play in the section between the verb 'to return [*šûb*]' and 'to take captive [*šbh*]'), and confess their sin, facing land, city and Temple (with great pathos all three are for the first time listed, each with a special epithet), God will vindicate their right and forgive them. Once again God's all-prevailing power is indicated by the citing of his cosmic dwelling place: God's universal dominion is irresistible.

The two petitions, with which the prayer ends, are introduced by the formula, 'and now'. They resume the two-fold petition introduced by the same formula, 'and now', in vv. 16-17.

The first petition, further, matches v. 20 in content; it is a virtual resumption of it. That link is strengthened by the MT paragraph sign *after* v. 40: the intervening verses are an exposition of what it means for God to have 'open eyes and ears' to the prayers of the suppliant.

The ending of the prayer is quite different in the two versions. In Kings, the stress is on the forgiveness of Israel because of their privileged position as the LORD's people and their separateness from the other nations of the earth. C, by contrast, ends with two petitions in parallel (vv. 40-42): the first is about the role of the Temple as the place or focus of prayers, such as have been listed in vv. 22-39; the second provides the whole basis on which such prayers can be confidently offered.

For C, the true climax comes in vv. 41-42. The LORD is entreated to assume cosmic control. This is expressed sacramentally by the ascent of the ark into the Temple. By depositing the ark, the symbol of the LORD's presence on the field of battle, in the Temple as its place of rest, the pacification of the world by God is represented. There is no further need for him to sally out to do battle (these associations of the ark and rest have already occurred in 1 Chron. 6.31; 22.9; 28.2). But this earthly pacification is simply the visible expression of the cosmic power of God. It is by virtue of God's prevailing power at the cosmic level that humanity's supplications can be heard.

This sacramental significance of the ark is made clear by the way in which vv. 41-42 freely makes use of two other passages of Scripture. 'Arise…to your rest' makes use of two key terms from Num. 10.33-36, the passage about the role of the ark in the wilderness wandering: it went before Israel to find for it 'a place of rest', that is, the camping places on the way to the Promised Land, which was the final 'place of rest'. When the ark left the camp of Israel, Moses petitioned before it, 'Arise [the same verb as in v. 41], O LORD, and let your enemies be scattered…', and when it returned ('rested', again the same verb as in v. 41), 'Return, O LORD, to the ten thousand thousands of Israel'.

These ideas have been taken up in the celebration of the bringing of the ark into the Temple of Jerusalem in Psalm 132, which, as part of the 'hymn and prayer book' of the community, must have provided it perennially with a means of celebrating that act and of appropriating its significance. Verbal reminiscences of that Psalm, indeed, in part direct quotations of Ps. 132.8-9, are present here in C. Solomon makes three specific petitions: for the Temple, that God will indeed express his reign of peace for all the world through it; for the priests and people, that they will appropriate for themselves the new life of harmony with God (key terms from the roots of 'salvation', 1 Chron. 11.14; 'joy', 1 Chron. 12.40; 'good', 1 Chron. 16.34); and for the anointed kings of the house of David (cf. 1 Chron. 11.3), that they may be accepted by God to play their role as his agents on earth.

In contrast to the Psalm where God is addressed only once, by the intimate Israelite 'LORD', each of these petitions in C contains an insistent direct address to God as 'LORD God': not only the local, but the universal terms for deity are used.

The Psalm is more localized in stressing the Temple as '*place* of rest': C speaks more generally of 'rest' as a state of being.

'You and the ark of your might' is a direct quotation.

'May your priests be clothed with salvation [cf. Ps. 132.16] and your loyal people rejoice in welfare' is more specific and more balanced than the Psalm (v. 9), 'May your priests be clothed with righteousness and your loyal people shout aloud'—the last verb may have been modified because C has used that root in connection with the cries of distress in v. 19.

Verse 42 quotes again directly from the Psalm: 'do not reject the face of your anointed'.

The last phrase of v. 42, 'be mindful of the faithful deeds of David, your servant', is not a direct quotation but contains echoes of vv. 1 ('remember') and 10 ('David your servant'). The 'faithful deeds of David', though the term itself is not used, are expounded throughout the Psalm: specifically, David's recovery of the ark from neglect at Kiriath-jearim and preparations for the housing of it in the Temple.

3. *The Festival of Dedication (2 Chronicles 7.1-11)*

The section begins (vv. 1-4; demarcated as a subsection by MT) with two demonstrations of how God has indeed chosen 'to dwell with humankind on earth' (2 Chron. 6.18). The first is the descent of fire from heaven upon the altar; by that fire God declares his acceptance of the Temple worship, including the atonement cult (cf. 1 Chron. 21.26). The second is the wreathing incense smoke that fills the Temple, before which not even the priests can stand their ground; it is the veil which evidences and yet conceals the indwelling majesty of the LORD, the cosmic ruler. Of these the second is the more fundamental: the altar is not the end, but the essential prerequisite whereby God's sovereignty focused on the ark can once more be expressed.

As was noted above, v. 2 resumes 2 Chron. 5.14, v. 3 echoes 2 Chron. 5.13 and v. 6 corresponds to 2 Chron. 5.11-13: this resumption, symmetrically disposed around ch. 6, suggests that the whole process recounted in these chapters of installing the ark, sacrifice and prayer of dedication is being presented as one concerted event. The rather complex structure of vv. 1-4 confirms this impression:

– There are significant modifications of 1 Kgs 8.54aα, 62 text. The parallels begin with the first phrase in v. 1, but then break off, not to be resumed until v. 4.

The intervening verses are radically different in the two versions. While C is concerned with the fire and the cloud, 1 Kgs 8.54aβ-61 recounts Solomon's blessing of the people.

– Whereas Kings records a series of events, C describes a set of simultaneous circumstances. The first phrase in C (2 Chron.

7.1aα) makes that clear: for the, 'When Solomon had finished praying' of (1 Kgs 8.54aα, C reads, 'As Solomon was finishing praying'. Similarly the last phrase, v. 4, 'while the king and all the people were sacrificing communion sacrifices before the LORD', is used by C as a conclusion (in the MT of C it marks the end of a paragraph), rather than, as in Samuel–Kings, the beginning of a new phase of the narrative.

C's reading in v. 4, 'the king and all the people', stresses the solidarity of the whole community, rather than the leadership of the king, as in 1 Kgs 8.62: 'the king and all Israel with him'.

- The tenses of the verbs in the intervening material, all of which is peculiar to C, equally express simultaneous circumstances. Verse 1 breaks off from the construction of the parent text in Kings to resume: 'Now the fire had descended from the heavens...while the glory of the LORD was filling the house'. Verse 3 similarly describes continuing circumstances: 'Meantime all Israel were observing the descent of the fire and the glory of the LORD upon the house'.
- The references to the 'whole burnt offering and the communion sacrifices' (v. 1, not in the Kings parallel) can only be to what has gone before in 2 Chron. 5.6.

This contemporaneous presentation shows how the action of God is not in mere response to human initiative; rather, human action is taken up into the divine. There is a oneness in the action that is wholly expressive of the new relationship with God inaugurated in the dedication of the Temple that God himself has planned and endorsed.

A further important statement is made in this section: the descent of fire upon the altar and the glory of God filling the sanctuary show that Solomon's Temple has indeed been endorsed as the successor to Moses' Tabernacle in the wilderness, for it too had been sanctified by means of similar manifestations (Lev. 9.24; Exod. 40.34). Solomon's act of incorporating all the furnishings of the old Tabernacle and Tent of Meeting, not least the ark (2 Chron. 5.5), has been approved by God. Solomon's declaration before God (2 Chron. 6.1-2) has been graciously answered.

The parallels between 2 Chron. 7.1 and Exod. 40.34 are particularly close: the phrase, 'and the glory of the LORD filled the [tabernacle/Temple]' is identical in each. The preceding phrase in Exod. 40.33 begins with the same verb as in C: 'So Moses *completed* the work'. Lev. 9.24 is not so close: there the fire 'came out from the presence of the LORD' to consume the sacrifice.

The response of the community at large (v. 3) is prostration in worship on the pavement in the great concourse, using in their praise the psalm already ordained by David to be sung before the ark (1 Chron. 16.34, 41).

The word for pavement recurs again of the Jerusalem Temple only in Ezekiel (e.g. 40.17), where again it is used of the outer court.

Verses 5-6 (a separate subsection in MT) list the unprecedented number of sacrifices Solomon makes in honour of the occasion: 22,000 cattle and 120,000 sheep (the unsurpassed scale of this offering can be appreciated when it is compared with other statistics for sacrifices; see 1 Chron. 29.21).

C makes one major change in v. 5 from the parallel text in 1 Kgs 8.63. The word 'communion sacrifices' (so again at the end of v. 7), which makes it clear that these were sacrifices in which the laity participated, is omitted. It is in keeping with C's concern for holiness, expressed physically in terms of the hierarchy of sacred space, to exclude the laity from immediate association with the altar and its rites.

In this, C reflects the diminishing role of the communion sacrifice elsewhere in the Hebrew Bible (for example, it does not appear in the list of stated offerings in Num. 28–29).

C's other variations from Kings in v. 5 are more minor: he adds 'the king' before Solomon's name. The universal name 'God' is used rather than the Israelite 'the LORD'; 'the king and all the people' is again used at the end of the verse as in v. 4 instead of 'the king and all the Israelites'.

Verse 6, on the instrumental and vocal music provided by the priests and the Levites, is added by C. The sacrificial cult is not the end in itself; it is accompanied by priests standing in their appointed place (cf. 1 Chron. 6.31; 2 Chron. 31.16; 35.2) in front of the whole assembly with their trumpets, announcing the self-manifestation of God. The response to that appearance by God himself to his people is led by the Levites in psalms as ordained by God through David (cf. 1 Chron. 15.16–16.42; 2 Chron. 5.12-13).

The narrative returns in v. 7 to the unparalleled scale of the sacrifices (vv. 7-11 are a separate subsection in MT). Because of their sheer volume the altar itself is unable to consume the sacrifices and their accompanying offerings (as specified in, e.g., Lev. 7.7-8). Unprecedented scale leads to unprecedented measures: the whole centre of the inner courtyard is dedicated as altar for the duration of the festival.

The archaic elements of the communion sacrifice are retained by C: in particular, the burning of the fat portions of the victim on the altar, as specified in the legislation on the communion sacrifice (e.g. Lev. 3.3).

The 1 Kgs 8.64 parallel to v. 7 begins the verse with a temporal phrase, 'on that day'. C with his stress on contemporaneity has no interest in signalizing these acts as sequential. Kings reads, 'the king', for 'Solomon'; Solomon's status is of no particular concern to C here. C abbreviates Kings slightly by omitting the first mention on the accompanying cereal offerings. C's rendering, 'for the bronze altar which Solomon had made was not able to contain the holocausts...', stresses the abundance of the offerings, while Kings has 'for the bronze altar which was before the LORD was too small to contain the holocausts...', merely emphasizes the inadequacy of the altar.

In vv. 8-10, C provides some chronological data on the duration of the festival of dedication itself (the precise date of this dedication within the reign of Solomon, except that it is the culmination of the first twenty years of his reign, still does not concern C). This makes it clear that for him the festival exactly coincides with the standard length of the Feast of Tabernacles as laid down in, for example, Lev. 23.33-36: seven days culminating, in addition, in an eighth day of solemn commitment.

The same technical term for the concluding day of the festival recurs in Deut. 16.8 for the final day of the festival of Passover, which, there are good grounds for believing, relates to covenant-making as expressed in Exod. 24.3-8.

The chronology in C differs from that in Kings. C has suppressed the note in 1 Kgs 8.65 that the dedication plus the Feast of Tabernacles lasted for 14 days; he adds his own v. 9 equating dedication and Feast of Tabernacles. C provides, equally, an adjustment at the beginning of v. 10, which makes the dating relative to the Feast of Tabernacles unambiguous: 'On the twenty-third day of the seventh month he dismissed the people to their tents' for the 'On the eighth day [of the second period of seven days] he dismissed the people and they blessed the king and went to their tents...' of 1 Kgs 8.66. From C's hierarchical view-point there can be no question of the people blessing the king.

For C, this festival of dedication, merged with the festival of Tabernacles, is not additional to an established round of festivals, but is the definitive beginning of all Temple worship (in the MT of v. 8 he promotes it to a more prominent position than in 1 Kgs 8.65). The dedication is specifically of the altar. But the context of the dedication is the Feast of Tabernacles. As is clear from such passages as Lev. 23.23, 33-36 and Zech. 14.16-19, the Feast of Tabernacles is associated with the celebration of the sovereignty of God as focused sacramentally by the ark. This week of festival, centred on the two foci of altar and ark, accordingly affirms the fundamental truths of Israel's life: atonement, and vocation to holiness as the agents of God's reign in the world of the nations. All of Israel's life hereafter can at its best only reaffirm the significance of this foundational event; it is the decisive restart of Israel's life and expression of its destiny. The archaic phrase in v. 10, 'he dismissed the people to their tents', retains fittingly the image of Israel as a war-camp (1 Chron. 12.22), ready for the campaign to carry out the LORD's commission. For the gladness at the goodness of the LORD with which they depart, see 2 Chron. 6.41. The totality of the effect on the life of the people is indicated by the comprehensiveness of the assembly: all are there from furthest north to south (C even adds 'very' to the 'great *qāhāl*' of 1 Kgs 8.65; for the direction north–south contrast 1 Chron. 21.2; 2 Chron. 30.5 in C's own material).

> C makes a slight adjustment to the last phrase of v. 10 to accord Solomon his rightful place: for 1 Kgs 8.66: 'because of all the goodness which the LORD had shown to David his servant and to Israel his people', C reads '...to David and to Solomon and to Israel his people'.

Verse 11 is a summary statement on the first half of Solomon's reign from Solomon's point of view. His efforts, to finish all the actions necessary to carry out his commission to build, equip and dedicate the Temple, have been crowned with total success. Also mentioned in passing is the fact that he has completed his own residence (cf. 2 Chron. 2.1). This passage thus picks up two of the key thematic terms of the whole presentation of the Davidic monarchy: 'house' (cf. 1 Chron. 17 and its recapitulations in 1 Chron. 22.7-16; 2 Chron. 6.7-11) and 'succeed/prosper' (cf. 1 Chron. 22.11; 29.23). Both Temple and royal palace are described by the same word, 'house': as the LORD has a 'house' on earth as a visible token of his universal dominion, so it is appropriate that the LORD's agent on earth should also have a 'house' as the visible expression of his rule in the LORD's name. By means of his total obedience to the demands of the task, Solomon has succeeded in building these edifices in which the earthly and the heavenly are brought into perfect correspondence, each with the other.

The variations in C from the parent text in 1 Kgs 9.1 highlight these points. In Kings this verse marks the beginning of the next section: 'When Solomon had completed...'; in C, by contrast, it marks the summary of what has gone before: 'So Solomon completed...' In Kings the scope of the action is more limited: it is merely, 'When Solomon had completed *building* the house of the LORD...' C omits the verb 'building', thus making the phrase more comprehensive: 'So Solomon completed the house of the LORD'. Similarly, the 'all Solomon's desire that he desired to do' of Kings has become, 'anything that occurred to Solomon'.

4. *The Appearing of the LORD to Solomon (2 Chronicles 7.12-22)*

This section (also unitary in MT), recording the response by God to all the actions of Solomon, marks the summary on the first half of the reign of Solomon from the point of view of God. It corresponds closely to Solomon's prayer in 2 Chronicles 6. As in 2 Chron. 1.7, the direct access of Solomon to the LORD is noteworthy: in perfect harmony with the divine purpose, he has no need of prophetic intermediary.

In Kings this passage cross-refers to a quite different occasion—to the first appearance of God to Solomon in Gibeon (the occasion paralleled in 2 Chron. 1.3-13). It begins in 1 Kgs 9.2, 'The LORD appeared to Solomon a second time, as he had appeared to him at Gibeon'. C suppresses 'a second time' and any reference to Gibeon, reading simply 'by night' (as in 2 Chron. 1.7).

God's response (v. 12) picks up specifically Solomon's central petition in 2 Chron. 6.19, that God will 'hear his prayer'. The role affirmed by Solomon for Jerusalem in 2 Chron. 6.6, 34, 38 is accepted for the Temple. Its function is defined as a 'house of sacrifice': the vocabulary used is not that of the atonement cult as such but of the fellowship sacrifice of the 'peace offering'. The Temple will be the place where the restored harmony between God and his people will be celebrated.

The LORD's response picks up in v. 13 the petitions which Solomon has made in 2 Chron. 6.22-39 about specific crises:

- lack of rain (2 Chron. 6.26);
- locusts (2 Chron. 6.28, though now different words are used);
- pestilence (2 Chron. 6.28, again with slightly different vocabulary).

In all these cases, and, by implication, all the others in 2 Chronicles 6 not specified again here, the LORD for his part will fulfil his people's petitions (v. 14): he will indeed 'hear from heaven' (a phrase resuming the vocabulary at the end of all except one of the seven petitions of 2 Chron. 6.22-39). This hearing will involve the two central concerns of C's whole presentation: he will 'forgive their sin' (as requested in 2 Chron. 6.21, 25, 27, 30, 39); but atonement is not an end in itself—it is only the prelude to the full restoration of the land, 'I shall heal their land' (a phrase otherwise unparalleled in the Hebrew Bible; for 'heal', see 2 Chron. 16.12). Atonement has been made for the sin that caused the abandonment of the land; the way to return is now open.

But this restoration is not unconditional. Israel is indeed God's special people, 'those over whom my name is called' (v. 14, a term for ownership already used in 2 Chron. 6.33 and fragmentarily in 1 Chron. 13.6). But Israel can only realize that status on terms which lie very close to the heart of C's message: it must 'humble itself, pray, seek God's face and turn from its evil ways'. That is, it must by deliberate decision make God the central focus of its life and accord God his place. This vocabulary provides variations on the central themes of C. 'Humbling oneself' (root *kn'*) before God, used here in this theological sense for the first time in C, is about to become a recurrent expression in the rest of the work (2 Chron. 12.6, 12; 32.26; 33.12, 19, 23; 34.27; 36.12; ideally elsewhere it is used of David's subjugation of foreign peoples, 1 Chron. 17.10; 18.1; 20.4; it is used of Israel when Israel fails in its role, 2 Chron. 28.19). It is notable that, in 2 Chron. 28.19; 33.19, it is associated with C's key thematic term, *ma'al*, 'unfaithfulness'. 'Seek God's face' is a synonym of *drš* 'resort to God' (they are found in parallel in 1 Chron. 16.11; 2 Chron. 15.2, 4; 20.3-4); it was Saul's failure to consult God that had been the fundamental fault at the start of the whole history of the monarchy (1 Chron. 10.13-14).

These conditions, thus, apply not just to the people but all the more to the designated leaders of the community. Appropriately, therefore, at this the end of the account of the first twenty years of Solomon's reign, God's response turns to Solomon's own responsibility and to the responsibility of all his successors on the throne. For them, too, God has faithfully fulfilled his part. Once again (v. 15), God makes direct response to Solomon's plea: 'my eyes will be open and my ears attentive' picks up the precise vocabulary of 2 Chron. 6.20, 40. He has indeed 'chosen this house and sanctified it as the place where his name dwells', where, in an astonishing—and unparalleled—anthropomorphism for the awareness and concern of God, his 'eyes and heart will always be' (contrast Isa. 44.18).

But, if God fulfils his part (v. 16), Solomon and the Davidic house must fulfil theirs (vv. 17-18). Their obligation is defined in terms of following the example of David and of obedience to God's Law (the metaphor of 'walk' as in 2 Chron. 6.16). In that case, the petition of 2 Chron. 6.16-17 can be fulfilled.

With v. 16, C returns to the parent text of Kings. His addition is marked at the beginning and end by the verb 'and I will choose' (v. 12)/ 'and now I have chosen' (v. 16). 'I will sanctify this house' resumes the 'I have sanctified this house', in 1 Kgs 9.3. For the 'which you have built where my name may be placed for ever' of Kings, C reads more simply, 'where my name may be for ever'.

There are a number of modifications of detail. In v. 17, C again abbreviates, omitting 'in integrity of heart and uprightness' after 'David your father'; so in v. 18, where 'over Israel for ever' is omitted after 'the throne of your kingship', and 'one ruling over Israel' replaces 'one from upon the throne of Israel' (though that has been read in 2 Chron. 6.10, 16). On the other hand, in v. 18 the expression is strengthened: 'as I covenanted with David', for 'as I spoke to David' in 1 Kgs 9.5.

Again, entirely in consistency with the argument of the whole work, the consequences of failure to observe these conditions, expressed fundamentally in the worship of other gods, are spelled out (v. 19). Disobedience to the Law by the kings, God's designated agents, will result in forfeiture of the land, '*my* land', as it is expressed with great force (v. 20). Equally, the Temple, built by the same royal agency, will be rejected and in its devastation become a horrific byword and object lesson for all humanity. What had been intended to be the channel of universal restoration has through the failure of its commissioned agents become an object of universal derision (vv. 21-22).

In v. 19 C abbreviates the first phrase and replaces the words of 1 Kgs 9.6: 'do not observe my commandments, my statutes' with 'forsake', one of the thematic terms for unfaithfulness about to be used frequently in the ensuing account of the monarchy (cf. already 1 Chron. 28.9). Suitably to the context concerning the kings, C reads in v. 20, 'I will remove them [the successors of David] from upon my ground' for 'I will cut Israel off from upon the face of the ground' in 1 Kgs 9.7. Similarly, the Temple itself will become a byword, whereas in Kings it is Israel. In v. 21 the melancholy note is sounded that Temple '*was* supreme', whereas in 1 Kgs 9.8 it is foretold that it '*will be*...'. C abbreviates the appalled response of the passer-by to the ruined Temple and devastated land, omitting 'he will whistle'. In v. 22, C reads 'because they abandoned the LORD, the God of their fathers [1 Chron. 5.25], who brought them out of the land of Egypt' for the '...their God who brought their fathers out of the land of Egypt' of 1 Kgs 9.9 and abbreviates by omitting the second occurrence of 'LORD'.

2 CHRONICLES 8.1–9.31: THE UNIVERSAL RECOGNITION OF SOLOMON'S REIGN

Less than one third of the space devoted to the presentation of the first twenty years of Solomon's reign in 2 Chronicles 1–7 is now given to the second period of twenty years in 2 Chronicles 8–9 (as noted in the introduction to 2 Chronicles 1–9).

The fundamental purpose of Solomon's reign—the inauguration of Temple worship—has been achieved. The account of the remainder of his reign records the benefits that flow from this expression of duty totally fulfilled towards God. These benefits are universal recognition, the establishment of harmonious relations with the neighbouring states, and the growth of trade, leading to unparalleled prosperity within Israel. The visit of the Queen of Sheba, attracted by Solomon's fame and the wisdom acknowledged to underwrite that prosperity, is the signal event of the second half of the reign. Even so, a significant proportion of the material of these chapters remains focused on the Temple.

These two chapters deal with a series of interlocking themes—status, acknowledgment, tribute and trade—which are grouped in the following way (so, broadly, MT):

(1) 2 Chron. 8.1-9: Solomon's building works at home and abroad as the expression of his dominion;
(2) 2 Chron. 8.10-11: Solomon's garrisons and foreign marriage as further testimony to his standing;
(3) 2 Chron. 8.12-16: at the centre of Solomon's reign lies the punctilious carrying out of the rites of the Temple;
(4) 2 Chron. 8.17-18: Solomon's demonstration of dominion: lucrative voyages in the Red Sea.
(5) 2 Chron. 9.1-12: the acknowledgment of Solomon by the Queen of Sheba;
(6) 2 Chron. 9.13-16: the acknowledgment of Solomon by subject kings: their tribute used to affirm his dominion;

(7) 2 Chron. 9.17-21: further affirmation of Solomon's dominion: his throne constructed from the tribute of remotest regions;
(8) 2 Chron. 9.22-24: the acknowledgment of Solomon by all the kings of the world;
(9) 2 Chron. 9.25-28: Solomon's military might;
(10) 2 Chron. 9.29-31: concluding annalistic notes on Solomon's reign (MT combines [9] and [10]).

There are some echoes in (1) of the opening of the first section on Solomon's reign in 2 Chron. 1.14. (8) resumes the theme of the beginning of this section, 2 Chron. 8.1-11; but its close echoing of the language of the beginning of the whole presentation of Solomon's reign in 2 Chron. 1.14-17 shows that it is designed to round off the whole Solomon narrative.

For the parallels to Samuel–Kings, see Introduction to 2 Chronicles 1–9.

1. *2 Chronicles 8.1-9: Solomon's Building Works at Home and Abroad as the Expression of his Dominion*

Six times in these verses the verb 'to build' is used and the section is dominated by the outcome of such activity: Temple, palace, cities in new territories, fortresses, and depots in conquered lands and in Israel proper. All these are an expression of Solomon's role as the representative of the divine king on earth: his purpose is to express fitly in physical terms the implications of the divine order.

The section opens with a link to the first part—and major task—of Solomon's reign: the building of the Temple in Jerusalem (v. 1). The Temple is the visible expression of the dominion of the LORD on earth and the means whereby the relationship between God and his representative can be maintained.

The related task of building a palace as an equivalent expression of sovereignty for God's representative is also mentioned (v. 1). Given the nature of the Israelite monarchy as the visible expression of the divine rule on earth, it is appropriate that the two structures are here co-ordinated with one another (cf. 2 Chron. 2.1; 7.11).

C, having consistently underplayed Solomon's activities in connection with the building of the royal palace in order not to detract from the status of the Temple, reformulates the 1 Kgs 9.10 expression, 'the two houses, the house of the LORD and the house of the king', which stresses the distinctiveness of the two buildings.

Verse 2 notes that Solomon has also rounded out the habitable area for his people. Huram, king of Tyre (cf. 1 Chron. 14.1; 2 Chron. 2.3-16), has given Solomon cities; these Solomon has rebuilt and populated with Israelites.

This note contrasts markedly with 1 Kgs 9.11-14, where it is Solomon who cedes to the king of Tyre twenty cities in Galilee. C also omits a reference in Kings to the forced labour required for the building of the Temple, palace, fortifications of Jerusalem and cities of Hazor, Megiddo and Gezer, and the narrative of how Gezer had come into Israel's possession in the first place as the dowry brought by Solomon's bride, the daughter of Pharaoh (1 Kgs 9.15-16; cf. 2 Chron. 8.11).

With these fundamental achievements behind him (the word order in v. 2 indicates that that verse belongs to the period of Temple building), Solomon can now turn his attention to the wider region (vv. 3, 4), the world of the nations round about, whom it is his duty to pacify in the name of the divine king. Accordingly, he advances to Hamath on the river Orontes in northern Syria and reasserts his authority over it (the key term, *ḥzq*, is used, 1 Chron. 11.10).

Uniquely in the Hebrew Bible it is called here 'Hamath-zobah'. Zobah is elsewhere a separate, Aramaean state, once conquered by David (cf. 1 Chron. 18.3-8; 19.6). By contrast, Hamath was a state friendly to David (1 Chron. 18.9-11), regarded as lying outside Israel's northern frontier (1 Chron. 13.5; 2 Chron. 7.8). Hamath is not mentioned by Kings in this context. The likelihood is that Hamath has been brought in from the end of v. 4: in C's sketch of universal dominion he has ahistorically combined the two.

There he builds store-cities. It is not stated precisely what the purpose of these cities was (the same word is used as in Exod. 1.11 of the store-cities that the Israelites had to build for Pharaoh in Egypt), whether they were depots for tribute paid, goods exacted, merchandise or garrison support. He is credited here also with the construction of Tadmor (the later Palmyra), some 150 km east in the Syrian desert.

The likelihood of highly ideological writing once again is suggested by the consonantal text of 1 Kgs 9.18 where, though the parallels are a little difficult to align, for C's 'Tadmor', 'Tamar in the desert in the land', that is, a much more local settlement south of the Dead Sea, is read. C is maximizing Solomon's imperial power.

Within the territory of Israel proper (vv. 5, 6), Solomon builds fortresses ('impregnable with walls, gates and bars'), garrison towns for his cavalry and, again, store-cities at strategic sites (cf. 2 Chron. 16.4; 17.12): the citizen army and the defence of the realm are thus organized. Apart from Jerusalem itself, three are mentioned: Upper and Lower Beth-horon commanding the approaches to Jerusalem from the north-west from the coastal plain and Baalath to the west. Throughout 'the whole territory of his dominion', whether in Israel proper or in the wider regions of inland Lebanon and Syria, Solomon, as the LORD's vicegerent, imposes his rule 'at will'. His victory is the sacramental expression of the victory won and the peace established by God; so, for example, 2 Chron. 11.5; 14.6; 17.12; 21.3; 26.9; 27.3, 4; 32.5; 33.14).

Verses 7-9 comment on the labour force employed in Solomon's building works. The requirement in no way impaired Solomon's military capability for pacifying the region, for only the descendants of the pre-Israelite indigenous population were subjected to perpetual forced labour. The free-born Israelites enjoyed the status of those whose privilege it was to bear arms in the wars of the LORD as the LORD's host: to fight as warriors and elite corps of charioteers and cavalrymen.

C slightly softens the reference to 'those who are left of the descendants' of the indigenous people. He contents himself with saying, 'those whom Israel had not destroyed', as opposed to the 1 Kgs 9.21 version: 'those whom the Israelites had not been able to place under ban of destruction'.

2. *2 Chronicles 8.10-11: Solomon's Garrisons and Foreign Marriage as Further Testimony to his Standing*

The precise reference of v. 10 is obscure in C. The end of the verse is not very explicit: Solomon has 250 officers who 'exercise authority over the people', but who the people are and for what purpose authority is exercised over them is not made clear. The difficulty is compounded by the double reading in Hebrew in the first phrase of the verse: either 'these are the officers of the garrisons' (*kethib*) or 'these are the officers of those appointed' (*qere*).

The parallel in 1 Kgs 9.23 is much clearer (though not entirely so) and supports the *qere* reading in C: 'These were the officers of those who were set in charge of Solomon's works: 550, who exercized authority over the people who were labouring in the works'. As it stands, the Kings text seems to envisage three classes who were involved in Solomon's public works: 550 royal officers, the foremen and the labourers [NRSV tacitly emends the Kings text by equating the officers and the foremen]. Kings relates the verse by content closely to the preceding: it concerns the supervision of the labour force of resident aliens who are involved in Solomon's public works. It is presumably to be related to the data that C has located at 2 Chron. 2.2, 17-18, where the foremen and the labourers are listed, and now adds to those data a tier of royal officers.

It is not clear that this is C's intention. The MT of C puts in the stronger paragraph divider between v. 10 and the foregoing, and has suppressed any reference in v. 10 to Solomon's public works. This makes it likely that the *kethib* reading should be preferred in the first phrase, for it alone provides any indication in the context of the purpose of these officials. The verse is not about the public works at all (that is to allow the Kings reading to print through); it is about the garrison posts throughout the land, which are under the control of a smaller number of royal officers than in Kings, 250 in all (for such garrison posts in Israel, which are integral to the military standing of Israel as the LORD's host, see 2 Chron. 17.2). Thus, while the *qere* reading relates to the construction, the *kethib* reading relates to the manning of the garrisons: the reference is to those whose task it is to express the order derived from the order imposed by God.

The note on Solomon's marriage to Pharaoh's daughter (v. 11) seems at first sight inconsequential (the occurrence yet again of the verb 'to build' might lead one to associate it with vv. 1-9). But it is striking that the note on David's wives comes in at a rather analogous point in 1 Chron. 14.3-7: the court and its composition are all part of the standing and international recognition of the Davidic king. Solomon's marriage to the daughter of Pharaoh is thus testimony to the recognition which he has secured even among the traditionally most threatening of Israel's neighbours, and to the positive relations that can prevail when the nations are in harmony through that recognition.

> Once again, the interpretation of Kings must not be allowed to print through—the disapproval of Solomon's foreign marriages. C has kept resolute silence over Solomon's amours—this is the only time in his account when he refers to a marriage of Solomon: he has not introduced the material on Pharaoh's daughter herself from 1 Kgs 3.1 and 9.16 nor on Solomon's vast harem in 1 Kgs 11.1-4—the kind of point he does not fail to introduce in his unfavourable portrayal of Solomon's son and

successor, Rehoboam, in 2 Chron. 11.21. Here the action of Solomon is regarded as wholly admirable.

The point of Solomon's constructing a palace for his only queen is that it lies outside the city. The problem posed by his wife is not her foreignness, but her marital status. At the heart of the issue lies the holiness of Jerusalem, and the degrees of holiness represented by the Temple, as the end of v. 11 makes clear. No wife of Solomon can then reside in Jerusalem (cf. the sexual abstinence enjoined on Israel as part of the measures in preparation to encounter God in Exod. 19.14-15 or the legislation on purification from emission of semen or discharge of blood in Lev. 15.16-24). The maintenance of purity at the centre of his rule is an absolute prerequisite for his maintenance of the holiness that is Israel's vocation.

C stresses the initiative of Solomon by making him the subject of the verse: whereas in 1 Kgs 9.24 'Pharaoh's daughter went up from the city of David to her house', here, Solomon himself removes her to the residence prepared for her. C omits the mention in Kings of other building activities in the second half of the verse in order to add his own theological comment.

3. *2 Chronicles 8.12-16: At the Centre of Solomon's Reign Lies the Punctilious Carrying Out of the Rites of the Temple*

The following section, therefore, returns to that core of Solomon's rule: the Temple and its rites. This section is at pains to confirm that Solomon, having undertaken the building of the Temple in the first half of his reign, does not then forsake his obligations, but ensures that in all perpetuity the rites of the Temple are observed. These rites are the strict round of sacrifices to be offered year by year as defined in such lists of sacrifices as in Numbers 28–29: there are prescribed the sacrifices which are to be offered each day, each sabbath, each new moon and on each of the three great annual pilgrimage festivals, Unleavened Bread, Weeks and Tabernacles (cf. 1 Chron. 23.31; 2 Chron. 2.4). To perform these sacrifices the priesthood has to be organized in accordance with their divisions. They have to be supported by the Levites to offer praise and play the musical instruments and the door-keepers have to be in post to regulate admission to the appropriate individuals to the appropriate areas of the Temple precincts (for all these see especially, 1 Chron. 23.6–24.31). The store-houses (v. 15) are also central to C's concerns (cf. 1 Chron. 26.20-32): it is there that the sacred offerings are laid up which are testimony to the dedication of the people as a whole and which it is the task of the Levites to monitor.

Verse 15 introduces an antonym, *sûr*, 'turn aside', of the key word, *drš* (1 Chron. 10.13-14); cf. 2 Chron. 20.32; 25.27; 34.2, 33; 35.15.

All this organization is given ultimate sanction. At the basis of it all lies the authority of Moses (v. 13): it is by the divine will revealed through him that the whole sacrificial system is enjoined. (The authority of Moses has already been appealed to in C in 1 Chron. 6.49; 15.15; 21.29; 22.13; 2 Chron. 1.3; 5.10.) The organization of this worship has been the contribution of David; for the first and only time he is given here the highest title, frequently reserved for the prophets and for Moses himself (1 Chron. 23.14), 'man of God'. There could be no higher claim: the system conceived in Moses and realized in David, both accredited by God in the highest terms possible, has now been put into operation by Solomon and continued in operation by him. The Temple is complete: not just its construction, but the whole system which expresses and imparts wholeness in the life of the people.

Once again, as in, for example, 2 Chron. 6.12-13; 7.1, C quotes Kings in order to provide a corrective commentary upon it. The passage opens with a text from 1 Kgs 9.25 which is extensively modified in the quotation; it is then expanded by three and a half verses to show how it could be modified to fit into C's theological system. The Kings text begins: 'Solomon used to offer three times per year whole burnt offerings and communion sacrifices on the altar which he had built to the LORD'. This text is itself modified by C. It begins with 'Then', the only fragment that is left from the suppressed second half of the preceding verse in Kings. It continues by suppressing the frequentative tense 'used to' and the 'three times per year': Solomon may once for all have inaugurated the cult in the Temple, but its continuation is the responsibility of the priests and Levites of the Davidic organization, as the following verses make clear. At most, Solomon '*caused* whole burnt offerings to be made'—by the clergy duly appointed. Further, the 'communion sacrifices' of the laity are suppressed: those who do not possess the sufficient degree of holiness are not permitted to enter the inner court of the Temple. Finally, the altar that Solomon built is described in matter of fact spatial terms: it is 'in front of the porch'. In its conception and use as the LORD's altar, the priests and Levites have exclusive right above Solomon. The following difficult phrase in Kings, 'and he used to offer therewith before the LORD incense offerings' (?), is simply suppressed. The remainder of the verse in Kings is continued in 2 Chron. 8.16b, but with a slight change: not 'thus he [Solomon] completed the Temple', but 'the house of the LORD was complete'. The intervening passage in 2 Chron. 8.13-16a reproduces the normative account of the sacrifices of Exodus to Numbers—precisely, indeed, the 'law of Moses' (v. 13).

4. *2 Chronicles 8.17-18: Solomon's Demonstration of Dominion: Lucrative Voyages in the Red Sea*

Verses 17-18 begin to explain how the 'treasuries' of v. 15 were filled by the tokens of endorsement, both divine and human, of Solomon's reign. Solomon's status as God's representative on earth is affirmed by the building of Temple and Palace. It is secured by the practice of holiness. C now turns to portray the consequences. He documents the successes of Solomon's reign as evidence of the blessings in terms of world-wide acknowledgment that flow from this ideal realized.

The first area instanced is the exotic lands of the south. Huram of Tyre, as king of a sea-faring nation, sends to Solomon ships and navigators to assist his men to sail the waters of the Red Sea. Since they use the seaports at the head of the Gulf of Aqaba, Edom too must have been quietly co-operative in Solomon's enterprise (cf. 1 Chron. 18.13). They reach as far as Ophir (South Arabia? East Africa? [cf. KBS]) and bring back from there 450 talents of gold.

> 1 Kgs 9.28 reads 420 talents. How this gold is acquired is not stated, whether by trade, tribute or plunder. For the comparative value of this large quantity see table at 1 Chron. 29.3. Kings eases the problem of how Huram could send ships to Solomon across land by reading that Solomon constructed the fleet, which was then partly manned by sailors from Tyre. Again C is not troubled by mundane practicalities (the construction of Phoenician ships in kit form from wood from Lebanon is not beyond the bounds of possibility).[1]

5. *2 Chronicles 9.1-12: The Acknowledgment of Solomon by the Queen of Sheba*

The visit of the queen from Sheba in southern Arabia falls naturally within the context of the voyage of Solomon's sailors to Ophir and is

1. W. Johnstone, 'The Signs', in H. Frost (ed.), *The Marsala Punic Ship* (Rome: Notizie degli Scavi, Accademia dei Lincei, 1981), pp. 191-240.

so placed by C (2 Chron. 8.17-18; 9.10-11). It was their exploits (such as bringing exotic materials for the furnishing of the Temple and Palace, even to equipping the minstrels with wood for their instruments), that had spread his fame. Here now is the most glittering prize of all.

Fundamental to this encounter is Solomon's wisdom (mentioned four times explicitly in this passage, vv. 3, 5, 6, 7), that gift which he had requested at Gibeon at the beginning of his reign and which acts as part of the framework of his entire reign (2 Chron. 1.10-12; 2.12; cf. 9.22). C does not make much overt use elsewhere in his work of the quality of wisdom as the traditional foundation of monarchy and is largely reproducing material inherited from Kings here. Kings emphasizes Solomon's role as patron of wisdom (cf. 1 Kgs 3.16-28; 4.29-34, which C does not use), that capacity to live life successfully because the person who possess it has insight into the way in which God has created and ordered the world. The king as God's representative on earth is, ideally, fully endowed with this capacity (cf., e.g., Isa. 11.2). C adds his own emphasis to the status of the Davidic king in v. 8, where, once again, the royal throne is identified as, in principle, the throne of God himself (cf. 1 Chron. 28.5). It is from this gift of divine wisdom—that insight into the inner workings of the universe itself—that all else follows in Solomon's reign: the position of preeminence and leadership among the nations and the wealth, fame, and deference that accompany it.

All this is fully exemplified in the visit of the Queen of Sheba. She has heard of his wisdom and the fabulous wealth which is the external sign of that wisdom. With her retinue, she herself cuts no mean figure and seeks to express her own status and impress with the unparalleled lavishness of her gifts (120 talents of gold [cf. 1 Chron. 29.3], precious stones and the spices [cf. 1 Chron. 9.29-30] for which her country was famous). Is Solomon so very impressive? She comes to test his wisdom and to verify that his wealth is a fair index of that wisdom and that it is as it has been fabled. The riddles with which she probes Solomon's understanding are a familiar element of the stock in trade of the wise men and women of the Hebrew Bible (Prov. 1.6; the most famous of these riddles is Samson's in Judg. 14.12-19). Solomon passes the scrutiny with the highest distinction and even adds to his reputation. There is no conundrum that she can pose that he does not answer. The physical circumstances match the dazzling intellectual display: the wealth and opulence of Solomon's court, the luxurious food and garments of his courtiers, surpass every expectation and are crowned by the private ascent into the Temple itself that betokens Solomon's status as the LORD's viceroy. The impact is totally overwhelming.

The climax of the Queen of Sheba's response is the theological statement in v. 8. Her acknowledgment of Solomon leads, as in the case of Huram (2 Chron. 2.11-12) though not quite so fulsomely, to a recognition of the LORD's role in the elevation of Solomon as his earthly representative on his own throne and in the perpetuation of the Davidic house. Much of the vocabulary of 2 Chron. 2.11-12 is repeated (the additions here in brackets): 'Blessed be the LORD [your] God [who has been pleased...]. In the love [of your God for Israel...he has] set you over them as king'. There is the same emphasis on wisdom and equation of Solomon's reign with the reign of God. In 2 Chron. 2.11 Huram naturally also makes mention of the assured succession to his old friend, David; here, that dimension is mentioned less specifically in terms of 'establishing Israel for ever'. It is through this rule of the house of David that the fundamental expression and benefits of this sacral reign will flow: justice and righteousness, the same qualities which marked the reign of David (1 Chron. 18.14, reflecting the LORD's own nature, 2 Chron. 12.6) and of every ideal king, according to the tradition of Jerusalem theology (e.g. Isa. 9.7).

The overall drift of the passage is similar in both C and 1 Kgs 10.1-13. There are numerous small adjustments, the most important of which are as follows. A significant sounding but obscure phrase in v. 1, 'because of the LORD's name', is omitted. Where Kings has 'the whole burnt offerings which he offered in the Temple', C by the addition of a single consonant reads 'the ascent by which he went up to the Temple' (wrongly, in my view, emended by NRSV; see the commentary on the whole burnt offerings that C has provided in 2 Chron. 8.12-16). The theological status of Solomon is heightened in v. 8: C reads 'the LORD your God, who was pleased with you to set you on his throne as king for the LORD your God'; Kings just reads, '...to set you over the throne of Israel'. The permanence of the promise to the Davidic house is obliquely referred to in the same verse by the addition of the verb 'to establish it [Israel] for ever'. In v. 10 C adds 'the servants of Solomon' to the fleet of Huram, to emphasize Israel's participation in the enterprise to Ophir. It is not entirely clear what the wood ('algum' as in 2 Chron. 2.7 for 'almug' in Kings) is used for in either Kings or C apart from the musical instruments, though different words are used, 'support' in Kings, 'banks' in C (v. 11). In the last verse C has 'quite apart from what she had brought the king' for the 'quite apart from what he had given her' of Kings; for C it is Solomon who gets the recognition, not the foreign sovereign, as befits the theology of Israel's monarchy.

6. *2 Chronicles 9.13-16: The Acknowledgment of Solomon by Subject Kings: Their Tribute Used to Affirm his Dominion*

Solomon's annual acquisition of gold is 666 talents (cf. 1 Chron. 29.3), quite apart from the wealth brought in by traders and their agents. This gold comes from the tribute of the nations round about, 'all the kings of the Arabs and the governors', the latter being presumably those appointed by Solomon in the various lands of his dominion (Hamath and the various Aramaean states, 2 Chron. 8.3, and Edom, 2 Chron. 8.17, besides the conquests inherited from his father, 1 Chron. 18–20). Silver, too, was brought, but C does not even bother to list its value (cf. v. 20).

Solomon uses gold from this source for the decoration of one of the chambers of his palace, the great hall with cedar columns called, appropriately, 'the house of the forest of Lebanon'. He makes 200 shields of beaten gold each weighing 600 shekels and 300 bucklers each weighing 300 shekels.

On the assumption that 1 talent = 3000 shekels (cf. Table at 1 Chron. 29.3), these shields would have used up only a small fraction of one year of income from this source. The shields at 120,000 shekels and the bucklers at 90,000, that is, 210,000 shekels altogether, make up only 70 talents.

For the bucklers 1 Kgs 10.17 reads much more: '300 minas'. On the usual assumption that the mina is 50 shekels [KBS], each of the bucklers would weigh 5 talents (smaller but 25 times heavier). Shields and bucklers would then come to 1540 talents, roughly two-and-a-half times the annual income.

The shields are highly symbolical as defensive equipment (e.g. Deut. 33.29; also—surprisingly—offensive, e.g. 2 Kgs 19.32), they stand here, by the figure of speech of 'part for the whole', for the rulers of the world as defenders of their people (cf. Pss. 47.9; 84.9; 89.18). The surrender of their shields to Solomon represents their acknowledgment of his protection for their people (cf. 2 Chron. 12.9-10; 23.9; 32.27).

'The house of the forest of Lebanon' is described in 1 Kgs 7.2-5 (not reproduced by C), where it is part of the complex of buildings leading up to the throne where judgment was pronounced. It is appropriate that, in this physical approach to the place where order is imposed in the name of the LORD, these symbols of acknowledgment of world dominion should be in evidence.

7. 2 Chronicles 9.17-21: Further Affirmation of Solomon's Dominion: His Throne Constructed from the Tribute of Remotest Regions

The next section is the mirror image of the last: it begins with the construction of the throne and concludes with a note on the source of the tribute used to make it.

It is appropriate that Solomon's throne should now be described, given its location in relation to the house of the forest of Lebanon just mentioned in the previous section and about to be mentioned with it in this.

The physical features of the throne serve to express its significance. The throne itself is made of ivory overlaid with gold. Beside the armrests stand a pair of lions. A golden footstool and a flight of six steps lead up to the throne; each step is flanked by another pair of lions. In both the throne-room and the house of the forest of Lebanon only solid gold cups are used.

This is the seat of the representative on earth of the divine king of the universe. No other kingdom on earth can have such a throne (it is not quite clear to what the claim to uniqueness precisely refers, whether the six steps, or the pair of lions on each step, or, indeed, both): by definition, Solomon's throne is taller and more magnificent than all (one might compare the figure of Zion as the highest mountain, Isa. 2.2).

To him all the leaders of the nations do homage. The gold and the ivory are not produced in Israel itself: they are the most precious and exotic substances, and symbolize the best that the world of the nations can provide. The theme of the ultimate in the exotic and dramatically splendid is carried on by the apes and peacocks which, along with the gold and the ivory, Solomon's mariners bring home from their triennial voyages to Tarshish. Such was the opulence of the time that silver was not accounted of any significance.

Tarshish is usually identified with Tartessus in Spain, though that would hardly be the place of origin of such merchandise. 1 Kgs 10.22 reads only, 'ships of Tarshish', which might mean no more than ocean-going vessels such as are capable of plying the whole Mediterranean [KBS].

Everything is designed to awe anyone who approaches this place where the absoluteness of the divine dominion is put into effect: the flight of steps leading up to the throne, the footstool and the pairs of lions on each side. Lions are used elsewhere in the Hebrew Bible as symbols of Israel's power and dominance (e.g. in Num. 23.24) or of the utterance of the LORD that causes the earth to tremble (e.g. Amos 3.8).

The word for 'footstool' (v. 18) is unique to this context in the Hebrew Bible (1 Kgs 10.19 has a different text, 'round-backed'). It is an appropriate symbol of dominion, being related to the verb 'to subdue' as in Gen. 1.28. It corresponds in significance to the other word for 'footstool', used in association with the ark as the footstool of the LORD (cf. 1 Chron. 28.2).

8. *2 Chronicles 9.22-24: The Acknowledgment of Solomon by all the Kings of the World*

After these specific examples, the account of the recognition of Solomon ends in a generalized summary. Solomon indeed exceeds all the kings of the earth in wealth, the outward manifestation of status, and in wisdom, its inner substance. Therefore, all the kings of the earth come to learn from Solomon's wisdom and to acknowledge his status with their tribute (1 Chron. 16.29). But his status is not just comparatively higher than theirs; it is absolutely superior. For he is the viceroy on earth of the divine king; only one appointed by God can attain this status. God himself has endowed him with all the gifts required. Thus they come 'to seek his face', a phrase used elsewhere in C of God (1 Chron. 16.11; 2 Chron. 7.14). This is an annual acknowledgment. These kings are not free to exercise rule in their own right. Instead of the annual celebration of their own coronations and empowerment by their gods, they express year by year, through their tribute, their wealth, military capability and other emblems of royalty, the fruits of the arts of peace and of war, their subjection to Solomon and their dependence on the wisdom imparted by his God. It is thus that the pacific rule of Solomon, the man of peace (1 Chron. 22.9), is realized.

C makes this theological point of qualitative difference between Solomon and all potential rival claimants clearer by reading in v. 23 'all the kings of the earth' for the 'all the earth' of 1 Kgs 10.24.

9. *2 Chronicles 9.25-28: Solomon's Military Might*

As noted at the beginning of the discussion of Solomon's reign, this second last section picks up material from the second section in 2 Chron. 1.14-17, thus rounding off the whole presentation.

Only the opening shows much difference: 'Solomon had 4000 stalls of horses and chariots' for 'Solomon gathered chariots and horsemen; he had 1400 chariots' (so too the parallel text in 1 Kgs 10.26). Verse 25aβ, b (the '12,000 horsemen' which Solomon 'stationed in the chariot cities and with the king in Jerusalem') is identical with 2 Chron. 1.14aβ, b and v. 27 with 2 Chron. 1.15 ('the king made silver and gold as common in Jerusalem as stone and cedar as common as the sycamore in the lowlands' except for the omission of 'and gold'). Verse 28, 'They were importing horses from Egypt for Solomon' summarizes 2 Chron. 1.17 but generalizes, 'and from all the lands', from 'the kings of the Hittites and Syrians', appropriately, in the light of the presentation of the world-wide dominion of Solomon as representative of the divine king in the previous chapters. The only verse not in the parallel in 2 Chronicles 1 is v. 26, which gives the extent of Solomon's rule 'over all the kings from the Euphrates...to the frontier of Egypt'; that verse is derived from 1 Kgs 5.1a, with the reading 'kings' rather than 'kingdoms'.

In consonance with his portrayal of Solomon as the ideal exponent of the role of Davidic king, C omits the material in 1 Kgs 10.28b to the end of 1 Kings 11, which places Solomon in an adverse light, especially his introduction of foreign religious cults and the dire consequences of rebellion among his subjects.

These verses on military capability are not to be regarded as an anticlimax. In sacramental theology, total physical preparedness is the appropriate expression of God's sovereignty (cf. 1 Chron. 14.10-16).

10. *2 Chronicles 9.29-31: Concluding Annalistic Notes on Solomon's reign*

The bare chronological statistics of the reign of Solomon are now given—his 40-year rule in Jerusalem. But among the bare annalistic material C mentions factors that are now to be of central significance in the continuing story of Israel's life. C is perfectly aware of the decline and division which now await Israel in the long years of trying to continue to realize in the Davidic house the ideals that have been stated from 1 Chronicles 11–2 Chronicles 9. He is not concerned to trace the historical roots of these divisions even within the reign of Solomon (and David), as Samuel–Kings has done. He plunges straight on into the narrative, introducing now for the first time (apart from the genealogy in 1 Chron. 3.10) Rehoboam (v. 31), Solomon's son and successor, and his rival in power, Jeroboam (v. 29), who is to be instrumental in splitting the kingdom.

But C is aware of the momentousness of this transition. With the pain of the division that is about to take place all too present in his mind, he retains the nostalgic note of the ideal unity that should have been taken for granted but which can now be only an eschatological hope, 'Solomon reigned in Jerusalem over all Israel' (v. 30).

For the elucidation of the background to the impending disaster, he refers the reader not to a secular source (as in 1 Kgs 11.41) but to the works of three generations of prophets and seers (see the three prophetic accounts of the reign of David referred to in 1 Chron. 29.29). As in 1 Chron. 29.29, these prophetic figures and their writings appear, not to satisfy the idly curious with information about a past world, but in order to stand in readiness as the LORD's emissaries to pronounce a word of judgment, if those divinely instituted for duty fail in the carrying out of their task (see introduction to 2 Chronicles 10–36). The three prophets mentioned are Nathan, Ahijah of Shiloh and Iddo the seer.

Nathan, the prophetic intermediary at a great turning-point of David's reign (1 Chron. 17), has already been credited with a record of the events of David's reign in 1 Chron. 29.29. As in the case of Samuel with David, he cannot have had much to record about the reign of Solomon.

Ahijah is referred to in C only here and in 2 Chron. 10.15. In Samuel–Kings he plays a prominent role in the insurrection of Jeroboam. C clearly presupposes in 2 Chron. 10.15 the account of the prophecy of Ahijah—presumably that referred to here, despite its being linked to the next figure, Jedo—to Jeroboam in 1 Kgs 11.29-39, which C has not reproduced in his own work. Ahijah's prophecy is that Jeroboam, the superintendent of the forced labour that Solomon has imposed on the northern tribes of Ephraim and Manasseh, will remove the ten northern tribes from loyalty to the house of David, thus negating the role of the house of David in fulfilling the destiny of Israel in the future of humankind.

The third prophetic figure is here called Jedo, assumed to be the same as Iddo, who figures in 2 Chron. 12.15 and 13.22 as the chronicler of Solomon's son, Rehoboam, and of his grandson, Abijah. Of his vision nothing further is known (see, again, introduction to 2 Chron. 10–36).

BIBLIOGRAPHY

This bibliography is far from being an exhaustive list of the secondary literature on C and its related questions. It is more of an account of works used in the process of writing the commentary and some further leads, which themselves provide substantial bibliographies.

A commentary is written not because the interpreter knows, but because he or she needs to know. It has to be the inductive description of the material in the work itself, written with as few preconceptions as possible about what the theme or themes may turn out to be. The Hebrew text has to be patiently read with, as chief tool, the Hebrew concordance to enable the main interconnections of language within the work and between the work and the rest of the Hebrew Bible to be traced. This is the policy I have tried to follow. I apologize to my predecessors for the inevitable occasions where insights are duplicated, with earlier work unacknowledged. My conclusions have been reached, for the most part, independently: where I am conscious of indebtedness, I have tried to acknowledge it.

Fuller discussion of individual topics has also to be left on one side. I have offered studies of some special areas elsewhere, noted below.

The commentary has been drafted on the basis of the Hebrew Text (*BHK* and *BHS*) and with extensive use of the Hebrew concordance, both manual (Mandelkern, on the whole for single words) and computerized (macBible™, Zondervan Electronic Publishing, Grand Rapids, 1990, usually for combinations of words and phrases). Where access to a range of informed scholarly opinion has been required, I have used the standard lexica (BDB, KBS), and representative modern English Versions (NEB, JPSV, NIV, and NRSV; where the rendering differs from NRSV, it is my own, unless otherwise stated). For geographical matters, I have used Grollenberg's atlas (occasionally J.B. Pritchard's 'Times', 1987, but on Jerusalem, the main crux, it provides little help); for historical, Bright's *History of Israel*, not because I always agree with it, but because it has been a standard textbook, which, simply because I do disagree with much of it, helps to provide a certain degree of objectivity. Where proper names have not been sufficiently differentiated by Mandelkern (e.g. under Mattithiah, '*nonnulli viri*'), I have consulted the standard Hebrew–English Lexicon, BDB. For technical terms (such as discussion of identification of precious stones or architectural features), I have consulted the review of opinions in KBS.

The secondary literature on C is growing rapidly. The mention of, perforce, only a fraction gives, perhaps, sufficient leads into the extensive discussion.

While within the confines of this commentary it is not possible to engage in debate with the work of one's predecessors, I have reviewed some of the commentaries available up to 1989 in 'Which is the best commentary?: The Chronicler's Work', *ExpTim* 102 (1990–91), pp. 6-11 (E.L Curtis, A.A. Madsen, ICC, 1910; J.M. Myers, Anchor, 1965; P.R. Ackroyd, Torch, 1973; R.J. Coggins, Cambridge, 1976; H.G.M. Williamson, New Century, 1982; J.G. McConville, Daily Study, 1984; R. Braun, R.B. Dillard, Word, 1986-87).

Since then, a number of commentaries have appeared: S.J. de Vries, *1 and 2 Chronicles*; S. Japhet, *I & II Chronicles*, which complements her, still essential, earlier work, *The Ideology of the Book of Chronicles and its Place in Biblical Thought* (I have offered a critical appraisal of some of her conclusions in my essay, 'The Use of Leviticus in Chronicles', noted below); M.J. Selman, *1 and 2 Chronicles.*

The most magisterial commentary of all to date will be T. Willi, *Chronik* (in progress).

An overview of issues and proposals in interpreting Chronicles is provided by: P.R. Ackroyd, *The Chronicler in his Age* (a collection of essays written over some thirty-five years) and, especially, G.H. Jones, *1 and 2 Chronicles*. Studies of special features are to be found in the monographs by: Gray, Kleinig, Riley, Kalimi, Steins, Weinberg and Kelly.

Ackroyd, P.R., *The Chronicler in his Age* (JSOTSup, 101; Sheffield: JSOT Press, 1991).
Bright, J., *A History of Israel* (London: SCM Press, 3rd edn, 1981).
de Vries, S.J., *1 and 2 Chronicles* (FOTL, 11; Grand Rapids: Eerdmans, 1989).
Douglas, Mary, 'Sacred Contagion', in J.F.A. Sawyer (ed.), *Rending Leviticus* (JSOTSup, 227; Sheffield: JSOT Press, 1996), pp. 86-106.
Graham, M. Patrick, Kenneth G. Hoglund, McKenzie, Steven, *The Chronicles as Historian* (JSOTSup, 238; Sheffield: Sheffield Academic Press, 1997).
Gray, J., *The Biblical Doctrine of the Reign of God* (Edinburgh: T. & T. Clark, 1979).
Grollenberg, L.H., *Atlas of the Bible* (London: Nelson, 1956).
Japhet, Sara, *The Ideology of the Book of Chronicles and its Place in Biblical Thought* (Frankfurt: Peter Lang, 1989).
—*I & II Chronicles* (London: SCM Press, 1993).
Johnstone, W., 'The Signs', in H. Frost (ed.), *The Marsala Punic Ship* (Rome: Notizie degli Scavi, Accademia dei Lincei, 1981), pp. 191-240.
—'Guilt and Atonement: The Theme of 1 and 2 Chronicles', in J.D. Martin and P.R. Davies (eds.), *A Word in Season: Essays in Honour of William McKane* (JSOTSup, 42; Sheffield: JSOT Press, 1986), pp. 113-38.
—'Reactivating the Chronicles Analogy in Pentateuchal Studies, with Special Reference to the Sinai Pericope in Exodus', *ZAW* (1987), pp. 16-37.
—'Justification by Faith Revisited', *ExpTim* 104 (1992–93), pp. 67-71.
—'Solomon's Prayer: Is Intentionalism such a Fallacy?', *ST* 47 (1993), pp. 119-33.
—'The Use of Leviticus in Chronicles', in J.F.A. Sawyer (ed.), *Reading Leviticus* (JSOTSup, 227; Sheffield: Sheffield Academic Press, 1996), pp. 243-55.
Jones, G.H., *1&2 Chronicles* (OTG, Sheffield: JSOT Press), 1993.
Kalimi, I., *Zur Geschichtsschreibung des Chronisten: Literarisch-historiographische Abweichungen der Chronik von ihren Paralleltexten in den Samuel- und Königsbüchern* (BZAW, 226; Berlin: de Gruyter, 1995).

Kelly, B.E., *Retribution and Eschatology in Chronicles* (JSOTSup, 211; Sheffield: JSOT Press, 1996).
Kleinig, J.E., *The LORD's Song: The Basis, Function and Significance of Choral Music in Chronicles* (JSOTSup, 156; Sheffield: JSOT Press, 1993).
Mandelkern, S., *Concordance to the Old Testament* (repr.; Tel Aviv: Schocken Books, 1962).
Milgrom, J., *Cult and Conscience: The Asham and the Priestly Doctrine of Repentance* (SJLA, 18; Leiden: Brill, 1976).
Neusner, J., *Between Time and Eternity* (Encino: Dickenson, 1975), p. 52.
Riley, W., *King and Cultus in Chronicles: Worship and the Reinterpretation of History* (JSOTSup, 160; Sheffield: JSOT Press, 1993).
Selman, M.J., *1 and 2 Chronicles* (London: Tyndale Press, 1994).
Steins, G., *Die Chronik als kanonisches Abschlussphänomen: Studien zur Entstehung und Theologie von 1/2 Chronik* (BBB, 93, Weinheim: Beltz Athenäum, 1995).
Weinberg, J.P., *Der Chronist in seiner Mitwelt* (BZAW, 239; Berlin: de Gruyter, 1996).
Westermann, C., *Basic Forms of Prophetic Speech* (trans. Hugh Clayton White; London: Lutterworth, 1967).
Willi, T., *Chronik* (BKAT, 24; Neukirchen–Vluyn: Neukirchener Verlag, 1991–in progress).

INDEXES

INDEX OF REFERENCES

OLD TESTAMENT

Index of Selected Key Terms

(words are listed in the order of the Hebrew alphabet, vowelled forms first)

JOURNAL FOR THE STUDY OF THE OLD TESTAMENT SUPPLEMENT SERIES

110 N.P. Lemche, *The Canaanites and their Land: The Tradition of the Canaanites*
111 J.G. Taylor, *Yahweh and the Sun: The Biblical and Archaeological Evidence for Sun Worship in Ancient Israel*
112 L.G. Perdue, *Wisdom in Revolt: Metaphorical Theology in the Book of Job*
113 R. Westbrook, *Property and the Family in Biblical Law*
114 D. Cohn-Sherbok (ed.), *A Traditional Quest: Essays in Honour of Louis Jacobs*
115 V. Hurowitz, *I Have Built You an Exalted House: Temple Building in the Bible in Light of Mesopotamian and Northwest Semitic Writings*
116 D.M. Gunn (ed.), *Narrative and Novella in Samuel: Studies by Hugo Gressmann and Other Scholars, 1906–1923* (trans. D.E. Orton)
117 P.R. Davies (ed.), *Second Temple Studies. I. Persian Period*
118 R.J. Tournay, *Seeing and Hearing God with the Psalms: The Prophetic Liturgy of the Second Temple in Jerusalem*
119 D.J.A. Clines & T.C. Eskenazi (eds.), *Telling Queen Michal's Story: An Experiment in Comparative Interpretation*
120 R.H. Lowery, *The Reforming Kings: Cult and Society in First Temple Judah*
121 D.V. Edelman, *King Saul in the Historiography of Judah*
122 L. Alexander (ed.), *Images of Empire*
123 E. Bloch-Smith, *Judahite Burial Practices and Beliefs about the Dead*
124 B. Halpern & D.W. Hobson (eds.), *Law and Ideology in Monarchic Israel*
125 G.A. Anderson & S.M. Olyan (eds.), *Priesthood and Cult in Ancient Israel*
126 J.W. Rogerson, *W.M.L. de Wette, Founder of Modern Biblical Criticism: An Intellectual Biography*
127 D.V. Edelman (ed.), *The Fabric of History: Text, Artifact and Israel's Past*
128 T.P. McCreesh, *Biblical Sound and Sense: Poetic Sound Patterns in Proverbs 10–29*
129 Z. Stefanovic, *The Aramaic of Daniel in the Light of Old Aramaic*
130 M. Butterworth, *Structure and the Book of Zechariah*
131 L. Holden, *Forms of Deformity*
132 M.D. Carroll R., *Contexts for Amos: Prophetic Poetics in Latin American Perspective*
133 R. Syrén, *The Forsaken Firstborn: A Study of a Recurrent Motif in the Patriarchal Narratives*
134 G. Mitchell, *Together in the Land: A Reading of the Book of Joshua*
135 G.F. Davies, *Israel in Egypt: Reading Exodus 1–2*
136 P. Morris & D. Sawyer (eds.), *A Walk in the Garden: Biblical, Iconographical and Literary Images of Eden*
137 H.G. Reventlow & Y. Hoffman (eds.), *Justice and Righteousness: Biblical Themes and their Influence*
138 R.P. Carroll (ed.), *Text as Pretext: Essays in Honour of Robert Davidson*

139 J.W. Watts, *Psalm and Story: Inset Hymns in Hebrew Narrative*
140 W. Houston, *Purity and Monotheism: Clean and Unclean Animals in Biblical Law*
141 G.C. Chirichigno, *Debt-Slavery in Israel and the Ancient Near East*
142 F.H. Cryer, *Divination in Ancient Israel and its Near Eastern Environment: A Socio-Historical Investigation*
143 D.J.A. Clines & J.C. Exum (eds.), *The New Literary Criticism and the Hebrew Bible*
144 P.R. Davies & D.J.A. Clines (eds.), *Language, Imagery and Structure in the Prophetic Writings*
145 C.S. Shaw, *The Speeches of Micah: A Rhetorical-Historical Analysis*
146 G.W. Ahlström, *The History of Ancient Palestine from the Palaeolithic Period to Alexander's Conquest* (ed. D. Edelman, with a contribution by G.O. Rollefson)
147 T.W. Cartledge, *Vows in the Hebrew Bible and the Ancient Near East*
148 P.R. Davies, *In Search of 'Ancient Israel'*
149 E. Ulrich, J.W. Wright, R.P. Carroll & P.R. Davies (eds.), *Priests, Prophets and Scribes: Essays on the Formation and Heritage of Second Temple Judaism in Honour of Joseph Blenkinsopp*
150 J.E. Tollington, *Tradition and Innovation in Haggai and Zechariah 1–8*
151 J.P. Weinberg, *The Citizen-Temple Community*
152 A.G. Auld (ed.), *Understanding Poets and Prophets: Essays in Honour of George Wishart Anderson*
153 D.K. Berry, *The Psalms and their Readers: Interpretive Strategies for Psalm 18*
154 M. Brettler & M. Fishbane (eds.), *Minḥah le-Naḥum: Biblical and Other Studies Presented to Nahum M. Sarna in Honour of his 70th Birthday*
155 J.A. Fager, *Land Tenure and the Biblical Jubilee: Uncovering Hebrew Ethics through the Sociology of Knowledge*
156 J.W. Kleinig, *The Lord's Song: The Basis, Function and Significance of Choral Music in Chronicles*
157 G.R. Clark, *The Word Ḥesed in the Hebrew Bible*
158 M. Douglas, *In the Wilderness: The Doctrine of Defilement in the Book of Numbers*
159 J.C. McCann (ed.), *The Shape and Shaping of the Psalter*
160 W. Riley, *King and Cultus in Chronicles: Worship and the Reinterpretation of History*
161 G.W. Coats, *The Moses Tradition*
162 H.A. McKay & D.J.A. Clines (eds.), *Of Prophet's Visions and the Wisdom of Sages: Essays in Honour of R. Norman Whybray on his Seventieth Birthday*
163 J.C. Exum, *Fragmented Women: Feminist (Sub)versions of Biblical Narratives*
164 L. Eslinger, *House of God or House of David: The Rhetoric of 2 Samuel 7*
166 D.R.G. Beattie & M.J. McNamara (eds.), *The Aramaic Bible: Targums in their Historical Context*

167 R.F. Person, *Second Zechariah and the Deuteronomic School*
168 R.N. Whybray, *The Composition of the Book of Proverbs*
169 B. Dicou, *Edom, Israel's Brother and Antagonist: The Role of Edom in Biblical Prophecy and Story*
170 W.G.E. Watson, *Traditional Techniques in Classical Hebrew Verse*
171 H.G. Reventlow, Y. Hoffman & B. Uffenheimer (eds.), *Politics and Theopolitics in the Bible and Postbiblical Literature*
172 V. Fritz, *An Introduction to Biblical Archaeology*
173 M.P. Graham, W.P. Brown & J.K. Kuan (eds.), *History and Interpretation: Essays in Honour of John H. Hayes*
174 J.M. Sprinkle, *'The Book of the Covenant': A Literary Approach*
175 T.C. Eskenazi & K.H. Richards (eds.), *Second Temple Studies.* II. *Temple and Community in the Persian Period*
176 G. Brin, *Studies in Biblical Law: From the Hebrew Bible to the Dead Sea Scrolls*
177 D.A. Dawson, *Text-Linguistics and Biblical Hebrew*
178 M.R. Hauge, *Between Sheol and Temple: Motif Structure and Function in the I-Psalms*
179 J.G. McConville & J.G. Millar, *Time and Place in Deuteronomy*
180 R. Schultz, *The Search for Quotation: Verbal Parallels in the Prophets*
181 B.M. Levinson (ed.), *Theory and Method in Biblical and Cuneiform Law: Revision, Interpolation and Development*
182 S.L. McKenzie & M.P. Graham (eds.), *The History of Israel's Traditions: The Heritage of Martin Noth*
183 J. Day (ed.), *Lectures on the Religion of the Semites (Second and Third Series) by William Robertson Smith*
184 J.C. Reeves & J. Kampen (eds.), *Pursuing the Text: Studies in Honour of Ben Zion Wacholder on the Occasion of his Seventieth Birthday*
185 S.D. Kunin, *The Logic of Incest: A Structuralist Analysis of Hebrew Mythology*
186 L. Day, *Three Faces of a Queen: Characterization in the Books of Esther*
187 C.V. Dorothy, *The Books of Esther: Structure, Genre and Textual Integrity*
188 R.H. O'Connell, *Concentricity and Continuity: The Literary Structure of Isaiah*
189 W. Johnstone (ed.), *William Robertson Smith: Essays in Reassessment*
190 S.W. Holloway & L.K. Handy (eds.), *The Pitcher is Broken: Memorial Essays for Gösta W. Ahlström*
192 H.G. Reventlow & W. Farmer (eds.), *Biblical Studies and the Shifting of Paradigms, 1850–1914*
193 B. Schramm, *The Opponents of Third Isaiah: Reconstructing the Cultic History of the Restoration*
194 E.K. Holt, *Prophesying the Past: The Use of Israel's History in the Book of Hosea*
195 J. Davies, G. Harvey & W.G.E. Watson (eds.), *Words Remembered, Texts Renewed: Essays in Honour of John F.A. Sawyer*
196 J.S. Kaminsky, *Corporate Responsibility in the Hebrew Bible*

197 W.M. Schniedewind, *The Word of God in Transition: From Prophet to Exegete in the Second Temple Period*
198 T.J. Meadowcroft, *Aramaic Daniel and Greek Daniel: A Literary Comparison*
199 J.H. Eaton, *Psalms of the Way and the Kingdom: A Conference with the Commentators*
200 M.D. Carroll R., D.J.A. Clines & P.R. Davies (eds.), *The Bible in Human Society: Essays in Honour of John Rogerson*
201 J.W. Rogerson, *The Bible and Criticism in Victorian Britain: Profiles of F.D. Maurice and William Robertson Smith*
202 N. Stahl, *Law and Liminality in the Bible*
203 J.M. Munro, *Spikenard and Saffron: The Imagery of the Song of Songs*
204 P.R. Davies, *Whose Bible Is It Anyway?*
205 D.J.A. Clines, *Interested Parties: The Ideology of Writers and Readers of the Hebrew Bible*
206 M. Müller, *The First Bible of the Church: A Plea for the Septuagint*
207 J.W. Rogerson, M. Davies & M.D. Carroll R. (eds.), *The Bible in Ethics: The Second Sheffield Colloquium*
208 B.J. Stratton, *Out of Eden: Reading, Rhetoric, and Ideology in Genesis 2–3*
209 P. Dutcher-Walls, *Narrative Art, Political Rhetoric: The Case of Athaliah and Joash*
210 J. Berlinerblau, *The Vow and the 'Popular Religious Groups' of Ancient Israel: A Philological and Sociological Inquiry*
211 B.E. Kelly, *Retribution and Eschatology in Chronicles*
212 Y. Sherwood, *The Prostitute and the Prophet: Hosea's Marriage in Literary-Theoretical Perspective*
213 Y.A. Hoffman, *A Blemished Perfection: The Book of Job in Context*
214 R.F. Melugin & M.A. Sweeney (eds.), *New Visions of Isaiah*
215 J.C. Exum, *Plotted, Shot and Painted: Cultural Representations of Biblical Women*
216 J.E. McKinlay, *Gendering Wisdom the Host: Biblical Invitations to Eat and Drink*
217 J.F.D. Creach, *Yahweh as Refuge and the Editing of the Hebrew Psalter*
218 G. Glazov, *The Bridling of the Tongue and the Opening of the Mouth in Biblical Prophecy*
219 G. Morris, *Prophecy, Poetry and Hosea*
220 R.F. Person, Jr, *In Conversation with Jonah: Conversation Analysis, Literary Criticism, and the Book of Jonah*
221 G. Keys, *The Wages of Sin: A Reappraisal of the 'Succession Narrative'*
222 R.N. Whybray, *Reading the Psalms as a Book*
223 S.B. Noegel, *Janus Parallelism in the Book of Job*
224 P.J. Kissling, *Reliable Characters in the Primary History: Profiles of Moses, Joshua, Elijah and Elisha*
225 R.D. Weiss & D.M. Carr (eds.), *A Gift of God in Due Season: Essays on Scripture and Community in Honor of James A. Sanders*

226 L.L. Rowlett, *Joshua and the Rhetoric of Violence: A New Historicist Analysis*
227 J.F.A. Sawyer (ed.), *Reading Leviticus: Responses to Mary Douglas*
228 V. Fritz and P.R. Davies (eds.), *The Origins of the Ancient Israelite States*
229 S.B. Reid (ed.), *Prophets and Paradigms: Essays in Honor of Gene M. Tucker*
230 K.J. Cathcart and M.J. Maher (eds.), *Targumic and Cognate Studies: Essays in Honour of Martin McNamara*
231 W.W. Fields, *Sodom and Gomorrah: History and Motif in Biblical Narrative*
232 T. Binger, *Asherah: Goddesses in Ugarit, Israel and the Old Testament*
233 M.D. Goulder, *The Psalms of Asaph and the Pentateuch: Studies in the Psalter, III*
234 K. Stone, *Sex, Honor, and Power in the Deuteronomistic History*
235 J.W. Watts and P.R. House (eds.), *Forming Prophetic Literature: Essays on Isaiah and the Twelve in Honor of John D.W. Watts*
236 T.M. Bolin, *Freedom beyond Forgiveness: The Book of Jonah Re-Examined*
237 N.A. Silberman and D. Small (eds.), *The Archaeology of Israel: Constructing the Past, Interpreting the Present*
238 M.P. Graham, K.G. Hoglund and S.L. McKenzie (eds.), *The Chronicler as Historian*
239 M.S. Smith, *The Pilgrimage Pattern in Exodus* (with contributions by Elizabeth M. Bloch-Smith)
240 E.E. Carpenter (ed.), *A Biblical Itinerary: In Search of Method, Form and Content. Essays in Honor of George W. Coats*
241 R.K. Gnuse, *No Other Gods: Emergent Monotheism in Israel*
242 K.L. Noll, *The Faces of David*
243 H.G. Reventlow, *Eschatology in the Bible and in Jewish and Christian Tradition*
244 W.E. Aufrecht, N.A. Mirau and S.W. Gauley (eds.), *Aspects of Urbanism in Antiquity: From Mesopotamia to Crete*
245 L.L. Grabbe, *Can a 'History of Israel' Be Written?*
246 G.M. Bediako, *Primal Religion and the Bible: William Robertson Smith and his Heritage*
248 E. Nodet, *A Search for the Origins of Judaism: From Joshua to the Mishnah*
249 W.P. Griffin, *The God of the Prophets: An Analysis of Divine Action*
251 F.A.J. Nielsen, *The Tragedy in History: Herodotus and the Deuteronomistic History*
252 D.C. Mitchell, *The Message of the Psalter: An Eschatological Programme in the Book of Psalms*
253 W. Johnstone, *1 and 2 Chronicles. Volume 1. 1 Chronicles 1–2 Chronicles 9: Israel's Place among the Nations*
254 W. Johnstone, *1 and 2 Chronicles. Volume 2. 2 Chronicles 10–36: Guilt and Atonement*
255 L.L. Lyke, *King David with the Wise Woman of Tekoa: The Resonance of Tradition in Parabolic Narrative*